21st CENTURY OPPORTUNITIES AND CHALLENGES:

An Age of Destruction or An Age of Transformation

Edited and with a Preface by
Howard F. Didsbury, Jr.

World Future Society
Bethesda, Maryland
U.S.A.

Editor: Howard F. Didsbury, Jr.

Manuscript Editor: Cynthia G. Wagner

Project Director: Susan Echard

Production Editor: Anne Silk

Assistant Editor: Tanya Parwani-Jaimes

Consulting Editor: Edward Cornish

Business Manager: Jefferson Cornish

Cover Design: Lisa Mathias

Published by:

World Future Society
7910 Woodmont Avenue
Suite 450
Bethesda, Maryland 20814
USA

International Standard Book Number: 0-930242-58-0

Printed in the United States

CONTENTS

EDUCATION

THE QUESTION OF CORPORATE INTEGRITY

ETHICAL VALUES

ON THE HORIZON

FOUR MISCELLANEOUS TOPICS

NOTE

21st Century Opportunities and Challenges: An Age of Destruction or An Age of Transformation is the World Future Society's conference volume for its San Francisco meeting, July 18-20, 2003, at the Hyatt Regency San Francisco.

The World Future Society staff, in addition to their many responsibilities, assisted greatly in the overall preparation of this conference volume with timely suggestions and critical insights.

The papers presented here were selected from a large number submitted. They are not necessarily papers presented by their authors at this conference. A number of distinguished papers whose subject matter did not lie within the limits of the volume could not be included.

As is our practice in general, footnotes and other academic paraphernalia have been minimized to avoid interruption in the flow of the author's ideas and insights.

With a great sense of loss, we report the death of Duane Smith on March 6th of this year. In addition to his long, outstanding service to the Ameritech Corporation, Duane made remarkable contributions to the World Future Society and THE FUTURIST. He was a volunteer who gave tirelessly and generously of his time for the progress and growth of the Society. He left a fine legacy to us all for the 21st century.

PREFACE

THE TYRANNY OF THE RIGHTEOUS

by

Howard F. Didsbury, Jr.

[Author's Note: This essay was originally in *Through the '80s* published by the World Future Society in 1980. As of 1995, this paper is listed in the electronic library of the Joint Chiefs of Staff, Defense Department.]

There are two universal processes of transformation at work on the planet today. One involves the modernization of undeveloped traditional societies, the other involves the advent of postindustrial (technological) civilization in highly developed societies. They both portend a great many good things for mankind. Undeveloped societies seek to modernize and gain the benefits of modernization as quickly as possible. Developed countries welcome the advent of postindustrial society. What's frequently overlooked, however, is that each of these processes, modernization and postindustrial society, at this juncture in world history creates conditions which encourage the rise and growth of extremist movements; in particular, a rebirth of religious fanaticism. This disturbing prognosis envisions an "enthusiasm" for intolerance and hatred wedded to a creed of absolute surrender. It is a reaction to the process of modernization in the undeveloped traditional society. In both of these cases all sorts of forces are in turmoil, values and attitudes are in flux. Large segments of the population feel bewildered, insecure, "lost" and insignificant. Out of such contemporary matrices, future extremist movements, either Left or Right, secular or religious, may take shape and grow. Religious fanaticism seems an especially frightening aspect of the general dynamics of present-day extremism.

THE IMPACT OF MODERNIZATION ON DEVELOPED TRADITIONAL SOCIETY

No rational person would challenge the many desirable features and genuine benefits resulting from the rise in the general standard of living and quality of life associated with modernization. There is, however, a potential danger in the process of modernization in the contemporary age which seems to create a peculiar receptivity to political and religious extremisms.

Almost simultaneously, an emerging society undergoes the wrenching experiences of modernization: disruption of the familiar way of life; disintegration of the traditional structure of family and

Howard F. Didsbury, Jr. *is director of Special Projects for the World Future Society and president of Alternative Futures Research Associates, Washington, D.C. He may be contacted at didsbury@wfs.org.*

community; individual and group tensions and stresses, bewilderment at the rapidity of change; confusion and uncertainty attendant upon current contradictory cultural values; the loss of traditionally guaranteed status; a new, sharpened awareness of social, economic and political incongruities; and a growing sense of "isolation" in an "atomistic" society. In addition, the demands and dictates of modernization, with its emphasis upon the prestige of science and technology, serve to unravel the ancient fabric of faith.

The process of industrialization and modernization in the late twentieth century is taking place in a global context, one very different from that which existed in the late eighteenth and nineteenth centuries when Europe and the United States industrialized. Modernization in the late twentieth century is not a single revolutionary event. It encompasses an a whole complex of revolutions. An immense series of radical changes in economics, politics and society in general are being compressed into such a short period of time that those involved are hard pressed in adjusting to the shock waves. People engaged in modernization are affected by industrialization and its social, political and economic ramifications: "the revolution of rising expectations," the advent of the nuclear age, population increase, energy and natural-resource challenges, and the increasing and compelling impact of telecommunications.

In past examples of industrialization and modernization, when the societies ultimately achieved the status of developed nations, the cornucopia of goods and services which such status made possible, together with the passage of time, ameliorated the harsh condition of the transition period. In time, an adjustment and accommodation to the new order of life took place.

Also, in the earlier age of industrialization there was no global system of telecommunications which now serves as the nerve cells of humanity. Today the pressure and complexity of events, a superabundance of information, and continuous examples of rapid change are conveyed vividly and immediately. Feelings of disquiet and unease can readily be exacerbated! Some years ago, Alexander H. Leighton, writing in *Human Relations in the Changing World*, summed up one aspect of the problem of change succinctly: "As part of the accelerated changes and contradictory cross-currents in society, values today are probably more confused for more people than they have ever been in the history of the world. Consistency and stability can only be found in a few remote and simple cultures, and even these are disappearing year by year under the impact of increasing communications and greater and greater interdependency of all parts of the world."

THE EMERGENCE OF POSTINDUSTRIAL SOCIETY

Among a host of writers who have described the characteristics of postindustrial society, one may cite Daniel Bell, *The Coming of Post-*

Industrial Society and *The Cultural Contradictions of Capitalism*; Martin Pawley, *The Private Future*; and Robert L. Heilbroner, *Business Civilization in Decline*. The cultural ethos of such a society is one which places great emphasis upon the self, personal freedom and personal rights, instant gratification, "self-actualization," permissiveness, and "consumerism."

In postindustrial society there are dramatic indications of a drift from the conception of the person as a citizen with obligations and responsibilities to family, friends, community, and nation to a conception of the person as a self-centered "consumer" seeking easy and quick satisfaction. His appetites are whetted by artificial, ingeniously contrived stimulation by means of advertising. Trivialities are glamorized. The self, comfort, and convenience are proselytized electronically. Such a cultural milieu may produce a comfortable life but may also produce a life barren of genuine meaning. Such a society, in the words of Oscar Wilde, "knows the price of everything and the value of nothing." Decades ago the late Erich Fromm observed: "Freedom has a twofold meaning for modern man: that he has been freed from traditional authorities and has become an 'individual,' but that at the same time, has become isolated, powerless, and an instrument of purposes outside of himself, alienated from himself and others; furthermore, that this statement undermines his self, weakens and frightens him, and makes him ready for submission to new kinds of bondage."

In a society which inordinately stresses human freedom, individuality an opportunity, how does one account for those who fail? If all are free and have many opportunities to succeed, the answer is clear and simple: It is the individual himself who is at fault for failure! In such a situation the result may be disgust with oneself and resentment towards others. This can be one among many of the factors in the likely growth of extremism and religious fanaticism in postindustrial societies. Trapped in a vortex of change, dwarfed by technological giantism and organizational impersonality, many people are lost and frustrated. The more uncertain and threatening the future the greater the appeal of "absolute" simple answers, be they cults, creeds or ideologies. Cults "serve to fill a need which science and technology have created by cutting away the power of the old established religions." For individuals confronted with the kaleidoscope change of postindustrial society there is "the tendency to give up the independence of one's own individual self and to fuse oneself with somebody or something outside of oneself in order to acquire the strength which the individual self is lacking."

THE RISE OF FANATICISM

In the process of modernization and the undeveloped traditional society, forces are unleashed which make the emergence of extremism, especially religious fanaticism, likely. In a traditional society undergoing the trauma of modernization, there is an ambivalent attitude toward the whole process of modernization. While seeking the obvious benefits accompanying modernization, there is a fear and hatred of its unsettling effects upon the society and its values. All kinds of attempts are made to reap the benefits yet avoid the socially destructive concomitant aspects. Such attempts prove futile and increase the level of hatred and reaction.

In the older, highly industrialized or postindustrial society, the rampant spirit of permissiveness, egotism, cynicism, relativism and hedonism likewise encourage the advent of intolerance. Though these two cultural matrices are different, the extremist reaction tends to be similar.

Total commitment to a creed or ideology brings relief from the anxiety of making individual decisions with respect to values and meaning in life. By following a leader, a creed or an ideology, the anxious, confused individual finds completeness and fulfillment. The cost is simply the abdication of one's personal judgment and responsibility. As Fromm notes, so much of the life "of the individual in modern society has increased the helplessness and insecurity of the average individual. Thus, he is ready to submit to new authorities which offer him security and relief from doubt."

Another way of finding meaning in the confusing environment of modernization or in the fluid world of postindustrial society is to try to "recapture" the past. This usually takes the form of an affirmation of loyalty to a prior "Golden Age" of patriotism or of faith. Notwithstanding the fact that such a vision of a golden age is largely a product of an unreflective nostalgic distortion of the past, its appeal is strong, particularly in an age of change and uncertainties. With the reaffirmation of the time-old faith, secular or religious, the individual finds a safe harbor from the troubled seas of "convulsive change."

The quest for meaning and the need for total commitment is one means of coping with an epoch of unsettling complexity. The affirmation of the "simple faith" and the relief gained by total willful commitment fires the exuberance of the fanatic. All too easily the personal ecstasy of the "true believer" can become a virulent hatred for "non-believers" or, even worse, backsliders. The communal bond of likeminded haters should never be underestimated. An intense common hatred for sinners passes all too quickly into an unconscious hatred for humanity.

As has been noted, the act of total commitment solves the problems created by a gnawing sense of doubt or insecurity. The absolute surrender to the faith, secular or religious, provides an enviable "simplification" of life for the follower. For such a person, a sharp line is drawn. It separates the good people from the wicked ones; the saints from the sinners. Filled with a firm conviction and a sense of mission, the "Righteous" go forth to set the world aright. All too often, the Reign of the Righteous ends in a Reign of Terror for all, as the "incorruptibles" and virtuous seek to redeem their fallen fellow man. One recalls with justified fear the enthusiasm with which the Cromwells and Robespierres embarked on the pursuit of such worthy ends.

Extremists need some group to despise, chastise or reform. In this endeavor the adherents, unconsciously, have ample opportunities to vent their deep-seated frustrations, resentment and envy and, at the same time, relish a conviction of superiority. All of this is done in genuine spirit of righteousness. The distinguished theologian C.S. Lewis describes this spirit well in *God in the Dock*:

> Of all tyrannies a tyranny exercised for the good of its victims may be the most oppressive. It may be better to live under robber barons than under omnipotent moral busybodies. The robber baron's cruelty may sometimes sleep, his cupidity may at some point be satiated; but those who torment us for our own good will torment us without end for they do so with the approval of their own conscience. They may be more likely to go to Heaven yet at the same time likelier to make Hell on earth.

Indeed, political extremists may not pose a great peril to the future well-being of people; they are concerned with more worldly ends. Conceivably, the extremist authoritarian may weaken or mellow and, given time, he may even grow to see the wisdom and profit of restraint or compromise. One is less sanguine with the religious fanatic whose character has about it the brittleness of the authoritarian but also the delusion of divine sanction for his mission.

The alarming prospect for the future is that the process of modernization in some parts of the world and of postindustrial civilization in others may be contributing to the rebirth of this disquieting phenomenon. Stunted in their own inability to enjoy the richness of personal development, self-appointed moral censors convince themselves that they are peculiarly conversant with divine wishes for human conduct. In God's name they can inflict great suffering and even destruction. Devoid of any regret or remorse, they can wreak havoc!

Tolerance achieved in the course of centuries of dedication and sacrifice is jeopardized by the rebirth of such movements of religious fanaticism. The fanatic regards tolerance not as a positive good but a necessary evil. The Righteous, were he in power, would espouse intolerance. In former times, behind the unctuous utterances of concern for the wayward, the Righteous had the dungeon, the rack and the block to ensure compliance.

The unfortunate fact of human existence may be that many people are incapable of knowing how to enjoy life. Human contentment, notwithstanding all the philosophers, may be the result of good judgment and good luck—both of which may be in extremely short supply among man. Fanaticism, either religious or ideological, may serve as a sublimation of unhappiness and frustration. For many, the perilous uncertain times now and ahead of us make submission to an absolute authority increasingly attractive, if not necessary.

INTRODUCTION

The World Future Society conference volume for the San Francisco conference, July 18-20, 2003, consists of 26 papers grouped under six major headings, plus a seventh embracing less-easily categorizable subjects:

- **Assessing Scientific and Technological Innovations**
- **The Impact of Globalization**
- **Education**
- **The Question of Corporate Integrity**
- **Ethical Values**
- **On the Horizon**
- **Four Miscellaneous Topics**

Professor Lynn Elen Burton's "Convergence and Collision: Assessing the Impacts of Emerging Scientific and Technological Innovations by Using Applied Foresight" is an enlightening overview of the European Community's concern with the need for foresight. The scope for foresight, she notes, can be any issue of social relevance in which knowledge and science and/or technology help us understand the possibility of different futures. This gives us the opportunity of shaping our futures, enhancing flexibility in policy making and implementation, broadening perspective, and encouraging creative thinking about possible, plausible, probable, and preferred futures and their potential impacts.

"Technology Forecasting and Assessment in the United States: Status and Prospects" by Vary T. Coates is a remarkably lucid account of the history of technology assessment for the United States Congress and of its demise. She then draws the reader's attention to technological assessment developments among European countries and the importance they attach to such an undertaking.

As Coates informs us, the Office of Technology Assessment (OTA) was an attempt to make the knowledge of the "experts" inform and serve, rather than manipulate or control, the people's representatives. It was to be of service to Congress, whose members are generally unsophisticated about science and technology. They are oriented toward reacting to problems rather than anticipating and avoiding them and leery of stepping ahead of the daily preoccupations of their constituents. OTA began in 1973 and issued more than 600 reports between 1975 and 1994.

Twenty-five years ago, the United States was a leader in exploring new methods for managing technological society. Now, Coates argues, the nation has allowed its foresight capabilities to become stagnant and its assessment institutions to be sacrificed in the name of downsizing and budget trimming. Before long, however, we may see a renaissance of technology forecasting. In the United States, the practice of roadmapping by corporations, industry associations, government agencies, the National Research Council, and professional groups is increasingly popular, even *de riguer*.

Among the current horrors galore that human beings have to face today, Jerome C. Glenn and Theodore J. Gordon, in "Global Science and Technology Risk Identification and Management," cite likely new ones awaiting us. For example, genetically engineered bioweapons development and proliferation over the next 25 years could become far more pervasive and unmanageable. Imagine AIDS or the Ebola virus engineered to go airborne. Civilian applications of genetic engineering that become inheritable social traits could alter humanity, they warn. This certainly suggests that the science and technology management elements outlined by Glenn and Gordon are in order indeed!

In "State of the Future Index (SOFI): A Method for Improving Decision Making that Affects the Future" Theodore J. Gordon asks, "Is the outlook for the future changing? If so, has it improved or worsened over the last decade? Is it likely to improve over the next few years? If so, what is responsible for the changed outlook?" The Index is an attempt to answer those questions.

The lure of such an Index is that it offers the hope of identifying positive and negative changes and points of leverage for policy. It also provides balance in answering questions about the outlook for the future.

Douglas Mulhall raises extremely important questions in "Reassessing Risk Management." Environmentalists and even some scientists have attacked nanotechnologies as too risky to continue with until we know more about them (a position that is opposed by many other scientists). Yet both sides are missing the elephant in the room, according to Mulhall. Conventional risk assessment methods fail to consider three important trends: Our technologies are beginning to merge with the natural environment; enhanced intelligence is transforming our interpretive capacities; and newly discovered natural threats are upending the risk-benefit equation. Neither proponents nor detractors of nanotechnology account for these factors in their analysis methods; therefore, Mulhall concludes with a call to create a forum that assembles experts in these areas so that more accurate evaluations can be developed.

"Globalization: Social Disruption Right Ahead" by J. Ørstrøm Møller makes several important points about the deterioration of the political and economic architecture holding societies together and governing international relations since 1945. Growing economic and social disparities are dividing most nations into two groups: an internationally oriented elite minority vs. a tradition-bound national-istic majority.

Complicating the situation is that the nation-state and sovereignty are dying, Møller believes. International interventionism has entered the stage, economically, politically, and militarily. The present system invented in the late 1940s and working extremely well for almost five decades is simply not up to the task.

"The passion, anger, and volume generated in almost any

discussion of *globalization* often stems from a lack of understanding that *globalization* is not one phenomenon but two—economic globalization and cultural globalization," notes Donovan D. Rypkema in his essay, "Globalization, Heritage Buildings, and the 21st Century Economy." And even when critics do "get it" that there are two forms of globalization, they mistakenly think that the two are inseparable and that the benefits of one must be accompanied by the ill effects of the other.

Rypkema argues that economic globalization is not only unavoidable, but is absolutely necessary to lift the world's impoverished to a standard of living that a world citizen of the 21st century has a right to expect. Cultural globalization, on the other hand, is a potential threat. It not only has adverse sociological and political impacts but also, in the longer term, adverse economic impacts. But the point to remember is that cultural globalization is not an inevitable outcome of economic globalization.

Barry H. Minkin's "Keep the *CON* in *Eco*nomics: Why Economic Forecasting Doesn't Work" lays out quite a case for the premise in his paper's subtitle.

He notes that the International Monetary Fund in 2000 projected global economic growth at 4.7%, the fastest in a decade, and that rapid expansion would continue in 2001. There were few signs of trouble, and the appraisal came near the end of a remarkable half-century that witnessed unprecedented global economic growth. Even with occasional financial disruptions, the IMF report seemed to imply that such growth would continue indefinitely.

But can it? Minkin thinks not, citing the current US recession, which has lasted longer and has been much deeper than many of the so-called "experts" ever expected. Minkin predicts that the US economy, which is linked to the economies of most countries, will soon collapse into a depression, which, like the one in 1929, will not respond to government monetary policy.

"The Need for a Multi-Level Educational Approach for the Future" by Donald B. Louria, Howard F. Didsbury, Jr., and Fred Ellerbusch proposes a change in our educational approach that could make a huge difference to future society: incorporating the teaching of societally connected thinking as an intrinsic part of the curriculum.

Students at all educational levels must learn to think in a societally connected way, or we will continue to develop decision makers who are unable to cope with the increasing complexity of the world and a public that will not participate in seeking solutions to major problems. This could lead to a societal catastrophe.

In "Whole Brain Education for the Digital Age," Professor Michael T. Romano describes a technology-enhanced curriculum designed to engage both the left and the right sides of the brain by fueling the teaching/learning process with both images and words. This would serve as an evolutionary approach to education that eliminates the book/chalkboard/teacher-talk/Industrial Age model in favor of an educational model in line with the Digital Age.

In "Four Urgent Requests from Future Generations," futurist Allen Tough imagines what tomorrow's society would ask of us, if they could, in order to secure their futures: (1) adopt a long-term perspective; (2) conduct more future-relevant research; (3) develop future-relevant education; and (4) make learning, caring, and meaningfulness a societal priority.

In short, Tough believes, future generations would simply want us to take their needs as seriously as our own.

Professor David J. Staley has a number of interesting things to say about the future of physical books (books as we have known them in contrast to their replacement by e-books in the new high-tech world). In "The Future of the Book in a Digital Age," he notes that many observers once believed computers would render physical books irrelevant, with textual information easily distributed through cyberspace. Readers would look at books on computer terminals or on small handheld e-books. But Staley offers another image of the future. Rather than displacing books, digital technology may be enhancing our ability to produce and distribute them. Future books may include interactive smart paper while retaining the same look and feel of physical books.

The future of the book, Staley maintains, will be determined by which model of the economics of information emerges: one in which information becomes a "commons," or one in which the concept of intellectual property remains in place. This subject reminds many of us of the certainty that the computer age would usher in the "paperless" society.

Richard A. Slaughter's "Changing Methods in Futures Studies" argues that three distinct methodologies have operated within FS over the past decades, moving from *forecasting*, an attempt to assert control and a measure of certainty over an unknown future, to *scenarios*, an attempt to explore diversity within the forward view, to *critical futures work*, which seeks to consciously and deliberately lead toward more humanly viable futures than those currently in prospect. As Slaughter points out, all these approaches coexist in the futures enterprise, each part of a broad, transdisciplinary field that welcomes a range of tools, methods, approaches and ways of knowing.

David Pearce Snyder, Gregg Edwards, and Chris Folsom argue in "The Strategic Context of Education in America: 2000 to 2020" that the superintendents, deans, principals, union officials, and board members who lead education should be more familiar with the "reliably forecastable realities" affecting their institutions' futures. Education is *about* the future: The primary purpose of schooling is to prepare people for imperatives and opportunities that they will encounter in their future lives. Thus, potential changes in education's future operating environment force school leaders to plan not only for changes in how much education will be needed and how education will be delivered, but also for changes in the content of education itself.

"Can corporations have integrity?" Marvin T. Brown asks in his paper, "Is Corporate Integrity Possible?" If not, then we need to dismantle them. If so, then we need to know what to expect from them. Brown demonstrates how to examine a corporation's integrity by exploring the communicative patterns that constitute a corporation's life, such as at the cultural level, the organizational level, the civic level, and the environmental level. He shows how integrity may be assessed at each of these levels and what actions would make integrity possible. Brown concludes that for corporations integrity may always be a matter of degree.

Ian Wilson's paper "Beyond Regulation, What? The Case for Corporate Self-Reform" concentrates on just two priorities for reform: the need to rethink both the purpose of the corporation and its system of governance and accountability.

In "New Futures and the Eternal Struggle between Good and Evil," Wendell Bell argues that our modern world is still contending with age-old millennial beliefs in the supernatural, good and evil, a coming apocalyptic upheaval, and a day of judgment—beliefs that are still widely held throughout the world. Bell contends that most evildoers are ordinary people who might use evil means to achieve their ends. Other people demonize their enemies and so do horrendous things to them in the name of destroying evil. Doing so, they start a tragic circle of escalating retaliation, cruelty and violence. But people can learn to restrain their evil acts with the help of some principles of futures studies, such as foresight that encourages people to consider the future consequences of their actions.

In "Cognitive Enhancement and Cognitive Liberty: Comments to the President's Council on Bioethics," Wrye Sentencia takes on the complex ethical issues at stake in new and developing technologies for improving human cognition. She addresses cognitive enhancement from the legal and ethical notion of "cognitive liberty," defined as every person's fundamental right to think independently, to use the full spectrum of his or her mind, and to have autonomy over his or her own brain chemistry.

"National Governments Are Moving into a New Stage in Electronic Government: How Fast Will They Evolve?" by Francis A. McDonough is a fine overview of what is under way. All developed countries have made good progress in electronic government, or e-Gov. Yet, there are barriers to further development: There are no models of success to reference and to copy, for example.

Many e-Gov leaders are asking whether they are making the right decisions. McDonough analyzes the progress in e-Gov in 16 nations, providing some answers for government officials responsible for making e-Gov investment decisions.

John Smart, in "Considering the Singularity: A Coming World of Autonomous Intelligence (A.I.)," argues that within the next 20 to 140 years the ever-increasing rate of technological change will reach a "singularity," becoming effectively instantaneous from the perspective of current biological humanity. After that, the events will become "future-incomprehensible" to existing humanity.

Smart disagrees, however. In fact, our technological systems have already grown so complex and interconnected as to leave most of us perplexed, and yet these systems are amazingly stable, he points out.

Hazel Henderson, in "Transition Paths to Sustainability: Information, Energy and Matter," argues that the shift from fossil-fueled industrialism to sustainable production and renewable-resource use is driving a paradigm shift in economics. Now, economics is becoming more interdisciplinary, embracing models of human behavior from psychology, for example. Henderson discusses new concepts and models, from new indicators of national progress beyond GNP, to the use of thermodynamics, non-equilibrium modelling and chaos theory.

In "Future of Information Era Communications Technologies," Graham T.T. Molitor asks a provocative question: "Are knowledge, information, education, and entertainment enterprises—accounting for 50% of all jobs in the United States during the 1970s, and 66% now—about to run their course?" Molitor's response covers a world history of communications technology and progress, from transmission speeds of one grunt/gesture per second to quadrillion bits per second and one-millisecond transmission of all Library of Congress books. Where *do* we go from there indeed?

Professor Raymond S. Kulzick's paper entitled "Managing in the Future: What Management Skills Will be Needed?" offers a number of insights into "business strategies of growing importance." He argues that the skills a manager needs to succeed in a competitive organizational environment are ultimately determined by outside forces acting upon the firm. Current trends mandate integrating three strategic approaches: (1) delivering real value to customers; (2) anticipating and taking advantage of rapid change; and (3) thriving in an increasingly complex, ethical and technical environment.

Kulzick identifies 15 business strategies of growing importance that require new skills and behaviors. He concludes by identifying the 12 core competencies that the manager of tomorrow's growth-oriented organization will need to succeed in an increasingly difficult managerial environment.

Professor Amitai Etzioni's essay "Diversity Within Unity" concerns a topic of great importance—a new framework for addressing the relationships that majority populations have with immigrant and minority communities. In response to the rising level of tension in countries in Europe and elsewhere, Etzioni, founder and director of the Communitarian Network, drafted a new framework for addressing the relationships among native and immigrant groups. In time, he and a group of scholars from around the world crafted a new project entitled "Diversity Within Unity." The DWU approach presumes that all members of a given society will fully respect the basic, shared values and institutions of the society. At the same time, each group in society should be free to maintain its distinct subculture.

In "The Modern Significance of Women's Liberation and Marriage for Love," Charlotte Waterlow outlines the huge problems the world now faces—including nuclear and chemical warfare, the gulf between the rich and the poor, an exploding population, etc.—concluding that we'll have to "grow up or blow up." A basic feature of this dire global situation is the inequality of men and women, in personal relations, in living conditions, in work. Waterlow argues that as women come into their own as equal partners with men, this spiritual partnership will inspire the growing up of the human race; its problems will be solved not by war and greed, but by love, wisdom, caring and sharing.

In "Labor Unions, Computer Power and the Near Future," Arthur B. Shostak argues that if labor is to reinvent itself rapidly, thoroughly, and meaningfully, it needs a new model. Shostak offers an ambitious and creative alternative that incorporates four matters newly enhanced by computer uses—namely, futuristics, innovations, services, and labor traditions (F-I-S-T).

These essays outline a very few of the great global challenges we must overcome in order to create a peaceful world and wholesome lives for everyone. In contemplating these great challenges, we would do well to adopt the stance of "tempered optimism." A "tempered optimist" is someone who operates on the assumption that with knowledge, wisdom, good will, and determination we can create a desirable future. In turn, future generations will be animated by a sense of moral responsibility to pass on a similar legacy to the ages to follow. And while there is that hope, there is life.

Let these assembled authors inspire us to tap our collective creative imagination, utilize our scientific and technological expertise, and unleash our spirit to create a future that is rich and bright with wonderful possibilities for the entire human family.

Howard F. Didsbury Jr.
Washington, D.C.
June 2003

ASSESSING SCIENTIFIC AND TECHNOLOGICAL INNOVATIONS

CONVERGENCE AND COLLISION: ASSESSING THE IMPACTS OF EMERGING SCIENTIFIC AND TECHNOLOGICAL INNOVATIONS BY USING APPLIED FORESIGHT

by

Lynn Elen Burton

We live in an exciting, tumultuous era, during which our environment and experiences will change more than during any comparable span in history. Humanity has never experienced the convergence—and, in some cases, the collision—of global forces of such magnitude and diversity. Understandably, we have extraordinary difficulty imagining the complexity of events that approach us so rapidly.

As these forces merge, recombine, and even crash into each other, they cause successive second- and third-order events. The resulting interlinked complexity often catches us—ourselves, our communities and corporations, our nations and international organizations—off balance.

John L. Petersen, Arlington Institute[1]

With this in mind, it is clear that science and technology both drive change and respond to the needs of society. Since the November 19, 1932, British Broadcasting Corporation transmission where H.G. Wells called for Professors of Foresight to think about ways to adapt our lives and ideas to new conditions, scientific and technological innovation has accelerated exponentially.

In this broadcast, Wells talked about how unprepared the world was for the motor-car. He claimed that, "the motor-car ought to have been anticipated at the beginning of this century. It was bound to come. It was bound to be cheapened and made abundant. It was bound to change our roads, take passenger and goods traffic from railways, alter the distribution of our population, and congest our towns with traffic. It was bound to make it possible for a man to commit a robbery or murder in Devonshire overnight and breakfast in London or Birmingham." He further said that while we could have, we did nothing to work out the potential impacts of the motor-car before our roads were choked, the railways were bankrupt, and the police were dealing with the likes of Bonnie and Clyde.[2]

In the 70 years since the BBC broadcast where H.G. Wells called for Professors of Foresight, scientists have put a man on the moon, mapped the human genome, cloned Dolly the sheep, crossed the strawberry with the Arctic char, designed our babies, and advanced artificial intelligence, robotics, and nano-technologies, among many

Lynn Elen Burton *is associate professor of futures studies at Simon Fraser University, Vancouver, British Columbia, Canada. She may be contacted at leburton@sfu.ca.*

other technological innovations. At the same time, there has been very little progress in assessing both the positive and negative impacts of these burgeoning innovations, much less developing plans to seize any hidden opportunities or lessen any negative effects. As a society we have paid very little attention to developing a cross-disciplinary early warning system "to bridge the now gaping chasm between science and technology, and policy.... We should resist the temptation to leap hastily and unthinkingly on the new technology bandwagon. In order to do that, there has to be a formal process for examining, analyzing—and even anticipating— relevant technologies and the impacts they have."[3]

Think about it this way: The first computer filled a huge room and was seen by many as a costly folly. Today, powerful computers that fit in the pocket have revolutionized the way we live and work. Likewise, for over a hundred years, while the casing may have changed, the telephone remained the same. Clearly recent improvements such as computer and fax connections, voicemail, conference calls, 800 numbers, and cellular phones are revolutionizing the way we communicate. In this case, few could "anticipate the trajectory of future improvements over the original innovation and the economic consequences of those improvements."[4]

At a time when the higher education community is increasingly being exhorted to be more "relevant" in terms of social and economic needs, isn't it time to begin to cross the stovepipe disciplines and contribute our unique perspectives to the collective wisdom on managing change? "Even if the rate of information growth only holds constant until 2020—and it has been accelerating—the second decade of the new millennium will be hugely different from the present. [In 1999], information [was] doubling every 18 months. This startling rate of change is reflected in every major field that touches our lives: social values, science, technology, and our physical environment and the planet's growth."[5]

Our surroundings and experiences are changing more now than at any other time in history. Never before has humanity experienced "global forces of such magnitude and diversity.... As fundamental shifts in science, technology, social values, global population, and physical environment merge, recombine, and even crash into each other, they cause successive second- and third-order events. As the developed world's support systems are constantly being reinvented to accommodate the extraordinary transformations of the information age, this explosion in capability raises the number of possible places of big failure or change."[6] To address some of the critical issues related to this change, a number of new initiatives have recently been started in Europe and elsewhere.

In one such example, CORDIS, the communications group of the European Community, defines foresight as:

a systematic, participatory, future intelligence gathering and medium-to-long-term vision-building process aimed at present-day decisions and mobilizing joint actions. As such foresight can improve anticipatory intelligence and contribute to an increased awareness of knowledge resources and strategic orientations of the actors that participated in the foresight activities. Foresight can be carried out by a broad set of analytical and participatory methods ranging from desktop research, expert groups, and stakeholder involvement in interactive brainstorming processes or broad participatory arrangements. The scope for foresight can be any issue of societal relevance, in which knowledge, and science and/or technology plays a considerable role such as:

• Understanding the possibility of different futures, and hence the opportunity of shaping our futures,

• Enhancing flexibility in policy making and implementation,

• Broadening perspectives,

• Encouraging creative thinking [about possible, plausible, probable, and preferable futures and their potential impacts].[7]

In another example, in July of 2002, the Chief Science Advisor in the United Kingdom held a brainstorming session to kick off the process of selecting new foresight projects. In the identification of the key issues and radical science projects, they said

All foresight projects should deliver:

• Thorough and up-to-date information and analysis of recent developments in science and technology, including an international perspective, and forecasts of what the next developments will be;

• Visions of the future, reflecting the potential impact of science and technology, and of social and economic trends, i.e., what will success look like;

• Recommendations for action, by research funders, business, Government or others, to make the most of science and technology; and

• Networks of people who recognize the importance of the issues to be addressed by the project, and are key to take the recommendations forward.[8]

Much earlier, in 1990, the Organization for Economic Cooperation and Development (OECD) established the International Futures Programme designed to help decision makers in government and industry deal with "a complex and uncertain world, in which the assessment of the trends shaping our long term future has become a formidable challenge." A world where "economic, social, and technological forces are combining to drive change along at great speed and in sometimes unexpected directions" and where "a growing deluge of information is making it increasingly hard to discern the key factors affecting the long term."

To begin to do this, the OECD International Futures Programme consists of four related and mutually supportive elements:

• *OECD Forum for the Future:* a platform for informal high level meetings with the aim of testing new ideas, developing fresh perspectives on problems and advancing the understanding of strategic and social issues.

• *OECD Futures Projects:* focused multi-disciplinary research and policy analysis on special themes, largely as spin offs from the Forum for the Future conferences.

• *OECD Future Studies Information Base:* a documentation system providing in succinct form the key findings and conclusions of published and unpublished literature selected from the world-wide output of futures analysis.

• *OECD International Futures Network:* a global network of some 600 people in government, industry and business, and research institutions who share common interest in long term developments and policy related issues.[9]

In an example within the post-secondary context, Professor Richard Slaughter, director of the recently established Australian Foresight Institute and president of the World Futures Studies Federation, talks about the need for both a symbolic domain and an applied field of practice. He claims that high quality foresight will be a cornerstone of organizational success and social viability in the 21st century.[10]

Finally, with all of these examples in mind, isn't it about time that we in North America define a new role for H.G. Wells's Professors of Foresight? Isn't it time to create a trans-disciplinary field, reaching beyond futures studies to applied foresight—a field which would include members from across the disciplines to provide their unique views on emerging issues? Drawing from a term commonly used by adult educators, we would employ *praxis.* We would be putting theory into action. But where do we begin? Similar to recent initiatives in Europe and Australia, perhaps a small task group under the aegis of the World Future Society could be formed to further explore this idea within the North American context.

In conclusion, as we think about the possible development of a new field of Applied Foresight, I'm reminded of a conversation in *Alice in Wonderland*:

> "Cheshire Puss, would you tell me please, which way we ought to go from here?" asked Alice. To which the cat responded, "That depends a good deal on where you want to get to."

NOTES

1. John L. Petersen, *Out of the Blue: How to Anticipate Big Future Surprises* (Lanham, MD: Madison Books, 1999), 1.
2. H.G. Wells, "Wanted Professors of Foresight!" *Futures Research Quarterly* (Bethesda, MD: World Future Society, Spring 1987), 90.
3. Arnold Brown, "Sometimes the Luddites Are Right," *The Futurist*, ed. Edward Cornish (Bethesda, MD: World Future Society), September-October 2001, 41.
4. Nathan Rosenberg, "Why Technology Forecasts Often Fail," *Exploring Your Future*, ed. Edward Cornish (Bethesda, MD: World Future Society, 1996), 74.
5. John L. Petersen, ibid. pg. 1.
6. John L. Petersen, ibid. pg. 1.
7. www.cordis.lu/rtd2002/foresight/chapter1.htm.
8. www.foresight.gov.uk.
9. www1.oecd.org/sge/au/oecdifp.htm.
10. www.swin.edu.au/afi/.

TECHNOLOGY FORECASTING AND ASSESSMENT IN THE UNITED STATES: STATUS AND PROSPECTS

by

Vary T. Coates

Technology forecasting and technology assessment are closely related fields of futures studies. Technology forecasting (TF) tries to foresee the emergence of new technologies, or to describe the developmental trajectory, future parameters, dissemination, and use of existing technologies. Technology assessment (TA) analyzes potential direct and indirect consequences of new or changing technology. It identifies possible impacts on the environment, the economy, social institutions and behaviors, and personal and collective quality of life. TA should incorporate and build on information and insights provided by TF.

TF can sharpen decision making in both the private and public sectors by better defining possibilities and priorities for research and development. TA, on the other hand, whether done by government, foundations, academic institutes, or other organizations, is intended primarily to support public policy making. It has the potential for helping government both to more wisely evaluate its own R&D resources and to incentivize the private sector to design and develop socially desirable technologies. TA can also identify ways to avoid, mitigate, or compensate for any undesirable secondary impacts of technology, whether these are unacceptable risks, such as loss of life, destruction of property, or environmental degradation, or the less severe disruptions that often accompany even highly desirable technologies, such as sector unemployment or boom-town stresses on regional infrastructure.

In theory, therefore, technology forecasting and assessment, which had quite different origins, should be closely linked through:

- their common recognition of the central role of technology in society

- their systematic, disciplined exploration of possible future states of society

- their utility for private and public sector policy formulation and decision making

- their common development and evaluation of methods and techniques, including trend projection, modeling and simulation, and Delphi surveys.

Vary T. Coates *was formerly senior associate, Office of Technology Assessment, US Congress, and is an associate editor of* Futures Research Quarterly, *Washington, D.C. She may be contacted at vcoates@concentric.net.*

These links were recognized in the late 1960s' proposals for a technology assessment institution to serve the US Congress; it was at first described as an "early warning system" for legislators. Today, far more than in the past, the boundaries between public and private sector activities have become blurred—less through "big government" intervention in commerce than through the technologizing of all common activities, the scale and power of huge corporations and commercial agglomerations, the reliance on "self-regulation" for industries as diverse as stock trading and transportation, and the privatizing of services such as criminal incarceration and hospitalization. In many areas, governments have effectively ceded to businesses the responsibility for public health, safety, and welfare. TF and TA, then, should be expected in both public and private sector decision making. Yet in both, interest in the development of TA and TF appears to have lagged, especially in the United States.

It is widely recognized that our economic prosperity, our national security, our personal health and longevity, and our global environment are critically dependent on continuing advances in technology. But decision makers in both sectors often seem skeptical of the benefits that might be gained from TF and TA. Neither discipline has realized the promise, which seemed clear in the 1970s, of further methodological development and institutional support.

Both corporate and government managers have become accustomed to utilizing the forecasts of demographers, economists, meteorologists, and traffic engineers; but they are still slow to take into account the projections of technological development and even more reluctant to anticipate its inevitable waves of societal impacts. This is especially true of legislators, who are generally unsophisticated about science and technology, are oriented toward reacting to problems rather than anticipating and avoiding them, and are leery of stepping ahead of the daily preoccupations of their constituents.

All branches and all levels of government, and businesses of all sizes, are beyond doubt much more aware of the swift pace of technological change than they were a generation ago. Almost weekly announcements, pronouncements, promises, and warnings about computer networks, medical discoveries, and gene transfers have made it clear to even the most scientifically naïve that tomorrow's technology will not be like today's technology. But instead of moving strongly to improve the capability to cope wisely with radically new technological opportunities, Congress has reacted in two opposed but equally ineffective ways. In some cases, especially with information technology and genetically altered crops, Congress has progressively abdicated responsibility to the chaos of raw business competition. In other cases, listening to the dire warnings of ethicists with poorly articulated sets of values, Congress has reacted with know-nothing prohibitions or constraints on research, for example on stem-cell research.

The executive branch has done somewhat better at dealing with advances in information technology, genetics, and medicine, but it is only edging cautiously forward, and making little attempt systematically to improve the capability to get ahead of the game with foresight and assessment.

The United States, which 25 years ago was a leader in exploring new methods for managing technological society, has allowed its foresight capability to become stagnant and its assessment institutions to be sacrificed in the name of "downsizing" and budget trimming.

TECHNOLOGY FORECASTING

Many practitioners now make a distinction between "technology forecasting" and "technological forecasting." They limit the latter, longer label to more quantitative, "scientific" techniques incorporating empirical and statistical data—trend extrapolation, curve fitting, etc. The broader term technology forecasting includes qualitative, judgment-based, or imaging techniques such as Delphi and scenario writing, planning tools such as technology roadmapping, and sometimes creativity-enhancing methods such as morphological box and futures wheels.[1] Following this distinction, it appears that "technology forecasting" is flourishing, while "technological forecasting" has declined in popularity and volume. The theme of this brief review, however, is that methodological development across the entire spectrum has been lagging for well over a decade. The semantic distinction is therefore noted, but will not be pursued further here.

Modern TF is generally said to have its roots in military planning during and immediately after World War II. The ground had been prepared earlier by Dr. S. Colum Gilfillan, beginning in 1920 with his Columbia University master's thesis on how expectations about technology are shaped. Historically, he said, useful predictions were derived both from extrapolation of past patterns or cycles and from understanding of inventors' motivations and goals and the barriers to their realization.[2] After the war, the military sponsored sporadic attempts at TF. In 1945 an Army Air Force Scientific Advisory Group was created to chart military R&D for the next 20 years; its report, *Towards New Horizons*, was mostly classified and therefore never well known. By contrast, a 1957 Army Ordinance effort, *Technical Capabilities Forecast, FY 59-60*, was widely circulated. In 1960, the chief of R&D for the Army began a continuing project on Long Range Technological Forecasts.

In the same year, Ralph C. Lentz, of the Air Force, wrote a widely distributed report that helped to establish TF as "an intellectually coherent activity and occupation."[3] Lentz reviewed the methods used by forecasters in fields ranging from natural events to financial affairs and business cycles, and showed how these methods might be applied to technology forecasting. He described growth curves, trend extrapolation, precursor events analysis, and biological analogies. (Although the Delphi method had already been developed, it did not appear in open literature until some months later.)

Thereafter, the Air Force, and then the Army and Navy, made TF an explicit and formal part of their planning procedures. Civilian applications also began. The RAND Corporation, which had begun as an Air Force think tank emphasizing TF techniques, spun off the Hudson Institute spearheaded by Herman Kahn, which went further into TF and then into socioeconomic forecasting and studies of technology transfer. Several excellent TF journals and textbooks appeared, giving further currency to TF.[4]

Dr. Eric Jantsch, in a 1966 report commissioned by the OECD, *Technological Forecasting in Perspective,* found TF projects in at least 13 countries, although he concluded that the military was clearly the leader in technology forecasting. This military interest was driven by the Cold War and the fear in the late 1950s and 1960s that the USSR might surpass the United States in military technology, a fear underlined by the putative "missile gap" and Sputnik.

Some of the 13 countries surveyed by Jantsch already had a background in futures studies. For example, in the late 1950s, Gaston Berger, in France, had established a Center for Prospective Studies, and later Pierre Masse and Bertrand de Jouvenel worked to encourage long-range economic and social planning, including technological development. Futures research and long-range planning were developed further in the 1970s in Holland, Great Britain, Sweden, Norway, West Germany, Africa, and Italy.[5] National Academies of Science in the USSR, the United States, Austria, Hungary, Romania, and other countries sponsored or carried out studies with elements of technology forecasting and assessment. Most of these activities were, however, oriented toward economic, social, natural resource, and environmental trends rather than chiefly or directly on technological change.[6]

A number of international or transnational institutions were formed to carry out studies of future technology; two of them, still at the forefront, are:

• The International Institute for Applied Systems Analysis (IIASA) in Austria, a joint undertaking of the scientific academies and governments on both sides of the Cold War, chiefly the United States and the Soviet Union, has been a leader in forecasts and assessments particularly in the technology fields of energy, agriculture, and transportation.

• The Club of Rome, an organization of 80 business and political leaders from many countries, founded by an Italian, Aurelio Peccei, and a Briton, Alexander King, commissioned the groundbreaking *Limits to Growth* study and subsequent studies of global futures, emphasizing environmental, resource, and related political trends.

It is clear in hindsight that interest in TF was already sagging during the 1970s. By this time, the Cold War had become a familiar and therefore less frightening part of the political environment, and observers had begun to suspect that the USSR was falling behind in technological development. In the 1980s, research and development became more and more the province of the private sector, and government fell into the assumption that competitive markets could determine the direction of technological change without support, direction, encouragement, or constraint from national security agencies, R&D funders, or regulators.

Another damper on TF methodology development was a growing sense, among theorists and practitioners, of its limitations. James Bright, a leader in promulgating TF to corporate managers, warned in the late 1970s, "Broad and scholarly development of rigorous techniques for forecasting technology is just beginning," and he articulated some of the problems:[7]

• The hypotheses behind many approaches are largely unproved.

• With rare exceptions, comprehensive and consistently based time series of technological parameters have not been compiled. The database for technology has not been accumulated or organized as it has been in economics or census statistics. This is a major problem with the field.

• Results of technology forecasting must be treated with caution. The distinction between predictions of experimental technological accomplishments and predictions of technology that will reach wide social adoption is especially critical to sound forecasting, and is the major source of confusion and error in technology forecasting.

But Bright continued, "We do have a start.... The possibilities, limitations, potential, and ... understanding are far advanced (in 1978) over those existing in 1965.... Technological change is too serious to be ignored until it descends upon.... There must be some-thing—some methodology—that is better than random opinion or nothing."

About the same time another leader in the field, Olaf Helmer of RAND, set out the challenges to be met:[8]

• Improving judgmental data such as that produced by the Delphi technique (it is, he said, "rarely based on a well-articulat-ed theoretical procedure but more often is intuitive and pre-theoretical")

- learning how to do model construction using "soft" or judgmental data, including developing a "defensible" cross-impact matrix procedure

- developing and demonstrating the validity of simulation as "pseudo-experimentation" about the future

- finding ways to appropriately relate non-monetary social costs to monetary costs so that overall systems costs can be meaningfully estimated

- learning to develop appropriate sets of social and other indicators in terms of which future social benefits can be identified and estimated

- refining the theory of scenarios—how to single out a manageably small set of "representative" scenarios to meaningfully portray the range of possible futures.

These challenges still stand; the promise of TF as a developing intellectual discipline has not materialized. Since the early 1970s, in fact, few or no significant advances have been made in forecasting methodology. Ironically, Delphi—the technique that Olaf Helmer (along with Ted Gordon, Norman Dalkey, and others) invented as far back as the 1950s, and that Helmer himself characterized as "intuitive and pre-theoretical"—is the technique that may be most widely used today, although usually in a much attenuated form. The Delphi indeed represents a shrug of despair—we will simply lean on the collective judgment of experts (or even non-informed observers) in spite of the fact that they can't really tell the basis of their predictions.

Even the Delphi, however, today appears to be used more frequently and systematically in other countries than in the United States. Japan has conducted a national Delphi on technological development every five years since the mid-1970s, and other countries, including Germany and Britain, have also utilized the technique. Some practitioners in those countries, however, privately admit to uncertainty about how, and to what extent, their forecasts are used by decision makers in either government or industry.

In general, interest in TF may until recently have been stronger in other countries than in the United States; for example, Harold Linstone, editor of *Technological Forecasting and Social Change*, notes that in 1974, 49% of subscribers to the journal were in countries other than the United States, but in 1999, 66% were foreign.[9] Nevertheless, corporate interest in technology forecasting has boomed in the last five years, although it appears that quantitative techniques of trend extrapolation—what was referred to earlier as "technological forecasting"—is mostly limited to a few industries—aerospace, electronics, and energy. In the United States, perhaps a score of consulting firms and research organizations specialize in futures studies, for both corporate and government clients. This growing business interest is reflected in a burgeoning literature on the future, some focusing on economic, political, and social trends, but much of it framed around the potential effects of emerging scientific discoveries and technological developments. One futures firm, for example, has collected and reviewed for corporate clients over 600 such forecasts from professional, scientific, and trade journals, the press, and popular literature.[10]

We may indeed be on the brink of a renaissance of TF. In the United States, the practice of "roadmapping," by corporations, industry associations, government agencies, the National Research Council, and professional groups such as the IEEE, is increasingly popular, even *de rigueur*. Technology roadmapping describes a goal or desirable path of development for a specific kind of technology and then attempts to lay out alternative paths—R&D, production techniques, supporting technologies, and market development—that will be necessary to reach that goal. Usually these initiatives are carried out by panels of experts assembled from industry, government, and research groups, as a kind of real-time Delphi.

The National Research Council has issued a long series of technology outlook papers prepared by committees of experts.[11] The Advanced Technology Program of the Department of Commerce does a kind of normative TF in selecting areas and specific research initiatives which it will support in partnership with corporations. The Department of Energy has a similar program called "Industries of the Future."

These expanding activities aimed at technology foresight are not surprising, given the short generation cycles of today's dominant technologies, the competitive pressure from globalization, and rapid-fire developments in biology, genetics and medicine. It should be emphasized, however, that almost none of these or the many similar foresight and planning activities in business and government include attention to the development, testing, or refinement of forecasting methodology. That has not significantly progressed since the 1970s.

There are some rays of hope. The development of huge and accessible databases and new methods of computer analysis, modeling, and simulation may eventually produce new techniques for technological forecasting.[12] The "Y2K problem" has called attention to the societal vulnerabilities that arise from complex technological systems and networks. By absorbing tremendous resources to find and fix the problem, Y2K got the attention of corporate executives and legislators, forcing many to realize the need to pay attention to the future implications of technologies introduced today.

Linstone says that "the most exciting development in the systems area in recent years ... is that of complexity science, focusing on nonlinear, dynamic, adaptive systems." He believes this may well contribute to entirely new techniques of forecasting.[13] In the past, Linstone notes, forecasting focused on the purely technological aspects of complex systems, a form of "reductionism [that] ignores the fact that complex sociotechnical systems are nonlinear" and "often show counterintuitive behavior, randomness, and instability." In speaking of sociotechnical systems, Linstone echoes Helmer and Bright in recognizing as one of the limitations of technology forecasting that technology is always embedded in institutions, economies, markets, and social behavior patterns that necessarily condition its parameters and its further development in ways that frustrate forecasters.[14] It may indeed be that the emerging techniques associated with complexity theory will lead to new ways of technology forecasting. By viewing technology in its full socioeconomic context, moreover, such an approach will also reaffirm the tie between technology forecasting and technology assessment.

TECHNOLOGY ASSESSMENT

The concept of TA developed in the mid-1960s from the clash of three strong cultural themes:

• our faith in technology as the vehicle of progress, a dominant paradigm of American culture

• countered by growing unease and then rising indignation about many of its unanticipated effects

• an upsurge of the peculiarly American tension between Congress and the executive branch of government.

All three themes were particularly strong in the 1960s, during one of the recurring periods when Congress was struggling to reassert its powers in the face of the "imperial Presidency" that had developed during the war years and afterward. With their constituents protesting about industrial pollution, ecological destruction, and community disruption by highway construction and urban renewal, legislators came to strongly distrust the information they got from executive agencies in support of administration projects and programs.

The proposal, first floated in 1966, to provide Congress with a source of technical advice not dependent on bureaucracies commanded by the executive branch should be seen as a great experiment, an innovation in democratic government. Many philosophers and futurists were then questioning whether democratic governance could survive and be effective in the world of the future, in which institutions, events, the natural world, and human behavior were overwhelmingly shaped by advanced technology.[15] Would the real decisions inexorably shift into the hands of experts or "technocrats," because the representatives of the people could not understand the implications and consequences of technological change? The Office of Technology Assessment was in essence an attempt to make the knowledge of the "experts" inform and serve, rather than manipulate or control, the will of representatives of the people.

In the six years between the first proposal of an Office of Technology Assessment in 1967 and its beginning operations in 1973, the concept of technology assessment[16] was explored, fleshed out, and tested in an amazing outpouring of interest and comment. The congressional committee considering the proposal took the unusual step of asking the National Academy of Science, the National Academy of Engineering, and the National Academy of Public Administration to consider and report back on the concept of TA and how it might be made operational. Their three reports were widely disseminated and became the basis of a large number of sessions in various professional, scientific, and industry association meetings and academic seminars, and these in turn evoked scores of papers in scientific and professional journals and articles in news magazines.

The National Science Foundation (NSF) had during the 1960s inaugurated a program of grants for applied interdisciplinary research called "Research Applied to National Needs" (RANN). Technology assessment was made one of the foci of the RANN program. A number of technology assessments were conducted by interdisciplinary teams on topics including weather modification, undersea petroleum extraction, alternative work scheduling, etc., making use of the insights and recommendations from the National Academy studies. Through these and similar assessments, and through workshops and meetings of the investigators, a model framework and methodology for TA evolved, which was subsequently incorporated in a number of academic TA courses and textbooks.

Spurred by these developments and the demands fostered by the environmental movement (and new legislation requiring an Environmental Impact Statement for major governmental technological projects), government agencies were already moving to broaden the range of social and environmental factors considered in planning and defending projects. A survey of federal agencies in 1970-71 identified 97 technology assessments or partial assessments done within, or sponsored by, offices responsible for technological projects and programs. About a dozen organizational units within federal agencies had been set up specifically to meet the new demand for impact identification and evaluation.[17]

The third of the cultural factors mentioned above, the tension between legislative and executive branches of the government, determined the structure of the Congressional Office of Technology Assessment when it began in 1973. It became one of the small number of congressional agencies (joining the General Accounting Office and the Congressional Research Service) charged with responding only to congressional committees, and was given a bipartisan governing board of senators and representatives. OTA's first major reports emerged only in 1975. There was some initial floundering as the agency developed a staff and a work process. None of the senior staff were experienced in managing contractual research, their first efforts were failures, and from then on, research and analysis were done internally with minor contributions from consultants and contractors. Between 1975 and 1994 OTA produced more than 600 reports. Its achievements might be briefly summarized thusly:

• OTA reports were almost universally respected as comprehensive, thorough, sound, well-balanced, and nonpartisan. They set a standard still recognized around the world.

• OTA quickly evolved a process that systematically reached out to experts in industry, universities, and governments; to "interested parties" and advocacy groups; and to opinion leaders. A strong effort was made to find all who could contribute either information or insights to the questions at hand, and to involve them through advisory groups, workshops, and one-on-one discussions. During the course of a study, drafts of report chapters were sent to scores of these contributors for comments and corrections. It was this process that largely insured the comprehensiveness and balance of OTA reports.

• OTA maintained independence and objectivity in the highly political environment of the congressional milieu. Moreover, although its reports underwent thorough review by high-level advisory panels, external reviewers, and internal research managers, the studies remained analyst-driven, in the sense that project directors and teams were encouraged to explain, document, and defend their work and were generally protected against one-sided or partisan pressures, and felt themselves responsible for sound conclusions.

• OTA reports, although directed at Congress, were widely accessible to decision makers throughout government and to the public. Substantively, OTA analysts were able "translators" between the language of science and the language of legislators and the public, making OTA reports readable and clear to the interested layperson. Operationally, OTA reports were easily available in government document sales rooms and libraries; and several thousand copies of each report were routinely mailed to citizens who had inquired about or contributed information to the work in progress, and to journalists and academics. Most OTA analysts were easily reached by telephone for questions or comments from the public.

• OTA reports were effective in "raising the level of public discourse," by discrediting false information, loose claims, and biased arguments. They were often appealed to in debates over issues both in Congress and in the press. Congressional members were challenged by knowledgeable constituents if they took positions or supported arguments implicitly refuted by OTA reports (which did not include recommendations, but did analyze and compare "options," or alternative legislative courses of action). Some OTA studies directly influenced legislation—although more often through interactions between OTA analysts and congressional staff than through the printed reports, and perhaps overall not as often as OTA and its supporters assumed, or hoped, for reasons to be discussed.

OTA's virtues have been much celebrated, during its existence and after its demise, but some faults and weaknesses should also be recognized:

• From its beginning, OTA failed to take advantage of, and even actively rejected, the TA frameworks and methods that had been developed through the NSF TA program and through academic and professional deliberations from 1966 through 1973 and beyond. Analysts newly recruited to OTA never had the concepts and theories of TA presented to them and got no hint that there existed a body of TA experience and a voluminous TA literature. Many studies suffered from inadequate or incomplete identification of potential long-range and secondary impacts, concentration on near-term developments, often a failure to identify latent interests and affected parties who were unorganized and the inarticulate. OTA sacrificed the opportunity either to try out useful assessment techniques or develop new ones that could advance the practice and increase the usefulness of TA.

• OTA was often criticized by activists for making little use of public participation in its assessments. Although there were usually attempts to represent both recognized interest groups and sometimes "ordinary citizens or potentially affected parties" in OTA workshops, this was not systematic or consistent across projects, and tended to diminish over time.

• OTA's congressional directors and agency management very early abjured the possibility of providing "an early warning system" for Congress. There was little or no attempt to use or to develop competence in technology forecasting, and in fact the effective time horizon of OTA studies was generally quite short.

• Although the OTA Director had a limited right to initiate some studies, the policy was to limit the work to topics that committees requested (or could be persuaded to request). In practice, this meant that an issue had to be important to the members already, or at least be easily recognized as likely to become important in the near future, for the request to be made. But the OTA process, which in its essence consisted of exhaustive outreach for information and reiterative review and revision, meant that full OTA studies nearly always took a year, more often two years, and in some cases three or four years. By the time they were finished, congressional interest had often faded, or the issue may already have been resolved. This greatly reduced the opportunity for OTA to have a direct and demonstrable impact on legislative actions, although, as already noted, its informal and indirect effect was undoubtedly greater.

• OTA studies, sound and balanced as they were, cannot be credited with proposing any creative, new, or imaginative legislation—for example, no Environmental Protection Act. The reports often laid out "options," but these were usually general, dealing with broad avenues of legislation rather than specifics, either because OTA analysts were somewhat removed from the daily negotiations necessary in framing legislation or they were wary of encroaching too directly on the turf of committee staff. Congress, unlike most parliaments, has a large professional staff both in members' offices and attached to committees.

• As part of OTA management's rejection of pre-OTA experience and methodological development, OTA's connections with the academic TA community weakened over time. Appointments to the Technology Assessment Advisory Council (TAAC), which was part of OTA's legislative mandate, became a way for the TA board—senators and representatives—to compliment well-known constituents in universities and corporations, whether or not they had any knowledge of or interest in impact assessment. The TAAC was unlikely to criticize the failure to practice or develop techniques of impact assessment. When OTA came under sudden and severe attack, in 1994, it could not quickly and effectively mobilize an external constituency to its defense; indeed OTA's insular and complacent managers did not even recognize the possibility of doing so.

The agency's position as a congressional agency—a creature of Congress, yet somewhat removed from the daily grind and firestorms of legislative politics, and resolutely "nonpolitical"—ultimately proved to be a weakness. The length of its projects often put it out of step with the legislative agenda, and made it less useful to individual members than the Congressional Research Service, whose analysts responded to questions from member offices often within a few weeks or even days. Because its projects were requested by committee chairmen, who for all of OTA's 20 years had been Democrats, it was suspect in the minds of some Republicans, in spite of its reputation for objectivity.

In 1994, Republicans gained control of both houses of Congress for the first time in two decades, and the revolution was led by a cadre of freshmen representatives with a single-minded priority: budget cutting and "downsizing" government. OTA became an early and easy target; it allowed the new congressional members to demonstrate their willingness to "start in their own backyard," i.e., with a congressional agency, and one whose value few of the newcomers were aware of. Although the six Republican members of OTA's bipartisan Board of Directors, long-seated and powerful legislators, rallied strongly to its defense, OTA was killed by a margin of a few votes.

What has survived—as much the legacy of the 1960s TA and environmental movements as of OTA's experience—is the general expectation that technological initiatives should be subject to questions about their environmental, economic, and social consequences. Bureaucrats today usually take into account a broader range of considerations in planning and designing technological programs. Public-interest groups do raise questions of accountability that they would not have ventured 40 years ago. Regulatory agencies and courts do give their challenges standing and credibility.

At present, there is no dedicated source of impact assessment or technology policy research for Congress, or for that matter, for the federal government. The Congressional Research Service (CRS) responds to senators and representatives on questions of science and technology, but their responses are to the requesters and are not readily available to the public. Their work lacks the interdisciplinary team approach and the systematic and exhaustive outreach that made OTA reports both balanced and comprehensive. CRS answers the questions that congressmen (or their staff) ask, but makes little attempt to broaden or reformulate the questions, or to raise additional ones, particularly regarding unintended consequences.

The National Academies of Science and Engineering release public reports on issues related to technology, many of them requested by government. Some are similar to OTA reports. They tend to address technical issues more than policy issues; and typically there is not thorough consideration of secondary or unplanned impacts. They are committee-generated rather than analyst-driven; they lack the independence, interdisciplinarity, and broad outreach and public review that OTA enjoyed; they reflect the outlook and interests of esteemed experts and businessmen but seldom of their critics.

There are many public-interest organizations that ably study and report on technology-related issues, especially in regard to environmental issues. Some of their reports show a less-than-complete perspective and a lack of balance. At best, they lack the credibility that a congressional agency enjoyed. Finally, there are study foundations such as the Brookings or the Cato Institute. Reports from some of these institutions are the work of individual statesmen and scholars and contribute to the public discourse; others are suspect because of strong ideological or political biases of the authors, the institutions, or both.

Congress may be, for the moment, content with these sources of information, or the information eagerly provided by lobbyists on every technology-related issue. Many citizens feel that more is badly needed. Several European countries followed the example and created governmental TA organizations. It may be that these TA institutions in other countries will in the future provide a model for the United States in reconstituting a TA capability for policy makers.

INTERNATIONAL TA INSTITUTIONS AS MODELS

In the mid- and late-1970s in a number of countries, including Great Britain, Germany, and Japan, attempts were made to set up OTA-like institutions. These attempts did not at first succeed. Most were conceived of as legislative support organs, following the OTA model. But parliamentary systems lack the separation-of-powers characteristic of government that had motivated Congress to create its own sources of policy analysis. Parliaments are less likely than the US Congress to have their own legislative priorities or agendas. The party or coalition of parties that controls a parliament also controls government and its ministries and bureaucracies. At any given time, the "out" party might wish for an OTA to inform its policy makers, but when it becomes the "in" party, it is less likely to create a policy-analysis organization beyond its legitimate control.

Nevertheless, in the 1980s, technology issues increasingly occupied government decision makers. Issues related to energy, environment, communications, and agriculture marked legislative agendas in every country. As OTA reports gained international attention and respect, one result was a renewed wave of European interest in TA, from which came successful institutional innovation in many countries.

Like OTA, these institutions are intended to help their countries' decision makers improve their understanding of technology and its potential impacts. Otherwise none of these organizations much resemble OTA; they are much smaller, and they have been designed to suit parliamentary systems and the needs and the institutions of their respective countries. They vary considerably in organizational form and position and in work modes, but less so in their products. France created an *Office Parliamentaire d'Evaluation des Choix Scientifiques et Technologiques* (Parliamentary Office of Assessment of Scientific and Technological Choices), or OPCEST, in 1983. This oldest of the European TA offices is also probably the least known. OPCEST responds to requests from parliamentary leaders or committees, operating like a small specialized staff for the leadership. In general, OPCEST products are not widely distributed or publicized, but by all reports the office is respected by and useful to the legislators. An example is a study of biotechnology applications in agriculture and the food industry, which was requested by a parliamentary committee in 1990, to help French legislators develop a position in regard to a European Union directive then being developed on the subject. Responsibility for the study was assigned to an OPCEST parliamentary member. When the resulting report was submitted to the requesting committee it included a series of strong recommendations for strengthening French biotechnology research, and for giving both Parliament and the French public better information to "demystify" the subject, clarify the issues, and call attention to the technology's benefits.[18]

The Netherlands Organization for Technology Assessment (NOTA) was created in 1986. As first proposed, NOTA was to be part of the Prime Minister's Office. After going through some structural changes, it was recommissioned in 1994 and renamed the Rathenau Institute. It is a part of the Netherlands Academy of Sciences, reporting to the Ministry of Education and Sciences. (The Netherlands Academy of Sciences has a dual mandate, to advise government and to carry out some management functions with regard to scientific research.) Since Parliament does not initiate legislation, the Rathenau Institute does TA for the government as a whole, but its work and its program planning is reviewed by Parliament every two years. The Institute, with a staff of six to ten professionals, lets contracts to university groups and research institutes for data collection and analysis but plans its studies and prepares "policy chapters" internally. Its recent programs have emphasized genetic engineering, communications technologies, and environmental protection. Many of the projects include a strong element of public participation, including workshops, panels, and conferencing.

Denmark's *Tecnolog-Rådet* (usually translated as "Board of Technology") was created in 1987 as a quasi-governmental unit, and was re-chartered in 1995 by the Danish Folketing, or parliament, as a "permanent, independent institution," charged to both advise the parliament and to "further technological debate and assess technological impacts." In structure and size it is much like the Rathenau Institute. It has been a leader in developing and relying on participatory technology assessment. The agency developed a process called "consensus conferencing," which has been picked up and copied in other counties, including The Netherlands, Sweden, and Britain, and some nongovernmental organizations in the United States. In consensus conferencing, two panels are set up: one of experts in a technology to be assessed, and the other of "representative" citizens drawn from a wide range of demographic, income, occupational, and interest categories. The expert panel delivers information to and answers questions from the citizens as objectively and comprehensively as possible. During several days of intense effort (often two successive weekends), the panel of citizens considers possible impacts, identifies issues, and formulates policy recommendations based on—hopefully—a group consensus. Their reports, prepared with staff support from the TA institute, generally get strong attention and consideration from government officials.

Austria has an Institute for Technology Assessment attached to the Austrian Academy of Sciences, which provides a quarter of the Institute's budget (another quarter comes from the Ministry of Science and Transport, and the rest from studies done under contract for other agencies). Some TA work is also done by the Ministry for Economic Affairs and by the Ministry of Science and Transport.

Britain has had since 1987 a Parliamentary Office of Science and Technology (POST) to carry out technology assessment for both Houses of the Parliament. It has a staff of only five professionals, but draws on contributions from knowledgeable participants in academia and industry. POST responds to Parliament's needs for specific information and analysis, whether they arise from the needs of individual members or select committees, but its legislative charter says that POST may also anticipate the needs of Parliament on issues "where policy cannot be satisfactorily formulated without a fuller understanding of the scientific and technological implications." This would appear to mean that POST is able to act as an early warning system when its professionals feel this is warranted. However, in practice POST has limited itself to strictly factual reports on issues directly and immediately of interest to members, and usually of narrow domestic concern. In another year, Parliament will decide whether to renew its support of POST and perhaps make it a permanent establishment, which could encourage a somewhat broader and more analytical perspective.

The German legislature, after several earlier attempts, in 1989 established the *Büro für Technikfolgen-Abschätzung beim Deutcchen Bundestag* (TAB). Much of its work is contracted out to an Institute for Technology Assessment and Systems Analysis located within the highly respected Fraunhofer Institute, a very large research organization. Among effective TAB studies was, for example, an assessment of biological safety in the Office of Genetic Engineering (1992), and an assessment of genetic mapping in 1993. There is also, at the *Land* or state level of the German federation, a Center of Technology Assessment in Baden-Wüttenberg. Switzerland has an organization for Biosafety Research and Assessment of Technology Impacts (BATS).

As yet there is no formal TA office or institute in Russia or other former members of the Soviet Union, or Eastern Europe, but interest is building in Russia.

Predating some of these national TA institutions was the European Parliament's Scientific and Technological Options Programme (STOA), formed in 1987 to provide members with sources of information and advice on complex scientific and technological issues. In 1990, after the national TA organizations were functioning, the European Parliament Technology Assessment network (EPTA) was set up to help coordinate their projects and interests. EPTA itself has commissioned some technology-related studies, including a pilot project on climate change. Finally, there is the European Union's Institute for Prospective Technological Studies (IPTS). The Organization for Economic Cooperation and Development (OECD) also carries out technology forecasts and assessments throughout its complex organization, especially in the Directorate of Science, Technology, and Industry.

The International Association of Technology Assessment and Forecasting Institutions (IATAFI) is hosted and supported by Norwegian government agencies and the Norwegian Science Foundation, but it is an international organization. It was created in 1993 after a UN conference in Bergen on sustainable development, as a nongovernmental organization (NGO) associated with the United Nations Department of Economy and Social Development. IATAFI's purpose is to encourage the use and sharing of knowledge between worldwide TA and TF organizations, including both governmental units and major industrial organizations. It operates principally through holding international conferences on issues and topics related to impacts of technology and to sustainable development, and through informal networking between member organizations.

PROSPECTS

In the United States, the legislation authorizing OTA still exists; the agency was simply zero-budgeted, and in theory could be reconstituted by majority vote in both Houses. There has as yet been no movement to do so. With some of the most stalwart congressional advocates for OTA having died or left Congress, even a return to Democratic control of Congress would not make likely a rebirth of OTA as it once was.

But there could be a new burst of interest in TA. Some things that would make it more likely are:

• a series of technology-driven disasters such as widespread crop failures blamed on genetically engineered seed or epidemics of immune-system collapse from pharmaceutical mistakes

• growing resistance to more subtle societal or environmental impacts of technology, such as loss of privacy, structural unemployment, or an increasing income-education-health-housing gap between rich and poor Americans

• awareness that social benefits have been sacrificed or opportunities missed because of regulatory indifference or corporate market-driven or profit-maximizing R&D strategies

• evidence that TA-like institutions in other countries had helped to avoid, or at least called governments' attention to, such impacts.

More likely than a direct resurrection of the defunct Office of Technology Assessment, and much more promising, is the creation of TA capability in some new institutional form. The thriving TA institutions in other countries, differing in organizational position, structure, and processes, suggest many possibilities for a new Office of Technology Assessment in the United States. It might, for example, take the form of a small government-subsidized foundation or research institute. It might be authorized to carry out assessments and forecasts of independently selected emerging technologies and technology-related issues, for the dual purpose of sparking and informing public discussion and alerting governments to potential impacts and issues. It might serve both federal and state legislatures. It might operate with a small internal staff of policy analysts able to contract out larger forecasting and assessment studies, when needed, to universities and research organizations. It might produce several kinds of products, ranging from comprehensive multidisciplinary studies to short and timely issue briefs. It might make frequent use of public participation techniques such as consensus conferencing. It might attempt to develop and experiment with new forecasting and assessment methodologies, as well as reviving the classic, well-tested model developed by the National Science Foundation in the late 1960s. It might, in short, constitute a new experiment in melding technological expertise and the wisdom of democratic citizens and their elected representatives.

NOTES

1. Some judgment-based or opinion-based techniques—Delphi and cross-impact matrices—are delivered in mathematical form; a frequent criticism has been that this may encourage unsophisticated users to misunderstand, or misstate, their limitations.
2. James R. Bright, *Practical Technology Forecasting*, The Industrial Management Center, Austin, TX, 1978, Chapter 2.
3. Joseph P. Martino, "Technological Forecasting," in Jib Fowles, ed., *Handbook of Futures Research*, Greenwood Press, 1978.
4. One of the first, and perhaps the best, of the journals was, and is, *Technological Forecasting and Social Change* (Elsevier Science Inc.) under editor Harold Linstone, himself a distinguished TF/TA methodologist. See his *Multiple Perspectives for Decision Making*, North-Holland, 1984, and *Decision Making for Technology Executives*, Artech Books, 1999. Among the TF methods textbooks referred to are Robert Ayres, *Technological Forecasting and Long-Range Planning*, McGraw Hill, 1969; James Bright, *Technological Forecasting for Industry and Government*,

Prentice-Hall, 1968; and *Practical Technology Forecasting: Concepts and Exercises*, Industrial Management Center (Austin, TX), 1970; and Joseph Martino, *Technological Forecasting for Decision Making*, Elsevier, 1972.

5. Eleonora Barbieri Masini, "The Global Diffusion of Futures Research," in Jib Fowles, ed., *op.cit.*

6. Most of these activities were located in university or independent research institutes. A few, however, were directly located in or in support of government decision making, such as the Swedish Secretariat for Futures Studies, which originated in 1971 within the Office of the Prime Minister.

7. James R. Bright, Preface to *Practical Technology Forecasting*, Technology Futures, Inc. (Austin, TX) and The Industrial Management Center (North Edgecomb, ME), 1978.

8. Olaf Helmer, "The Research Tasks Before Us," in Jib Fowles, *Handbook of Futures Research*, (Greenwood Press, 1978) pp.763-778.

9. See the editor's preface to the 30th anniversary issue of this journal, Vol. 62, No. 1-2, winter, 1999.

10. Coates and Jarratt, Inc., Washington, D.C.

11. For example, *Defense Manufacturing in 2020 and Beyond*, 1999; *Separation Technologies for the Industry of the Future*, 1998; *Space Technology for the New Century*, 1998; *The Future Highway Transportation System and Society*, 1997; *Innovations in Ground Water and Soil Cleanup*, 1997; *Nonconventional Concrete Technologies*, 1997; *Microelectromechanical Systems*, 1997.

12. See the article on bibliometric analysis and forecasting by Professor Alan Porter, "Tech Forecasting: An Empirical Perspective," in *Technology Forecasting and Social Change*, Vol. 62, No. 1-2 (1999).

13. Harold Linstone, "Complexity Science: Implications for Forecasting," *Technological Forecasting and Social Change*, Vol. 62, No. 1-2 (1999).

14. In this regard, see Tim Mack, "Technology Forecasting in an Imperfect World," *Futures Research Quarterly*, Vol. 15, No. 1 (Spring 1999).

15. Remember Jacques Ellul, *The Technological Society* (Knopf, 1964); Zbigniew Brzezinski, *Between Two Ages: America's Role in the Technetronic Age* (Viking Press, 1968); Victor Ferkiss, *Technological Man* (Mentor, 1969); Daniel Bell, *The Coming of Post-Industrial Society* (Basic Books, 1973), *The Cultural Contradictions of Capitalism* (Basic Books, 1974), and earlier papers.

16. It was often argued that "technology assessment" might better be called "impact assessment," especially because the former term was often used in engineering and business literature for strictly technical evaluation of the performance of a technology or device. But a

congressman who proposed OTA chose the term "technology assessment" to ensure that his and related legislative proposals would be referred to the subcommittee on Science and Technology, which he chaired.

17. Vary T. Coates, *Technology and Public Policy: The Process of Technology Assessment in the Federal Government*, doctoral dissertation, The George Washington University, 1972, published as a report of the Program of Policy Studies in Science and Technology, The George Washington University, July 1972.

18. Christine Mironesco, "Parliamentary Technology Assessment of Biotechnologies: A Review of Major TA Reports in the European Union and the USA," *Science and Public Policy*, October 1998.

GLOBAL SCIENCE AND TECHNOLOGY RISK IDENTIFICATION AND MANAGEMENT

by

Jerome C. Glenn and Theodore J. Gordon

[Authors' Note: Much of this article is drawn from Millennium Project research funded by the Office of Science, US Department of Energy, published in the 2002 *State of the Future*.]

Since computer capacity improves faster than biology, some authorities have argued that we must take seriously the future possibilities of robots taking over, nanotech self-organizing machines covering everything with a "gray goo," and "artificial life" growing beyond human control. Genetically engineered bioweapons development and proliferation over the next 25 years could become far more pervasive and difficult to manage than nuclear weapons technology. Consider AIDS or Ebola engineered to go airborne. Civilian applications of genetic engineering that become inheritable social traits could alter humanity. These and other potential unintentional (as well as intentional) future threats go far beyond almost anything experienced in the past. Governments and the global community seem unsure how to manage such risks.

Many political leaders around the world make decisions involving science and technology (S&T) matters about which they have little understanding. These and other political decisions would benefit from input from the S&T community, but that input is too often not sought or is offered in a form that is not useful to the decision maker or is disregarded by them entirely. The public's perceptions about evolving S&T also lags far behind the profound S&T developments that will radically and rapidly change their lives. As democracy develops, political leaders have to be more responsive to public perceptions in the policy process. Both the general public and political decision makers seem to be left behind in the advancing S&T knowledge revolution.

There were two schools of thought about controlling S&T risks. One school believed that regulations would simply drive research underground or to other countries. Regulators would have no chance to keep up with the accelerating pace of advances. The way to manage risks was to educate global opinion about S&T and to train scientists to be more ethical and to self-manage risks. The other school believed that the potential scale of intended and unintended impacts of S&T on the future of humanity requires that there be glob-

Jerome C. Glenn *is executive director of the American Council for the United Nations University and director of the Millennium Project in Washington, D.C. He may be contacted at jglenn@igc.org.* **Theodore J. Gordon** *is senior research fellow for the Millennium Project, American Council for the United Nations University and resides in Old Lyme, Connecticut. He is the founder of The Futures Group, Glastonbury, Connecticut. He may be contacted at tedjgordon@att.net.*

al systems to forecast and assess the risks from S&T and to design regulations and enforce agreements. Since the impacts can be worldwide, global systems are justified.

An analysis of the content of Millennium Project interviews conducted with policy makers and R&D managers around the world showed that there is enough common ground between these two views to begin to consider developing a global risk identification and management system. This system has seven interdependent elements, as shown below:

- formulate international definitions and guidelines via eminent experts;
- establish an International S&T Organization (ISTO) for dissemination of information about risk and opportunity;
- add roles for university education;
- create a global S&T fund;
- produce annual Davos-like S&T forums;
- engage media to improve the public S&T discussion and engage politicians;
- create international treaties as consensus evolves.

INTERNATIONAL DEFINITIONS AND INITIAL GUIDELINES

The formulation of international definitions and initial guidelines has to begin with an "elite consensus" that moves to social consensus within advanced nations, and then culminates in robust international agreements. Since there is little likelihood of complete agreement about the risk of a scientific research project or technological application, the assessment model chosen is critical to the success of this approach.

Working groups of widely acknowledged wise and eminent S&T leaders should be convened to create an "elite consensus." The participants would be selected through national academies, Inter-Academy Panel on International Issues, the International Council of Scientific Unions, S&T interest groups, Nobel laureates, and private sector R&D firms working in the areas where catastrophic risks are identified.[1]

Generalists as well as specialists should be included. To avoid subjectivity and capture by vested interests, subcommittees may have to be ad hoc with limited duration, acting like nodes and networks that make their information public, rather than standing committees making decisions in secret.

The tasks of these eminent groups would be to formulate standards of acceptable risk; define codes of conduct (for scientists and scientific organizations); write a Scientific Oath (like the Hippocratic Oath); draft initial texts for international treaties, including possible sanctions and criteria for intervention; and suggest the creation and missions for ongoing systems such as an international S&T organization, university education, media, global S&T fund, and global S&T forums.

The initial group might begin by developing a statement of basic principles (similar in nature to the UN Declaration of Human Rights) that are rather general and unquestionable, so that everybody agrees, and then move on to more difficult issues. The range of issues that the eminent group might then address could include: How can we forecast research that will accidentally unleash destructive powers that would otherwise not have been anticipated by the scientists (such as creation of a particle accelerator that would give the initial conditions of the Big Bang or the creation of new viruses or germs that would devastate human populations)? When should dangerous research be undertaken by the scientific community despite antici- pated risks? How can we identify and address dangerous or morally questionable research undertaken by rogue scientists working underground for the sake of science? Or for military or terrorist purposes? How can a monitoring mechanism assess and prevent risk?

Some factors the eminent group might consider when assessing future technology include:

• Undesirable developments coexist with desirable ones. Risk management cannot be viewed as an analysis of just the negative outcomes.

• Costs and benefits may not be balanced across the population. Group A may get all the benefits, Group B all the costs.

• It may not be possible to find a valuation method that will permit trade-offs between differing packages of costs and benefits, or for that matter between two sets of undesirable outcomes. How would one choose between two dam locations if one resulted in 15% land loss and 12% salmon loss, while the other had a 17% land loss and a 10% salmon loss?

• Even without trade-offs, valuation will vary within a popula- tion. A cure for cancer will be more important to people with a history of cancer in their family.

• Within the public policy arena, a blending of the notions of risk (meaning costs) and uncertainty (meaning incomplete information) is expected. The two concepts are related: For example, if the risks are known and high, then the project is unacceptable, while if the risks are known and low, the project is acceptable. But if the risk is uncertain, then it may always be unacceptable.

• Familiarity with a technology will alter perception of risk. A hamburger is normally considered safe, even though it can cause heart disease. A bun with genetically modified wheat in it could be considered risky, even though there is no evidence of risk.

• The public is predisposed to view some technologies as more suspect than others. Nuclear technology is considered dangerous, genetic modification is considered risky. Medical and computer research are always good.

Each time the eminent group reaches a consensus, it should be discussed around the world to create a broader social consensus. This is essential for democratic societies where decisions are ratified and turned into laws and regulations that have to have broad public support. To help international understanding, a special kind of scientific interpretation of meanings may be necessary for judging different concepts and meanings. As the broader social consensus becomes clear, elements of the strategy can be implemented, such as those discussed in this section.

INTERNATIONAL S&T ORGANIZATION

The ISTO would not be a regulatory agency, but an information system to forecast and assess S&T threats and opportunities on an ongoing basis. It would forecast to create S&T maps that would expose possible risks far enough in the future to allow enough time to create technologies and protocols to prevent such problems. It would produce information and guidelines, not controls. It should have some affiliation with the UN, but function as a professional scientific organization rather than a political one—it would not be an intergovernmental body with country members on its board.

To avoid becoming an outdated, irrelevant bureaucracy, the ISTO should be a constantly changing and loose affiliation of networks and nodes like those that recommended the eminent persons previously described. It would also recognize and include self-assemblies of risk improvement communities and like-minded enlightened people on common issues as they arise. It would use ad hoc rather than standing panels, though a standing staff would be required for administrative continuity.

The ISTO would understand, forecast, assess impacts, and monitor both risk and opportunities. Building on the work of the eminent persons, the organization would suggest international norms or regulations for risk management and foster development of technical safeguards, such as technological immune systems, computer-assisted surveillance systems, and biological weapon and nanotech weapon "off-switches."

The vetted feedback system would have protocols to help increase collective intelligence. It would identify and create databases on S&T risk and opportunities. These would include facts, informed judgments, and conjectures about both risks and opportunities in scientific research and technological applications, including potential management strategies, and would have alternative views about speed, impacts, and severity of impacts.

Nations could draw on this body of informed judgment, and identify the best expertise at the moment they need it as they formulate policy. It could also include conclusions and decisions on issues of public concern. This approach could also make it easier for each country to learn what other nations are doing. The National Academy of Science (www.nas.edu) in the United States and the AlphaGalileo Foundation (www.alphagalileo.org) in Europe provide a similar service in their countries. The InterAcademy Panel on International Issues of eighty countries also provides advice in science, engineering, and medicine.

Researchers who possess deadly materials (microorganisms, toxins, viruses, etc., that could pose a risk) should be required to register their collections with the ISTO databases as well as with their national systems. Where systems do not yet exist to register some deadly material, then the ISTO could initiate the database. The databases could help developing countries set priorities for their limited S&T resources.

Working with the nodes and networks of the ISTO, the staff developing the databases would:

• collect the information, map the potential futures, and identify the issues and the players;

• present this information to the larger community of nodes, networks, and institutions for assessments;

• based on this feedback, estimate and explain the risks and benefits to the different socio-cultural contexts and environmental life-support systems;

• promote discussion of responsible alternative views;

• enter results into the ISTO databases and widely publicize this work, leaving it to the concerned societies and nations to evolve their own risk management approaches in terms of risk avoidance, risk mitigation, risk acceptance, and any corresponding methods; and

• in cooperation with media and public S&T forums, translate results into suggested policies and politics.

Since many of the S&T issues today were previously anticipated, the issue is not just forecasting, but also setting priorities. This would be needed to bring the most important items to world attention. One set of criteria suggested by an interviewee was speed of the developments, uncertainty of results, and severity of impact if negative results occur. Delphis could be used to set priorities.

As the work of the ISTO progresses, the international control of S&T developments would be strengthened, directly and indirectly, similar to the restraining influence that the Food and Drug Administration activity in the United States has on the development of new medications in other countries. One participant suggested that incentives for compliance should also be created, as well as disincentives like sanctions.

UNIVERSITY EDUCATION

Since many thought that risk could be managed only through the training of honorable scientists, university S&T programs' roles in scientific ethics should be strengthened. While some university courses currently include such ethics, the international definitions, guidelines, and codes of conduct from the eminent group and the ongoing work of the ISTO should provide additional content in strengthening university curricula.

Science students should be obliged to sign a "Scientific Oath" that might be formulated by the eminent group described above. Similar to the Hippocratic Oath of medical doctors, signature would reinforce the awareness of potential implications of their work, and have a moral as well as a judicial significance.

An "Ethics of S&T" course should be required that explores the risks and benefits through the perspectives of environmental science, humanities, medicine, history of ethics, philosophy, religion, and global views of human affairs. Just as ethical thinking is an important first step in Kung Fu as a dangerous technology, so too ethical training should be a precondition to advanced S&T work.

GLOBAL S&T FUND

To make sure that defensive technologies and protective measures will evolve along with the S&T threats, a global S&T fund for such research and development should be considered. This would finance the development of safeguards and ways to reduce risk that might not be pursued through conventional means.

The fund's priorities could come from the ISTO. It might fund national labs, universities, or private-sector R&D firms to conduct the research. Results would be fed to the ISTO data bank and national S&T authorities.

Since the potential impacts are international, the cost of developing countermeasures should be shared internationally. One participant argued that funds from defense budgets should be used to create defensive technologies to counter potential dangers from biotech, nanotech, and robotics, and that for every dollar spent on new technologies that can improve our lives, another dollar should go to protect us from the negative impacts of those same technologies.

Since both risks and opportunities are to be assessed, the fund could support important R&D that cannot attract venture capital due to the long time for return on investment, such as non-greenhouse-gas global energy technologies that could avoid the risks of current options. Long-term financing of the fund could come from licensing the technologies developed from its funding.

S&T FORUMS

The international definitions and guidelines from the eminent group, research from the ISTO, funding agenda for the Global S&T Fund, and potential issues for international treaties could be topics for discussion at an annual Davos-like S&T Forum. Such forums would initiate broader public discussions to help build global consensus. Participants could include political leaders, national S&T policy officials, national lab scientists, corporate R&D managers, university research scientists, NGO S&T issue leaders, UN and other international organization S&T officials, news executives, science writers, software designers, and media producers (TV, radio, film, software). The forums could become "learning communities" of politicians, developers of technologies, scientists, and media, and could build on the experiences of the Global Science Forums of the OECD.

Such forums could provide input to national S&T goal-setting processes. They could provide the state-of-the-art S&T research for the media and universities to help educate the general public to overcome unwarranted fears of S&T. The European Commission (EC) has proposed conducting such forums on a regular basis for Europe beginning in 2004.

MEDIA

It would be impossible to generate a broad global consensus about acceptable risk without the media. More comments from the interviewees about improving the general relationship between the news media, the S&T community, and policy makers are presented in the next section; however, specific public discussion about S&T risk management has to be facilitated by the media. It can connect stories of stakeholder groups, the ISTO, university researchers, Global S&T Fund, and S&T Forums to foster enlightened public debate to contribute to collective consciousness for a commitment for the benefit of all. The media should explore all risks—from genetic counseling to biological warfare. One participant argued that this kind of public discussion is a type of information power for risk management that is better than the control by public administrators.

Unfortunately, integrity in the media can be compromised by the need to sell newspapers, which is done through exciting conflicts. Hence, they prefer to focus on differing points of view rather than "correctly" explaining the facts.

It used to be taboo to talk about research before it appeared in a professional journal. Today, papers are submitted to a preprint server on the Internet and the results are available around the world the next morning. The final judgment of the quality of the research is left to the rest of the world.

INTERNATIONAL TREATIES

As global consensus on any S&T risk is achieved, especially risks considered morally unacceptable, it is reasonable to expect international treaties will follow. There was a general tendency among the participants to prefer regulating technological applications more than basic science. Although some favored international treaties to define the conditions for intervention when risk is too great, it should be understood that the UN Security Council could authorize intervention without new S&T treaties. Both treaties and the Security Council could call for sanctions.

There was disagreement over intervention into S&T research even when the most extreme threats to planetary life support appear to exist. Several participants pointed out that there were no international interventions in the development and deployment of nuclear weapons; authorities in Moscow and Washington came to bilateral agreements. However, there was broad agreement that if treaties are to be created, then the first areas should be biotechnology and genetic engineering.

If S&T treaties are to be drafted, they should define "scientific crime." International standards have to be consistent with S&T changes and human evolution. One participant suggested that the responsibility for implementing the "treaty against abuse of scientific knowledge" should not be left exclusively in the hands of governments. History teaches that even democratic and liberal countries can mobilize scientific research for malicious goals. It was also pointed out that such a treaty should be also enforced personally upon the individual scientist. This could be a special case of crimes against humanity for the new International Criminal Court. Others pointed out that, thus far, legislative steps are far behind the progress in laboratories, and hence international treaties could be even further behind.

There was a broad range of views among those who did advocate principles for intervention and control. For example:

- In general, the more basic the research, the less the control; however, selective oversight in some areas of basic research is still necessary to prevent lethal accidents.

• The stronger the ethical issues involved, the broader the public dialogue prior to drafting treaty text.

• Intervention is justified only when there would be the loss of a significant percentage of humanity, environmental damage severe enough to prevent life support, or the undermining of civilization. One participant added that intervention is also justified when moral values are countered and spiritual development is stopped.

• Research should be controlled when the potential danger can occur with no further opportunity for intervention.

• Wider democratic processes should be involved in assessing S&T with strong ethical issues, such as human cloning. Without interrupting the research, information flows to the public should be continuous.

• Use Ashby's law of requisite variety to measure and manage control options while taking into account socio-cultural contexts.[2]

• Intervention and control should be limited to work that presents a clear and present danger, such as the production of extremely toxic materials. The production of technology can, in this way, be regulated like any other industry.

• Intervention is justified to prevent terrorists from getting S&T for weapons of mass destruction.

NOTES

1. One example of an S&T interest group is the Human Genome Organization, a forum through which the world's scientists can collaborate as they work to unravel our genetic code, and that allows them to discuss some of the social, legal, and commercial issues that spin off that research. The National Nanotechnology Initiative is another example, though initiated by the US government.
2. W.R. Ashby, *An Introduction to Cybernetics* (London: Chapman & Hall, 1973).

STATE OF THE FUTURE INDEX (SOFI):
A METHOD FOR IMPROVING
DECISION MAKING THAT AFFECTS THE FUTURE

by

Theodore J. Gordon

Is the outlook for the future changing? If so, has it improved or worsened over the last decade? Is it likely to improve over the next few years? If so, what is responsible for the changed outlook?

In answering questions like these, problems of the moment often obscure real progress or lasting threats; for example, many people (including decision makers) when asked if the future looks better or worse today than it did in the past, might respond in terms of the consequences of corporate shenanigans or the chaos in the Middle East (the problem of the moment) and overlook the real improvements of the last few decades in life expectancy, infant mortality, public health and increased literacy.

What is needed, we believe, to provide perspective to decision making is some measure of the state of the future. With such a measure, decision makers and others can evaluate the consequences of proposed actions in terms of their impacts on the future outlook, and questions about whether things are improving or worsening can be answered quantitatively. Finally, such an index would improve the sensitivity of decision makers to the issues of the future and the potential results of today's actions or inactions.

The SOFI is an experimental approach to the statistical combination of historical records and forecasts of selected global indicators. It is designed to depict whether the future promises to be better or worse, the directions and intensity of change and the factors responsible. If confidence were developed in such an index, it could be used in policy analysis at the global, national and local levels. Furthermore, nations could be ranked by their SOFI to determine if the future outlook in their regions was better or worse than the global outlook and the reasons for any differences.

Some warnings about the index should be considered. The future cannot be reduced to a single number. Combining many variables into a single index number can lead to loss of detail about the forces that move the index. Creating an index requires judgments not only in selecting the variables to include, but also in weighing them to create an aggregate number. An index of global conditions can mask variations, for better or worse, among regions, nations, or groups.

The apparent precision of an index can easily be mistaken for accuracy. For these reasons, many people interested in tracking social or economic conditions prefer to keep the variables that they consider

Theodore J. Gordon *is senior research fellow for the Millennium Project, American Council for the United Nations University and resides in Old Lyme, Connecticut. He is the founder of The Futures Group, Glastonbury, Connecticut. He may be contacted at tedjgordon@worldnet.att.net.*

important separate and distinct. Since the SOFI is designed to be a globally aggregated measure, it can mask differences among groups or nations: The SOFI could look very positive and yet, for some groups or nations, the situation could be worsening. Therefore, we believe that variable-by-variable and disaggregated SOFI analyses will always be important. These issues notwithstanding, the promise of a SOFI is alluring since it offers the hope of identifying positive and negative changes and points of leverage for policy, as well as achieving some measure of balance in answering questions about the outlook for the future.

In 2001 and 2002, the research program of The Millennium Project (a global activity of the American Council for the United Nations University) undertook an initial investigation into the development and potential use of a SOFI. Five important questions had to be resolved in this research:

1. *What variables should be included in a State of the Future Index?* If people say that the future seems promising, what do they mean? That life will be good for themselves and their family; that food, water and shelter will be sufficient; that fear will be absent and life fulfilled. What else should be included? The selection of variables forces a person to answer two key questions: What do I consider an improvement? And how would I know it if it happened?

2. *How can very different variables be combined?* It is necessary to make all the measures included in the SOFI commensurate—that is, expressed in terms that are comparable. Without some adjustments, the number representing the percent of the population that is literate cannot be added to, say, the number of AIDS deaths.

3. *How can the variables be forecast?* Measurement is not enough; since we are dealing with the future, the variables that make up the SOFI must be forecasted. How can this be done?

4. *How can the variables be weighted?* The SOFI elements are not all of equal importance to the future and must be weighted. But weighting leads to other problems: Different people may see one or the other of the measures as being more or less important, or even of different polarity—that is, some may see an increase in a variable as good while others see it as bad. (Percentage of the population that is urban, is an example of this duality.) The SOFI uses a new nonlinear weighting approach in order to balance the significance of the measures that are included in the index.

5. *How can double accounting be avoided?* This has to be consid-

ered or else one area could be over-represented. For example, should SOFI include both a measure of carbon dioxide concentration and global temperature? They measure different things but are important for the same reason.

The initial inputs for this analysis were obtained from a global survey of 600 futurists and scholars in over 50 countries who answered the question, What variables are important to the future outlook. What are the best and worst values that you see for these variables in the next 10 years? How relatively important are they?[1]
Based on this survey, the variables included in the index are:

• infant mortality rate
• food availability
• GNP per capita
• households with access to safe water
• carbon dioxide emissions
• annual population addition
• percent unemployed
• literacy rate, adult total
• annual AIDS deaths
• life expectancy
• number of armed conflicts
• developing-country debt
• forestlands
• rich/poor gap
• terrorist attacks
• violent crime rate
• population in countries that are not free
• secondary school enrollment
• population with access to local health care.

After obtaining two decades of historical data for each of these variables, the first step of computing the SOFI was to forecast each variable using time series to fit the historical data. These extrapolations make the implicit assumption that the future history of the variables can be determined solely by the past history; obviously, this is true only when no new forces of change impact on the extrapolation.

To avoid the tyranny of this "momentum" assumption, the extrapolative forecasts for the variables were modified to take account of perceptions about the impacts of future unprecedented developments. Using previous work of the Millennium Project, a list of some 80 future developments was assembled; these developments were chosen on the basis of their apparent potential to affect the future course of the SOFI variables. The statistical analysis method used then produced not only a new median forecast for each variable but also the ranges for each in view of the developments that were expected to affect it.

Examples of some of the most profound developments (profound in the sense that they were powerful in changing the forecast of the variables) are listed below:

• Biotech in agriculture: improved food availability as well as enhanced animal health, insect- and disease-resistant plants, etc.

• Social marketing by governments to effectively promote health care and other public objectives.

• Convergence of information/communication technologies (including Internet) lead to improved education.

• Global political order: more aspects of national sovereignty are subject to international decisions (e.g., weapons of mass destruction, human rights).

• Inexpensive very-long-term contraceptives: wide availability and low cost.

• Global economic depression resulting in drop of GDP per capita by 15%.

• Internet use by dissidents, criminals, terrorists for communications.

• The number of nuclear warheads diminished by half.

• Middle East or Chinese/Taiwan wars of large proportions (more than 50,000 casualties over four years).

• Organized crime groups becoming even more sophisticated global enterprises.

• Announcements by terrorists of the anticipated use of weapons of mass destruction to cause panic.

• Effective systems for augmenting human intelligence and improve decision making.

• Establishment of the International Criminal Court.

The SOFI was then computed on the basis of these new forecasts. The curves below illustrate the results of this variable-by-variable forecasting process. Only four variables are shown here, but all of those listed above were forecasted.

TABLE 1 - RESULTS OF VARIABLE-BY-VARIABLE FORECASTING PROCESS

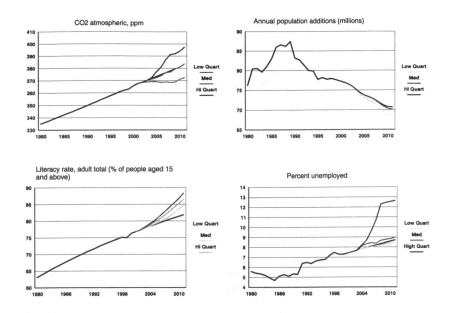

The computation of the SOFI involved:

• Use of judgments of the Global Lookout Panel about what the best (norm) and worst (dystopic) status was for each indicator in 2011 and the importance of reaching the norm or dystopic state.

• Scaling the data by assigning the value of 100 for the most desirable (normative state in 10 years) and 0 for the least desirable values (dystopic state in 10 years).

• Weighting the data using an "S"-shaped function that allows the weight of a variable to vary with the value of the variable.

This "S"-shaped weighting function is an innovation in the field of indexes as far as is known to the research team. In most cases, weights assigned to the variables in an index are held constant. But this is a great oversimplification. For example, the importance of food (as measured in calories per capita per day) is much higher for a hungry person than a satiated person. Therefore, in this work, the weights assigned to all of the variables changed as the variables themselves changed in value, and the best function for relationship was taken as an "S" shape.

TABLE 2 - STATE OF THE FUTURE INDEX

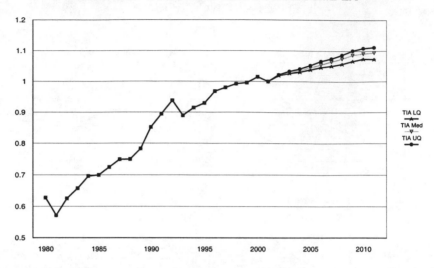

TIA=trend impact analysis

The two black curves define the upper and lower quartile forecasts—that is, the range in which 50% of the forecasted futures fall.

The outlook for the future is getting better due to the past 20 years of improvements in:

- infant mortality rate
- food availability in low-income countries
- GNP per capita
- share of households with access to safe water
- adult literacy rate
- life expectancy
- percent of world population living in countries that are not free
- secondary school enrollment
- share of population with access to local health care.

At the same time, it is getting worse due to deterioration in:

- carbon emissions
- percent of population unemployed
- forestlands
- ratio of global average income of top 5% to bottom 5%
- annual AIDS deaths
- developing-country debt.

We view the work to date as promising but still experimental. If the research continues, future steps would include:

- Improving the analysis programs to facilitate their use by others in sensitivity analyses and policy applications.

- Designing a more compelling presentation of the variables, perhaps in the form of a "dashboard."

- Systematizing the techniques for updating the historical data annually.

- Repeating the global inquiry, utilizing the Millennium Project's panels to again collect judgments about the most important variables, their forecasted normative and dystopic values, their weights, and perturbing future developments.

- Performing the analysis for a set of 50 countries or so to compare SOFIs and explain differences from a newly prepared global SOFI.

- Developing means for introducing selected decision makers to the concept and integrating it into their thinking.

The Silicon Valley node of the Millennium Project began the development of a much improved analysis program in the fall of 2002; the other steps may be initiated over the next three years. If undertaken, the work will involve the participation of all of the Millennium Project's nodes, and in particular, the participation of the Project's global panels.

NOTES

1. See Jerome C. Glenn and Theodore J. Gordon, *State of the Future 2002*, American Council for the United Nations University, July 2002, Washington, D.C., for details about the questionnaire and computational method.

REASSESSING RISK ASSESSMENT

by

Douglas Mulhall

INTRODUCTION AND BACKGROUND

Some environmentalists perceive the risk of nanomaterials as too great to go ahead with until we study them further.[1] Many scientists disagree and say that the potential benefits outweigh the potential risks.[2] I argue in my book, *Our Molecular Future*,[3] that both sides are missing the elephant in the room.

Environmental risk assessment is the foundation of our capacity to evaluate ecological impacts. Yet, a wave of scientific discovery is transforming the way that we perceive the ecology. This will force basic changes to how we evaluate risk.

Until we make such changes, it will not be possible for detractors or supporters of nanotechnologies to accurately evaluate risks and benefits.

NEW FACTORS THAT MAY TRANSFORM RISK ASSESSMENT

For my book, I conducted an extensive examination of emerging theories and technologies that may transform risk assessment methods. The evaluation drew on my own experiences developing and supervising Life Cycle Assessment methodologies:[4] These principal factors were identified:

Technologies That Merge with the Natural Environment

Ray Kurzweil, who pioneered technologies such as the flatbed scanner, argues that technology is a continuation of evolution by other means.[5] This implies that our technologies are becoming an integral part of the ecology. What are the physical manifestations of this?

Smart Dust[6] comprises a massive array of micromachines made of nanoscale components that ride on air or water currents, undetectable to the human eye. Each expendable machine can have a camera, communications device, and varying sensors for chemicals, temperature, and sound. It has its own rechargeable energy source. It can serve as the eyes, ears, nose, and guidance mechanism for everyone from soldiers to hurricane watchers. It costs a fraction of a penny to manufacture, and its prototype exists today. It forms part of a massive array that delivers information to one or hundreds of computers

Douglas Mulhall *is a technology journalist and former manager of Hamburg Environmental Institute where he developed and implemented environmental risk management methods. His new book* Has Heart Disease Been Cured? *examines the risks posed by nanoscale organisms. He may be contacted at webmaster@ourmolecularfuture.com.*

in one or many locations. It will soon be in our environment in the trillions, delivering information about everything from troop to sewage movements.

This nanoscale level of incursion into the ecology suggests emergence of an *intelligent environment*. Just as nature has its own intelligence by acting to balance environmental changes, so we are creating an intelligent human-built environment not just alongside that, but as part of it. An intelligent environment is able to sense virtually every part of the ecology, from the epicenter of earthquakes to the heart of a hurricane and the heartbeat of every species, then interpret what this means.

Such intelligent particles are also gaining the capacity to *self-assemble*. Several universities have pioneered self-assembling photovoltaic materials that generate and conduct an electric current.[7] These materials can be painted onto surfaces, thus eliminating the need for solar panels.

When we combine self-assembly with intelligent sensing at the nanometer scale, then multiply it a trillion-fold, we see that our technology is becoming an integral part of the ecology instead of just impacting it, and that human technologies may soon be indistinguishable from nature.

Enhanced Intelligence Changes the Groundrules

Hans Moravec, head of Carnegie Mellon's Robotics Institute, has shown convincingly—as have others—that the rate of acceleration in information processing is logarithmic.[8] Not only is the capacity to process ones and zeros multiplying, but the *rate* at which it is multiplying is also increasing.

For millennia, this exponential rate was barely perceptible, because it took thousands, then hundreds, then tens of years for such capacity to multiply, from the abacus to the microprocessor, and now the nanoprocessor.

Today, this exponential acceleration enables super-fast manufacturing by machines and software. An example of this is desktop manufacturing that is transforming desktop printing into three-dimensional desktop manufacturing of products.[9]

Such hyperchange is upending the ground rules for intelligence, and by extension for environmental risk management.

Most environmental risk assessment today implicitly assumes that evolution of human intelligence will proceed in the same way that it has over the past few thousands of years—that is, gradually.

Here are examples of why this assumption may be wrong.

In 2001, a computer used "genetic computing"[10] to build a thermostat and actuator that were superior to the counterparts designed by a human. The computer's programmers were unable to trace how the computer reached its conclusion. This is because genetic algorithms allow computers to solve problems in their own way without human intervention.

Machines with enhanced intelligence do certain things far faster and better than we do. Not everything, but many things. Stock brokers now use algorithms that forecast commodity markets more accurately than humans do.[11] Satellites that repair themselves and make unilateral data transmission decisions are already in orbit.[12]

Moreover, massive networks are enhancing our own intelligence. It is now possible for the layperson to perform Internet searches in real time to get answers to complex questions. This acceleration in data recovery *by the general population* constitutes a mass enhancement to our own memories.

At the more specialized level, remote robotic surgery is creating a networked medical "mind" that can perform operations in and from many locations at once.[13]

The merging of human intelligence with genetic algorithms and massive networks is being applied to modeling of, for example, climate change, but it has only just begun to be applied to real-time evaluation of phenomena such as those described below.

Punctuated Equilibrium

The theory of *punctuated equilibrium*[14] was first proposed in 1972 by Niles Eldredge and Harvard evolutionary biologist Stephen Jay Gould. This holds that evolutionary change occurs relatively rapidly in comparatively brief periods of environmental stress, separated by longer periods of evolutionary stability. After many years of skepticism, their theory is now gaining acceptance. This is because proof is emerging.

Intelligent tools, such as those described earlier, are helping us to discover that the natural ecology experiences periodic instability that threatens our society; not just in the extended time frames that we used to think.

In 1994, Comet Shoemaker-Levy 9 (SL9) hit Jupiter,[15] blasting holes the size of Earth in its atmosphere. Had this hit the Earth, human life would have been virtually extinguished.

Until then, it was thought that such upheavals happened only every few million years and that we'd have lots of time to see them coming. SL9 demolished this idea. It demonstrated that we live in a galaxy where life can be snuffed out on a planetary scale without warning.

Furthermore, scientists have found that smaller events have upset the ecology here on Earth. Ice core and tree ring records show that in the year A.D. 536 an unknown event triggered a catastrophic cooling of the Northern Hemisphere, resulting in two years without summers that led to wholesale crop failures and starvation.[16]

Thousands of samples taken from ice cores and tree rings around the world show that naturally induced climate flips have occurred far more frequently than we once thought, and that they do not occur over centuries but rather over a few years.[17]

At the regional scale, in 1700, a fracture at the Cascadia subduction zone produced a gigantic tsunami that scoured much of the Pacific coast for miles inland, where many of our cities now stand.[18] In 1958, a 1,500-foot wave swept away a forest after a mountain collapsed into Lituya Bay, Alaska.[19]

At the *nanometer* scale we are also getting a surprise. Nanoscale organisms a hundred times smaller than most bacteria have been discovered in vast numbers. In human ecology they have been labeled "nanobacterium sanguineum" or blood nanobacteria.[20] In geology, similar sized organisms are named "nanobacteria"[21] and "nano archaea."[22] For decades, researchers around the world have theorized that many prevalent diseases such as atherosclerosis are caused by infection.[23] This was proven for stomach ulcers decades ago, but for other illnesses no one could find a culprit. Now it seems that we have one. Skeptics claimed that nano organisms don't exist, but studies in 2002 by the Mayo Clinic and well-known universities confirm their existence.[24]

Furthermore, scientists have theorized that nanoscale organisms may represent the most plentiful form of biomass on Earth,[25] and that they drive most biochemical processes. Skeptics claim that this is nonsense, but the decoding of the DNA of such organisms in 2002 lends credence to this idea. If it turns out to be only partially valid, then it may still fundamentally alter our present understanding of how ecology works, and what constitutes an ecosystem.

Many of these nano- and macro-scale phenomena pose threats to our society. Yet agencies such as the Federal Emergency Management Agency (FEMA) and Environmental Protection Agency (EPA) have no defenses against them. They usually do not consider such threats because they are perceived as indefensible, or they haven't entered the awareness of the organizations yet.

Thus, punctuated equilibrium is not part of the environmental risk assessment framework, and as such a chunk of the equation is missing. This is especially true when considering the relative environmental risks and benefits posed by nanotechnologies. Such technologies may at once be driving the next "punctuation" in evolution, and give us the tools to protect ourselves from newly discovered big natural threats.

MATCH NATURE'S COMPLEXITY

The convergence of these discoveries may let us achieve something that we have only dreamed of until now: to match nature's complexity.

Right now, most of our technologies are unable to match the complexity of natural environments. For example, we use antibiotics to cure bacterial infections, but they lose their potency when the environment that they work in adapts to them. We build power lines to survive ice storms, but our miscalculation of the worst scenarios leads to collapses that paralyze our high-technology infrastructures.

Most of our agricultural, medical, energy, transportation, and housing systems are in a constant struggle to respond to the complexity of the natural environment.

Yet this imbalance may shift. Molecular technologies are empowering us to find solutions that replicate natural processes at the molecular level. We may see energy grids based on solar "paint" that slash the political and economic risks associated with fossil fuel infrastructures. Our drugs may be so precise that they backfire only occasionally instead of generating widespread immune responses as they do now.

This capacity to match nature's complexity constitutes the next big environmental revolution and may force us to redefine the boundaries of risk assessment.

WHAT TO DO

Newly understood natural phenomena are the elephants in the room of environmental activism and of environmental risk assessment. As such, they must be investigated in the context of emerging factors described in this paper.

For example, although nanoscale organisms have been identified in geological formations and the human body since the late 1980s, few projects have examined the implications for human or natural ecology or for environmental chemistry. NASA is studying it, as are the universities of Texas, McGill (Canada), Regensburg (Germany), Kuopio (Finland), Melbourne (Australia), and a few others. Yet, few if any EPA or FEMA projects examine newly discovered mega-scale anomalies such as the naturally induced climate flip of circa A.D. 536, or the giant west coast tsunami of 1700. These might disrupt natural ecosystems and American society if they recur today.

Finally, no EPA, FEMA, or environmental activist initiative examines how nanotechnologies might be used for adapting to such phenomena.

Due to the fundamental role of risk assessment in analyzing new technologies, I therefore suggest that a forum be sponsored by the World Future Society, "Matching Nature's Complexity: Using Advanced Technologies to Adapt to Newly Found Natural Threats at the Macro and Nano Scale."

The goal of such a forum would be to summarize newly understood natural threats, list advanced technologies that may help us adapt to them, then determine how risk assessment methods might be revised to evaluate such threats and responses.

Examples of such technologies to examine might include:

- Superstrong aerogels to let human settlements withstand hurricanes, earthquakes and tornadoes without causing environmental damage.

• Self-assembling solar cells that help us tolerate environmental shocks with a stable energy supply.

• Nanobiotic treatments that have shown to be effective in combating infectious environmental contaminants implicated in many prevalent diseases.

Such a forum would bring together experts who have never met, including:

• Biochemists, geologists, and physicians who discovered nano-bacteria in the environment and human body, and also developed a new treatment that reverses nanobacterial infections.

• Climatologists and geologists who have uncovered evidence of natural mega-events such as climate disruptions and giant tsunamis.

• Scientists who have developed adaptive technologies such as self-assembling photovoltaic materials that might help us adapt rapidly to big ecological changes.

• Computer scientists who have applied artificially intelligent software to technologies that might be used for environmental adaptation.

• Environmentalists who have proposed a ban on nanomaterials.

In this way, we might help to make risk assessment a more accurate tool for proponents, detractors, and users of advanced technologies.

NOTES

1. *The Big Down, Atomtech Technologies Converging at the Nano Scale*, ETC Group, January 2003, www.etcgroup.org/documents/TheBig Down.pdf.
2. Updates on the nanoethics debates, including rebuttals to the ETC position, are found in the December and February newsletter of CMP-Cientifica, www.cmpcientifica.com/cientifica/frameworks/generic/public_users/tnt_weekly/subscribe.htm.
3. Douglas Mulhall, *Our Molecular Future: How Nanotechnology, Robotics, Genetics, and Artificial Intelligence Will Transform Our World* (Amherst, NY: Prometheus Books, 2002).

4. Michael Braungart, Justus Engelfried, Douglas Mulhall, "Criteria for Sustainable Development of Products and Production," *Fresenius Environmental Bulletin* (Basel, Switzerland: Birkhauser Verlag, 1993), 2:70-77. Also, Douglas Mulhall, "Tools for Adapting to Big Ecosystem Changes," *Futures Research Quarterly*, Vol. 16, No. 3, 49-61. Also, Douglas Mulhall, "Redefining Earth: A Conceptual Framework for Nanoecology," *Nanotechnology Magazine*, December 2001.

5. Ray Kurzweil, "Are We Spiritual Machines?," *The Material World: "Is That All There Is?*, Future Positive, June 18, 2002, futurepos itive.synearth.net/2002/06/20.

6. "Smart Dust," DARPA research Web site describing project on micro air vehicles, robotics.eecs.berkeley.edu/~pister/SmartDust/ (accessed March 15, 2003).

7. "Solar Cells Go Organic," *The Economist, Technology Quarterly*, July 20, 2002, www.economist.com/science/tq/displayStory.cfm?story_id= 1176099 (accessed March 14, 2003).

8. Hans Moravec, "Robot," *Power and Presence* (Oxford, 1998), 60. "The number of MIPS in $1,000 of computer from 1900 to the present," www.frc.ri.cmu.edu/~hpm/book98/fig.ch3/p060.html (accessed March 15, 2003).

9. "Personal Fabrication on Demand," *Wired Magazine*, Vol. 9, No. 4 (April 9, 2001).

10. John R. Koza (Stanford University), Forrest H. Bennett III (Genetic Programming Inc.), David Andre (University of California, Berkeley), Martin A. Keane (Econometrics Inc.), "Genetic Programming III: Darwinian Invention and Problem Solving" (Morgan Kaufmann, 1999) Chapter V. *Automated Synthesis of Analog Electrical Circuits.*

11. Dave Cliff, *Artificial Trading Agents for Online Auction Marketplaces,* HP Labs, Bristol, www-uk.hpl.hp.com/people/dave_cliff/traders.htm (accessed March 15, 2003).

12. "Satellite Trio to Test Artificial Intelligence Software," Aviation-Now.com, *Aviation Week* (May 30, 2001), www.aviationnow.com/ avnow/news/channel_space.jsp?view=story&id=news/ssat0530.xml (accessed March 15, 2003).

13. *FDA Approves New Robotic Surgery Device*, Food & Drug Administration news release (July 11, 2000), www.fda.gov/bbs/topics/ NEWS/NEW00732.html.

14. Stephen Jay Gould, "Darwinian Fundamentalism," *New York Review of Books* (June 12, 1997), www.nybooks.com/articles/1151 (accessed March 17, 2003).

15. Dan Bruton, *Frequently Asked Questions About the Impact of Comet Shoemaker-Levy 9 with Jupiter*, Institute for Scientific Computation (February 2, 1996), www.isc.tamu.edu/~astro/sl9/cometfaq2.html# Q3.1 (accessed August 29, 2001).

16. R.B. Stothers, "Mystery Cloud of 536 A.D," *Science Frontiers*. No. 33 (May-June 1984), reprinted from R.B. Stothers, "Mystery Cloud of AD 536," *Nature*, 307 (1984), 344, www.science-frontiers.com/sf033/sf033p19.htm (accessed August 12, 2001).

17. Richard B. Alley, *The Two Mile Time Machine: Ice Core, Abrupt Climate Change, and Our Future* (Princeton, NJ: Princeton University Press, 2000). Also, M.G.L. Baillie, *A Slice Through Time: Dendrochronology and Precision Dating* (London: Routledge, 1995).

18. Nelson et al, "Radiocarbon Evidence for Extensive Plate Boundary Rupture About 300 Years Ago at the Cascadia Subduction Zone," *Nature* 378 (November 23, 1995).

19. *The 1958 Lituya Bay Tsunami*, University of Southern California Tsunami Research Group, www.usc.edu/dept/tsunamis/alaska/1958/webpages/index.html (accessed March 17, 2003).

20. E. Olavi Kajandera, Neva Ciftcioglua, Marcia A. Miller-Hjelleb, J. Thomas Hjelleb, "Nanobacteria: Controversial Pathogens in Nephrolithiasis and Polycystic Kidney Disease," *Current Opinion in Nephrology and Hypertension*, 2001: 10: 445-452.

21. Robert L. Folk, "Nanobacteria: Surely Not Figments, But What Under Heaven Are They?," *Natural Science* (March 4, 1997), naturalscience.com/ns/articles/01-03/ns_folk.html (accessed January 25, 2003).

22. Harald Huber, Michael J. Hohn, Reinhard Rachel, Tanja Fuchs, Verena C. Wimmer and Karl O. Stetter, "A New Phylum of Archaea Represented by a Nanosized Hyperthermophilic Symbiont," *Nature*, 417, 63-67, May 2, 2002.

23. Steven D. Mawhorter and Michael A. Lauer, "Is Atherosclerosis an Infectious Disease?," *Cleveland Clinic Journal of Medicine*, Vol. 68, No. 5, May 2001.

24. Todd E. Rasmussen, Brenda L. Kirkland, Jon Charlesworth, George P. Rodgers, Sandra R. Severson, Jeri Rodgers, Robert L. Folk, Virginia M. Miller, *Electron Microscope and Immunological Evidence of Nanobacterial-Like Structures in Calcified Carotid Arteries, Aortic Aneurysms and Cardiac Valves*, Mayo Clinic and Foundation, Rochester, Minnesota; University of Texas, Austin, March 6, 2002.

25. Robert L. Folk, "Nanobacteria: Surely Not Figments, But What Under Heaven Are They?," *Natural Science* (March 4, 1997), naturalscience.com/ns/articles/01-03/ns_folk.html (accessed January 25, 2003).

THE IMPACT OF GLOBALIZATION

GLOBALIZATION: SOCIAL DISRUPTION RIGHT AHEAD

by

J. Ørstrøm Møller

ANALYSIS

At the end of the 18th century the world saw the technology of power destroying the social fabric of the agricultural and feudal society. The visible conflict was the Napoleonic wars, but beneath the surface it was really a social conflict between a society based upon feudalism and the new industrial society.

More than one hundred years ago a similar conflict was brewing and erupted in 1914 with World War I. The second industrial revolution introduced technology of transformation in the sense that mankind possessed the ability to transform its surroundings (e.g., electricity could turn night into day). Again, the social structures were ripped apart. They could not accommodate the strive for opportunities and wealth.

What seems to be the common denominator for both cases is:

- growing disparities with regard to income, wealth, education and access to knowledge in an unprecedented scale

- creation of tremendous wealth outside the established groups or classes of society

- accompanied by destruction of wealth inside the established groups of society

- the emergence of new political forces shaping evolution of our societies.

Our present societies epitomize exactly such a development. It can be seen inside the nation-states and it can be seen internationally between the nation-states. It can, with some justification, be said that this is not really new, that we have seen it and known it for a long time. Yes, but what is new is the strength, the speed and the strong repercussions on our societies.

It is difficult to challenge the statement that inside nation-states and between rich and poor nation-states disparities are growing. All statistical evidence points to that effect.

It is equally difficult to challenge the view that tremendous wealth is being created outside the well-known circles of society. The new technology makes people rich to the tune of millions of US

J. Ørstrøm Møller *is adjunct professor at the Copenhagen Business School and Ambassador of Denmark to Singapore, New Zealand, and Australia. He may be contacted at jormol@denmark.com.sg.*

dollars from one day to the next. This new wealth simply dwarfs conventional economic and social wisdom. The wizards of the new global and high-tech economy operates with sums of several billion US dollars compared to the US development assistance equivalent to about $8 billion per year.

The establishment is being crowded out by this onslaught of mighty economic and technological forces. The traditionally rich part of society, having accumulated some sense of social responsibility, is losing influence because its wealth fades away. The newborn rich do not find it necessary to shoulder burdens vis-à-vis society and their country or the international community. Why should they? They owe nothing to anyone other than themselves! The *nouveaux riches* have acquired their wealth by breaking away from the existing society to which they feel no allegiance while all those having lost jobs, income or wealth do in fact belong to the core groups of precisely that society. No reconciliation is in the cards—on the contrary. The *nouveaux riches* are distancing themselves from political and social responsibility, conveying the impression that this is not worthwhile and that those operating in these circles are losers. It is said that Bill Gates received the loudest applause some years ago speaking in California when answering "no" to a question on whether he contemplated entering politics.

One hundred years ago we saw the working class coming to power. As yet we have not seen a new determining political class, but we have seen the well-established coalitions inside nation-states breaking up. In Britain, Margaret Thatcher ripped apart the post World War II political consensus. She could work a new coalition while in power, but her successors cannot. In the United States, Ronald Reagan was the last president presiding over some kind of political coalition. Neither Bill Clinton nor George W. Bush has been able to shape a new coalition. Traditional and workable political constellations have been blown apart without any visible lasting and workable new structure being born. The political forces are ephemeral and malleable, not foundations for a lasting social and political consensus creating stability. There is growing uneasiness that this may pave the way for a decade dominated by nationalistic, maybe even populist politicians after the policy-oriented politicians in the 1980s and the management politicians of the 1990s.

KEY OBSERVATION

We are fast approaching some kind of full circle in the sense that a new social explosion lies ahead of us. On top of threats to the social fabric having surfaced at the two earlier occasions, we have three new and maybe even more dangerous trends.

The Elite vs. the Majority of the Population

The nation-state used to be a strong player in shaping national and international politics, albeit it is losing influence and power—and fast. Where it has been losing "fastest and mostest" is in its own domestic political and social cohesion. In short: The elite goes more and more international while the majority of the population is being left in its slipstream to fight for themselves as best they can.

The elite takes its clue from the global and international development. It buys international, it gets its information from international channels, it sends its children to internationally recognized universities, it communicates with the elite in other nation-states and not with the population inside the nation-states. The common identity linking elite and population is fast disappearing.

The elite is supposed to lead the way and show that globalization is to the advantage of the nation-state as a whole, but instead it reserves all the advantages for itself and leaves the rest of the population to wonder about the advantages, if any, for them.

Long Live Retrenchment!

This happens exactly at the time when business leaders are applauded by politicians and most of the elite has come to the conclusion that the best manager is the man who retrenches the largest part of the workforce in the enterprise he is supposed to lead. For an economist of the old school it is indeed strange to read business pages in the leading papers and journals. Column after column is filled with news of retrenchment and laying-off in this or that enterprise. That may or may not be necessary to survive in an increasingly competitive world, but the tone is that this is mighty good.

Formerly, economic science was about welfare and good living conditions for the majority of people. The objective of all economic activities was or should be consumption—what else? A whole string of the fathers of economic theory wrestled with the problem of how to increase welfare and consumption for the population as a whole. Not so, anymore. Now, focus is upon creating wealth regardless of its distribution. The beacons of business are those who create more wealth for an enterprise or themselves by reducing wealth for a large number of persons being retrenched. You do not need to be a detective to spot this. Just read the papers and see on one page retrenchment and on another page how the managers in charge reward themselves with stock options and/or other means of enrichment.

The Minorities Begin to See Their Chance

This political, economic and social challenge to stability is being aggravated by a cultural revolution breaking with almost 200 years of uninterrupted evolution: the revolt of the minorities inside nation-states. Potentially this may be the most dangerous threat to the political and economic architecture built since the industrial revolution. The nation-state was created to promote the industrial society. Minorities were enrolled against their wishes, but they benefited like the majorities from the industrial development, which could not take place without the political, social and technical infrastructure. This kept the Scots inside Britain, the Bretons inside France, the Catalans inside Spain, the people in Lombardy inside Italy, the Ukrainians inside Russia, etc.—the list is endless.

They were willing to surrender some, albeit not all, their cultural identity on the altar of economic progress. And so they did.

But now the industrial society is no longer necessary. Indeed, in many cases it has become an obstacle to economic progress, so they revolt. We see it most clearly in Europe, where the industrial revolution started.

The minorities are no longer ready to surrender part or all of their identity to belong to a nation-state that for decades, even centuries, exercised cultural imperialism, as it is no longer capable of furthering economic growth.

History may pronounce the verdict that the European Union was most successful in picking up this trend and providing the people of Western Europe with exactly the right mix of economic international-ization and cultural decentralization. The prospect of joining this model explains why Central and Eastern Europe did not erupt into clashes between majorities and minorities as most observers thought would happen after the collapse of the Soviet and Russian empire in 1990.

The plain fact is that the minorities no longer feel attached to the nation-state. In many cases, the nation-state is regarded as an enemy. Instead, they look to the international community as the midwife to deliver them. And, in many cases, the international community delivers.

WHY IS GLOBALIZATION IN THE FRONTLINE?

Quite simply, globalization is in the frontline because a rising share of economic transactions and dissemination of knowledge and information take place at the international level. In the industrial society, most people could live a whole and active life without much connection to international economic transactions. Not so today. People are employed by supranational companies, they are being promoted or retrenched by companies with headquarters in other nation-states, and they get much of their information and entertain-ment from international channels. The sheer size of the global economy and its impact on the nation-states guarantee that most people feel the consequences of the global economy.

But the majority of people do not associate capital movements, trade and transfer of technology with the global economy. For them, it is either abstract or they take it for national activities.

For them, the global economy and internationalism is represented by the institutions trying to rein in the activities of the supranational companies and constitute some kind of political framework—the EU, the WTO and the IMF just to mention a few. The majority of the people aim their criticism and indeed anger at these institutions. This is what they understand and what they read about.

Most people still prefer the national political decision-making process, even if it has become more or less devoid of substance, because the parameters it tries to control have gone international. They believe that internationalism is brought to them by the institutions instead of realizing that the institutions represent their only chance of getting influence in the same way as they have in the national political system.

This is why it is so difficult to move the political institutions on to the same level—international—as the substance (trade, capital movements, transfer of technology) it tries to control. One of the paradoxes of our time.

A powerful political coalition is being forged these years constituted by:

- political leaders from a number of semi-developed nation-states questioning the conventional wisdom that globalization is good for their countries

- political leaders from developed countries adopting a nationalistic, not to say populist, policy

- activists such as the Attac movement rejecting globalization

- pressure groups such as Greenpeace trying to curb the progress of economic globalization

- a large part of the population in developing nations putting the question about globalization on the political agenda: Where is the beef for us?"

- a rising share of the population inside developed nations seeing globalization as a threat to their welfare and not as a challenge or an opportunity.

The dichotomy between the elite and the majority of the population, the retrenchment produced by supranational companies and the voice of the minorities, boost this political coalition while those who want and are capable of delivering a strong defense of the benefits accruing to our societies from globalization constitute a silent group—having chosen to be silent!

The elite does not really bother to take a stand and defend globalization. Why should it? It is doing quite nicely anyway, and probably the threat toward globalization does not need to be taken seriously! Anyway, it is too burdensome to communicate with the population.

The supranational companies use the freedom of localization to shift production from country to country, thus aggravating the criticism. They demand more and more liberal rules and use them to wriggle free from efforts to control their activities and/or constitute a framework like the one we have on the national level.

The minorities emphasize their cultural identity instead of economic progress as they used to during the industrial age. In many cases, we clearly see a willingness to prefer identity (culture, religion, ethics) instead of higher production, productivity or competitiveness.

This last point may be a very dangerous one. In many parts of the world the political leaders confront dissatisfied groups of minorities saying that if they do not accept enrollment in the programs offered by society to prepare for the international competition, they may not be able to maintain a rising living standard. Until recently the reaction was acceptance—grudgingly, maybe, but acceptance—but now we see and hear the following answer: "That may be so, but we are willing to pay that price."

This reaction or answer put the proponents of globalization on the spot. If the minorities are ready to accept a lower living standard to safeguard what they regard as their own cultural identity, there is no argument left in favor of globalization. But there is a consequence. And that consequence is a breaking up of many societies between the elite accompanied by a part of the population taking part in the globalization and another part of the population rejecting globalization because it, in their eyes, represents a threat toward their cultural identity.

For those convinced that globalization is the best model, the challenge is to combine the benefit of economic internationalization with the right to maintain and even develop cultural identity regardless of whether we speak of majorities or minorities inside the nation-states. If we do not master that problem, nation-states will gradually break up, propelled by nationalism, and thus not only herald the end of internationalism but announce economic, cultural, ethnic and religious confrontations probably of a very ugly nature. What we have seen in the Balkans for the last decade will not be the final chapter of political misconduct 100 years ago but a new pattern of international and national behavior.

POLICY PRESCRIPTIONS

It would indeed be a great help if political leaders perceived this threat as the greatest challenge to the world instead of being captivated by strategic thinking belonging to the Cold War based upon military instruments and enemies vs. allies. The challenge today is to shape a system to facilitate global cooperation—to think and act like internationalists—and not to find out who is the next enemy 20 years ahead and how are we going to prevent that potential enemy from growing stronger.

The political and economic infrastructure governing the Western world (domestically and internationally) since 1945 was shaped by the exigencies posed by the Cold War. The Cold War itself ended in 1990. The infrastructure belonging to the era of the Cold War died in the beginning of 2003. We can go one step further. The main characteristic of the international system, as it now emerges, is the end of the sovereignty of the nation-state, telling us that the Westphalian system introduced in 1648 guarding the nation-state and making it the cornerstone of the international system is out, dead, gone and forever.

Such a turnaround in strategy away from conflict to define problems and solutions in common would pave the way for the following policies:

• The world badly needs a set of common values. This is not what some call monoculture, or a misguided attempt to harmonize culture and behavior, but simply an idea of what is good and what is bad. Without such a set of common values it will not be possible to reconcile the elite and the majority, nor will it be possible to avoid a clash between those who give priority to their cultural identity and those who favor economic progress. It served the world tremendously well after World War II that there actually was such a set of common values pointing to an increase in economic and social welfare as priority number one, with few if any dissidents. The main problem right now is that this, let us call it common understanding, is slipping away.

• Nationally, a common set of values keeps the nation together and, if mutually agreed upon and applied successfully, produces a solid, even robust nation-state. A common mind-set presents an almost insurmountable obstacle to fragmentation, disintegration and disorganization. By upbringing and tradition, people react according to some kind of common denominator defined by the underlying set of values. Are we prepared to introduce a set of values on the international level to safeguard the identity of people irrespective of ethnicity and/or religion, neglecting nationality as criterion for rights and obligations?

• Is the world prepared to rein in the use of power and subject it to agreed rules and norms, and can the powerful nations be counted upon to respect these rules in the interest of internationalism? Power in itself does not legitimize intervention. Only by maintaining the moral high ground can international use of power be warranted. And even more difficult: Are we mentally capable of reining in the use of power by the powerful while, at the same time, confronting, even imposing upon, violent minorities rules of behavior as a quid pro quo? The majorities must recognize the cultural identity of minorities. Minorities must exercise their distinctive character in conformity with and not against the grain of the community in which they live.

• This is where tolerance comes into the picture. Tolerance does not mean opening the floodgates for everybody to behave as they like. Tolerance constitutes the right to think and act differently from other people but within a mutually agreed framework. Tolerance defined in this way forces us to know precisely where we stand ourselves. Other opinions must be measured against our own opinion. We must know what we think and why we think in the way we do—what is our mindset, why do we have it, and why do we think it is the right one for us? Thinking in this way opens the door for realizing that what is best for us may not necessarily be best for others. And that gives birth to the crucial observation that the heart of tolerance is that we care for other people's destiny even if we do not agree with them.

• Doubts are cast over international actions even where a lot of good will is present. The International Monetary Fund is heavily criticized for its action to help Indonesia even if the objectives of the IMF were unquestionably laudable. The NATO action in Kosovo aroused suspicion and misgivings in other parts of the world despite the fact that NATO governments felt that they were moving in to avoid a genocide. In these and other cases, international action becomes more and more difficult, even suspicious, because it takes place without the implicit backing of a common set of values removing any doubt about the purpose of intervention and what those performing it actually have in mind.

• International intervention inside the nation-state becomes gradually the rule rather than the exception. But if or when it takes place outside an agreed set of values, the fear arises— warranted or unwarranted—that the yardstick is sheer power exercised by those having the power instead of a common set of values opening the door for the weak nation-states to have their say in shaping and operating the international system.

• Our political systems and our economic models are gradually moving toward value-based and value-controlled systems. This is a complete break with the past, where both systems were mainly guided and tested by economic considerations. It is no longer decisive for elections whether the economy is doing more or less well. Thinking back to the slogan from Bill Clinton's campaign in 1992, "It's the economy, stupid," seems to have been wrong. It was the idea of government and its relations to people that helped Clinton win the White House. It was the threat to the American homeland and the focus upon American values that helped George W. Bush-backed Republicans to win the mid-term election in 2002 despite a depressing economic outlook. In the same vein, it can be said that consumers are increasingly being guided by values when choosing what to buy. Enterprises are being pushed, with or against their will, to produce not only economic accounts but also environmental accounts, social accounts and now value-based accounts—what do they stand for and what have they achieved in pushing their values?

• Most people can identify themselves with the national political system even if it does not work properly to their mind (as they would like it). But they cannot identify themselves with the international system. It is not theirs. It is not transparent, it does not embody accountability and it loses legitimacy because it blurs the picture about who is actually responsible for which decisions. People feel that in the national system they can reward and punish politicians according to the scoreboard, but not so in the international system.

• This is why political actions outside the normal pattern take place on the international scene. NGOs and other fora for pressure groups, plus the large supranational companies, have more or less given up pursuing their objectives by patterns known from the domestic political game. They do not find such patterns on the international scene. They then fall back on non-parliamentarian actions, which the national parliamentarians take as an affront. This produces a stalemate between the outworn national system, which has not been able to transfer its main instruments to the international arena, and the players on this arena, which demand channels to political decision making and would be more than happy to find such channels but unfortunately, time after time, come to the conclusion that they do not exist.

• The world needs such channels to accommodate the international players, which sometimes, but not always, are the same as the players in the national arena. It is no longer any use to pretend that companies like Microsoft, pressure groups like Greenpeace, and minorities inside nation-states do not influence the political and economic development—they do. The system must incorporate them in decision making or it will undermine itself.

• Various international organizations, be it UN, EU, or NAFTA, must be better-geared to draw the distinction between what they can usefully do and what they should definitely not do. A big conference to draw up a catalogue would be the certain road to disaster, but the politicians masterminding these organizations should do it in the way that they leave to lower levels in the political decision-making process what they can and only deal with what demands international action and accordingly can be justified in a dialogue with the population.

• The plain fact is the majority of people are not against globalization or internationalization or whatever it is called, as long as they understand and see the advantages by decisions in common instead of individual decisions by each nation-state. Where they refuse to take part is where the advantages are doubtful or even absent, so that the whole exercise resembles an academic endeavor serving nobody except a handful of politicians and civil servants.

• International actions justified to achieve objectives that are supported by a large majority of the population usually find broad support provided that the politicians explain to the population what they are doing, how they are doing it and why they are doing it. Unfortunately, this is rarely being done, because most politicians inside international political decision making perceive the process as fulfilled when they leave the meeting room. Indeed, this is where it starts, because now they have to go back to their constituencies to rally the necessary support.

What is in doubt, severe doubt, is whether this is the case for the present international system.

REFERENCES

J. Ørstrøm Møller, *The Future European Model: Economic Internationalization and Cultural Decentralization*, with a foreword by the Honorable James A. Baker III (Westport, CT: Greenwood Publishing House, 1995).

J. Ørstrøm Møller, *The End of Internationalism or World Governance*, with a foreword by President of the European Commission, Jacques Santer (Westport, CT: Greenwood Publishing House, 2000).

GLOBALIZATION, HERITAGE BUILDINGS, AND THE 21ST CENTURY ECONOMY

by

Donovan D. Rypkema

INTRODUCTION

Just over fifteen years ago the American urbanologist Jane Jacobs wrote, "...all developing economic life depends on city economies.... All expanding economic life depends on working links with cities."[1] Although that book, *Cities and the Wealth of Nations*, is still cited as a pivotal work in urban economics, the word *globalization* doesn't even appear in Jacobs's index. Today, how could one ponder the role or the future of cities without considering globalization?

The question then becomes, "In a globalized economy does economic life still depend on city economies?" Urban economist Richard Knight in his book, *Cities in a Global Society*, seems to think so as he writes, "Now that development is being driven more by globalization than by nationalization, the role of cities is increasing. Power comes from global economies that are realized by integrating national economies into the global economy, and cities provide the strategic linkage functions."[2]

It is not my intention here to argue the merits of economic globalization aside from the following: (1) economic globalization is inevitable in the 21st century; (2) there are 1.2 billion people in the world living in poverty—most of them people of color—and the industrial world will never tax itself enough to end that hunger; (3) the only escape from poverty is the ability to sell goods and services around the world; and (4) while there will be some places that choose to opt out of the world economy for reasons of provincial ideology, protectionist isolationism, or political IOUs, the citizens of those places will be the losers. I also concur with Jacobs and Knight that the decisive role in a globalized economy will be played by cities.

But there has been a misunderstanding of globalization by both its advocates and its critics. That misunderstanding is this: that *globalization* implies both economic globalization and cultural globalization. I will argue that those are two different phenomenon that while interrelated are not inexorably linked. Further, I would suggest that, while economic globalization has many positive impacts, cultural globalization has few if any benefits but has significant adverse social and political consequences in the short term, and negative economic consequences in the long term.

If cities are to succeed in the challenge of economic globalization they will not only have to be competitive with other cities in their

Donovan D. Rypkema *is principal of Place Economics, a real estate and economic development consulting firm located in Washington, D.C. He may be contacted at drypkema@placeeconomics.com.*

nation or region, but be competitive worldwide. However, their success will be measured not just by their ability to foster economic globalization, but also by their ability to diminish and mitigate cultural globalization. In both cases a city's historic built environment will play a central role.

As the world has quickly passed into the 21st century, the context and environment of local economic development is rapidly evolving. The purpose of this paper is to identify some of the realities of that evolving context, establish a set of principles that will underlie economic development in the 21st century, enumerate the "five senses" that each city will need to be competitive, and suggest that the preservation of the historic built environment, far from being a hamper to economic growth, can be a critical vehicle to make it happen. This paper is not intended to be an exhaustive discussion of any of these issues; rather, it is hoped to be a checklist of economic development components against which a variety of specialists can consider their own areas of expertise.

REALITIES OF THE 21ST CENTURY ECONOMY

Before the role of the city can be understood, it is necessary to step back and understand the realities of this century's economy. Four such realities are already obvious.

First, the 21st century will be a globalized economy. This will affect every national economy regardless of political or economic system.

Second, the most significant impacts of the global economy will not be at the national or even the provincial level. The biggest impacts will be local. Akito Marito, founder of Sony, called this "Global Localization."[3] Harvard professor Michael Porter writes in *The Competitive Advantage of Nations*, "The process of creating skills and the important influences on the rate of improvement and innovation are intensely local." Paradoxically, then, more open global competition makes the home base more, not less, important.[4]

Third, there will be a rapidly growing demand for products worldwide. But the manufacture of those products will require fewer and fewer people. Likewise, the need for agricultural products will only increase with world population growth, but fewer agricultural workers will be necessary to grow that food.

Fourth, the areas of the economy that will grow, both in output and in employment, are these: services; ideas; one-of-a-kind products, individually produced; culture; entertainment; communication; travel; and education. For each of these growth areas, quality and authenticity will be major variables in consumer choice.

PRINCIPLES OF 21ST CENTURY ECONOMIC DEVELOPMENT

The cities and their citizens who will be successful in this century's economic development will be those that recognize these realities and respond by embracing five principles.

The first principle is globalization itself. To ignore the reality of a globalized economy, or to recognize it but not respond, will make many cities the victim rather than the beneficiary of globalization. To adopt globalization as a principle allows a city the opportunity to identify its own characteristics that can be competitive in the global marketplace and to establish measures that mitigate the adverse impacts that a globalized economy can carry. Even such a staunch globalist as Kenichi Ohmae writes, "As the borderless and interlinked economy develops, regional- and city-level interests come more and more into play."[5]

The second principle is localization. The definition of what "economic development" means needs to be a local one. It needs to be specific and measurable. Many local economic development yardsticks in the 21st Century will be qualitative rather than quantitative. Localization will always necessitate identifying local assets (human, natural, physical, locational, functional, cultural) that can be utilized to respond to globalization. Those assets need to be first identified, then protected, then enhanced. In his book *Post-Capitalist Society*, the American business guru Peter Drucker writes, "Tomorrow's educated person will have to be prepared for life in a global world. He or she must become a 'citizen of the world'—in vision, horizon, information. But he or she will also have to draw nourishment from their local roots and, in turn, enrich and nourish their own local culture."[6]

Diversity is the third of these principles. Biologists were the first to understand the importance of diversity to a healthy ecological system. But the English words "ecology" and "economy" come from the same root, the Greek word *oikos*, which means "house." Economic development analysts—based on the models of the ecologists—have discovered that what is necessary to keep our economic house in order is the same as it takes to keep our ecological house in order and that, in part, is diversity.

The concept of diversity has three different facets in relation to economic development principles:

- As populations are more mobile and more diverse—particularly in cities—there will need to be an accommodation of human diversity in economic development and an appreciation of the valuable alternative perspectives that diversity can provide in an economic context.

- Cities will have to have a diverse local economy to provide protection from the volatile patterns of demand in the marketplace. Excessive reliance on a single source of employment, production, and economic activity leaves cities inordinately vulnerable.

• With economic globalization as a given, the extension is that potential customers for goods and services will be exceedingly diverse. Successful economic development will specialize and customize to meet the needs of diverse markets rather than standardize and homogenize, ignoring customer diversity.

The fourth principle of 21st century economic development is sustainability. Sustainability has for sometime been recognized by the resource industries—the necessity to pace extraction or renew resources so that the local economy is sustainable over the long term. A broadened principle of sustainability recognizes the importance of the functional sustainability of public infrastructure, the fiscal sustainability of a local government, the physical sustainability of the built environment, and the cultural sustainability of local traditions, customs, and skills.

The final principle is responsibility. While in most parts of the world there will be provincial, national and international resources that can occasionally be tapped for use in enhancing a city's economy, the vast majority of the efforts will take place at the local level. This, then, requires that each city take a large measure of responsibility for its own economic future. Certainly local government has a part to play in that process, but so do the private sector when it exists, NGOs, and citizens at large. Each must recognize the responsibility at the local level to define and pursue a citywide economic development strategy.

THE *FIVE SENSES* OF COMPETITIVE CITIES

In the past the economic fate of a given city was largely driven by locational and resource factors. Is it near a port? Is there timber to be cut? Is transportation available by waterway? Is there copper that can be mined? Certainly these and similar factors will continue to play a major role in the economic future for many locations. But in the 21st century there will be a shift from location economics to place economics. Many of the variables that will influence a city's economic opportunity will not be locationally driven. The most important variables will be qualitative and place-based rather than quantitative and location-based. These are referred to as the Five Senses of Competitive Cities and will, in the intermediate and long term, have considerable impact on the economic health of individual cities.

The first sense is the Sense of Place. Both the built and the natural environments will need to be used to express the particularity of *this* place. That this city is neither "anyplace" nor "no place" but "someplace," unduplicated anywhere. Four hundred years ago the Italian philosopher Giordano Bruno recognized that "Where there is no differentiation, there is no distinction of quality."[7]

The second sense is the Sense of Identity. In economics it is the differentiated product that commands a monetary premium. A city that in the long term wants to be a "valuable place," however that is defined, needs to identify its attributes that add to its differentiation from anywhere else. The cultural as well as the physical attributes of a city will be critical to that differentiation.

The third sense is the Sense of Evolution. Quality, living cities will neither be frozen in time as museum relics nor look like they were built yesterday. The physical fabric of a city should reflect its functional, cultural, aesthetic and historical evolution. Writing in his book *Citistates*, Neal Pierce emphasizes the need to "Reaffirm the critical importance of the citistate's heart—its historic center city and neighborhoods.... This means urban design, waterfront planning, streetscapes, and historic preservation are important issues for a citistate's presentation to the world."[8]

The fourth sense of competitive cities is the Sense of Ownership. If there needs to be responsibility exercised at the local level to create and benefit from economic health, then there has to be a sense of ownership of the city by each of the sectors. This does not mean ownership in a legal or property sense, but ownership more broadly, a feeling of an individual stake arising from that particular place and fellow citizens. An American mayor, Daniel Kemmis—one of the few American politicians who is also a scholar—wrote, "A good city has always been one that teaches citizenship, in the deepest sense of the word, and such cities are not only teachers, but are themselves always learning how to be better cities."[9]

Finally, there is the Sense of Community. A sense of ownership acknowledges an individual benefit from, an individual stake in, and an individual responsibility for one's place. A sense of community acknowledges the obligations to and interconnectedness with the other residents of that place. Robert Bellah has spent a career examining this amorphous concept of *community* around the world and has concluded, "Communities, in the sense in which we are using the term, have a history—in an important sense they are constituted by their past—and for this reason we can speak of a real community as a 'community of memory,' one that does not forget its past."[10]

ECONOMIC GLOBALIZATION WITHOUT CULTURAL GLOBALIZATION

Cities, then, will need to respond to the principles of the 21st century economy—globalization, localization, sustainability, diversity, and responsibility. Competitive cities will cultivate and promote the five senses—sense of place, sense of identity, sense of evolution, sense of ownership and sense of community.

This will be necessary both to foster economic globalization and to mitigate cultural globalization. For all of the potential benefits of a globalized economy (and there are many) it carries with it the substantial risk of a globalized culture, of which there are few if any benefits.

But it is not inherently necessary that a globalized economy leads to a globalized culture. In fact, it is crucial for economic as well as other reasons that it does not. That will require decisions at the national and regional level but particularly at the city level to make sure a globalized local culture does not occur.

In parallel to the above, the "modernization" of local communities in infrastructure, public health, convenience, and quality of life *does not* necessitate the "Westernization" of the built environment. The copy of a built environment from elsewhere will never be as good as the original. An imitative strategy for the built form quickly leads a city from being "someplace" to "anyplace." And the distance from "anyplace" to "no place" is short indeed.

HERITAGE CONSERVATION AS AN ECONOMIC DEVELOPMENT STRATEGY

Heritage conservation has often been portrayed as the alternative to economic development—"either we have historic preservation or we have economic growth." This is absolutely a false choice. Increasingly, around the world, historic preservation is becoming a uniquely effective vehicle for economic growth.

Historic preservation has moved from being an end in itself (save old buildings in order to save old buildings) to being a vehicle of broader ends—center city revitalization, job creation, cultural stewardship, small business incubation, housing, tourism, and others. The successful strategies of utilizing historic preservation as a tool of economic development seem to have several common denominators:

1. Major landmarks and monuments need to be identified and protected, but
2. Historic resources are far more than monuments and often are vernacular buildings.
3. Groups of buildings rather than individual structures are often what are important.
4. The vast majority of buildings of "historic importance" have their importance defined by their local significance, not national or international importance.
5. Adaptive reuse of functionally obsolete buildings is central to an effective heritage conservation as economic development strategy.
6. Authenticity is an important element in sustainable historic preservation-based success.

With those understandings, a historic preservation-based economic development strategy has several measurable benefits:

• *Job creation.* The labor intensity of building rehabilitation generally means that there is a greater local economic impact in jobs and income than with the same amount spent on new construction.

• *Job training and skills passing.* The local craftsmanship of the building process can often be nearly lost in a generation but instead can be passed on through historic preservation, creating jobs and skills simultaneously.

• *Import substitution.* A central strategy in building a sustainable local economy is import substitution—creating locally what otherwise would have to be purchased elsewhere. Almost by definition, historic preservation is locally based, using expertise, labor, and materials from the local market. Often new construction is the opposite, requiring the importation of expertise, materials, and often labor from elsewhere.

• *Compatibility with modernization.* There are certainly many historic buildings that don't currently meet today's standards for comfort, convenience, and safety. But over the last two decades great strides have been made around the world in the methods of bringing historic buildings into compliance with modern demands without harming their physical structure or their architectural character. Most components for modernization—water and sewer lines, telephone cables, electric wires, even high speed computer data transmission lines—can be put in place almost invisibly, often underground, without jeopardizing the individual historic resources or their important context and interrelationships.

• *Compatibility with evolution.* Once there is an acknowledgement that effective historic preservation isn't just museums and the concept of adaptive reuse is adopted, historic buildings have proven themselves remarkably versatile in responding to the demands of the widest imaginable range of uses.

• *Reflects product differentiation.* In economics it is the differentiated product that commands a monetary premium. If in the long run a city wants to attract capital, to attract investment, it must differentiate itself from anywhere else. It is the built environment that expresses, perhaps better than anything else, a city's diversity, identity, individuality—in short, its differentiation.

• *Most effective venue for cultural goods and services.* For communities that have cultural assets and crafts products that represent economic opportunity, historic buildings often constitute the most appropriate physical locations for the manufacture, sale, and display of goods and the presentation of products. The physical context of the historic building adds to the sense of authenticity, originality, and indigenousness of the art.

• *Natural business incubator for small enterprises.* Regardless of a nation's overall economic or social system, entrepreneurship nearly always begins on a small scale—a one- or two-person operation. The size, location, character, and often pricing of historic buildings means that they frequently serve as natural incubators of emerging enterprises.

• *Opportunity for tourism.* While tourism will be one of the fastest growing segments of the world's economy in the 21st century, not every city can or should look to tourism as a major portion of its economic base. There are cultural, economic, logistical, sometimes even religious reasons why tourism isn't appropriate for every locale. Further, it would be a mistake to inflexibly connect "historic resources" and "tourism"—there are far more avenues by which historic buildings can be used. In the US, for example, 99% of all of the historic resources in productive use have nothing whatsoever to do with tourism. That having been said, when tourism is identified locally as a component of an overall economic development strategy, the identification, protection and enhancement of the city's historic resources will be vital for a successful tourism effort.

Those are heritage conservation's measurable benefits. But there are two other benefits that are perhaps even more important albeit less directly measurable. Globalization, be it economic or cultural, means change—change at a pace that can be disruptive politically, economically, socially, and/or psychologically. The Swiss born deconstructionist architect Bernard Tschumi writes, "Architecture's [ultimate] importance resides in its ability to accelerate society's transformation."[11] Accelerate society's transformation? Why in the world is there a need to accelerate society's transformation? Its current pace is destabilizing enough. The adaptive reuse of the historic built environment can provide a touchstone, a sense of stability, a sense of continuity both to individuals and to societies that counteracts the disruption and acceleration that too much of contemporary deconstructionist architecture certainly exacerbates.

The second of the less measurable benefits of reusing historic buildings lies in the philosophical examination of the relative significance of space versus the importance of place. Not long ago with the creation of the Internet, the growth of telecommunications, and the ability to work around the globe from one's house, there were predictions that the significance of one's physical place would diminish in importance. In fact the opposite has been true. The ability to work anywhere, the ability to electronically be everywhere, has increased our need to be somewhere—somewhere in particular, somewhere differentiated. Thomas Friedman is surely one of the world's most articulate globalization advocates. But here's what he says in his book, *The Lexus and the Olive Tree*: "Yes, globalization and the internet can bring people together who have never communicated before ... [but] can we build cybercommunities that replace real communities? I'm very dubious."[12] The Internet exists only in space; humans who use the Internet need a real place, a place of both substance and quality. But as the sociologist E.V. Walter wrote, "The quality of a place depends on a human context shaped by memories and expectations, by stories of real and imagined events—this is by the historical experience located there."[13] Historic buildings are the physical manifestation of that historical experience.

PUBLIC POLICY REASONS FOR HERITAGE CONSERVATION AS ECONOMIC DEVELOPMENT

Heritage conservation also has numerous attributes that warrant using preservation as an economic development tool from a public policy perspective.

Targeted areas. Historic buildings are usually located in areas that are otherwise determined as appropriate targets for public intervention—center cities, close-in residential neighborhoods, rural villages.

Not a zero-sum game. Many approaches to economic development are essentially zero-sum games. That is to say, for city A to succeed, city B has to lose (a factory recruited from place A to relocate to place B, for example). Because nearly every city has its own historic resources that can be used to house a variety of activities, for one city to benefit from the adaptive reuse of its historic structures in no way precludes another city from doing so as well.

Geographically dispersed. Related to the above, public officials and NGO institutions do not have to limit a strategy to a single geographic area (city instead of village or coast instead of inland, for example). Because cities are geographically dispersed throughout a province, an economic development strategy based on the use of historic resources also automatically becomes a geographically dispersed strategy.

Range of project scales. A variety of factors will affect the public sector's ability to implement plans on a large scale. Financial constraints, political factors, environmental concerns are all reasons that the "big project" is often delayed or shelved. Historic preservation, however, can be done at virtually every scale, from the smallest shop building to the massive revitalization of areas in large metropolitan regions. The smaller projects can proceed while larger ones are still on the drawing board.

Counter-cyclical. One obvious result of globalization is that today no city in either a market or a non-market economy is immune to the ups and downs of worldwide economic cycles. Because of their scale, cost and labor intensity, heritage conservation projects are often possible even in down cycle periods, providing a measure of job and income stability to a local economy.

Incremental change. It isn't inherently change that seriously adversely affects a local economy and its culture; it is change that is rapid, massive, and beyond local control. Historic preservation by definition is an incremental strategy within the framework of an existing city, not an immediate and overwhelming type of change, which often leads to feelings of powerlessness locally and a decline in the sense of community.

Good base to build NGOs. Non-governmental organizations (NGOs) have proven themselves to be singularly effective in responding to serious issues on a grassroots level in every corner of the globe. They have tackled and solved local problems that neither government nor, in market economies, the private sector have been able to effectively address. In historic preservation in particular, the NGO sector has been most effective in advocacy, in education, and in the creative reuse of historic buildings. The Aga Kahn Trust for Culture has been especially effective in assisting and encouraging local NGOs in heritage conservation throughout the Arab world. If it is public policy to encourage and support a strong NGO sector, historic preservation activities can be an effective means to do so.

Modernization without Westernization. Historic preservation as an active public policy is an effective way to allow for modernization to meet the public safety, comfort, and convenience needs of citizens without the Westernization or Americanization or McDonaldization of the local built environment and the concomitant loss of local character.

CONCLUSIONS

Historic preservation as an economic development strategy is consistent with all five principles of 21st century economic development: globalization, localization, diversity, sustainability, and responsibility.

Heritage conservation reinforces the five senses of quality communities: sense of place, sense of identity, sense of evolution, sense of ownership, and sense of community.

Historic preservation can meet the test of both "quality" and "authenticity" that will be critical elements in economic development in the next century.

The cultural assets of a city—dance, theater, music, visual arts, crafts, and others—are inherently influenced and enhanced by the physical context within which they were created and evolved over the centuries. If cultural resources are to become and remain an economic asset for a city, then the physical context that has always influenced their creation needs to be maintained. Otherwise more than just the physical buildings are at risk; the quality, character, differentiation, and sustainability of the other assets are in jeopardy as well.

Historic preservation allows a city to participate in the positive benefits of a globalized economy while resisting the adverse impacts of a globalized culture.

Historic preservation allows a city the opportunity to modernize without having to Westernize. More than that—historic preservation is the irreplaceable variable to achieve modernization without Westernization.

For the 21st century only the foolish city will make the choice between historic preservation and economic development. The wise city will effectively utilize its historic built environment to meet the economic, social and cultural needs of its citizens well into the future. Early in the 20th century, Oswald Spengler wrote, "We cannot comprehend political and economic history at all unless we realize that the city ... is the determinative form to which the course and sense of higher history generally conforms. World history is city history."[14] And the political and economic history of the 21st century will surely be written in cities as well.

NOTES

1. Jane Jacobs, *Cities and the Wealth of Nations* (New York: Vintage Books, 1985), 132.
2. Richard V. Knight, *Cities in a Global Society* (Newbury Park, California: Sage Publications, 1989), 327.
3. Akio Morita cited in *The Borderless World*, by Kenichi Ohmae (New York: Harper Business, 1990), 93.
4. Michael E. Porter, *The Competitive Advantage of Nations* (New York: The Free Press, 1990), 158.
5. Kenichi Ohmae, *The Borderless World* (New York: Harper Business, 1990), 82.
6. Peter F. Drucker, *Post-Capitalist Society* (New York: Harper Business, 1993), 214-215.
7. Giordano Bruno, "On the Infinite Universe and Worlds," as cited in *The Fate of Place* (Berkeley: University of California Press, 1997), Edward S. Casey, 120.
8. Neal R. Pierce, *Citistates* (Washington, DC: Seven Locks Press, 1993), 298.
9. Daniel Kemmis, *The Good City and The Good Life* (New York: Houghton Mifflin, 1995), 31.
10. Robert Bellah et al., *Habits of the Heart* (New York: Harper and Row, 1985), 153.
11. Bernard Tschumi, "Event Cities," as cited in *The Fate of Place* (Berkeley: University of California Press, 1997), Edward S. Casey, 309.

12. Thomas L. Friedman, *The Lexus and the Olive Tree* (New York: Anchor Books, 2000), 473.
13. E.V. Walter, *Placeways: A Theory of the Human Environment* (Chapel Hill: University of North Carolina Press, 1988), 117.
14. Oswald Spengler, "The Decline of the West," ed. James A. Clapp, *The City* (New Brunswick: Center for Urban Policy Research, 1987), 223.

KEEP THE *CON* IN E*CON*OMICS: WHY ECONOMIC FORECASTING DOESN'T WORK

by

Barry H. Minkin

INTRODUCTION

In its fall 2000 semiannual economic assessment, the International Monetary Fund (IMF) projected global economic growth at 4.7%, the fastest in a decade. Further, it forecast that rapid expansion would continue in 2001. There were few signs of trouble: Inflation was low, budget deficits were shrinking in the leading economies, and international trade and capital flow were expanding. The report, as the *Financial Times* observed, presents one of the most glowing accounts of global economic prospects in decades

The appraisal came near the end of a remarkable half-century that witnessed unprecedented global economic growth. The global output of goods and services grew from just under $5 trillion in 1950 to more than $31 trillion in 2000, a sixfold expansion. From 1990-2000, it grew $10 trillion, doubling the growth from the beginning of civilization to 1950. This brought widespread economic and social progress. Worldwide, life expectancy climbed from 47 years in 1950 to over 63 years today. Literacy rates rose on every continent while diets were also improving.

Even with occasional financial disruptions, the IMF report seemed to imply that such growth would continue indefinitely. *But can it?*

One of the most important concerns for most on this planet is how the global economy will impact their lives. Indeed, right now the United States seems to be in a recession that has lasted longer and has been much deeper than many of the so-called "experts" ever predicted. Everyone, from top-level managers to department store clerks, is worrying about his or her job. Businesses are subsisting hand-to-mouth, waiting for the recovery to get going in earnest.

I predict that the US economy, which is linked to the economies of most countries, is soon to collapse into a depression that will be similar in many ways to that of the 1930s. Hundreds of companies will go bankrupt. Real estate markets will drop 30% in some areas. Unemployment will reach 15%, putting many middle-class families out of their homes. Retirees will find their investments and pensions turning into dust.

This won't happen all at once. For a while, perhaps as long as a year, a recovery may appear to have started. But by mid-2004, growth will stall, business will keep cutting costs by laying off work-ers, and scared consumers will stop spending, making business conditions even worse. The 2004 recession, like the one in 1929, will

Barry H. Minkin *is a futurist, author, and global management consultant with Minkin Affiliates (www.minkinaffiliates.com) in Redwood City, California. He may be contacted at barryminkin@msn.com.*

not respond to government monetary policy.

THE MISTAKEN FORECASTS

The so-called "experts," the economists and big-picture types, don't see the depth of our problems. This is because they haven't been looking in the right places. By focusing on the "big picture," they're overlooking the fact that the ground we are standing on is shaky. Even the pessimists are looking in the wrong direction. They've been looking at today's problems as a cyclical financial collapse when the real problems facing our economy are structural and cannot be solved by monetary policy or reliance on an automatic self-correcting "business cycle rebound."

The Earth is flat; the sun moves around the Earth; man could never have evolved from the apes. Think of the impact on societies if our basic economic theories are as wrong as those that were held by the power structure during the time of Columbus, Galileo or Darwin. Like Galileo, who tried to change the conventional beliefs about astronomy held by the academic and political leadership of his time, it is time we challenge the *very foundation and value of current economic thought.* Changing current economic dogma is important since it is currently masking a near-term global depression as will determine how we analyze and solve global economic problems in the future.

PART ONE—THE GLOBAL CRISIS: WHY IT'S INEVITABLE, WHAT WILL HAPPEN

They were not prepared for the storm today, so they have all been thrown into great confusion. They do not possess a compass for ordinarily when the weather is fine; they follow the old tradition and steer by the stars in the sky without making serious mistakes regarding their direction. This is what we call "depending upon heaven for existence."

But now they have run into bad weather so they have nothing to rely upon. It is not that they don't want to do well, only they do not know the direction and so the further they go the more mistakes they make.

Travels of Lao Can by Liu E.
Beijing, China, 1905

Why the Tales of Gloom?

Even the most pessimistic of economists predict continued growth in the 2000s, so why the doom and gloom? In Part One, I am going to point out the fourteen deepest and most damaging economic trends that I've been watching. Once you have seen the fourteen "C's," you will understand why I see economic trouble ahead.

C1: Connectivity

Remember when your stockbroker recommended foreign investment as a hedge against problems in the US economy? If you do, you will also recall that, as global markets connected, they tended to mimic each other. As we first learned from the Mexican peso fiasco and were reminded by similar problems in Thailand, South Korea, Hong Kong, Indonesia, and Russia, economic problems elsewhere in the world can cause serious economic problems in the United States. This pattern will continue—and worsen in the future. Why? Because the United States is the largest net investor in these emerging markets.

The problem stretches both ways. Just as the United States cushions potential downturns in its domestic economy with foreign investment, foreign banks invest in the United States as a hedge against problems that could develop in their own countries. But, when the United States experiences a cataclysm such as the October 1997 market crash, these investors panic. In fact, foreign central banks liquidated $7 billion in US government securities during the crash, which dragged our markets even lower.

Bear in mind things could get worse—Japan holds $291 billion in US treasury bonds. If the Nikkei, Japan's stock market, plunges, Japan's 20 biggest lenders would collectively face $96 billion in portfolio losses, sending not only Japan but also many other countries into a downward cycle.

C2: Complexity

Not long ago, investors could profit from foreign exchange transactions simply by learning about and acting on news likely to impact financial markets. Today, with the world watching CNN and other international media sites, everyone learns what is happening at the same time with the result that foreign exchange is a far less profitable pursuit. Consequently, in order to make money, investment houses have developed more complex strategies, such as the use of derivatives that were a major cause of a hedge fund collapse.

Complexity has caused a breakdown of our early warning systems. No one can possibly understand what is happening in the economy!

For example, what if principals in a couple of large investment houses decided over lunch in Geneva to quietly buy a huge quantity of copper as a hedge against winter wheat or some other commodity? I doubt that any economist would understand that fluctuations in the price of copper the next day were traceable to that transaction. And I know, not even with the assistance of powerful computer programs can any economist possibly understand the impact of $3 trillion a day of such cross-border financial transactions.

Complexity adds the element of surprise to economic scenarios, with the result that economic predictions are way off the mark. Indeed, the Asian Development Bank's predictions of growth in Asia have been off by 50%. Coin flips are more accurate!

C3: Capacity

This is the first time in many years that global over-capacity exists in most industries. The excess supply will only grow as Asia tries to export itself out of trouble. Take the automobile industry: An oversupply of autos forced Toyota to close two new plants in Thailand, further hurting the ailing Japanese and Thai economies. At the same time, Indonesia and Malaysia are developing national car programs, adding to the difficulty of car companies trying to survive in the weakening Asian economy.

It's not just the automobile sector where over-capacity is happening. Take semiconductors: Taiwan is building a dozen new billion-dollar plants despite an 82% crash in prices for the basic D-RAM chip. Moreover, chemicals are also at over-capacity with prices for petrochemicals down 36%. Yet, Indonesia, Thailand, South Korea, China, and Taiwan are blindly sinking billions into sprawling petrochemical complexes.

C4: Corporate Profits

The ripple effect of Asian over-capacity impacts other regions of the world. The Mexican garment industry is an example. It received trade breaks with NAFTA, but cannot raise prices because it still competes with Asia. Prices for goods and services are also stagnating in the United States because they are forced to compete with goods and services from parts of the world where labor is considerably cheaper. Indeed, falling or stable prices currently characterize two-thirds of US manufacturing production.

My optimistic colleagues would argue that keeping prices down is good for consumers. That's true, and car buyers were pleased when the cost of a new car came down somewhat in 2002. But lower prices mean less profit. Indeed, a 1% drop in price will cause a 12.3% drop in profits in the average Standard and Poor 1000 company. Drops of this magnitude can provoke serious economic havoc. No wonder we are seeing record bankruptcies and debt!

In the "Great Depression" of the 1930s, a deflation spiral sank prices 10% annually, and moderately leveraged companies went belly up, unemployment soared and the stock market plunged.

C5: Consolidation

To keep profits up, companies are going through a record round of merger and acquisition activity. Average corporate profits are inflated by 20% simply because of M&A activity. Moreover, a major contributing factor to the growing army of unemployed is the unprecedented rash of corporate mergers, acquisitions, consolidations, and bankruptcies. A significant part of my consulting practice involves identifying acquisition candidates for companies worldwide. The practice has presented me a broad perspective on the rapidly narrowing industrial landscape.

Consolidation means fewer jobs. And the hardest hit segment is the middle class. For the first time, there is no relationship between the growth in corporate profits and the growth in salaried jobs. Indeed, the inverse is true—salaried workers, which represent about 40% of the workforce, suffered about 62% of recent layoffs. Moreover, the high-tech sector which became the new engine of the economy when we shipped most of our manufacturing jobs overseas, is continuing to unravel.

That's not just an economic pothole, it's a chasm, because for every job lost in manufacturing or high technology, 6.2 jobs in the service sector are eliminated. The service sector in Silicon Valley is currently suffering the ripple effect of recent high-tech layoffs. Together, these consolidations present a serious and long-range problem that will become an icy downhill slope for US employment for years to come.

C6: Costs

Labor costs are not as attractive as they once were. In Korea, for example, thanks to their labor unions, labor cost is no longer lower than in most Western countries. Because it lost its competitive edge, Pohang Steel was forced to layoff 20,000 employees. Historically, 70% of Japan's investment in Asia went into the manufacturing sector. With the weak yen and other economic problems, Japan is bringing manufacturing projects back home, causing problems for less-developed countries that relied on this business.

C7: China

Moving from Mao to McDonald's in one decade is quite dramatic, but China has serious problems that will lead to global turmoil. Seventy percent of loans given by China's banks go to state-run enterprises even though 40% of the 100,000 state-run enterprises are spilling red ink. Weak markets make it very difficult for small entrepreneurs to get capital.

Most of China's growth has been based on foreign investment

rather than domestic growth. Foreign investment is responsible for the Asian miracle. Asia's developing countries received $916 billion in capital investment—a sum slightly larger than foreign investment into the United States. But with foreign-financed office buildings having only 35% occupancy rates in places like Shanghai, it's no wonder investors have begun to charge a risk premium for doing business in China. To make matters worse, China lacks infrastructure. Poor highways and ports plus pollution and population problems will continue to make China a hellish place to live and work.

C8: Corporate Planning

Long-term planning, the "keen eyes" that can gaze into the future to spot potential threats and maximize future opportunities, has fallen out of fashion. What was once the most glamorous and richly rewarded preoccupation in corporate America now commands little attention among top management.

The consequences for many of the management consultants, formerly godlike in their ability to shape the corporate future, were demotion—both symbolic and actual. Once vision had been focused down to what is happening the next quarter, consultants did their bit for re-engineering. By chipping away at operational inefficiencies or hacking off bureaucratic flab, consultants became the masters of corporate liposuction.

The result of the bloody deed helped corporations record profits, but they also cut expenditures essential for future growth. R&D as a percentage of GDP continues to drop, as do expenditures for new plant and equipment. And for all the rhetoric about wanting skilled workers, spending on training is at the lowest levels since the 1980s. Unfortunately, a lean-and-mean company can lack the muscle and stamina required for long-range success and survival.

C9: Competition

US difficulty in being competitive internationally is becoming evident. The Council on Competitiveness estimates that the United States is lagging behind in one-third of our cutting-edge technologies. One that particularly troubles me is LCDs—liquid crystal displays that are found in our laptop computers and power the high defini-tion televisions of the future. Even now, companies like IBM are forced to buy these displays offshore, further increasing our negative trade balance with Asia. Speaking of IBM: It seems only yesterday that IBM was the only game in town; more than 300 IBM clones now compete for the PC business.

C10: Confused Investors

There is little correlation between the declining corporate

performance and stock prices, yet the percentage of our money tied up in the market is at record levels. People's expectations of making it big in the market are clearly unrealistic. Moreover, the low interest rates on savings, money market accounts and certificates of deposit have forced investors to hold on to declining stock portfolios.

C11: Cash Out

There is movement toward both income poles, shrinking the middle-class consumer as a percentage of the population. This phenomenon, particularly evident in the United States, is a distressing fact for business to contemplate. The proportion of low-wage earners in the global workforce will continue to rise, creating an underclass in a two-tier wage structure. Already, a sizeable proportion of US workers are paid markedly less than comparable workers in other advanced countries. However, high-paid US workers still earn more than their counterparts in most other nations.

The affluent control the discretionary income (DI) in the United States. Only one-third of US households have DI, with the average amount being $12,300. Not surprisingly, the rich have most of the DI —just over one-quarter of US households earn over $40,000 a year. However, they comprise about two-thirds of the households in the DI group and control almost 90% of the nation's DI.

The outlook for the poor and middle class is bleak. The world has done very little to reduce the poor population, and there is nothing on the horizon that will pull any significant percentage of them into the middle-class ranks.

C12: Conspicuously Absent Consumption

In our mature economy, most of us have enough clothes in the closet and computers that are fast enough to do what needs to be done online. Without a major breakthrough like computers, there may be problems for individual firms, but in the overall quality of life, how much difference does it make? With less discretionary income due to declining wages and increasing unemployment, expect more shopping but less buying, further shrinking our bloated service sector.

We are entering a world where more of us will have less money to make discretionary purchases. Particularly hard hit will be nonessential high-tech firms that provide increased productivity tools. The problem for companies is not one of productivity but simply needing more work. Also hurt will be those commercial construction companies and their financial services backers. Those firms that did not learn the lessons of excess overbuilding in the 1980s are about to relearn them again. Expect, as companies continue to run out of capital, we will see more vacancy signs all over the country.

C13: Capitalism Crumbles

Our economy is in a pivotal period, changing from one that was market driven to one shaped by government spending. Already, about one-third of our gross domestic product (GDP) is affected by government, whether at the federal, state, or local level, and more than 16% of us are employed by the government.

Another economic fault line is that state and local governments will be getting more obligations and less cash from the federal government. Growing budget deficits at the state and local level will force many program cutbacks and add to the growing legion of the unemployed.

C14: Capital Crunch

Small businesses employ the most people, but they are the least likely to benefit from low-interest loans. In the high-tech sector, the publicized explosion of venture capital and favorable bank rates does little to help startup companies. Indeed, more than seven out of every 10 Americans starting a business rely on personal savings and loans from relatives and friends.

Also, venture capitalists (VCs), having backed so many losers have become extremely risk adverse, making it almost impossible for a new firm to get VC financing. Moreover, the pension funds and institutions that provide most of the VC funds are looking for safe opportunities with good short-term profit possibilities.

No Bounce Back

The recent problems of international business failure and the stagnation and consolidation of the US manufacturing, high-tech and service sectors have created situations that are *not* cyclical in nature but are structural. The economy is not "simply weak" or "sick." It has been stricken with profound, fundamental internal problems that no amount of economic pump-priming by the Fed can ever cure. The layoffs will not be temporary; these jobs will be permanently lost. Foreign ownership of US business is virtually irreversible. The record number of mergers and bankruptcies has dug economic holes that no "upturn" can ever fill. The list of economic woes is a long one: intense global competition, record government employment and regulations, global over-capacity, unbridled consumer debt, stagnating incomes, bad bank loans, declining education levels, and insufficient corporate and government planning. These issues will paralyze our economic, social and political environment for years to come.

Hopefully, Part One of this paper has opened your eyes to the negative economic reality that is now unfolding. Part Two will explain why economic predictions continue to miss the mark. Part

Three will outline some steps toward getting us out of our economic quagmire.

PART TWO—ECONOMISTS AND OTHER PUNDITS: WHY THE EXPERTS ARE MISSING IT

He's naked!
by Hans Christian Andersen,
"The Emperor's New Clothes"

If, as I suggest, we are about to enter a depression of historical magnitude, why don't economists, futurists, the Federal Reserve, and politicians from both parties understand the depth of the problem? Obviously, they and I perceive the signals the economy is sending differently. This section will discuss how the invalidated but nevertheless accepted theories of economic history have blinded today's leaders, who are still charting their course by inadequate measures and outdated techniques.

Economists love to go on programs like the *Lehrer News Hour* and debate ferociously over the potential effect of proposals like President Bush's tax cut proposals. One says it will stimulate us right back into the happiest of economic times, while the other will smirk and suggest that tax cuts are not needed since the current downturn is just a normal part of the economic cycle and that we should see a rebound by the third quarter of this year.

The casual viewer might think these people have few beliefs in common. Nothing could be further from the truth. Virtually all leading economists share one unifying belief: They make their living predicting how tomorrow will be like yesterday. Because they are forever looking backward into the rear-view mirror of the past, they do not see—indeed *cannot* see—the coming "econoquake." In Part Two, we demystify and challenge basic economic thought, methodology and tools.

Recycling Business Cycles

Most economists and business forecasters believe in what is called "the business cycle" and the ability of monetary policy to control its effects. They view this current downturn as a natural and expected event as part of the boom and bust pattern of US economic activity for more than a century. Economists believe they can predict the path of these cycles and predict our economic direction. Indeed, we hear them every night on TV with their latest prediction on when the economy is about to rebound and how strong the recovery will be. For the laymen, let me summarize the business cycle dogma.

First comes an expansion phase usually lasting three to four years. This phase is believed to start when interest rates and inflation are low, *which is where the economy is now*. At this point, the "experts" would expect consumers to borrow money to make purchases of big-ticket items such as cars, homes, furniture, and appliances. Corporations, predicting increased consumer demand and greater profits, borrow money to increase production to meet heightened consumer demand. Institutional and individual investors buy stocks, anticipating corporate profits. The service and high-tech sectors typically expand as the manufacturing sector requires more products and services.

As demand for credit increases and more borrowers compete for loans, interest rates start to rise. Inflation increases as the rising demand for goods and services sparks price and wage increases. A decline in spending occurs as tightened credit cuts back demand for the more expensive products. This decline is a signal that the contraction phase in the business cycle is under way. Factories and the service sector cut back production and lower prices to move inventory. Consumer and business borrowing declines. Investors sell stock, anticipating lower corporate profits. Layoffs increase, and consumer spending decreases. After some months at this point, we are in a recession.

Why These Fluctuations?

Wave-like expansion and contractions in business can be traced almost back to the founding of the United States. Economists have continually seen cyclical movements in employment, factory output, interest rates, and bank credit, as well as in such far removed phenomenon as marriage, birth, and divorce rates. By studying many economic times series, the National Bureau of Economic Research (NBER) believes that it has identified 30 complete business cycles between 1834 and 1958 having an average line of just over four years. Cycles of three to five years are called the Kitchin cycle, named for Joseph Kitchin, who first wrote about them. The Kitchin cycle, that the government and the mass media most frequently cite, tracks inventories, wholesale prices, interest rates, and bank clearings.

Over the decades, Kitchin cycles have differed markedly in amplitude. Every second or third cycle has been more violent than the preceding one. Peaks which cumulated in about 1899, 1907, 1913, 1920, 1929, and 1944 seemed to have ended in major booms followed by severe declines in business. These six peaks are thought to enclose five such major cycles, lasting 45 years altogether, with an average duration of nine years. Major cycles averaging eight to 11 years in length have been called "Juglar cycles," for a Frenchman who wrote about them over 130 years ago.

Nicolai Kondratieff, a Russian economist, found statistical evidence of cycles of even longer duration, at least in the case of commodity prices and interest rates. These cycles are purported to have an average duration of between 40 and 50 years.

Do These Cycles Really Exist?

Mainstream economists rely so much on business cycle theory that they no longer question its existence or value as a predictor of economic events, such as the next recovery. I question its existence, and so have some others in the past.

W. Allen Wallis, former professor of statistics in economics at the University of Chicago, said flatly that they don't exist. He believes these so-called business cycles are not cycles with the rigid periodicity implied by the term "cycles," but oscillations of variable and (unpredictable) duration and amplitude. "Almost any series, if stared at long enough begins to shape up into patterns and cycles," he states. "An enterprising new Rorschach (founder of the famous inkblot test in psychology) may someday develop a test of statistical personality based on a standard set of random correlated times series."

Two other respected observers believed that the business cycle, forming the basis of current economic forecasting, is a psychological rather than a real-world tool. They are Arthur F. Burns and Wesley C. Mitchell, former experts with the NBER, who first identified the short cycle that today's economist and politicians are so patiently waiting to rebound. Burns and Mitchell warned, "that when we speak of observing business cycles we use figurative language. For like other concepts, business cycles can be seen only in the mind's eye."

Some cyclical theories fall of their own weight—or lack thereof. British economist William Jevons (1834-1882) found a correlation between sunspot cycles of 11 years, a similar cycle of rainfall in the Ohio and Mississippi valleys, and a cycle of the same length in business conditions. A recalculation of sunspot data and a decline in the relative importance of the Ohio and Mississippi valleys as influences on the world's wheat supply killed that theory.

Harold Barger, a former professor of money and banking at Columbia University, noted that no two cycles are exactly alike in duration, amplitude, or even in the area of the economy principally affected. Even no two Kitchin cycles, averaging only four years, are alike. Their peaks and valleys vary considerably, and some peaks were followed by severe financial crisis while others were succeeded by declines so gradual that nobody even recognized the decline until many months later. Barger asked the obvious question, "If individual business cycles display so many differences, how can we say anything useful about business cycles in general?" I agree with writers who have denied the existence of cycles in business, claiming that the fluctuations we observe are essentially random in nature.

Reliance on "Macro Measures"

Most of what we hear in the media these days consists of

economists discussing such indicators as gross domestic product (GDP), changes in money aggregates and so on. Supposedly, these tell us about the health and direction of the economy. But these measures are so "macro" that observing them produces little in the way of knowledge of what's going on in the real world. The fact is that we ought to be extremely cautious about the value of data received and used by economists, futurists, government, and other pundits when it comes to the economy.

Robert Eisner, of Northwestern University, said in an address to the American Economic Association, "Economic statistics often do not measure what economic theory pretends they do." Somehow econometricians, theorists, and economic analysts of all stripes have lost essential communication with the compilers and synthesizers of their data. He wrote, "To put it bluntly, many of us have literally not known what we are talking about, or have confused our listeners—and ourselves—into thinking that what we are talking about is directly relevant to the matters with which we are concerned."

As Burns and Mitchell noted, what we have seen over the last century and a half is not a uniform rising and falling of economic activities in unison. Instead, what we have seen has been changed readings taken from many recording instruments of varying reliability. These readings have to be decomposed for our purposes; then one set of components must be put together in a new fashion. The whole procedure is far removed from what actually happens in the real world. Whether its results will be worth having cannot be assured in advance and can be determined only by pragmatic tests after the results have been attained.

This predicament is common to all observational sciences. A familiar example is meteorology. We laypeople observe the weather directly through our senses. We see blue sky, clouds, snow, and lightning; we hear thunder; we feel the wind, temperature, and humidity. The meteorologist makes direct observations as well, but instead of relying upon his sense impressions, he uses a battery of recording instruments—thermographs, barographs, anemometers, weather vanes, and so on. In other words, he transforms much that he can sense, and some things that he cannot sense, into numerous sets of symbols void of all qualities of personal experience. It is the symbols from his own station, combined with similar symbols sent by other observers dotted over continents, that he works.

All of us can observe economic activities as easily and directly as we can observe the weather, for we have merely to watch ourselves and our associates work and spend. What we observe has a wealth of meanings no symbols can convey. We know more or less intimately the plans and problems, successes and failures of ourselves and the people we are in direct contact with. But we also realize what happens to us and our narrow circle is determined largely by what is being done by millions of unidentified strangers. What these unknowns are doing is important to us, but we cannot observe it directly.

Someone tending an open-hearth furnace has a close-up view of steel production. But what they see, care, and smell is only a tiny segment of the vast process. They work at one furnace, but cannot see the hundreds of other furnaces in operation in the country. And smelting is only one stage in the process that includes mining and transporting iron, limestone, and coal; raising capital; hiring and training workers; making and selling goods that give rise to a demand for steel; and setting prices.

No one can personally watch all these activities. The people dependent on the steel industry need an overall view of what is happening. To get it, they, like meteorologists, use symbols that bear no semblance of actual processes. The complex steel making process is reduced to a column of numbers purporting to show how many tons of units have been turned out in a given area for successive days or weeks.

We can readily see that the tonnage reports in the complex steel operation have little connection with the real world. Yet "GDP" and most of the economic indicators used to forecast our economic weather are the cumulative results of the combined output reports of many widely diverse businesses, from steel to beef. The price fluctuations and their effects on the supply and demand for beef and the time it takes to bring cattle to market are just a few factors that determine the health of the beef business. Think of scores of other industries, each with its own complex processes, being combined with the cattle business to provide an economic measure, and you'll have to agree that economists can't tell cow manure from knowledge.

The View from Top Down: How the 1970s and 1980s were Viewed by and Significantly Impacted the Current Idols of Economics

• *Keynes: The Classics*—Maynard Keynes was born in the 1880s. Though not a highly trained economist, he dominated economic policy until the 1970s. This economic idol thought you could spend your way out of a recession and increase employment by cutting taxes and boosting government spending.

The centerpiece of Keynesian economics was the "multiplier." By running a deficit, the government "injected" money into the economy, and as this "injection" ripples through the economy it produces a far larger boost in gross national product. The question of course is where does the government get this money it "injects" into the economy? Well it borrows it. But if you borrow from Peter to pay Paul, what is there to be multiplied?

The Keynesian also believed in the so-called "Phillips curve." Simply put, they believed there was a tradeoff between unemployment and inflation. In other words, the cure for unemployment was a little more inflation. But when the 1970s dealt more inflation and more unemployment simultaneously the whole

Keynesian universe imploded.

The stagflation of the 1970s upset the political universe as well as the economic orthodoxy. The simultaneous stagnation and inflation of the 1970s not only bewildered policy makers, but ruptured the prevailing consensus of the economics profession. Prime Minister Callaghan, a former head of Britain's Labor government, said about Keynesian economics, "I tell you, in all candor, that option no longer exists, and that insofar as it ever did exist, it only worked by injecting bigger doses of inflation into the economy followed by higher levels of unemployment as the next step. That is the history of the last twenty years."

The important point to remember is that as late as the 1970s what was being taught to generations of current economists was a failed theory, and it is still being advocated by some of them today.

• *The Monetarists: The Neo Classical*—Milton Friedman led the modern assault on Keynes' theory from the University of Chicago. Friedman's centerpiece was controlling the money supply. To oversimplify, draw a small circle in the middle of piece of paper and call this M-1, the total of all of the US currency and checking deposits. A concentric circle overlaying M-1, call M-2, which includes M-1 plus savings deposits. A large concentric circle overlaying the M-1 and M-2 circles is called "utilized trade credit"—that is whatever you can charge on the credit cards in your pocket.

The monetarists believed that they can control domestic inflation and control the money available to business by simply controlling M-1 and M-2 through the interest rates they charge member banks.

Like the Keynes theory that failed in the 1970s, the monetarists took their blows about 1981, when M-1 signaled money growth was too slow and M-2 said it was too fast. As 1981 developed, inflation headed down but interest rates refused to follow, correspondingly, bond prices plunged. The falling bond prices would normally be a sign to economists of expected future inflation, but the signal was confounded by disinflation in other markets, such as gold and the dollar being strong in foreign exchange markets.

In his *Newsweek* column, Milton Friedman, the monetarist guru, ruled out the obvious answers to this unexpected confusion and concluded perhaps this bubble would burst, "If it does not—back to the computer."

Unfortunately, these discredited, unproven, fiscal and monetary theories and policies are still the major tools used by the Fed to control interest rates and inflation.

• *The Supply Siders*—The premise of supply-side economics,

whose small elite group carped at both the Keynesians and the Monetarists, was that you fight inflation with tight monetary policy. And you offset possible reversionary impact of tight monetary policy with the incentive effects of reductions in marginal tax rates.

This policy, also called "Reaganomics," was blamed for one of the most costly recessions since the Great Depression. Indeed, unemployment hit 11%.

Irving Kristol, in November of 1982, however, stated that the reason for the collapse was not Reaganomics but was a collision between the swollen Carter budget for 1981 and the tight money policies of the Fed. The supply-siders would not take blame for the 1982 recession but continue to take credit for the seven fat years that followed, starting in 1983 and ending in a 1990 recession. These proponents are behind some of the current Bush economic policy that includes targeted tax cuts to promote a rebirth of entrepreneurial vigor.

Bush senior, you might remember, called Reaganomics "voodoo economics," and others have said it is nothing but smoke and mirrors.

Looking Up: My Real Worldview of the Economy, 1970-1980s

Now we reach the halfway house; half the world's economy are auto related; half the world resources are auto devoted; and, half the world will be involved in an auto accident at some time in their lives.

"Autogeddon," a fact based poem
by Heathcote Williams

My thesis is that you have to get "into it to understand it." You cannot expect to stand on Wall Street or among the eucalyptus groves at Stanford University and talk meaningfully about the US economy based on what you've read, analyzed, or viewed from the latest M-1 or other figures. Nor can one hearken back to unproven economic strategies whose outcomes are a continual surprise to economists. Astrology has more meaning—probably more. If you truly understand what makes the economy work, your outcomes should be predictable. In the 1970s, I was the first to predict a major decline in the US manufacturing sector, that had been growing steadily until then.

The basis of my dissonance with current economic thought is not that I am smarter or claim some special gifts. It was simply a matter of being at the right place at the right time—in my case, working as a project leader for SRI International and consulting to America's Midwestern heartland, as well as the Japanese auto manufacturers. During the 1970s and 1980s, I interviewed scores of companies in all of the two-digit SIC codes about the factors that will determine their economic success or failure.

The real economic engine of the United States in the 1970s was the manufacturing sector, and the auto industry was the heart of the economy. I listened and learned what really made the US economy tick.

The 1950s were the happy days for the US auto manufacturers and then blue-collar union employees. Then, US manufacturers built three out of every four cars produced in the world, with the United States importing less than 1% of domestic sales. When the foreign cars appeared on the scene, Detroit could have built better smaller cars, but instead US automobiles grew even bigger and gaudier and sported absolutely useless tail-fins.

By the time Eisenhower left office in 1960, United States accounted for just 50% of the world automobile market and imports had captured at 10% share of American sales. Ironically, the Cold War played a minor role in the foreign invasion. Hundreds of thousands of US troops stationed in Europe were allowed a peculiar fringe benefit. They could ship home free of charge one foreign-purchased automobile. While the total number actually shipped was probably fewer than 100,000, the presence of foreign cars on US highways served as rolling advertisements for Volkswagen, Austin Healy, and other European manufacturers, whose postwar factories were producing record numbers of vehicles. Volkswagen's advertising led the way catching Americans imagination, and soon the VW Beetle became a kind of anti-snobbery status symbol.

The period 1950-1973 was called the "Golden Age" in an OECD "Study of the Century." Then came the oil embargo of 1973. All across the country, millions of Americans waited in long gas lines, and the longer they waited the more many of them calculated for the first time just how precious few miles their guzzlers could go on a gallon of gas. Suddenly, Americans were interested in small cars in a big way! The US auto manufacturers, however, continued to ignore the sales charts. They did not have the products the market demanded, and sales of the domestically produced cars fell sharply. Honda, on the other hand, had the right product, and its growth was dramatic.

By 1977 and 1978, memories of gas lines had faded, and domestic car sales rose to new heights. Detroit executives popped champagne corks and toasted their own wisdom. Unfortunately, Detroit success in 1977 and 1978 led to the dangerous and erroneous misperception that without high energy prices consumers felt no need to economize or buy fuel-efficient cars.

The party did not last long. The second gas crunch accompanied the Iranian revolution in the spring of 1979. But unlike the sequence of events that followed the oil embargo of 1973, this time buyers failed to return to larger vehicles after the initial fuel shock wore off. Domestic manufacturers found themselves selling all the small cars they could produce but fewer larger models. Detroit was forced to wait for new generations of small fuel-efficient cars that were still only on the drawing boards. In fact, Detroit had committed to spend more money on massive redesign programs than it cost to send the Apollo mission to the moon. In other words, our "can do" management was spending $1 billion for every half-mile improvement in average fleet fuel economy.

While Detroit was trying to make a U-turn, domestic car sales plummeted for four years from 1979 to 1982—making it easy for me to predict that recession was coming. *This was the longest period of falling car sales in US history.* Sales in 1982 were incredible 45% below the 1978 sales. Instead of meeting the challenge head-on with vaunted Yankee ingenuity, Detroit instead began waving the white flag. Plant after domestic plant closed, and over 55,000 workers lost jobs. And as a result, the small car fever that gripped the nation was a boon for foreign manufacturers, who had long concentrated their attention on the small car segment of the marketplace.

My Midwest experience taught me not to believe the still accepted econo-babble of Washington and Wall Street as summarized by Robert Bartley, editor of *The Wall Street Journal*: "The 1982 recession was caused by monetary policy, for better or for worse. Or, to view it more instructively, it was caused by a timing mismatch. The tight money part of the policy mix was put in place as early as October 1979 and especially in the fall of 1980. The tax cuts didn't start until October 1981, and were not effective on a net basis until January 1983. In between there was a recession."

The economic elite completely ignored the fact that the engine running the US economy, the automobile business, had stopped for reasons having nothing to do with the intellectual masturbation being practiced by our leading economists.

University of Maryland professor of economics Melville Ulmer more eloquently summed up my thinking about economics and practitioners of this black art: "Since mainstream economics is by nature dogmatic, and most often ideological to boot, experience has proved to be an ineffective teacher. Facts do not disturb deductive reason based on arbitrary assumptions. Moreover, professional reputations, including Nobel prizes, continue to rest on faithful devotion to sacred mysteries of mainstream methodology. The weight of such personal investments has calcified into a self-perpetuating cult with guild like restrictions on apprenticeships and approved research procedures. This is why no perspective turnabout appears to be in the offing, at least not one generated within the professional mainstream itself.

"The prestige of no professional group—doctors, lawyers or politicians—can plummet indefinitely without courting the complete rejection of its consuming public. Economics cannot be exempted. Competition in the world of ideas seems certain to enforce a return to standards that will ensure its ultimate survival: Plain speaking, testable theories, and verifiable evidence, whether inspired by present or future dissidents in the prevailing mainstream. Until the counter-revolution arises as it must in time, the authority of economics and economists which is already fallen so far will no doubt fall even lower."

PART THREE—INSIGHT AND POLICY IDEAS

> There is no rest for a messenger till the message is delivered.
>   Joseph Conrad

I learned firsthand that organizations are as individual as people are. The factors affecting the success or failure of companies, even within the same industry, can be quite different. Therefore, a one-size- fits-all top-down approach will be of little value.

I also observed that most of the determinants of organization success were not the type of data collected and analyzed by econo-mists or others charged with determining our economic direction. Economic forecasting must be based on those factors that do impact organizations and propel economic growth.

Moreover, a bottom-up company specific approach will always produce more accurate forecasts than top-down macroeconomic tools and theories.

My Forecasting Technique

Based on what I learned from the field, I developed a simple and logical approach to forecasting. I call my model the Econo-2000 system and have been using it successfully for over a decade. What follows is the oversimplified six steps that the model is built around:

Step 1: *Indentify* the three or four major organization-specific factors that determine how a company will fare over the next three years.

Step 2: *Determine* how these factors will be affected by future scenario predicting declining growth.

Steps 3: *Make* predictions based on the interaction between determinants and the scenario.

Step 4: *Analyze* the ripple effects of declining growth scenario on other companies, industries and business sectors.

Step 5: *Roll up* your sleeves and estimate the impact on sales for all companies in your sample.

Steps 6: *Compile* the company-specific forecasts and you will develop a very accurate industry forecasts.

Some Policy Ideas

1. We must develop a practical valid economics and economic forecasting techniques.

I have hopefully shown that the problems of the auto industry and the ripple effect through the country, including the high-tech sector, were the real cause of the 1982 recession. It was not the machinations of economists and politicians, whose efforts still have little or no impact on the scores of companies in all economic sectors that are the real engines of the economy. If we had looked instead at the recovery in 1983-1987, the 1990 recession, or our current economic problems, we would have learned that they also were not caused nor cured by the Wizard of Oz, Alan Greenspan, or his predecessors. Indeed, the numerous interest cuts that the Fed has made over the last year or two and the president's tax cut have not ignited an economic recovery. This once again surprised and confused economists and politicians. We, however, should not be surprised if we can finally realize that most of the actions taken in Washington will have little impact on most of our industries (besides housing). Indeed, *the Federal Reserve Chairman is a puppeteer without the attached strings necessary to pull our economic engines.*

The economy is too important to trust to economists. We need a new economics that is based on how the real world works, not controlled by the entrenched economists who will continue to fail us. We would not use a lawyer to fix our plumbing. Yet, we rely on economists, most of whom have never worked outside government and the universities, to understand and solve economic problems which are really the sum total of the problems of individual businesses.

2. Regroup and get down to basics. As resources dwindle, our countries must clearly decide our various priorities, basic needs and direction.

3. Restructure and downsize the federal government. Turn the government pyramid over, with local government and private industry having more money and responsibility.

4. Develop an industrial policy based on state industrial extension programs. Support regional and state economic recovery groups made up of representatives of public, private and independent sectors.

5. The future rests with smaller market oriented firms. These firms need to explain what specific assistance would help them grow and become a source of additional employment. We must customize programs to meet their specific needs. We can no

longer afford to trickle down money into the economy through Washington. As the late Paul Tsongas noted, this is the equivalent of feeding oats to the horses to feed the birds.

6. Have a plan for massive public works programs similar to the 1930s and/or cash grants to assure the massive numbers of unemployed will have a long-term safety net during the tough times ahead.

7. Control illegal immigration; too many people on the safety net will break it.

8. A few hundred dollars in a tax cut won't solve our problems. With so many people below the disposable income level, this money will be used toward the next month's rent and food, not for the products needed to stimulate the economy. The money may have to be used to pay increased fees, another form of taxation being charged to consumers for everything from air travel and phones to using town facilities.

9. The time to act is now.

For taken together, the fault lines presented in Part One are undercutting our economy, driving it into a downward cycle that won't be easy to escape. Indeed, the US economic structure now bears a disturbing resemblance to a bucket with a lot of little holes at the bottom. The holes have been getting bigger for years, and it's going to be very hard to plug them all. Indeed, there are so many holes at the bottom of the bucket that the only thing left to do is throw the bucket away and start again—and this is a far more radical step then most people are willing to contemplate at this time.

EDUCATION

THE NEED FOR A MULTI-LEVEL EDUCATIONAL APPROACH FOR THE FUTURE

by

Donald B. Louria, M.D.; Howard F. Didsbury, Jr.; and Fred Ellerbusch

Our educational system is not teaching students how to think critically, and is not adequately preparing them for long-term commitment to solving major societal problems. It is thereby failing both young people and our society. Apparently mesmerized by the extraordinary advances in communications technologies and the capacity to gather information, we have hoodwinked ourselves into the assumption that information is understanding. They are not identical. Information may be required to develop understanding, but understanding is a far broader concept. Similarly, understanding by itself does not equal critical thinking, though it is usually an essential component. We propose a change in our educational approach that could make a huge difference; we believe we should include, as an intrinsic part of the curriculum, attempts to instill in students what we shall call societally-connected thinking, one form of critical thinking that blends interdisciplinary learning with systems thinking. This has not been an intrinsic component of the educational process; instead, for the last four decades, our educational efforts have, in large part, focused on incorporation of technological advances. As a consequence, we now have two whole generations of decision makers at local, state, national, or international levels who, in the aggregate, are inadequately trained to solve or even ameliorate major problems that threaten the future of our society.

Unless we imbue our students at all educational levels with the need to think in a societally connected way, we will continue to develop decision makers who are unable to cope with the increasing complexity of the world, and a public that is not committed to participate in seeking solutions to major problems. This could lead to a societal catastrophe.

There are three interrelated components of societally-connected thinking:

1. Mandatory Interdisciplinary Courses: At every educational level—junior high school, high school, college, graduate school—the curriculum should include mandatory interdisciplinary courses that cover the current major problems facing society

---

Donald B. Louria *is professor and chair emeritus, Department of Preventative Medicine and Community Health, New Jersey Medical School. He may be contacted at louriado@umdnj.edu.* **Howard F. Didsbury, Jr.**, *is director of Special Projects, World Future Society, and president of Alternative Futures Research Associates, Washington, D.C. He may be contacted at didsbury@wfs.org.* **Fred Ellerbusch** *is president of SYSTEMSTHINK, Warren, New Jersey. He may be contacted at fred@systemsthink.com.*

at local, state, national, and international levels, as well as the critical problems we are likely to face in future years, decades, and centuries. The courses *must* be interdisciplinary, obligatory, and learning-focused.

2. Systems (Non-Linear) Thinking: Students must be taught to think about these problems in a manner that is comprehensive, integrated, and holistic, and that uses the principles of systems thinking. That is the bedrock of our proposal.

Learning communities and systems thinking in particular, as championed by Peter M. Senge (*The Fifth Discipline*, Doubleday 1990; *Schools That Learn*, Doubleday, 2000) is a framework for identifying interrelationships and patterns, for seeing the whole rather than just the parts. It integrates various learning disciplines and requires that we think in terms of systems that are composed of circles of influence with various feedback loops and leverage points to exert change, instead of the linear (straight line) approach that characterizes most of our thinking processes. It helps us remember that, while we must often reduce problems into component parts to solve them, we must also place the problems and solutions back into the context of their system.

3. Commitment to Problem Solving: Our educational system must conscientiously and deliberately seek to instill in students a long-term part-time, or even full-time, commitment to addressing major societal problems and a commitment to lifelong learning. Active individual participation in problem solving can be at local, state, national, or international levels.

In decades past, we taught civics, making the assumption it would engender commitment; it infrequently did. Currently, some schools require participation in community projects, but this, too, is not likely to result in lifetime dedication to solving or ameliorating critical societal problems unless the concept of commitment is vigorously nurtured throughout students' educational experience.

One problem is that many young people will be concerned that, as individuals, they can have no significant impact on major societal problems. As Sidney Smith, a 19th century British clergyman, noted (quotation slightly modified), "No man or woman makes a greater mistake than he or she who does nothing because he or she can only do a little." To cope with those concerns, attempts at instilling commitment must be accompanied by specific involvements that are rewarding enough to persuade students they can indeed make a difference.

Four examples will illustrate the usefulness of the systems approach.

THE POTENTIAL FOR LIVING TO 120 TO 180 YEARS OR LONGER

The extraordinary scientific discoveries being reported with ever-increasing frequency offer the potential for literally resetting our biological time clocks, allowing life expectancy to increase in coming decades or centuries to 120 to 180 years. These monumental scientific advances are focused on understanding the genetic and molecular determinants of aging and have three basic tenets:

• aging should be regarded as a disease

• if we understand the basic mechanisms, we can intervene to profoundly prolong longevity

• what science can do in regard to aging, science should do, leaving any concerns about the societal consequences for consideration at some later time.

This technologically dominated thinking leads to the following linear approach:

Determine the mechanisms of aging → develop pharmacologic agents that change the aging process → allow people to live extraordinarily long lives.

That is a formula for potential societal catastrophe.

This is a perfect example of a potentially gargantuan problem that cries out for a holistic (systems) approach allowing the scientific advances to be accompanied by an intensive debate about the consequences of very long life for both the individual and the society.

A systems approach (see Figure 1, page 98) would raise the following questions and issues for thorough discussion and debate:

1. The world population is now more than 6 billion people. If the scientific endeavors are successful, as they are likely to be, potentially, at the dawn of the next century or the one after that, there could be four or five people on this planet for every one we have now, and more than one-half the population could be over 65 years, or even over 80 years, of age. The current life expectancy at birth worldwide is about 70 years. Each decade extension of life expectancy will add 1.35 billion people to the eventual population of planet Earth. That, in turn, requires assessment of the effects of a much larger world population on global warming, world ecosystems, food and drinking water availability, etc.

At what point is the number of people so large that it exceeds the carrying capacity of the planet, thus sowing the seeds for our own destruction?

At what point does the crush of human numbers make life miserable for the vast majority of humans and impossible for many other species?

2. What will the quality of life be for very old people?

3. Will changing the boundaries of aging be accompanied by health or will certain tissues and organs deteriorate even as life span is markedly prolonged? If you live 140 years, what will happen to your hearing, sight, mental function, musculoskeletal function?

4. Will we be expected to work, support ourselves, and pay taxes until age 80, or 90, or 110 or older?

5. What percentage of us will outlive our resources and spend our extended years living in poverty?

6. Will not having huge numbers of people over age 60, with limited and often inadequate incomes if they stop working, create intense adversarial relations between younger and older persons as they compete for limited jobs and resources?

7. In the United States, at present, 13% of the population (over age 65) consume more than 30% of health care dollars. What happens when the majority is over age 65? Over age 80? Over age 100?

8. What happens to a nation when more than one-half of its people are more than 80 or 100 years old? Is it able to compete with nations with much younger populations that might have greater per person productivity?

9. Above all, the overriding question: Where is the research on aging going, where do we want it to go, and what limitations, if any, do we want to impose on it?

Only a systems approach to increased longevity can allow us to "manage science and technology so they can help us get where we want to go" (Rene Dubos, quoted in Archibald MacLeish, "Master or Man," in *Riders on the Earth: Essays and Recollections*, Houghton Mifflin Co., 1978).

FIGURE 1 - A SYSTEMS APPROACH TO MARKEDLY INCREASED LIFE SPANS

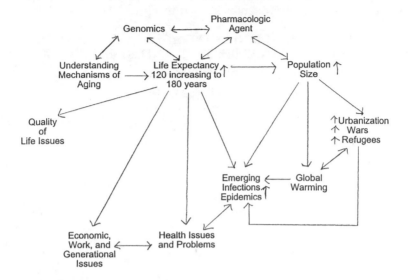

THE PROBLEM OF EMERGING INFECTIONS

Emerging infections are those that either are new or occur in a new geographic area. Re-emerging infections are those that have been dormant for a prolonged period and then reappear.

HIV/AIDS is the prototype of a ferocious emerging infection epidemic; diphtheria in the 1990s in Russia and ex-Soviet Union countries is an example of an infection that re-emerged, in large part, because of public health infrastructure breakdown.

In reacting to the concerns, the public health and scientific communities have focused on better surveillance to detect such epidemics early, rapid laboratory diagnosis, and prompt intervention. There is also emphasis on building better public health infrastructures in developing countries, and more effective immunization programs.

We are convinced that, in fact, the most effective way to control the frequency and severity of emerging infection epidemics is to do something about the critical societal variables that provide the milieu in which emerging infections arise and thrive. The two superordinating determinants are population growth and global warming; others include massive urbanization with disease-promoting slums, increase in the number of people living in poverty, larger numbers of refugees, wars, an aging population, the search for energy, malnutrition, increased international travel, and certain human behaviors.

The best way to look at this is as a gigantic system with intercon-

nected critical variables whose greater or lesser control or ameliora-
tion will lead to an output of more or less ferocious epidemics of
emerging infections. That makes it a virtual necessity to utilize a
systems thinking approach as shown in Figure 2.

FIGURE 2 - INTER-RELATEDNESS OF SOME MAJOR VARIABLES IN EMERGING AND RE-EMERGING INFECTIONS

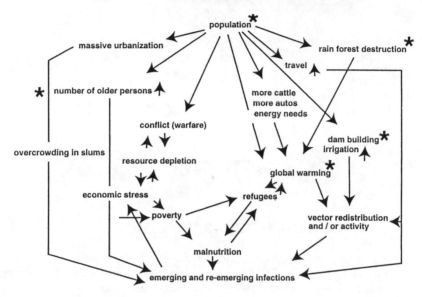

*leverage points

Some of the variables relate more to occurrence of emerging or
re-emerging infections, others to their propagation. Some of the listed
variables are obvious; others require some clarification.

• *Poverty.* Poverty promotes infections, in part, by crowding in
unhygienic conditions and, in part, because it leads to malnutrition. Billions of people on this planet suffer some degree of
under nutrition or malnutrition, 800 million experience major
under nutrition and 400 million suffer dire malnutrition. It used
to be thought that malnutrition made the individual (the host)
more susceptible by interfering with host defenses against
infection. Recent studies suggest that undernutrition in the host
can affect invading microbes, actually making them more
venomous by genetic changes in the microbes themselves.

• *Urbanization.* More people virtually guarantees more extensive
urbanization. At the start of the 20th century, 15% of the world's

population lived in cities; currently, that has increased to almost 50%; and by the year 2030, an estimated 65% of the approximately 8 billion people on planet Earth will live in cities. Most of these urban centers, particularly in so-called developing countries, will have extensive slums where people are crowded together in unhygienic circumstances, a situation in which mosquito and fly vectors and rodents will thrive, producing the setting for both point source epidemics and rapid person-to-person spread of infectious agents.

• *Activities of Man*. Nowhere is this more evident than the infectious disease consequences of irrigation and dam construction. As population size increases, there is an increasing need for both irrigation and dam building. In 1950, there were approximately 5,000 dams greater than 10 meters in height. Now, that figure has increased to 38,000; and, currently, there are approximately 1,200 more under construction, 60% of which will be greater than 30 meters in height. In developing countries, new infectious disease patterns have often been an untoward consequence of vector redistribution resulting from dam construction. Habitat advantages have been created, particularly for mosquitoes and snails. The Aswan Dam resulted in 200,000 new cases of the mosquito-borne viral infection Rift Valley Fever, as well as marked increases in schistosomiasis and malaria among populations with a relatively low prevalence of both. In Ghana, construction of a huge dam on the river Volta was followed by an increase in prevalence of *Schistosoma hematobium* in the Volta Basin area from approximately 10% to 90%. Additionally, large dams, such as the gargantuan one being constructed on the Yangtze River in China, require relocation of tens of thousands, or even millions, of people; this forced displacement is often associated with worse living conditions and increased poverty, both risk factors for increased infection rates. In some cases, the enormity of the construction project requires the recruiting of large numbers of workers from distant parts of the country or from other countries. These new "temporary" immigrants bring their own infections with them, creating the potential for emerging or re-emerging infections in inadequately protected local populations. Furthermore, the newly-created large bodies of water are subject to massive fecal contamination, increasing the likelihood of re-emerging pathogen epidemics (for example, cholera).

• *Warfare*. Perhaps no human activity is so conducive to emergence or re-emergence of infectious diseases as warfare, a human behavior that, measured by the number of people involved, becomes more extensive every century (in part because of population growth). The 20th century was the bloodiest in history. There were 150 wars in the last half of the century, resulting in more than 23 million deaths, two-thirds of them civilians.

Wars create the milieu for infection in many ways: massive injuries that invite microbial infection; forced migration of non-immunized persons into areas inhabited by disease-carrying vectors; crowding in refugee camps with inadequate sanitation facilities; migration of disease-carrying individuals into uninfected areas; exposure to disease-carrying rodents; malnutrition, even starvation; and destruction of public health infrastructures and safe water supply.

The prospects for less warfare are not good. Ethnic, religious, racial, and tribal strife that currently savage planet Earth will be exacerbated by population growth, crowding and rivalries over increasingly depleted natural resources. In future decades, competition for a decreasing supply of fresh water will be an ever more important motivation for combat. Water shortages will result from a combination of population growth, increased irrigation requirements to feed that growing population, and the effects of urbanization and industrialization; the latter depletion of water supplies can be mitigated by water treatment and recycling, but the resources required for industrial (as well as irrigation) conservation are likely to be either insufficient or inadequately utilized in less affluent countries, affected simultaneously by poverty, population explosion, and uncontrolled urbanization.

• *Population Growth and Global Warming.* Population growth will accelerate global warming by a variety of mechanisms. As populations increase so does the number of polluting automobiles and ruminants (such as cattle and sheep), which are major sources of methane, an important greenhouse gas. Forest destruction releases a great deal of the major greenhouse gas, carbon dioxide.

Changes in temperature will alter vector distribution and behavior. At higher temperatures, some mosquitoes tend to be more active, eat more voraciously, and bite more frequently. Additionally, they have shortened reproductive cycles and the extrinsic period for infectious agents (the time required for development in the mosquito) is lessened. Mosquitoes that have found higher elevations colder and less hospitable will be able to thrive in previously mosquito-free areas; this, in turn, will introduce certain diseases, such as malaria and dengue, to unexposed areas and, therefore, to non-immune populations. For those populations, diseases will emerge that may have been endemic for their general geographic areas, but which they have escaped because their geographic sub-area was free of the vectors. This introduction of infectious agents into non-immune populations as a result of vector redistribution is likely to be one of the major worldwide consequences of global warming.

Malaria, dengue, and schistosomiasis lead the list of infections likely to spread as a consequence of global warming.

• *An Aging Population.* Many older persons develop defects in their immune systems as part of the aging process. This increases their susceptibility to certain infections and makes others more severe. Thus, older persons can literally serve as incubators for emerging or re-emerging infections which can then spread to the rest of the population.

We have placed an asterisk (*) by variables for which there is a reasonable chance that intervention can have a predictably beneficial effect. These are called "leverage" points. With systems diagrams, it is important to identify leverage points that can modify the system, but it is equally important to understand it is unrealistic to assume all variables can be modified by specific actions. We can reduce population growth by intensive family-planning efforts, and we can ameliorate (but not entirely prevent) global warming. We can also reduce the severity of deforestation by establishing laws and regulations and enforcing them, as well as by other approaches. On the other hand, it is unrealistic to think we can have a predictable impact on urbanization or poverty or on the aging of the world population.

Any variable in a systems diagram can be approached; the leverage points tell us what is likely to be most effective.

For several years, one of us (DBL) traveled the country talking about emerging infections, emphasizing the societal determinants. First, I would list them, summarize the current status of each, relate each to specific infectious diseases, and then indicate that these variables were intertwined. By then, the audience was overwhelmed with somewhat disconnected data. Once I started with Figure 2 and told them to view emerging infections as a gigantic system with interrelated variables and all sorts of feedback mechanisms, they could far more readily conceptualize and appreciate the linked determinants that would influence whether we will be destined to have more or less venomous emerging infection epidemics in the coming decades or centuries.

RECOMMENDING AN INCREASE IN CONSUMPTION OF FATTY FISH

The scientific evidence now clearly shows that increasing dietary intake of omega-3 fatty acids that are found, in large part, in oily fish substantially reduces the risk of sudden death from severe abnormalities in heart rhythm that occur most often during a heart attack, but may occur in the absence of a heart attack. The evidence is so clear that adequate intake of omega-3 fatty acids saves lives that the current medical questions are now the following:

- What kinds of fish provide good amounts of omega-3 fatty acids?

- How often should they be eaten to achieve the maximum benefit?

- Instead of fish, can the available fish oil supplements be substituted?

- If fish oil supplements are used, what is the optimum dosage?

Is that all there is to it—scientific evidence and derivative health promoting recommendations? The answer is, absolutely not. In point of fact, the dietary recommendations that everybody include oily fish in the diet one or two times a week as a minimum must be put into a systems thinking paradigm. The derivative issues are:

- What is the impact on the dwindling fish populations if this recommendation is followed in the United States? In the world?

- What is the impact of this recommendation on the ecology of the oceans?

- If an increasing percentage of the oily fish originates from fish farms, what is the impact of these farms on the environment?

- What is fed to the fish on fish farms? If it is, in part, some sort of fish product, will this, in point of fact, accentuate the problem of profound reduction in the numbers of certain fish species?

- What is the source of the omega-3 fatty acids in the commercially available fish oil supplements? If these are from natural sources, will that not have potentially a major effect on the numbers of certain fish species in the oceans worldwide?

Then, of course, there are issues about the costs to the consumer of these oily fish, the percentages of the total dietary budget that will be required and the possible adverse effects for less affluent people in regard to the purchase and utilization of other essential nutrients. The questions raised represent the start of a systems approach to what, on the surface, would appear to be an evidence-based scientific and health recommendation. But, thus far, nobody appears to have considered the necessity for placing the dietary recommendation in a systems thinking context. Indeed, to our knowledge, this is the first time anyone has suggested that a recommendation for increasing the dietary intake of oily fish is not just a medical and health promotion issue, but also a societal issue requiring a systems approach.

ILLICIT DRUG USE

Drug abuse is a huge problem in our society. There are an estimated 500,000 to one million or more persons dependent on heroin or cocaine in the United States, and millions of heavy users of marijuana.

The reductionist linear approach by politicians, law enforcement, and the public is:

drug use→   treat or jail individual user and reduce supply

If the user has a medical or psychiatric complication of use and goes to a clinic or hospital emergency center, the usual linear approach is equally restricted:

drug user →   medical or →   treat the →   discharge to
                psychiatric   complication   community or
                complication   refer to drug
                                                 abuse treat-
                                                 ment

Figure 3 indicates that a systems approach is much more complex, but also provides more leverage points for specific interventions that could make a real difference. Thus, for example, a systems approach would encourage states, local communities, schools, and colleges to provide the resources to offer young persons adequate and interesting extracurricular activities that could keep them occupied and involved, avoid boredom, and create positive peer pressure. Boredom is a critical variable that promotes drug use both directly and by thrusting young people within the sphere of influence of unconstructive, drug using, peer groups. Providing adequate resources requires commitment of both personnel and money.

Understanding the drug scene, intervening effectively, and, most important, having the capacity to prevent extensive involvement by young people requires a systems focus.

FIGURE 3 - A SYSTEMS (HOLISTIC) APPROACH TO TEENAGE OR YOUNG ADULT ILLICIT DRUG USE

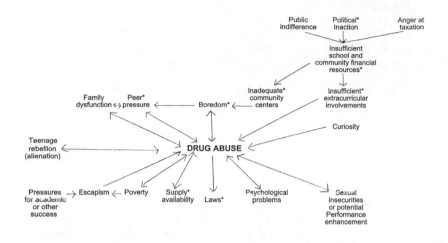

*leverage points

IMPLEMENTING EDUCATIONAL CHANGE

Once students understand and accept the tenets of systems thinking, it gives them the flexibility to adjust to the specific problems at hand, recognizing that some can be approached in a simpler linear fashion, whereas others require a broader systems focus.

These changes in our education system will not cost a lot of money, but will require a change in the way most educators think. Many resources, often at minimal cost, are now available for educators. A good starting point is The Creative Learning Exchange in Acton, Massachusetts, which can be reached online at www.clex change.org. They offer an excellent newsletter and links to other systems thinking resources that jumpstart the journey. It is really not difficult; all that is required is, where appropriate, changing from a linear approach to the circular focus with feedbacks and leverage points where intervention efforts are most likely to effect desirable change. Nobody should reject this approach on the false premise it is too complicated.

Many teachers make the mistake of assuming that teaching holistic thinking or the principles of systems thinking is all that is required. That is not correct. Teaching does not necessarily equate to learning. We must give students the learning opportunities to experience these thinking patterns, adopt them, and show that they can apply them. That, in turn, will require bringing the real interconnected world into the classroom, engaging students to take on a specific problem to test holistic-systems thinking approaches, and report back through oral presentations and/or essays on what they learned. Our objective should be to reinforce what students intuitively know: that they and their actions influence systems. We must make sure that the academic systems support life readiness.

Every high school student in the junior year (eleventh grade) could have a school year-long course titled "The World Ecosystem." In this huge system, almost everything is related to everything else. This one course, taught by transdisciplinary teams building on teachings in earlier school years, could expose students to the major problems facing the global society, to complex interrelationships, and show them that multiple perspectives improve problem definition and analysis. Additionally, it will teach them to think like futurists and to utilize a systems approach. That is essential. One of the aftermaths of the recent terrorist attack is a national feeling of anxiety. With the insistent talk about more terrorism and chemical, nuclear, and horrific biological weapons, one of the dangers is that we will come to believe we are a fey society and non-meliorist—that is, unable to solve our critical societal problems by the dint of our own efforts. Such perceptions could be catastrophic for the functioning and future of the global society.

If young people are trained to think like futurists, drawing up alternative scenarios for years or decades hence and selecting the most attractive scenario, that planning for the future instills at least a modicum of confidence that there will be a future, that we are still a meliorist society. Creating that perception by persuading young people to think like futurists is enormously important. Once they become immersed in analysis of and thinking about the ecosystem in which they live and have the potential to influence, there is a strong likelihood that a significant proportion will develop the kind of commitment to societal issues that is required if our global society is to thrive in future decades and centuries.

Educational modification is the vision; the three interrelated components are the goals within that vision. Once the educational establishment and the general public accept the vision and its goals, there are many and varied specific strategies and tactics that can be used by individual teachers, schools, institutions, and communities to achieve the goals and the overall vision. As noted, the proposed changes are intended for every level of the educational system, from junior high to graduate schools. Additionally, each person will have to decide for himself or herself which of the large number of societal problems deserve to be designated as important enough to merit that individual's particular attention and commitment.

The future of our society, indeed whether that society has a future, may well depend on how we teach our students to think about the major problems facing their society. Churchill said, "What is the use of living if it be not to make this muddled world a better place for those who will live in it after we are gone?" If we are going to follow that piece of Churchillian wisdom, we will almost certainly have to modify our educational system in accord with the three interconnected recommendations we have outlined.

ACKNOWLEDGMENT

The development of the educational approach has been supported by generous grants from The Healthcare Foundation of New Jersey.

WHOLE-BRAIN EDUCATION
FOR THE DIGITAL AGE

by

Michael T. Romano

INTRODUCTION

For over 30 years, research has confirmed the observation that each hemisphere of the human mind functions differently. It is almost 20 years since it has been proposed that this phenomenon has profound implications on how humans learn. As yet, this potentially consequential matter has not found its way into the mainstream of thought in the education establishment.

Additionally, for most of the 20th century, loud voices have contended that information technology and education would form an enduring, meaningful union. For decades, billions have been spent and enormous effort has been expended to make this happen. Today, there is ample evidence that educational technology has had no broad-scaled, quantifiable impact on academic achievement.

It is inevitable that sooner or later, these two tracks will converge and take hold on the educational landscape. It can be speculated that then, technology will empower teachers with a heightened capacity to impact on the mind and that this will markedly influence how our youth learn.

This paper looks beyond what is presently happening in classrooms and offers the vision of what can be termed a *whole-brain, technology-enhanced model of education for the digital age.*

ABOUT THE TWO-SIDED BRAIN

Albert Einstein made this statement in 1949:

The words or the language as they are spoken, *do not seem to play any role* in my mechanism of thought. The physical entities which seem to serve as elements in thought are signs and images.[1]

Apparently, this one-of-a-kind genius was "right-brain-dominant," as it came to be called decades later. It has been conjectured that Thomas Edison, Leonardo da Vinci, George S. Patton and Nelson Rockefeller are among others who demonstrated this trait.

Linda Williams in her 1983 book, *Teaching for the Two-Sided Mind*, notes that research regarding the two-hemisphere phenomenon has been reported as early as 1968. Essentially, it has been determined that the right and left sides of the brain process different types of

Michael T. Romano *is professor emeritus at the University of Kentucky. This paper is excerpted from his book,* Empowering Teachers With Technology. *He may be contacted at (859) 543-0099.*

information in a synergistic mode:[2]

• The left hemisphere is most efficient for processing verbal information; for encoding and decoding speech. The processing moves from one point to the next in a sequential manner.

• The right hemisphere does not move linearly but processes all information simultaneously. It is most efficient at visual and spatial processing (images). Words seem to play little part in its functioning.

We do not think with one hemisphere or the other; the whole brain is involved in higher cognitive processes. However, it has been determined that some individuals are right-brain dominant, while others appear to favor the left-brain in processing information. What is the relationship between this phenomenon and what happens in the classroom?

In 1980, Jean Houston, a sociobiologist, offered some enlightening observations. She notes that before going to school, from infancy children learn to think and to function from a much larger sensory and neurological base. They develop by relying on what they see, hear, feel, taste and smell. In the classroom, the great bulk of the sensory inputs are to the left brain. Our educational system and our understanding of intelligence, she contends, discriminate against one whole half of the brain. Her most disconcerting observation: So much of the behavioral problems and failures in school come directly out of boredom which itself comes directly out of the larger failure to stimulate all those areas in children's brains which could give them so many more ways of responding to their world.[3]

Jeffrey Freed in his 1998 book, *Right-Brained Children in a Left-Brained World*, sharpened the focus on this critical matter. Here are several quotes from his work:

• Why are we facing a crisis in education? Students today are fundamentally different. Our classrooms are being flooded by a new generation of right-brained, visual kids. While our school system plods along using the same teaching methods that were in vogue decades ago, students are finding it more and more difficult to learn that way. As our culture becomes more visual and our brain dominance shifts to the right, the chasm widens between teacher and pupil. *Our schools are no longer congruent with the way many children think.*[4]

• Most gifted and virtually all children with Attention Deficit Disorder (ADD) share the same learning style. They are all highly visual who learn by remembering the way things look and taking words and turning them into mental images. This is a simple yet revolutionary notion.[5]

• The 21st century child is the product of a culture that bombards us with rapid-fire images. From birth, his environment literally wires and rewires visual pathways in the brain.[6]

• Some educators point to the 1960s as the time when our schools "collapsed." That period of time coincides with the first generation of children raised with television.[7]

• If we have any hope of reaching the growing population of right-brained children, we have to understand how they think and learn.[8]

This is indeed leading-edge thinking. There is little indication the education establishment has yet grasped the enormous significance of the right/left brain matter. The *primacy of the word* in education has endured for centuries. It is the basis for a left-brain-oriented teaching/learning process handed down from the Industrial Age to the Digital Age. There is ample evidence that technology, skillfully adapted, will allow teachers to routinely create visually rich, whole-brain experiences for learners.

ABOUT THE TECHNOLOGY GAP

Today, young people live in two worlds. Outside the classroom they are immersed in a world of mind-grabbing marvels. It is the awesome Digital Age, and the young become technically-versatile with ease and enthusiasm. Actually, it is as though some develop a virtual *dependency* on their linkage to a compelling, whole-brain, electronic universe brought to their eyes and ears by television, computers and the Internet.

Then there is the world of the classroom. There, for the most part, the routine centers on books, chalkboards and teacher-talk. It was so for our parents, our grandparents and even our great grandparents. In today's technology-dependent society, this is difficult to rationalize.

It was in the 1950s when many believed a union between television and education would revolutionize how our youth learn. Since then, billions have been spent for technology in schools—*and it is everywhere.* In 1999, the CEO Forum, a school reform advocacy group financed by 20 of the nation's leading corporations, published its *School Technology and Readiness Report.* It concludes:

The *gap* between technology presence in schools and its effective use is still too wide. We continue to believe the quality of public education depends upon our collective ability to close the *gap* between technology presence and its effective use in the pursuit of school improvement.[9]

In spite of the enormous amounts of money spent on technology, it is pertinent to note that in 1972 the composite national SAT score was 1039; in 1999 it was 1016.

In simple terms, the technology gap exists because, as yet, we have not found a feasible way to do for teachers what has been done for pilots, surgeons, bankers and other professionals in our society: amplify their capacity to function by empowering them with technology. The US Department of Education announced in February of 2002 that it is mounting a $15 million, three-year study to determine how to integrate technology into the curriculum.

Teaching and learning is a process fueled by information. The teacher serves as the manager of the information fed into the process. Technology enhances the teacher's capacity to search for, configure, store and make information available to the learner, and all of this in multimedia: words, in print or sound; images, in motion or still. Hence, the potential of technology to provide teachers the capacity to more readily impact on the whole brain.

The fact that the most effective way to use technology in the classroom has not yet been devised is confirmed by several authoritative sources.

- 1995, US Congress Office of Technology Assessment: Teachers and administrators need a vision of how technology can best be deployed.[10]

- 1996, the Apple Classroom of Tomorrow Project: In the maze of reform efforts, the role of technology remains unclear.[11]

- 1999, the Milken Exchange on Education Technology Study: Digital resources are bursting on the scene, but no one is quite sure how to effectively use them.[12]

A final point. After over 40 years as an academician, I contend that regardless of how we deploy technology in the classroom, the approach must be based on this truth: *Human beings have always been conditioned to learn under the guidance of other humans.* Teaching and learning appear to be driven by emulation, shared aspirations and a special bond between someone with a "felt" need to learn and grow and someone dedicated to help meet that need.

This paper offers the vision of a whole-brain, technology-enhanced, Digital Age model of education that preserves what is best in our system of education: *the magical, and essential interface between teacher and learner.*

A STRATEGY FOR CLOSING THE TECHNOLOGY GAP IN EDUCATION

There can be identified four primary obstacles to the effective use of technology in education which must be surmounted:

1. *The expectations regarding "revolutions" in education are unrealistic. There can be no "great leap" in education—only skillfully managed evolution.*

Webster's dictionary defines "revolution" simply as "a sudden, radical, or complete change." Based on my decades as an educator, I instinctively believe it is best that there be no "sudden, radical, or complete change" in one of the keystone institutions of our society. For the good of all involved, I believe it is essential that continuity and stability in our education establishment remain uncompromised.

The first "revolution" was proclaimed early in the 20th century. It was the motion picture that would change forever how our youth learned. It did not happen. Then, 50 years ago, millions were spent in the hope that educational television would usher in "the revolution." Again, it simply did not happen.

Today, it is computers and the Internet. With great expectations, billions are being spent by government at all levels and a host of private agencies. For example, the corporate giant IBM has put in place a long-term, multimillion-dollar effort they call "Reinventing Education." Their objective: replace the existing system with a new, technology-intensive model.

Although their motive is commendable, they have failed to acknowledge that there is no way the educational system in place can be demolished and carted away like an old building. Without a doubt, the new must be linked firmly to what exists, *or there can be no progress.* This has been referred to in the literature as the "compatibility factor."[13] Thus, it is contended that:

> The routine, broad-scaled use of technology in education can only be achieved by a strategy based on a realistic appraisal of the existing system's capacity to assimilate change, not the perceived capacity of technology to create new and superior systems.

After studying decades of failure to achieve meaningful, broad-scaled education reform, Richard Reiser, in an article in *Instructional Communications* published in 1991, offered this conclusion:

> Our public education system has built up complex mechanisms that serve to maintain and support it. They exist in the form of administrative structures, organizational and cultural norms, and even legislative policies. That is why *innovations are either adapted to fit the existing system, or else they are sloughed off, allowing the system to remain essentially untouched* (italics added).[14]

2. *Teachers lack a clear understanding of how technology would empower them. Some erroneously perceive it as a threat to their professional security rather than an amplification of their capacity to function.*

Teachers harbor an understandable uneasiness that they might be replaced by an electronic terminal. Further, they appear to be locked into a seemingly rational mind-set: I function as proof that yesterday's approach to teaching works, therefore, if it worked for me it will work for my learners.

Traditionally, teachers are the gatekeepers of the classroom. They orchestrate the curriculum and greatly influence how technology fits into the classroom. If innovation is to be widely adopted, it must be carefully folded into:

> what teachers have been trained to do, what they can easily be re-trained to do, what they believe is best for their learners, what they believe is best for their careers, as well as the requirements of the curriculum in place and the constraints of the classroom support system.

3. *Efforts to train teachers to use technology are for the most part counterproductive. Often, teachers are confounded rather than enlightened.*

For several decades, the federal government has spent billions for research on developing effective utilization strategies for technology in the classroom. There is little doubt this effort has not been productive. It is an incongruity that in view of this reality, additional billions are spent, at all levels, to train teachers to use technology. Thus, teachers face a veritable "catch-22" situation:

> They are concerned that they actually do not know how to use technology; they are concerned that after they learn all they need to know, they will not have time to integrate technology into their curricula; and when they participate in the training programs, they come away without a definitive understanding of how to use technology—*because such an understanding does not exist.*

And thus, they retreat to their classrooms to teach in the same way they, their parents, and their grandparents had been taught.

4. *The crucial significance of course-specific software has not been generally acknowledged. Most of the time, "off-the-shelf" software does not adequately integrate into the curriculum, thus—for the most part—negating its effectiveness.*

What is a curriculum? Pilots have flight plans. Physicians have treatment plans. Coaches have game plans. Teachers have curricula.

It is a strategy put in place to specify *what* to teach, *when* to teach it, and *how* to teach it. It is not arbitrary; it is specific. It has time constraints, with little flexibility.

A curriculum is driven by information. Determined by specific learning objectives, the information is carefully selected and precisely sequenced. Any deviation will adversely affect the outcome.

It is essential that we do with the newer information technology what has been done with print—handouts, manuals and textbooks: provide teachers the support system necessary to create course-specific software. Anything less will compromise realizing the full potential of technology. This view is confirmed by a number of sources. Perhaps the most authoritative is the 10-year, Apple Classroom of Tomorrow Study, which reported:

> Technology use must be grounded firmly in curriculum goals, incorporated in a sound instructional process, and deeply integrated with subject matter content. Absent this grounding, which too often is neglected in the rush to glittery application, *changes in student performance are unlikely.*[15]

Finally, the matter of the Internet needs to be included in this discussion. Encouraged by the federal government, considerable funds are being spent to bring this potentially powerful information resource to every classroom. Again, the critical matter of curriculum-specific information needs to be reconciled. In a 1999 study, teachers noted that "it is too difficult and time-consuming to find appropriate Web sites, preview them and develop materials to bring them into lessons."[16] How teachers might best manage the overwhelming amount of "unprocessed" information delivered by the Internet is still unclear.

The *Whole-Brain Technology-Enhanced Curriculum* deals directly with the four obstacles discussed. Most importantly, it is designed by determining what teachers do, what technology does and then carefully folding them together.

EMPOWERING TEACHERS WITH TECHNOLOGY

Volumes can be written about the teacher's role in the teaching/learning process. For the purpose of this discussion, it will be divided into four primary tasks. These usually occur sequentially but can also take place in a random/repeat mode:

- *Planning:* All teaching/learning experiences require planning; the design of the curriculum depends upon the nature of the learning objectives.

- *Communication:* Although there is more to the total process, nothing happens unless information is made available to the learner.

• *Guidance:* The learner needs to be guided in applying and/or attempting to understand the information.

• *Evaluation:* The achievement of the learner needs to be assessed, feedback provided and remedial measures initiated.

It appears axiomatic that anything the teacher does to enhance any of these tasks should enhance learning. To elaborate:

• The *planning task:* It is the teacher's responsibility to decide *what* information is required to reach the objective and *when* it is to be sequenced into the curriculum. Computers and the Internet provide planners an additional, readily accessible, vast source of information beyond print.

• The *communication task:* Although each of the four tasks is integral to the process, the *communication of information to the mind of the learner* is the essence of education. Stated another way: *information is the fuel that powers the teaching/learning process.* Thus, anything the teacher does to improve the *quality* of the fuel—or the *fidelity* of the information—must have a positive impact on the outcome. The core information technologies—video and computers—allow the teacher to readily make *visually rich multimedia* available to the learner—*thus heightening the impact on the whole brain.*

• The *guidance task:* One-on-one interaction with the learner is how the teacher attempts to compensate for the disparity in each individual's capacity to learn. In the real world of the classroom the amount of guidance is seldom as much as the teacher would choose to provide. A computer programmed with course-specific software has the potential to increase the guidance available to learners—*based on their need, not the teacher's availability.*

• The *evaluation task:* Ideally, evaluation includes identifying deficiencies, providing feedback and initiating remedial measures. Again, *the extent to which teachers have the time to provide remedial tutoring for each learner varies markedly* from what might be considered ideal. Theoretically, the computer has the potential to allow teachers to provide as much remedial tutoring as the individual requires to meet achievement standards.

THE CRITICAL MATTER OF WORDS VS. IMAGES

For centuries, the teaching/learning process has been primarily fueled by words—the lecture and the book—mainly because until now, teachers have always found words easier to use, not because it was determined that words *impact on learners better than the combination of words and images*. To pursue this critical matter further: It is a shibboleth—and it has been around for a long time—"*a picture is worth a thousand words....*"

The logic seems irrefutable; yet, it implies that a thousand words can be substituted for a picture. How many words would it take to describe a sunset? Or the look on Jacqueline Kennedy's face on that fateful day in November 1963 as she watched Lyndon Johnson take the oath succeeding her slain husband as President of the United States? A thousand words do not begin to communicate all there is etched in these images. The time has come to put a sharper edge to that age-old adage, which perhaps understates reality:

> A verbal description alone of anything that can be seen must be considered a compromise; a compromise made every day in classrooms everywhere.

Obviously, learners cannot be brought to an historical event as it happened. It is necessary, therefore, to create a *replica* or a substitute for the sensory experience of actually being there, which would be termed the *referent*. For example, the best replica possible of the moon landing would be a video of the event, accompanied by narration. Is there any doubt that there would be a more powerful impact on learners from a video than from a verbal description alone? Given the choice in 1969, how many in the world then would have chosen the obvious compromise of radio over television to experience the historic event? This compromise occurs in classrooms all over the world, every day, in an age when technology makes it unnecessary.

Another perspective: The gap between the referent and the replica, regardless of the medium used, determines what can be termed the *fidelity of the information*. Thus, it is axiomatic that in the classroom, the greater the *fidelity*—or stated another way, the smaller the gap between replica and referent—the greater the impact on the learner, *resulting in more effective learning*. In summary: Technology empowers teachers by allowing them to routinely replace left-brain-oriented print with the more powerful whole-brain-oriented multimedia.

THE WHOLE-BRAIN TECHNOLOGY-ENHANCED CURRICULUM

What Specifications were Used in Designing the WBTEC?

Primarily, it deals directly with the four obstacles to the effective use of technology previously defined. Most importantly, it is intended to be compatible with the existing system so that the change will be easily managed by all involved—particularly teachers. Finally, it serves as a universal template that can be applied to all levels of education and thus provide continuity.

How are Teachers Empowered by Technology in the WBTEC?

Basically, technology is used to amplify the teacher's capacity to communicate, guide and evaluate, and thus impact favorably on the outcome of the teaching/learning process. To summarize:

• It allows teachers to convert a print-based, left-brain-oriented process to a multimedia-based, interactive, whole-brain process. Technology allows teachers to routinely use a blend of images (still and motion), graphics, sounds, print and digits based on the objectives of the curriculum.

• Additionally, it allows teachers to more effectively compensate for the disparity in individual learning capacity by providing the opportunity for more one-on-one tutoring—based on the need of the learner.

This is accomplished by using technology in two basic modes: *Teacher-Narrated Video* and *Computerized Remedial Tutoring.* It should be noted that both can be used by teachers without major retraining.

What is Teacher-Narrated Video?

It evolves from the commonly used mode where teachers lecture "over" images from an overhead or slide projector. The teacher is provided video segments that add the dimensions of motion and sound to images and graphics.

The video segments are not complete productions with titling, music, etc. Instead, they are designed to permit the teacher to provide narration and interpretation "live," while still using the chalkboard and interacting with the class as is done traditionally. It can be considered "interactive multimedia." The multimedia is provided by technology; the teacher orchestrates the interaction.

Finally, it enhances the communication phase of teaching by eliminating the compromise of using verbal descriptions of all that can be seen or heard. It should be noted that the video segments might be retrieved by means of videotape, DVD or CD-ROM.

What is Computerized Remedial Tutoring?

It allows teachers to readily do for each learner what teachers do best, but are limited by time constraints: one-on-one evaluation and guidance.

Computers are programmed with software specifically created for a particular course. At specified checkpoints, they determine what each individual has learned and identify what has not been learned. Based on that assessment, the computer tutors the learner so that the gap between what they know and the achievement standards set for the course is narrowed.

It should be noted that in other areas of society that have become computer-dependent, there has emerged a major, universally adopted application. For instance, in air travel it is the reservation system. In banking it is account management. And in medicine it is computerized diagnostic imaging. It is proposed that *Computerized Remedial Tutoring* may be that primary, broad-scaled application in education.

However, it should be emphasized again that the key is not hardware but course-specific software. For over 25 years, we have had teachers select and attempt to fit into their curricula off-the-shelf software. The results have been discouraging. Admittedly, the challenge to create teacher-support services geared to produce course-specific software is formidable—but not prohibitive; not for a nation with a federal annual budget for education approaching $35 billion.

MORE ABOUT THE DIGITAL AGE CLASSROOM

Here are some examples of how *Teacher-Narrated Video* would heighten what happens in a high school classroom.

In one instance, learners—hand-in-hand with their teacher—become eyewitnesses to history. For example, she is the narrator standing next to the TV monitor as *they see, hear and feel* the exciting times of the Kennedy presidency. There is the drama of the election returns, the traditional pageantry of the inauguration, the keen disappointment of the Bay of Pigs, the intense anxiety of the Cuban missile crisis, the high exhilaration of the speech at the Berlin Wall and the heartbreak—the terrible heartbreak—of the assassination; and, *all in sight and sound*. They are there. They literally are participants. To add texture and depth, they absorb information from the textbook and, at intervals, the electronic images pause and—as always—the teacher is at the blackboard.

In physics, the teacher begins the year with a multi-session overview of the physical phenomena to be covered in the course. Narrating over video segments of the 1969 moon shot, he/she skillfully guides the class from the colossal launch pad to a tiny spot on the eerie surface of the moon, and all of this from the perspective of the many laws of physics that had to be managed—with infinite care—to make this unprecedented feat possible.

In sociology, learners are escorted to a magnificent spring ball, held in the midst of the Civil War in an elegant southern mansion. To create the grand illusion, the teacher uses segments of the epic 1939 motion picture, *Gone With the Wind*. The music, the refreshments, the finery, the furnishings, even the mores of the day are all authentically depicted as Rhett Butler dances with the newly widowed Scarlett O'Hara. *And, the class is there—eavesdropping, learning.*

In chemistry, the teacher uses images created by computer graphics to construct complex molecules. Then, as if by magic, he/she combines two, initiating a reaction depicted in slow motion, although it occurred in a flash, intriguing, multi-element structures disassembling and reassembling in new, intricate configurations and all orchestrated by a skilled teacher—*empowered with technology.*

Then, there is English literature. At the push of a button the teacher has King Lear leap from the pages of the textbook on to the face of the magic tube. And so, he/she shares with the class his/her all-time, favorite Shakespearean actor—perhaps the incomparable Richard Burton. At selected intervals, he is put on hold as *the teacher and learners talk, read aloud, interact, enjoy—and learn.*

It is minds interacting with minds—both sides, right and left. It is a synergism of textbook, blackboard, electronic images and sounds—and above all—a skilled teacher empowered with technology. It is the teaching/learning process at a new, evolutionary level.

The same video segments are used to produce the course-specific software for *Computerized Remedial Tutoring.* In regard to cost, it should be noted that every event in human history, every major literary work and every natural or physical phenomenon already exists on film or tape in the combined libraries of the news networks, Hollywood, the Public Broadcasting System, the Arts and Entertainment Network and the History Channel.

A final word about *Computerized Remedial Tutoring.* Programmed with course-specific software, computers provide each learner what every teacher has always strived to deliver: ample, additional, individualized tutoring so they might attain a higher level of achievement.

ONE FINAL THOUGHT

The *Whole-Brain Technology-Enhanced Curriculum* is not proposed as the leading edge of the vast potential of information technology in education—rather, it is a transitional, adaptation model. *It is an increment of change the system will accept.*

There are teachers who have advanced beyond *Teacher-Narrated Video* and *Computerized Remedial Tutoring;* but it has been established, conclusively, that these are the few. The many are still firmly entrenched behind a host of barriers and still teach as they were taught. In essence, the vision brought forth is about how to at last penetrate these formidable barriers and replace an Industrial Age model of education with a Digital Age model; and usher in the era of whole-brain education—*where no child is left behind.*

NOTES

1. J. Hadamard, *The Psychology of Invention in the Mathematical Field*, (Princeton, NJ: Princeton University Press, 1949), 24.
2. Linda V. Williams, *Teaching for the Two-Sided Mind* (New York: Simon and Schuster, 1986), 2.
3. Jean Houston, "Education and its Transformation," *Education: A Time for Decisions* (Washington, DC: World Future Society, 1980), 145.
4. J. Freed and L. Parsons, *Right-Brained Children in a Left-Brained World* (New York: Simon and Schuster, 1998), 76.
5. J. Freed, *Right-Brained Children*, 17.
6. J. Freed, *Right-Brained Children*, 33.
7. J. Freed, *Right-Brained Children*, 159.
8. J. Freed, *Right-Brained Children*, 161.
9. *School Technology and Readiness*, (Washington, DC: The CEO Forum, February, 1999).
10. US Congress, Office of Technology Assessment, *Teachers and Technology: Making the Connection*, OTA-EHR-616 (Washington, DC: US Government Printing Office, 1995), 125.
11. C. Fisher, D. Dwyer, and K. Yokum, *Education and Technology* (San Francisco, CA: Apple Press, 1996), 97.
12. E. Fatemi, "Building the Digital Curriculum," *Technology Counts '99* (Bethesda, MD: Education Week, 1999), 6.
13. E. Burkman, "Factors Affecting Utilization," *Instructional Technology: Foundations* (Hillside, NJ: Lawrence Erlbaum, 1987), 445.
14. R. Reiser, "Instructional Technology and Public Education in the United States," in *Instructional Communications* (Englewood, CO: Libraries Unlimited, 1991), 219.
15. Fisher, *Education and Technology*, 200.
16. M. Lehr, "Screening for the Best," *Technology Counts '99* (Bethesda, MD: Education Week, 1999), 19.

FOUR URGENT REQUESTS FROM FUTURE GENERATIONS

by

Allen Tough

What if future generations themselves were able to speak to us? Just what would future generations say to us if they could? If they had a voice today, what would they ask us to do for them?

Here is my best guess about some of the things they would like us to know and do. The rest of this essay is a message to us from future generations in their own words—what they would say to us if they could.

A MESSAGE FROM FUTURE GENERATIONS

Thank you for listening to this message from future generations—those of us who will inhabit this lovely planet for many decades to come. Our voices are usually overlooked by your generations, so we are very appreciative of your willingness to listen to our perspective.

You are alive at a pivotal moment in humanity's development. You are making some of the most important choices in human history. Your era is marked by positive and negative potentials of such newness and magnitude that you can hardly understand them. Through your public policies and daily lives, the people of your era have tremendous power to influence the future course of humanity's story. We strongly care about your choices, of course, since we benefit or suffer from them quite directly. We live downstream from you in time; whatever you put into the stream flows on to our era.

We will be very grateful if you devote your best efforts to four particular changes. These are the four things that we need most from you.

It is important for you to realize just how deep and pervasive these changes must be in order to give us equal opportunities. Individual behavior, social structures, economic assumptions, even paradigms and worldviews must all change. We know that these changes are not shallow or easy. But if you do not change vigorously and successfully, we will be much worse off than you are. The costs of the deterioration and losses will be far larger than the costs of making the changes in the first place would have been. If you continue your shortsighted selfishness, the consequences will be catastrophic, perhaps even beyond the stretch of your imagination. From our long-term perspective, we see how foolish and unfair you will be if you fail to make the required changes soon. How would you react to a bus driver who knew the brakes would give out soon

Allen Tough *is professor emeritus at the University of Toronto, Canada. His biography is at members.aol.com/welcomeeti/4.html and his e-mail address is future@ieti.org.*

but did not bother to get them fixed promptly? If you do make the changes, the benefits to ongoing humanity will be much greater than the costs of making the changes.

We appreciate your willingness to consider these four changes seriously.

Adopt a Long-Term Perspective

In all of your major decisions and actions, please consider our perspective and well-being along with your own. Take our needs as seriously as your own. Care about our welfare as well as your own. Our needs and rights are not inferior to yours. Please regard your generation and ours as equals. This is the principle of intergenerational equity—equal opportunities across the generations.

Reflect on your unique place in human history. You face the historic challenge of making the shift from a narrow, self-centered, short-term focus to a long-term global focus that takes into account our needs as well as your own. If you succeed in making this deep-seated shift toward a long-term perspective, your era will be remembered for saving human civilization and its planet from catastrophe and disintegration, and for building the foundation for a more positive world.

As members of future generations, we are particularly eager for you to designate a spokesperson for our needs in your various policy-making forums, planning processes, legislatures, parliaments, houses of representatives, senates, and so on. Because we are not yet alive in your era, we are unable to lobby or vote. We have no voice. We seem unreal and unimportant to many of your politicians because we have not yet been born. Our perspective and interests are rarely noted in any depth. This is why we are very enthusiastic about your era's diverse proposals for incorporating the views and needs of future generations into your legislative and policy-making processes. On the global level, we are pleased with your proposals for designated advocates and an international tribunal for future generations. We are also pleased with your additional proposals for particular nations.

We now urge you to move on from words and proposals to practical innovative experiments. As you experiment, you will gain greater insights and skills and thus be able to develop even better ways of incorporating our views into your public decision making. Please experiment with a spokesperson for future generations in the decision-making processes of the United Nations and its agencies, other international agencies, nongovernmental organizations, each religion, various levels of government, and all other major organizations. As you see what works, what does not, and why, you will be able to move ahead with wider use of spokespersons for those not yet born. Our ultimate hope, of course, is that *all* participants in public and corporate decision making will eventually adopt the perspective of future generations and will serve as spokespersons and guardians for our interests.

The overriding importance of *avoiding the worst catastrophes of all* will become obvious to you as you make progress in adopting a long-term perspective. Please begin now. Detect and study the entire range of potential catastrophes or trends that could eliminate or severely harm human civilization. Avoid losing the foundation that the previous hundred generations have built up for you and us. Take particularly vigorous and creative steps to avoid a severe world war—perhaps even to eliminate warfare entirely. Equally important, take vigorous actions to stabilize the size of the human population and to end the rapid deterioration of the planet. These two potential catastrophes—warfare and environment—are so probable and have such far-reaching consequences that they are clearly central in any list of priorities.

Future-Relevant Research

In order to achieve a satisfactory future, you need to rapidly expand your efforts to develop future-oriented knowledge, ideas, insights, understanding, visions, and wisdom. You need to know far more about world problems, social change, potential futures, the effectiveness of various possible paths, individual change, the personal foundations of caring about future generations, and several other future-relevant topics. This future-oriented inquiry can include not only research and development projects, but also creative visioning, speculative brainstorming, disciplined thinking, synthesis, conceptual frameworks, theory building, and wide-ranging dialogue.

Move toward a body of concepts, ideas, and knowledge that is profound, powerful, and well organized. Carefully examine your conceptual frameworks and paradigms. Organize your existing knowledge base more rigorously; don't be conceptually sloppy or lazy. Critique and build on the ideas and frameworks of others, instead of operating in intellectual isolation. Try to attract people with especially penetrating minds and thoughtful approaches, and then generously support their intellectual work.

The amount of effort going into creating knowledge that is profoundly significant to the long-term future is only about one-third of what it should be. The gap between the optimum effort and your current level is foolish and poignant. Your aim should be to multiply your future-oriented inquiry threefold over the next few years. The long-term benefits will far outweigh the costs.

For success, you need to increase your knowledge of world problems and social change much faster than the problems themselves increase. At present, the problems are outstripping your knowledge of how to deal with them. You are going to have to run much faster than now simply to catch up to all the major problems. Then you may find that the negative forces are running faster and faster, becoming more and more challenging. To develop the knowledge to outrun all these tendencies for civilization to deteriorate, you will need to increase your efforts even further. You certainly have the potential to win the race, but not by coasting along at your present level of future-oriented research.

Future-Relevant Education

Learning and teaching about the future provide an essential foundation for building a better world. You cannot achieve a positive future without far-reaching learning and changes by individuals around the world. These individuals include all of you, not just political leaders, government officials, policy experts, or business leaders. You no doubt recall the prescient words of one of your early futurists, H.G. Wells: "Human history becomes more and more a race between education and catastrophe." You can successfully navigate through the next few decades only if a large proportion of the world's population understands global problems and potential futures, cares about future generations, accepts the need for change, and takes a cooperative and constructive approach to dealing with hard choices. Once enough people care about future generations, implementing these four key priorities will become much easier.

Any path to a positive future will require deep changes in individual perspectives, values, and behavior. From early childhood to late adulthood, learning opportunities should be widespread. In every city on earth, at least some schools, colleges, adult education programs, and libraries should provide a wide array of methods for people to learn about the future prospects of their civilization and their region. In addition to various educational programs and institutions, these opportunities can include libraries, discussion groups, informal education, workshops, support groups, television, printed materials, electronic sources and hardware, and self-planned learning projects. This range of learning opportunities should help people of all ages understand global issues, think skeptically and critically when appropriate, treasure all life on earth, feel concern for other people, grasp the importance of caring about us future generations, grasp our perspective, feel committed to necessary changes, tolerate diverse cultures and views, cooperate for the common good, and pursue meaningful nonmaterial goals.

Educational institutions should provide courses in futures studies, with some emphasis on the perspective of future generations, using approaches that affect the head, heart, soul, and hands of people of all ages. Your education about the future could be greatly enhanced if you develop a better knowledge base about potential futures, conduct research on the processes of learning and teaching about the future, and experiment with innovative and profound approaches to such learning and teaching.

In addition, we urge you to consider a worldwide campaign to increase caring for future generations. This campaign could use various approaches, including:

• clear, moving, powerful books and booklets written for the general public and for students

• superb television programs and films that enable you to "experience" future generations, and to grasp the fact that we too are actual living people (in your future) rather than some abstract concept

• a major Web site, spearheaded by the World Future Society, where people around the world can quickly learn about significant world trends and forecasts

• classroom exercises, such as speaking with the voice of future people, of wild species, or of beings on other planets

• writing a pledge to future generations

• further growth of the World Future Society's publications and programs for the general public

• inspirational support groups

• transformative experiences that combine music, poetry, powerful prose, nature, rituals, inspirational meetings, and the voices of children and youth.

Learning, Caring, and Meaningfulness

Now we come to the final societal priority that we recommend for your era. This priority continues to be very important to us, so we hope it will soon become important to you, too.

In this final priority, we urge your society to focus plenty of attention and support on the deeper and softer aspects of individual lives. We refer specifically to three areas: (a) widespread individual learning about the most important questions of all; (b) caring based on deep connectedness to people, the planet, and future generations; and (c) a strong sense of meaning and purpose in life. Although we will discuss these three areas separately, they are actually closely interrelated. And all three contribute to the individual's deeper and softer side.

Your society could do much more toward widespread individual *learning* about the most important questions of all. You should encourage and help each individual to learn the accumulated knowledge on these questions, and also to think through their own best answers. Obviously they will be more successful in their quest if your society has fostered their ability to think clearly, flexibly, creatively, and skeptically about difficult and controversial questions. Here are some of the big questions that thoughtful individuals face:

- the origin of the universe

- cosmic evolution and the ultimate destination of the universe

- our place in the universe

- our relationship with other intelligent beings and civilizations in our galaxy

- the history and long-term future of humankind and human culture

- our appropriate relationship with the planet and its diverse forms of life

- core values

- finding a path to a positive human future

- how each individual can contribute to achieving that positive future.

Your society should do much more to help people feel a deep bonding or *connectedness* with all of humankind, with the planet and its diverse forms of life, and with future generations. Explore the usefulness of music, hymns, songs, poetry, prose, laser light shows, art, hiking, cathedrals, inspirational services, children, mountains, observation towers, zoos, nature reserves, and scenic beauty for this purpose. As more and more people experience a deep connectedness, they will care strongly about humanity, future generations, and the planet—and will act on that deep love and caring. They will eagerly want to make a positive difference to humanity and the planet. They will be happy to experience a bond with something ageless, something transcendent, something much larger than their own life.

Creating inspirational groups dedicated to future generations could be particularly useful. The people in these groups would feel bonded together by their deep caring for future generations, and by their efforts to build a better world. Various methods could be used to inspire and strengthen each member's sense of connectedness to humanity and its positive future. Inspirational gatherings, oral readings, silent reflection, discussion, and songs of gratitude and joy could all play a part. Members could share their feelings about the long-term future, reflect on the implications of recent events, and discuss their most significant unanswered questions. Members could also discuss their current efforts to contribute, including their strategies, obstacles, triumphs, and failures. Many people want to make a positive difference to the world, but lack a sympathetic and inspirational support group. Such groups could be built on love and reverence for human civilization and other societies in our galaxy, awe concerning the mysteries of the universe, and commitment to service on behalf of future generations. By supporting various efforts to build a positive long-term future, these groups could provide people with an inspiriting and transcendent purpose in life.

Your society should also focus much more attention and support on the individual's desire for a sense of *meaning and purpose* in life. A sense of meaning and purpose can easily pervade a society in which people share a sense of connectedness with the cosmos, with its diverse life, and with the continuous procession of generations.

REFLECTIONS

We worry that you will choose the tempting path that lies right in front of you, dissipating your efforts on alluring goals and priorities that will have little influence on long-term flourishing—squandering your time and energy not only on consumption, luxury, competition, quarrels, and violence, but also on the faddish projects and causes of the moment. Think of the pain and suffering that you will cause us—the bleak lives and barren planet, the harsh restrictions, the lost potential, the sense of malaise and futility. We cry when we think of what might come to pass. Perhaps you too will feel some tears as you think about what your era's lack of future-oriented caring and effort could inflict on us.

We agree with you that the four key changes that need to be made by individuals, organizations, and society are startlingly large, deep, and far reaching. But the alternative is for your grandchildren and the other members of their generation to spend much of their adult life in a social and physical environment that is bleak and nasty. The four profound changes are necessary in order to avoid such a negative outcome. They provide the best path to a positive future.

Of the four, the most important of all is a worldwide shift toward caring deeply about the well-being of all the people who will be alive over the next few decades, and the well-being of the planet. This perspective transformation or paradigm shift is necessary for citizens, policy makers, business leaders, and key people throughout governments. As more and more of you change your inner perspective, there is an excellent chance that the necessary outer changes will also occur. As a result, the ever-unfolding history of human civilization may alter course toward a happy and positive future!

Thank you for your deep and serious attention to our suggestions.

THE FUTURE OF THE BOOK IN A DIGITAL AGE

by

David J. Staley

It was widely believed in the 1990s that the end of the book was near. "The printed book," observed literary theorist Jay David Bolter, "seems destined to move to the margin of our literate culture." While there would still be literacy, while we would still engage in writing and reading, in the future these activities would be carried out on the screen, in an electronic environment. Moving literacy from book to screen was part of the larger history of writing; after all, had not the written word moved from clay to papyrus to vellum to paper? The shift from printed book to computer screen, reasoned Bolter, was part of this larger historical process. "We are living," Bolter concluded, "in the late age of print."[1]

Critical literary theorists well recognized that they were living in the twilight of the printed book. Jacques Derrida proclaimed the end of the book; poststructuralist critics described print culture as exhausted, dying, and vanishing. "Critical theorists," insisted the theorist George Landow, "continually confront the limitation —indeed, the exhaustion—of the culture of print." In contrast, theorists working with hypertext found in the computer a new writing space upon which to transcribe literate culture. The book was an old, exhausted technology, but the computer screen offered a new, invigorating space for literate culture. Hypertextual reading and writing would transcend the limitations of printed books. Hypertexts were nonlinear and participatory, blurring the boundaries between author and reader, providing readers the opportunity to interact with and alter texts in a way not possible in linear, author-dominated, out-dated printed books. Rather than lamenting the end of the book, these theorists welcomed the new Golden Age of writing on the screen.[2]

The view that we were living in the twilight of print culture was echoed even by technophobes. Sven Birkerts wrote *The Gutenberg Elegies: The Fate of Reading in an Electronic Age,* a collection of essays that noted with dismay the passing of the book. While Birkerts unrepentantly, if quixotically, proclaimed that "the bound book is the ideal vehicle for the written word," he was realistic enough to recognize the same historical transformation identified by Bolter, Landow, and Derrida. "The displacement of the page by the screen is not yet total (as evidenced by the book you are holding)—it may never be total—but the large-scale tendency in that direction has to be obvious to anyone who looks,"[3] Birkerts wrote in 1994. Birkerts, unlike hypertext theorists, was not pleased with this transformation, but seemed resigned to the fact, powerless to do anything about it.

David J. Staley *is an associate professor of history at Heidelberg College, Tiffin, Ohio. He may be contacted at dstaley@heidelberg.edu.*

Indeed, it seemed obvious to most thoughtful observers by the end of the 1990s that writing was inevitably migrating to the screen.

I include myself in this list of, if I may be permitted the conceit, thoughtful observers. I wrote a guest column for a student newspaper in 1996 that echoed many of the observations above. I noted that the television series *Star Trek: The Next Generation* presented a compelling picture of the future of literacy and of books; compelling, if disheartening to bibliophiles like myself. On the *Enterprise*, there was a great deal of reading and writing—look at all the textual information stored on the ship's computer, accessible on those little handheld devices—but there were very few books. Captain Picard read books in his leisure time, but hardly anyone else on the *Enterprise* did. The books Picard did read seemed old, as if no one had published a book in centuries. Picard read books the way museum patrons observe paintings by Old Masters: cultured sophisticates acquire books, but these are relics, collector's items for eccentrics, not a vital part of the lives of the crew. So, I told the students, you will still be reading and writing in the future, just not with printed books. Like Birkerts, I was resigned to the inevitability. Clearly, in the 1990s the belief that books were an old, dying technology was suffuse throughout both scholarly and popular culture.

I am not convinced that we can continue to hold to this belief in the year 2003. Book sales continue to remain brisk, and e-books and other digital products have hardly made a dent in the book market. While many in the 1990s predicted the imminent arrival of the paperless office—the harbinger of the end of the book—researchers Abigail J. Sellen and Richard H.R. Harper document that the paperless office has yet to emerge; in fact, according to their research, offices are actually using more paper.[4] In the same way historians change their view of the past when confronted with new evidence or a compelling new interpretation, so futurists must be ready to change their view of the future. While the end of the book is certainly a plausible scenario of the future, this is far from the inevitability predicted in the 1990s. Indeed, rather than hastening the end of the book, computers and other new technologies may in fact be enhancing our ability to produce and distribute printed books, ensuring that books will continue to be a part of our future.

There are several driving forces that will determine the future of the book, including the availability of specific digital technologies, the preferences of consumers, and the economics of information. Of the three, I believe economics will be the main driving force that will determine the future of the book. Specifically, the future of the book will be determined according to which model of the economics of information that emerges. Either: (1) books will disappear as a viable technology because digital information becomes a commons, or (2) books will remain a vital information technology because the concept of intellectual property will remain in place.

WILL THERE BE BOOKS IN THE FUTURE? NO.

If we truly live in the late age of print, this will be because the production and distribution of written words will increasingly migrate into cyberspace. Instead of holding a physical object, the reader of a "book" would be looking at a screen. This was the assumption of many futurists in the 1990s, such as Bolter and Landow, that the screen would replace the page as a reader's main interface with written language. This screen need not be the computer monitor that currently sits on our desk; handheld "e-books" may well be that interface. These devises may soon have the capabilities of wireless technologies, meaning that a reader could download an entire text into the e-book as one might download a file into a stationary hard drive. A college student would need only have access to an e-book, and then have all their textbooks downloaded. An entire bookbag worth of coursebooks could be easily stored in one e-book device.

E-books and e-journals are already commonplace among scholars, and advanced versions of these may become the common method for accessing all written materials.[5] Today, most writers compose their written works in electronic form, like on the word processor I am using now. I can write a journal article as a Word document and attach it to an e-mail to the editor of a journal, without ever creating a paper version. The journal editors then work with this electronic document, editing it and formatting it. Only at the end of the process does the production staff of that journal convert the electronic document into a printed paper version that can then be bound between covers and shipped to libraries. I work for an online journal that is very much like a print journal—especially in its editorial functions—except that the final product of the production process remains in electronic form. Rather than printing off and binding a paper version, our editors simply upload the electronic article to the Web site, which can be accessed by any reader who wishes to view it (and has the requisite technology, of course, a non-trivial consideration). Readers of our journal pay nothing to read the articles, which we can afford to do because, unlike a print journal, our distribution costs are essentially zero.

Modern economic theory is based on the study of the scarcity and exclusivity of material goods. The assumption underlying economics is that goods are scarce precisely because they can be used up, or used by only one person at a time. If I buy an automobile, I am the only one who can use it; you and I (or thousands of other people) cannot use the product at the same time. Moreover, for an object like a lump of coal, once I use the product, it is used up. I cannot burn a lump of coal and then in turn hand it over to you to use.

Information, on the other hand, is non-rival and non-excludable. When economists say that information is non-rival, they mean that two or more people can use it at the same time and at the same cost.

When reading an online version of a written text, thousands of people can read the same article at the same time. The cost to reproduce this article for all those readers is next to nothing, as opposed to a print version of the article. By having access to this digital article, a reader does not have exclusive use of the article. Because it can be easily and cheaply reproduced, reading the article does not exclude another reader from reading the same article. Unlike a lump of coal, many readers can use the same digital article, without ever "using up" the information; unlike a physical object, information cannot be exhausted. When produced and distributed digitally, information can retain its non-rival, non-excludable form. Information is not a material object, and the explosion of the Web has demonstrated that information is simply evanescent bits of data that are not subject to the conventional laws of economics.[6]

Prior to the arrival of the printing press, medieval scholars treated ideas as if they were held in common by all. "The indifference of medieval scholars to the precise identity of the authors whose books they studied is undeniable," observed E.P. Goldschmidt. "The writers themselves, on the other hand, did not always trouble to 'quote' what they took from other books or to indicate where they took it from; they were diffident about signing [their own works] even when it was clearly their own in an unambiguous and unmistakable manner."[7] For medieval thinkers, ideas were more like a commons rather than a form of property. A commons, as defined by legal scholar Lawrence Lessig, is a resource held in common, held jointly and enjoyed by a number of people, free to anyone who wishes to use it. Commons are often non-rival and non-excludable. The invention of the book acted as a type of intellectual enclosure movement around the commons of ideas.

The Internet was originally designed as a commons, argues Lessig, and the ideas that flow across it should similarly be viewed as a commons, not as "intellectual property." That ideas could be a type of property struck Thomas Jefferson as odd:

> If nature had made any one thing less susceptible than all others of exclusive property, it is the action of the thinking power called an idea, which an individual may exclusively possess as long as he keeps it to himself; but the moment it is divulged, it forces itself into the possession of everyone, and the receiver cannot dispossess himself of it. Its peculiar character, too, is that no one possess the less, because every other possess the whole of it. He who receives an idea from me, receives instruction himself without lessening mine; as he who lites his taper at mine, receives light without darkening me. That ideas should be freely spread from one to another over the globe, for the moral and mutual instruction of man, and improvement of his condition, seems to have been peculiarly and benevolently designed by nature, when she

made them, like fire, expansible over all space, without lessening their density at any point, and like the air in which we breathe, move, and have our physical being, incapable of confinement, or exclusive appropriation. Inventions then cannot, in nature, be a subject of property.[8]

Jefferson could very well have been describing the contemporary debate over books, intellectual property and the digitalization of information. When one "divulges an idea," one is "publishing" that idea, keeping in mind that the root of the word "publish" is "to make public." An idea in my mind is private; once this idea leaves my mind, however, I have made it public. Indeed, prior to the printing press, to publish was to make public an idea, either by reading aloud or by distributing in written form. As Goldschmidt noted, medieval writers did not lay personal claim to ideas; they cared little for citation or personal recognition for their works, in contrast to the printed author. Ideas, Jefferson recognized, are non-excludable and non-rival; while he does not use these exact terms, Jefferson does note that ideas are like a candle's flame: lighting your candle with mine does not diminish the amount of my flame. In arguing that ideas should spread over the globe, for the edification of mankind, Jefferson sounds as if he is describing the flow of bits of information through cyberspace, spreading freely for the benefit of all.

It should come as no surprise that this long quote from Jefferson forms the basis of Lessig's thinking about the future of ideas in cyberspace. He agrees with the Founding Fathers that authors and other creators should have some control over their creations for some limited time, but this should not mean control over ideas in perpetuity. Lessig is concerned with the suffocating influence of large media "middlemen": corporations who have, in Lessig's estimation, misused the idea of copyright to maintain stultifying control over ideas. Lessig is especially concerned with the ideas flowing through cyberspace, that these should not be "enclosed" by copyright and the control of media giants. Shutting down Napster is but the tip of the iceberg: Media giants will make every effort to maintain control over film, music, written words, computer code and a whole host of ideas that could potentially flow through cyberspace. These corporations are acting contrary to the original spirit of the Internet, which was designed to act just as Jefferson might have described it: to allow for the free flow of ideas, open to anyone, under the control of no one.

For the cartoonist Scott McCloud, such a system of production and distribution can change the economics of comic books (and possibly all books), to the benefit of the authors and their readers. Not unlike Lessig, McCloud sees digital technology as a way for artists, writers and other creators of content to maintain greater control of their work, and to keep more of the proceeds of this work. The average price of a comic book is about three dollars. "In the print industry," observes McCloud, "each step in the process (publishing, printing, distribution, warehousing) takes its cut, until that three dollars turns to thirty cents in the creator's pocket."[9] The system of production and distribution enabled by networked computing, on the other hand, has the potential to keep more money—and creative control—in the hands of authors. McCloud favors a subscription-based system, where a creator makes his creation available on the Web for a nominal cost (since there are no middlemen to increase costs), all of which the author keeps. In such a system, the middlemen of the print industry are eliminated, along with any control over content they may exert. McCloud's vision is based on the assumption that readers will be willing to pay for content on the Web, which even McCloud understands has been far from successful. Few people today have been willing to pay for on-line content, largely because of the high transaction costs and the dubious security of "online cash" (encryption of which drives up the costs of the transaction). But McCloud is confident that this problem will eventually be solved.

If Lessig's vision of the future unfolds, intellectual property will disappear because the physical containers for that property—including printed books—will have disappeared. Digitalization makes written language cheaply and easily reproduced, distributed instantaneously, to be used simultaneously by all. If the printed book was the container for the concept of intellectual property, the elimination of that container would spell the end of intellectual property as we have known it since the 15th century.

WILL THERE BE BOOKS IN THE FUTURE? YES.

The historical significance of the printed book was that it turned written information into "intellectual property," a physical commodity that was both rivalrous and excludable. As literary theorists have long maintained, the printing press enabled the invention of the "author," the individual who claimed ownership of an idea. Jefferson was not entirely correct: Once ideas and information are made material, as in the form of a book, they are subject to the same laws of supply and demand that govern all other physical objects. A printed book, in other words, turns written information into a commodity. This is McCloud's contention: "Print industries" exist to control the production and distribution of physical objects and the information contained within them.

If books continue to exist in the future, this may well be because authors and other copyright holders will want to maintain their intellectual property. Books will survive because they are material, because they are tangible objects—not in spite of this fact, as technophiles often claim. This is not the same as the argument that says that books will survive because readers find them "easier to take to the beach or in the bathtub." Instead, my argument is that the economics of intellectual property will necessitate its survival in printed, bound, "old-fashioned" book form.

The computer may be more like the printing press than we ever imagined before. Think of what the printing press did: It transformed the production and distribution of written codices.[10] Compare a medieval manuscript to a printed book. There are clearly physical differences between the two objects, in terms of the layout of the pages, the materials used in each, the labor required to manufacture both, the economies of scale, and the audience (and market) for each product. But when all is said and done, the form and structure of the written codex had changed very little. Both manuscripts and printed books contained pages enclosed with a binding. Printed books were clearly not scrolls or lumps of clay; manuscripts and books shared many physical commonalties. Many of the changes from one form to another had to do with the economics of books, the system of production and distribution. It is possible that the computer will have a similar effect on the production and distribution of printed books. Books in the future may very well be different from the books we read now. But in form, they will seem very familiar to us.

Computers may alter the production and distribution of book-making, but have little effect on the physical appearance of books. Consider print-on-demand technology, for instance. With print-on-demand, the written text is stored electronically; when a customer wants a copy of the book, it can be printed and bound (one or a hundred) and then shipped. Shoppers may one day find book-making kiosks in bookstores; in the same way that today one can order a custom-made card from a Hallmark kiosk, a customer in the future could order a book from a menu of choices, wait 15 minutes or so while the device prints off and binds a copy, and walk out of the store with a new book. We might even envision a similar technology in the home; rather than ordering a book from Amazon and waiting for it to be shipped via UPS, one could simply produce the book at home. Such "just in time" production methods means that a publisher can match supply and demand for books with some precision. Rather than producing 10,000 copies of a book, and selling only 500, a publisher can print off only the number of books that satisfies demand. In addition to serving the needs of self-publishers, the company iUniverse also does contract work for other publishers. Say a university press wishes to begin a monograph series; iUniverse will print off one or one thousand copies of the book. In theory, a book would never go "out of print"; it would simply idle in electronic form until ready to be made material in book form. Rather than spreading the electronic bits freely across cyberspace, however, the publisher would parcel out the information only to those who wish to pay for its material form. But note: The finished product of this computerized process is a physical object in book form.

While a book in the future might look very similar to the books of today, the pages in that book might look very different. Xerox's

PARC research lab recently unveiled "smart paper" technology called Gyricon.[11] This is a thin, flexible rubbery sheet made up of millions of small balls, black on one side, white on the other. When charged, the balls that are rotated to the black side would make a mark on the remaining white background. Smart paper looks something like an LCD screen, only the surface is not rigid but flexible, not unlike a sheet of paper. Imagine hundreds of smart paper pages bound within a cover (the "spine" of the resulting book would hold the electronic components). A reader could download a text like an e-book, yet enjoy the feel of a traditional printed book. At the same time, a smart paper book would be capable of displaying the kinds of dynamic and animated visual data that we associate with a computer screen.[12] A smart paper book would be as different from a printed book as the first printed books were from medieval manuscripts. But in physical, tangible form, a smart paper book would seem very familiar to a reader of a print book.

Rather than being replaced by computer screens, books of the future might also mimic those screens (even without the smart paper). Literary theorist N. Katherine Hayles believes that books in the future will be as multimedia and hypertextual as computer screens are today. Future books, she speculates, might appear like "artist's books," currently a minor art form but one which provide a model for the future appearance of books. Artist's books are characterized by "the innovative use of cutouts, textures, colors, movable parts, and page order, to name only a few."[13] Artist's books are multimedia objects, like digital hypertexts, except that these books are material and tangible. Hayles's book, *Writing Machines*, is itself an example of the kind of book of the future she envisions. Each page features printed words of different size, shape and font, interspersed with cutouts of images and other decorative flourishes. Rather than simply placing quotation marks around quotes, Hayles will reproduce the text in question, the differing font and letter size indicative of the quotation. Her book, quite apart from the arguments she makes in writing, is itself a visual and tactile object (the texture of the cover is ribbed). A reader cannot help but to look at and feel the object in his hand. In the future, books and "text on the screen" may coexist, but those books will increasingly imitate the multimedia space of the screen. In this scenario, the "materiality"of the book will not disappear; quite the contrary, books will become "hypermaterial."

THE ECONOMICS OF INFORMATION

If books survive, it will be because of their materiality, not in spite of their materiality. As a physical object, a book is rivalrous and excludable, conditions necessary to maintain intellectual property rights. To paraphrase Sven Birkerts, the bound book is the ideal vehicle for authors and publishers to maintain their intellectual property rights. If books survive as a vital information technology, it will be because it is in the economic interests of authors and publishers to maintain books in tangible, physical form.

A major reason why books have not yet disappeared—and may never disappear—is that a new economics of information has yet to replace intellectual property. Judging by sales, subscription-based electronic books of the type advocated by McCloud have not been warmly received by readers. The reason may be that if (digital) information is non-rival, and if cyberspace is the ideal vehicle for freely distributing this non-rival information, then why would anyone pay for such information? If digital authors want to be paid for their work, they might have to do as television broadcasters have done and charge for advertising space embedded within their electronic pages, not an unrealistic possibility. Electronic books might begin to look like so many Web pages do today, covered with advertisements, with others popping up in new windows. Electronic authors could also resort to PBS-style fund raising, in the same way public broadcasters provide content for free, and ask only for viewers to pledge money. "Without excludability," observe the economists J. Bradford DeLong and A. Michael Froomkin, "the relationship between producer and consumer becomes much more akin to a gift-exchange relationship than a purchase-and-sale one."[14] If digital "books" are going to remain non-rival and non-excludable, what incentive will there be for consumers to pay for them?

On the supply side of the equation, we might also ask what will be the incentive for authors to produce? Lessig envisions an online world where creators—of software code, of music, of written information—create their content and distribute it for free, because that was the original intention of the Internet. Creators would find it very difficult to profit in such a system; in fact, it would seem that only those who were independently wealthy or who had some other source of income would be able to create content, since they could not rely on their creations as a source of income. That is, Lessig's model of the future of information assumes that creators would be like today's academics. Most academics write not to make money but to establish an academic reputation; a line on their curriculum vita is its own kind of currency, and is usually payment enough for much of the writing they do. Such a similar "academic" system preceded the emergence of the printed book; the invention of the book allowed authors to live off the proceeds of their work, freeing them from the patronage system that had funded writers before them.[15] In Lessig's digital future, writers would either need to be gentleman amateur writers, academics or would once again require a patron in order to freely distribute their ideas.

If producers and consumers cease to think of information as property, if ideas return to their medieval roots as a freely available commons, then books will not be needed, since only the evanescent bits of information will matter. In fact, books would hinder access to this commons. We really would be living in the late age of print. However, the uncertain economic questions that have arisen about digital information—who will pay? who will produce?—might never be properly answered, ensuring the continuity of our current system of intellectual property rights well into the future. Stated another way, technological change alone will not hasten the end of the book. Rather, economic factors—the behavior of the producers and consumers of information—will play a more important role. If information remains a form of intellectual property, then authors and publishers will continue to maintain control over this property via the best available technology: the printed book.

NOTES

1. Jay David Bolter, *Writing Space: The Computer, Hypertext and the History of Writing* (Hillsdale, NJ: Lawrence Erlbaum Associates, Publishers, 1991), xiii.
2. George Landow, *Hypertext: The Convergence of Contemporary Critical Theory and Technology* (Baltimore: Johns Hopkins University Press, 1992), 87.
3. Sven Birkerts, *The Gutenberg Elegies: The Fate of Reading in an Electronic Age* (Boston, London: Faber and Faber, 1994), 3,6.
4. See Abigail J. Sellen and Richard H.R. Harper, *The Myth of the Paperless Office* (Cambridge, MA: The MIT Press, 2002).
5. See for example, the American Historical Association/Columbia University Gutenberg e-project, www.gutenberg-e.org.
6. See the very useful edited collection by Brian Kahin and Hal R. Varian, *Internet Publishing and Beyond: The Economics of Digital Information and Intellectual Property* (Cambridge, MA: The MIT Press, 2000).
7. Cited in Marshall McLuhan, *The Gutenberg Galaxy: The Making of Typographic Man* (Toronto: University of Toronto Press, 1962), 131.
8. Quoted in Lawrence Lessig, *The Future of Ideas: The Fate of the Commons in a Connected World* (New York: Vintage Books, 2001), 94.
9. Scott McCloud, *Reinventing Comics: How Imagination and Technology are Revolutionizing an Art Form* (New York: HarperCollins/Perennial, 2001), 182.
10. For an excellent introduction to this history, see Lucien Febvre and Henri-Jean Martin, *The Coming of the Book: The Impact of Printing 1450-1800* (London: Verso, 1984).
11. Jennifer Sullivan, "The New Papyrus, from Xerox," Wired.com (www.wired.com/news/business/0,1367,16028,00.html).
12. This would be not unlike the book described in Neal Stephenson's science fiction novel *The Diamond Age* (New York: Bantam Books, 1995).

13. N. Katherine Hayles, *Writing Machines* (Cambridge, MA: The MIT Press, 2002), 20.

14. J. Bradford DeLong and A. Michael Froomkin, "Speculative Microeconomics for Tomorrow's Economy," in Brian Kahin and Hal R. Varian, *Internet Publishing and Beyond: The Economics of Digital Information and Intellectual Property* (Cambridge, MA: The MIT Press, 2000).

15. Landow, 175.

CHANGING METHODS IN FUTURES STUDIES

by

Richard A. Slaughter

This chapter looks at shifts that have occurred in underlying methodologies in futures studies (FS) over three decades. It suggests a progression from forecasting to scenarios to social construction and seeks to account for the rise of the latter. As is now well known, all fields have collective frameworks that provide practitioners with accounts of the important questions to be studied and the methods that are to be employed. FS is no different. Those who become futurists use the available methods of the time and work with them over extended periods.

In the 1970s forecasting was regarded as a "cutting edge" methodology. Since then, however, we have seen forecasting become commonplace and witnessed the rise of scenario building, or scenario planning, as it is sometimes called. It was widely popularized and has long passed into public awareness, albeit in highly simplified forms.

When done well, scenarios can illuminate aspects of possible futures and then tie these back to assumptions, ways of thinking, decisions, etc., in the here-and-now. Yet, over time, they have become less and less satisfactory, especially conceived as a core methodology. This chapter attempts to explain why. It then sketches in aspects of an emerging methodology that may help to revise our view of this maturing discipline within the wider 21st century context.

FORECASTING AS A NECESSARY CONTRADICTION

Before dealing with forecasting per se it is helpful to deal briefly with the underlying issue of prediction. There are basically two views about this in the field. One, held most strongly by Wendell Bell, is that all forward-looking enquiry involves prediction in some form. Bell writes of "presumptively true or false predictions" and "terminally true or false predictions." The former are made before the validity of the prediction can be demonstrated; the latter are decided later depending on whether or not the predicted event actually occurred. Bell also makes a strong case for the functionality of predictions per se. He shows very clearly how human decisions—and, indeed, social life in general—are necessarily grounded in different types of predictions.[1]

In Bell's view, futures enquiry under whatever banner—foresight, forecasting, projection, etc.—always contains this notion of prediction. A more widely shared view within FS is that while the small-scale predictions made by individuals and groups are certainly useful, the

---

Richard A. Slaughter *is Foundation Professor of the Foresight Institute at Swinburne University of Technology in Melbourne, Australia. He may be contacted at rslaughter@groupwise.swin.edu.au.*

utility of predictions declines when they are applied more broadly to the futures of social systems per se. In other words, there is a general preference among practitioners for restricting predictions to micro- and medium-scale contexts. The exception, perhaps, is when large-scale systems are well enough understood for their movements to be predictable. The Earth's rotation around the sun is good example. But large-scale social predictions are problematic because societies obviously do not operate like "celestial clockwork."

Successful predictions convey power, and Bell quite reasonably makes the point that there is a reciprocal relation between control and prediction. If you know an eclipse or a flood is coming you can make appropriate preparations. But any desire to "predict the future" on a broad scale appears to be in conflict with the essential "un-knowability" or "non-measurability" of many aspects of society and culture, as well as the view of people as agents and makers of history. While many small-scale predictions convey certainty and power in various degrees, ambitious large-scale prediction takes us beyond what is possible and desirable. If the future could be fully known in any hard or final sense, many believe that it would render human beings as passive observers. Moreover such full-scale "foreknowledge" is simply unavailable. But humans, being humans, shapers and now would-be masters of this small planet, have a built-in need and capacity to direct, control and construct. The globe-spanning infrastructure that surrounds us today is conclusive evidence of that. Hence, futures enquiry takes place between these two poles of what is knowable and what is unknowable about the future.

Within that broad domain are many interests, situations, that absolutely require some foreknowledge or, at the very least, strong assumptions about the future. If you want build a house that will withstand strong winds you need to make judgements about how to construct it and with what materials. Similarly, if you want to build a bridge, you must anticipate how it will be used and what stresses it will have to bear. As the 20th century infrastructure developed, however, such physical problems were well understood (in most cases) by the applied discipline of engineering. Forecasting itself became a generalized tool of such wide use in so many areas that it seemed to quit the futures domain for other contexts, especially finance and economics. What would be the level of demand for the bridge, airport or power station? What return on investment (ROI) could be anticipated? How good an investment was it likely to be? Such questions have become very familiar.

In short, forecasting flourished in the late 20th century because it attempted to come to grips with such questions and to provide investors, corporations, governments and others with tools for making decisions. Yet, from a futures point of view, forecasting ceased to be interesting. It did so for a number of reasons, including (a) it was perceived as a largely technical exercise; (b) it was coopted by the powerful; and (c) it failed to challenge the status quo. It did not become redundant—far from it. It remains in wide use—necessary use—in countless instrumental contexts. Rather, what has been lost, and probably lost forever, is the notion that forecasting can tell us much of value about how we should operate in the world and, more particularly, how we should solve some of the very serious problems facing humankind. Such questions are bound up with complex social and human issues, but forecasting fell silent when confronted with the human predicament.

SCENARIOS AND THE EXPLORATION OF DIVERGENCE

The term "scenario" arose in late 19th century Italy and was introduced to FS by Herman Kahn during the mid-20th century. The first formal scenarios at the Hudson Institute in the 1960s and 1970s drew on latent human capacities that had existed from the dawn of time that allowed people to consider, and respond to, the not-here and the not-yet. The context that concerned Kahn, however, was that of the Cold War and, in particular, the strike/counter-strike ideology of the time. His works *On Thermonuclear War* and *Thinking About the Unthinkable* elevated the use of scenarios in drama, gaming and military contexts way beyond their earlier uses.[2] It took a little longer for this methodology to be domesticated and integrated into strategic planning and organizational decision making. But, over a decade or two, that is what happened.

By the 1980s and 1990s a flourishing industry had developed around the commercial and government uses of scenarios. The point was, and remains, that a useful response to the irreducible uncertainties associated with forecasting was to shift the focus of anticipatory work to new ground. That is, to set aside hopes for accurate forecasts in favor of two other valuable gains: exploration of divergence and preparation for change.

This was a very successful move. It led to the widespread use of scenarios in many different contexts. Moreover, the tools involved were less demanding than the maths that supported rigorous forecasts. You no longer needed a doctorate to use the new methods. All you really needed was a small group of willing participants, a whiteboard and a felt-tip pen! The commonest methodological starting points for scenario building are (a) conceptual exploration and (b) simple group processes. Henceforth, anyone could become a scenario builder. Inadequately trained consultants spread out through the boardrooms of commerce, the convocations of government and even, in some cases, the ivory towers of academia. The future had arrived! Or, rather, scenario building had. Since the approach was readily understood and easily mastered it spread out and assumed prominence as the central "keystone" methodology of futures work.

This was, it must be said, a huge success. People were now no longer just "talking scenarios"; a lot of them were actually creating them. Even schoolchildren could get their heads around the technique and create simple scenarios on demand. In one sense, therefore, they represent what could be considered the most successful example of the diffusion of a futures methodology. After all, they have a number of very attractive features. These include:

- ease of use
- a participatory method
- direct relevance to specific situations, and
- intrinsic flexibility.

Moreover, at the upper end of the market, scenarios could bring a new sophistication to strategy and decision making. Yet underlying this success there are a number of weaknesses that make scenarios a less than satisfactory method. Three are particularly worth mentioning.

First, while there are certainly interpretive elements in all scenario building, the focus is mostly on the *external* tracking of possible events and situations. In other words, these "future worlds" tend to focus on aspects of the external world and to hide, or overlook, non-empirical factors (see below). Second, standard approaches to scenario building tend to accept current social reality as unproblematic, as just "being there." They lack an awareness of the way all societies are constructed. This means that scenarios are readily assimilated into existing social structures, with all their inequities and dysfunctions, without anyone being aware of the fact. Third, and possibly the most serious criticism, is that standard scenario building allows, encourages, individuals and organizations to explore future divergence in a kind of "free-floating" way that bears little or no relation either to the actual dynamics of the global system (however conceived) or to the broader frameworks of understanding that are available. In other words, the widespread practice of scenario building, scenario planning, fails to reflect the depth of insight and understanding of its most advanced practitioners.[3]

Another consequence is that the value of scenario building can be overstated. A case in point is the oft-discussed Mont Fleur scenarios constructed in South Africa. Among those who have written about them is Adam Kahane, who stated that:

> The Mont Fleur project contributed to the building of a common language for talking across groups about the opportunities and challenges facing the country. This shared understanding ... eventually helped lead to the unprecedented "miraculous" transition from minority to majority rule in 1994.[4]

Don Beck, co-founder of Spiral Dynamics, looked at the situation quite differently and reached different conclusions. From a "spiral" perspective, the participants in the process were operating out of what might be called "different worlds of reference." The failure to understand and deal with this "inner" dimension meant that, according to Beck, "the scenario process in South Africa (has) failed in that they did not prepare the society for what was going to happen." Crucially, he adds "my key point is (that) until scenarios deal with the realities of the interiors, along with an understanding of natural habitats, then they will be useless and even dangerous."[5]

Clearly when scenarios are carefully conceived and well grounded they can indeed be very useful. At their best they are very successful tools at the highest levels of strategy and decision making. Their inherent weaknesses, however, mean that they are less useful when these conditions are not met. They may become problematic when faced with the challenging problems of a world facing quite new demands and challenges.

EMERGENCE OF CRITICAL FUTURES STUDIES

Critical Futures Studies (CFS) emerged, in part, from a doctoral dissertation written during the period 1978-1982—in other words, during the time when forecasting was giving way to the rise of scenario building.[6] From this perspective, the limitations of mainstream futures work became clearer. Some specific guidelines emerged. For example:

- there was a need for greater depth of understanding generally
- the roles of language, power and social interests needed to be accounted for
- the differential up-take by different social groups and organizations needed attention
- prescriptions for action based on limited views should be questioned, and
- an openness to other traditions and "ways of knowing" should be encouraged.

Such concerns apply in a range of fields. Yet a little understood, developing discipline such as FS necessarily had to attend to questions dealing with issues of quality and professional standards. One area of enquiry involved probing the powerful (yet commonly obscured) connections between FS and education. Yet, at the time, the available materials, approaches, methods and guiding ideas were inadequate. Appeals to the presumed dangers of "future shock" were powerless to challenge, and reform, anything so set in place as education systems. Equally, work that merely addressed the surfaces of the taken-for-granted, everyday world could not deal with deeply-embedded cultural and human dilemmas. More powerful tools and deeper insights were clearly needed.[7]

Over time, Critical Futures Studies began to shed new light on old problems and open up new lines of enquiry. It became clear, for example, that behind the façade of everyday life were a host of structures, processes, factors, realities, in fact, that should not be overlooked. Indeed, to understand the present it was necessary to cover two very different sub-domains of futures work. One is the past, and the question is: how did we get here? Why do we live in this particular world (and not the countless others that were once possible)? The other is the "depth" that is inherent in what we mean by "the present." In other words, here were at least two routes to what may be called "the inner world." Furthermore, understanding this had major consequences. For example, in some respects the "inner" world could, in some ways, be said to precede and underpin the "outer" one! Or, to put it differently, personal, organizational and cultural worldviews, or "ways of knowing," give rise to the humanly constructed external world which, in turn, exists in a dynamic and ambiguous relationship with the world of nature. This is by no means the whole of what we call "social reality." It did, however, indicate a domain that had hitherto been widely overlooked in futures studies.

The key point is *that the world "out there" is framed, understood and conditioned through the world "in here."* It has been a significant step toward disciplinary maturity for increasing numbers of futures practitioners to have discovered this and to be applying it in many different ways. Futures writers, teachers, consultants and practitioners are becoming aware of the ways that language, culture, ideology, worldview and so on are universally involved in our work. It follows that there is no objective account of the world, no privileged heights of Olympian understanding to attain, no way to disentangle ourselves from processes of cultural framing and cultural production.

In this view, what is crucial is not so much the single-minded pursuit of "outer" concerns that are, in some senses, "downstream" from the hidden sources. A central issue could now be framed thus: How can we gain sufficient clarity about the construction of our inner worlds to be able to intervene in "the way things are" in a worldview, in deeply held values, in presuppositions and a variety of social interests? Overlooking this level of enquiry weakens the futures enterprise, undercutting its drive for wider social and professional legitimation. It makes the emergence of a dystopian "overshoot and collapse" world far more likely.[8] Equally, incorporating it provides FS with greater symbolic and practical power.

The central concerns of Critical Futures work differ from those of prediction, forecasting and scenario building. They focus most centrally on (but are by no means limited to) *the re-negotiation of meanings.* Futures work so understood is therefore largely symbolic. If we acknowledge that all accounts of society are partly symbolic this might seem an unexceptional comment. Except that hitherto the dominance of pragmatic and applied futures work means that the symbolic foundations have been widely overlooked. It follows that perhaps the best way to gain access to the field is through what Wendy Schultz termed "futures literacy." It may be true that there is no one "right way" to train futures practitioners and to carry out futures work. But it makes sense to regard futures literacy as coming *prior to* the tools and methodologies of the field. Without a thorough grounding in these areas of symbolic depth the practice of futures work risks becoming "thin" and unproductive—which, strangely enough, is exactly the fate of many scenarios. They skate easily enough around the surface but, on the whole, fail to deal in depth with issues of people, organizations, cultures in stress and transformation.

LAYERED FUTURES WORK

On the other hand, critical approaches shed light both on the way things are as well as on the way they could be. This is not a predictive interest. Rather, it's an emancipatory one, just as Habermas suggested some years ago. The latter is not centrally about control. It's about the rights, freedoms and capacities of self-constitution in social contexts. Much futures work around the world is focused on real-world issues and problems. It takes place in planning departments, environmental protection agencies, the boardrooms of numerous organizations and many other locations. It attempts to deal with everyday concerns in appropriate and sensible ways. The main difficulty is that, given the global predicament, work at this level is simply not able to shift perceptions, priorities and actions. There remains a need to go deeper.

For example, if we take a standard political or business view on the idea of "growth," we'll likely see it as a highly desirable norm. After all, growth leads to income, profits, the ability to pay salaries and invest in new activities. We may even think that growth will provide the resources to deal with social and environmental problems. In other words, our view of growth as a positive norm will lead us strongly toward some actions and, at the same time, put out of contention any need to re-think priorities or evaluate different strategies. We'll be "locked into" commonly shared ways of thinking and acting. But if, on the other hand, we were to look into the foundations of the Western industrial worldview, we might also discover that the kinds of growth processes that appear so "normal" in our context are historically highly abnormal. We might even look at how notions of limits were actually abandoned in the recent historical past. We might, in other words, begin to "problematize" growth, to see it freshly, to understand that, once we question taken-for-granted notions of growth, entirely new challenges and options arise.

Some interesting questions could then be posed. What might a "steady state" economy look like? What system imperatives might be employed? What transitional strategies could help a global trading and finance system adapt to the end of growth as a superordinate goal? What kind of world is implied by a system that cannot learn to rein in growth? What social, economic and political innovations would be needed to operate successfully in a no-growth world? Clearly depth understandings of this kind quickly take on practical relevance when they are taken seriously. Nor are they confined to any single domain. One of the distinguishing features of high quality futures work is that it routinely ignores borders and moves across many different domains.

It is partly for this reason that productive futures work cannot be an individualistic enterprise. Most practitioners necessarily draw on the work of hundreds, perhaps thousands, of other people, mainly through literature, but also through global networks of invaluable colleagues and friends. It is here that futures organizations such as the World Future Society (WFS) and the World Futures Studies Federation (WFSF) play a key role. It was at a conference organized by the latter that Sohail Inayatullah saw a presentation about these various "layers" of futures work. It was part of his genius to see that this approach could be rendered as a method. Thus was born one of the first methodological developments of the new "inner" perspective: Causal Layered Analysis (CLA).[9] Despite its somewhat forbidding name it employs a simple—but productive—workshop method that is already proving valuable in a wide range of circumstances.

SOCIAL CONSTRUCTION OF REALITY

The various threads and developments of various fields arise in different places, at different times, and now and then meet up later, yielding the possibility of a new synthesis, or a series of them. A source work on the *Social Construction of Reality* (SCR) was published by Berger and Luckmann in 1967.[10] It intersected with other streams of innovation in sociology (such as the sociology of knowledge and studies of science and society). But it was not until later that the centrality of SCR to advanced futures work became clear. Some aspects appeared in the initial formulations of CFS.[11] Another who saw the potential of this work was Kate Miller. Her 1994 paper in the *WFSF Bulletin* provided a succinct and readable summary of the role of SCR within an advanced futures discourse.[12]

One starting point is the term "social reality" itself. As Miller puts it: "What is regarded by the public as social reality is a construction to which each member contributes by selecting from available information to develop a picture of the world."[13] In their now-classic text on the subject, Berger and Luckmann consider some of the ways that societies are constituted by history, culture, institutions, roles, etc. For example, they suggest that "the relationship between knowledge and its social base is a dialectical one, that is, knowledge is a social product and knowledge is a factor in social change."[14]

They consider the role of reification—the view that what has been created by humans has some sort of independent reality. Further, they suggest that when this occurs there has been a loss of memory of human authorship. Thus power slips away, is seen as external. The question is whether humans can retain the awareness "that, however objectivated, the social world was made by men—and therefore can be re-made by them."[15]

Such statements clearly resonate with some of the underlying purposes of CFS. But the relationship is much more than a vague resonance. The language and concepts of the SCR discourse feed directly and explicitly into the problematic which is central to both domains. Consider the following:

> The legitimation of the institutional order is ... faced with the ongoing necessity of keeping chaos at bay. All social reality is precarious. All societies are constructions in the face of chaos. The constant possibility of anomic terror is actualized whenever the legitimations that obscure the precariousness are threatened or collapse.[16]

Here we can see one source of society's necessary resistance to change, its fearfulness of social innovation, its fury when confronted with certain symbolic challenges (such as "growth" or "progress"). It is exactly within this territory that CFS operates. It is the social heartland, vital to the functioning of society on a day-to-day basis, yet contested in its very essence. Thus the strategies of social defence are very powerful. Logically, then, this is where questions of power (especially definitional power, the power to include or exclude) are unavoidable. It is worth re-emphasizing here that we are not only thinking of instrumental power (the power to re-shape the world externally) but symbolic power (the power to define the foundations of the social order).

Berger and Luckmann describe various sorts of social legitimation as "machineries of universe-maintenance" and comment that "the success of particular conceptual machineries is related to the power possessed by those who operate them."[17] Here is the nub of the issue: To what extent does CFS itself constitute a self-consistent, liberating and constructively powerful symbolic universe of its own? Is it coherent enough, is it sufficiently widely established, is it capable of being fully legitimated by sufficient numbers of thinking people to fulfil its potential as an agent of social progress and renewal?

CONCLUSION

The significance of social construction within the CFS view is as follows: *It decisively moves debates about the currently threatened world and its many futures options away from the arena of externals to the processes of self-understanding, self-constitution and issues of power and meaning at these formative levels.* Perhaps the central claim of CFS is that it is here, in the symbolic foundations of the social order, that the wellsprings of the present lie, as well as the seeds of many possible alternative futures. If the latter is indeed the key guiding concept of futures work generally, then it is unlikely to be effectively put into practice without a steady shift into the areas outlined above and a much wider engagement on the part of futures workers.

This chapter has argued that three distinct methodologies have operated within FS over the past decades. Forecasting was an attempt to assert control and a measure of certainty over an unknown future. Scenarios are an attempt to explore diversity within the forward view. In a futures context the social construction of reality is an attempt to put into practice the deepest purposes of critical futures work in ways that consciously and deliberately lead toward more humanly viable futures than those currently in prospect. Obviously all these approaches co-exist as different ways of enabling the futures enterprise.[18] Each has something essential to offer as part of a broad transdisciplinary field that welcomes a range of tools, methods, approaches and ways of knowing.

NOTES

1. W. Bell, *The Foundations of Futures Studies*, Vol. 1 (New Jersey: Transaction Publishers, 1997), 97-107 and 227-35.
2. H. Kahn, *On Thermonuclear War*, 1960, and *Thinking About the Unthinkable*, 1962.
3. See J. Ogilvy, "Futures Studies and the Human Sciences: The Case for Normative Scenarios," ed. R. Slaughter, *New Thinking for a New Millennium* (London: Routledge, 1996), 26-83. Also H. Tibbs, "Global Scenarios for the Millennium," in R. Slaughter, *Gone Today, Here Tomorrow: Millennium Previews* (Sydney: Prospect, 2000), 333-341. For an outline of Wilber's meta-framework for considering these questions, see K. Wilber, *A Brief History of Everything* (Melbourne: Hill of Content, 1996).
4. A. Kahane, "Changing the Winds," ed. R. Slaughter, *Gone Today, Here Tomorrow: Millennium Previews*, op cit, 2000, 33-40.
5. D. Beck, personal communication to Alex Buick, March 2002.
6. R. Slaughter, *Critical Futures Studies and Curriculum Renewal*, PhD, University of Lancaster, 1982.
7. R. Slaughter, "An Outline of Critical Futures Studies," *Futures for the Third Millennium—Enabling the Forward View* (Sydney: Prospect, 1999).
8. D. Meadows (et al), *Limits to Growth* (New York: Universe Books, 1972). Also see A. Atkisson, *Believing Cassandra* (Melbourne: Scribe, 1999), 203-230.

9. S. Inayatullah, "Causal Layered Analysis. Poststructuralism as Method," *Futures*, Vol. 30, No. 8 (1998), 815-830.

10. P. Berger and T. Luckmann, *The Social Construction of Reality* (London: Penguin, 1966).

11. See R. Slaughter op cit 2000.

12. K. Miller, "Constructing Future Realities," *WFSF Bulletin* 69, 21, 1 (1994), 1-16.

13. Ibid p. 4.

14. Berger and Luckmann op cit 1966 p. 104.

15. Ibid p. 106.

16. Ibid p. 121.

17. Ibid p. 123-126.

18. W. Bell, personal communication, May 2002.

THE STRATEGIC CONTEXT OF EDUCATION IN AMERICA: 2000 TO 2020

by

David Pearce Snyder, Gregg Edwards, and Chris Folsom

INTRODUCTION

As is true for the leadership of any other business or profession, the superintendents, deans, principals, union officials, and board members who lead education should be familiar with the reliably-forecastable realities that will be prominent features of their institutions' future operating environment. In fact, the relevance of the future to education transcends its relevance to other enterprises, since education is *about* the future. The primary purpose of schooling is to prepare people—collectively and individually—to deal with the daily tasks and the longer-term imperatives and opportunities that they will encounter in their future lives. Thus, significant projected changes in education's future operating environment would require school leaders to plan not only for changes in how much education will be needed and how education will be delivered, but also for changes in the content of education itself.

Of course, the future seems much less certain now than it did two or three years ago, when everything was "coming up roses." The dot.com bust, terrorist attacks and massive corporate malfeasance have dispersed many of our casual assumptions about the future. Economic forecasts have become less confident and more ambiguous. While some experts have concluded that the high tech boom was a flash in the pan, others argue that a bigger boom is yet to come. All of this speculation is duly reported, analyzed, and debated in the media, and the resulting cacophony in the public policy arena is obscuring the reliably forecastable long-term realities that we can be reasonably certain will reshape daily life and work in America during the decade ahead. And, because addressing these realities will be instrumental to the success of education—and thus, the success of the nation—it is particularly important at this turbulent and uncertain moment for educators to reflect upon what we know about the long-term future.

THE RANDOM FUTURE—9/11 AND OTHER "WILD CARDS"

Suicidal skyjackings and anthrax in our mail have led some people to ask, "In a world where apparently *anything* can happen,

David Pearce Snyder *is principal partner of The Snyder Family Enterprise, Bethesda, Maryland. He may be contacted at snyderfam1@aol.com.* **Gregg Edwards** *is director of the Academy for Advanced Strategic Studies, Washington, D.C. He may be contacted at ge@aa-ss.org.* **Chris Folsom** *is research associate at The Snyder Family Enterprise, Bethesda, Maryland. He may be contacted at snyderfam1 @aol.com.*

can anything about the future be certain?" To this legitimate question, the futurist must concede that many of the "surface features" of the future—including dramatic events and dynamic personalities—occur randomly over time, and cannot be reliably forecast. Some of the more prominent random features of the future include political actions, stock market behavior, economic performance, scientific breakthroughs and the weather.

Weather and Politics

While great strides have been made in improving short-term weather forecasts and in predicting voter behavior, unexpected weather and election upsets still occur routinely. Forecasting either the long-term atmospheric or political climate remains problematic at best. Our inability to reliably forecast long-term climate change is the principal reason why we have been unable to reach a political consensus on global warming. The long-term non-predictability of politics means that educators should not casually assume that the nation's past commitment to publicly-funded education will continue unabated, or that political initiatives will not dramatically alter the economics, the markets, the missions, the organizational structure, the curriculum content and the technology of educational institutions over the next five to ten years. Politics will remain as unpredictable in the future as it has been in the past, perhaps even more so.

Markets and Marketplaces

Similarly, educators—and those who manage their pensions and endowments—should not base crucial long-range decisions on assumptions about the future performance of the stock market. As statisticians have repeatedly demonstrated, all stock markets are "random walks" whose behavior is not reliably forecastable from hour to hour, let alone from one year to the next. One-third of post-secondary trusts and endowments are invested in stocks, and among the larger private schools, the end of the ten-year bull market has reportedly reduced the value of those funds by hundreds of millions of dollars. And, since most institutions disperse roughly 5% of their endowments each year to underwrite student grants and subsidize campus operations, shrinking endowments are causing tuition increases, hiring freezes, cuts in student aid and project/program delays and cancellations (Zhao, 2002).

Not only can we *not* reliably forecast how soon our endowments will regain their lost value, we can only guess at when the US economy will emerge from the current economic slow-down. The Business Cycle Dating Committee of the National Bureau of Economic Research didn't decide until November 2001 that the United States had actually entered a recession eight months *earlier*, in March 2001. Of course, according to the classic definition, a "recession" involves at least two consecutive calendar quarters of shrinkage in the GDP. And, while the US economy *did* shrink by 0.2% in the third quarter of 2001, it actually grew at a 1.7% annual rate during the fourth quarter, the fastest rate in over a year. Although some economists believe that the economy will resume shrinking later in 2003, the Federal Reserve Chairman pronounced that the shortest recession in history is already over, and the Treasury Secretary, Paul O'Neill, concluded that there wasn't any recession at all!

In short, there is no reliable means by which we can forecast changes in the performance of the economy. Economists predicted *none* of the ten US recessions or three US "booms" since World War II. This means that economists can offer little insight into how soon public educators can expect robust local economies to increase the flow of tax revenues to public schools. They are even less able to inform judgments concerning how soon recent declines in alumni donations might be reversed, since such largess is linked to the performance of both the stock market and the economy. And, for students approaching graduation, economists can make no reliable assertions with respect to when the job market will pick up.

Accidental Discoveries and Unexpected Breakthroughs

One last random component of the future that holds particular relevance for higher education is the pace and direction of scientific progress. We have no reliable means of forecasting the timing of specific scientific breakthroughs. How soon will we have a cure for Alzheimer's? When will we achieve sustained fusion? Maybe next week; maybe next century! Even in carefully designed research projects, most breakthrough discoveries are unintentional. As the late Herb Simon observed, "If you look at the Nobel Laureates, in case after case after case, the critical event was a surprise." Kevin Dunbar, a researcher at McGill University's Cognitive Neuroscience Center, had investigators look over the shoulders of scientists at eight North American biological research labs for two years. He found that 50% to 60% of all experimental results did not support the hypothesis that went into the design of the experiment, and that 50% to 70% of scientists' conclusions arose from those unexpected results (Weiss, 1998).

In spite of the unpredictability of scientific research, the economic benefits of breakthrough discoveries are so enormous that America spends more than a quarter of a trillion dollars a year on R&D, including nearly $40 billion annually on basic scientific research, over half of which is conducted by colleges and universities. In 2000, the total research activities of US colleges and universities involved expenditures of $36 billion, roughly 15% of the total operating budgets for all four-year institutions nationwide. Post-secondary institutions themselves underwrite less than one-fourth of their research, receiving the bulk of their funding—$20 billion in 2000—

from federal agencies or state and local governments.

Research is integral to both the classical and modern definitions of higher education. In theory, faculty maintain currency and fluency in what they teach by spending time probing the frontiers of knowledge in their fields. In fact, Daniel Rock, at the Educational Testing Service, has found that a distinguishing characteristic of demonstrably superior post-secondary academic programs is "student involvement in faculty projects" and "extra lab time." And, since economic research has demonstrated that more than half of the historic growth in US per capita income is attributable to advances in technology (Cohen, Noll, 1994), it would seem reasonable to assume that the public sector will continue to underwrite the nation's investment in basic research. *But such an assumption would constitute a political forecast, and as such, must be regarded as risky.*

In the mid-1950s, federal expenditures represented two-thirds of the nation's total annual investment in R&D. After Sputnik (1958), business expenditures on R&D rose steadily, matching federal outlays by the mid-1970s and rising in tandem until 1990, when both government and industry were each investing about $65 billion p.a. on research. But since 1990, annual business investments in R&D have nearly tripled, to $180 billion, while the federal research budget has remained essentially unchanged, and has actually dropped 5% in constant dollar terms. Historically, war has always provoked an increase in R&D, and by January 2002, federal agencies had announced over $2 billion in new anti-terrorism research. Both the Department of Health and Human Services and the Pentagon have issued wide-ranging invitations for research proposals. And John Marburger, recently confirmed as President Bush's science advisor, reports receiving a "huge, spontaneous outpouring of concepts and ideas," ranging from new ways to protect buildings, power lines and reservoirs to advanced systems for detecting chemical weapons and other bio-terror agents, and for maintaining cyber-security (Hayden, 2002).

Unfortunately, owing to current fiscal constraints, any new anti-terror research is likely to be funded by resources diverted from other research. Meanwhile, in the fall of 2001, Congress passed the "Patriot Act," which restricts researchers' access to thirty-six potential bio-terror agents. Additional legislation now pending in Congress would prevent foreign nationals from working with dangerous microbes, would bar publication of genetic research data and even ban publication of all research on what makes specific microbes dangerous. Such impediments, plus other recent and proposed restrictions on federally-funded research regarding stem cells, cloning, etc., all threaten to drive much academically-centered research into the private sector. And there are some who believe that would be a good idea.

In 1996, the University of Rhode Island released a comprehensive study of their own income and outlays, which showed that it costs the University more to get grants and administer research projects than the grants actually pay, leading to a negative cash flow that is made up by the students in the form of tuition increases. Without the operating losses arising from the University of Rhode Island's tens of millions of dollars in yearly research grants, the study concluded, average tuition could have been cut by $1,900, from $4,400 to $2,500. The *Chicago Tribune* has also reported that the preliminary findings of an audit of finances at the University of Michigan "seemed to show that the tuition checks of its students help bail out research programs that run in the red." This followed a previous study of tuition inflation over the prior nine years that concluded that "the rise in student fees has not been matched by any commensurate rise in expenditures on instruction or on student service support activities" (Grossman, Leroux, 1996).

After a decade during which tuitions rose more than twice as fast as the Consumer Price Index, the continued underfunding of university research and the legitimate relationship of R&D to higher education are both likely to be politically and economically problematic issues for academia in the decade ahead.

THE KNOWABLE FUTURE—BENCHMARKS FOR STRATEGY

The futurist can afford to concede the unpredictability of the foregoing random phenomena—and many others—largely because history strongly suggests that such factors do not *alter* the long-term course of human progress. However, they can—and do—speed up or retard the existing long-term forces of change. The long-term forces for change—i.e., those that we can reliably forecast some useful distance into the future—include:

1. The size and make-up of the adult population

2. The composition of the economy and the job market

3. The characteristics and capabilities of mass-market technologies.

Together, these three sets of forecastable realities are the principal features of the "knowable future"; they constitute the reasonable certainties upon which sound strategies can be built.

The Demographic Context of Education—2000 to 2015

The basic function of education is human resource development, and we know a great deal about the future of human resources in America. To begin with, we can be reasonably certain that there are going to be a lot more Americans in the future; the Census Bureau expects the US population to double during the 21st century—from

282 million today to 571 million by 2100. In consonance with that growth, the Department of Education projects K-12 school enrollment will rise from a record 53 million today to 94 million by century's end. At the other end of the age distribution, the number of people over the age of 65—numbering 34 million today—is expected to reach 131 million by the end of the century, making them nearly one-quarter of all Americans. And, as the population grows older, it will also become much more diverse. By 2100, Euro-descended Americans are expected to make up just 40% of the total US population; Hispanics will constitute 33%, while African- and Asian-Americans will each account for 13% (El Nasser, 2002).

To be sure, 100-year population forecasts are subject to considerable potential variability, and must be regarded as *reasonable probabilities* rather than certainties. As such, they cannot, strictly speaking, be regarded as part of the "knowable" future. Such long-term projections are, however, entirely valid indicators of where the American national enterprise is headed, and their implications are awesome. Twice as many Americans will require twice as much infrastructure as today. Twice as much suburban sprawl! Twice as many teachers and classrooms! Fortunately, this huge future is far enough distant in time that it need not concern us for the moment. Even more fortunately, for the nearer term future—i.e., the next 15 years—demographers can provide all institutional leaders—including those in education—with reliable, detailed information about their changing human resource environment.

It is possible to make precise, consistently reliable forecasts of the size and makeup of the adult population for the next 15 years simply because all of the people who will become adults during the next 15 years have already been born. This means we know exactly what our labor force and our consumer markets will be like through 2015, by age, race and gender, etc. Figure 1 displays the changing age make-up of the US adult population from 1950 to 2015. At a glance, it is clear that, at least in one respect, American society is about to become fundamentally different from what it has been for the past 50 years.

The "roller coaster" changes in age distribution that have characterized American society over the past half century are the direct result of adaptive social behavior. During the austerity and uncertainty of the Great Depression and the Second World War—1930 to 1945—US birthrates temporarily dropped one-third below average long-term levels. This "Birth Dearth" was immediately followed by the more famous "Baby Boom"—1946 to 1964—as fertility rates returned to long-term norms once peace and prosperity had been restored. The rolling disparities in our population age mix arising from society's adaptive behavior has given the Baby Boomers unusual leverage in the consumer marketplace and in the voting booth.

In the 40 years since the Boomers entered the US adult population, they have represented 50% to 100% more people than any other age group in society. As a consequence, the Boomers have not only dominated our tastes in food, clothing, music and lifestyles, but their values were instrumental in forging the political consensus that gave us the watershed progressive legislation of the 1960s and 1970s: e.g., the Civil Rights Act, the Environmental and Consumer Protection Acts, the Occupational Safety and Health Act, and the Freedom of Information and Privacy Protection Acts. Hundreds of thousands of 16- to 24-year-old Boomers, mobilized in the streets and at the polls, were the surrogates of the national consensus that coerced America out of Vietnam.

FIGURE 1 - AGE COMPOSITION OF THE US ADULT POPULATION 1950-2015

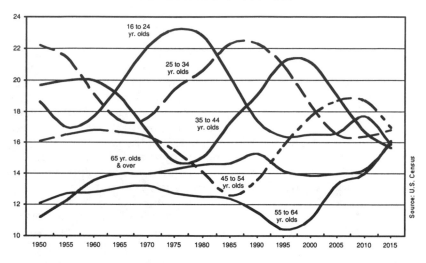

The creation of the US Department of Education (1979-81) was perhaps the last noteworthy political consequence of the Boomer consensus. Of course, since Baby Boomers remain the single largest age group of adult Americans, they may yet again mobilize in support of one or more issues to evoke a new national political consensus. (Political observers have long predicted that the Boomers will not take the institutional indignities of old age "lying down.") But by 2015, the Baby Boom's political leverage will have dramatically diminished, their huge numbers offset by their own maturing children and the rising tide of over-65-year-olds. By 2015, each of the six major age groups will constitute roughly one-sixth of all US adults: between 15.8% and 17% of the total.

Social demographers have suggested that, with each age cohort representing a roughly equivalent share of the US electorate, it will be more difficult to forge political consensus in the future than it has been in the past, especially with respect to the allocation of taxes and public funds. The producers of mass-market goods and services commonly expect that selling to a marketplace where there is no dominant, trend-setting age group will be much more challenging than marketing in the Baby Boom Era. And the labor-intensive components of our economy, including health care, the military and education, will find that, while the supply of entry-level workers—16 to 24-year-olds—will increase very slowly over the next 15 years, the numbers of employees of retirement age (55 to 64-year-olds)—will soar by more than 50%.

The Bureau of Labor Statistics (BLS) has projected that, between 1998 and 2008, 22.5% of all elementary school teachers (418,000), 30.5% of all secondary school teachers (378,000) and 15.0% of all college and university professors (195,000) will enter the 55- to 64-year-old age group, in which over 85% of all Americans retire. This will also be true for 178,000 education administrators, accounting for almost 40% of their ranks! Over the next 10 to 15 years, as the Boomers reach retirement age, every sector of the US economy expects to experience a similar exodus. The replacements for these retiring millions will be recruited largely from the Baby Boom Echo.

The Baby Boom Echo, which began in 1985, has already lasted longer than the original Boom (1946-1964), and has produced more babies (84 million vs. 78 million). What's more, the Echo Boom isn't over yet! Baby Boomer birthrates peaked in the early 1990s, and had begun falling when the renewed prosperity of the late 1990s inspired a second round of childbearing among younger Boomer households (35- to 44-year-olds). Currently, US birthrates are at a 30-year high, which accounts for today's burgeoning school enrollments.

During the next 10 years, however, as the Boomers pass out of their childbearing years, they will be supplanted by the offspring of the smaller "Baby Bust" cohort (born between 1965 and 1984), which will cause birthrates to moderate. Meanwhile, although the Echo Boom will produce substantially greater numbers of new Americans than did the original Boom, the US population has grown so much since the 1960s that the Echo Boom will cause only a modest, temporary increase in the 16- to-24-year-old share of our total population. (See Figure 1.) The original Baby Boom boosted US population by 44%; the Echo Boom is likely to add only 30% to the number of Americans.

The "good news" to be inferred from this reality is that we are *not* going to have to live through a repeat of the turbulent 1960s and 1970s, when nearly one-fourth of the adult population were immature idealists on testosterone. The bad news is that, unlike the 1960s and 1970s, when the Baby Boom made labor plentiful and cheap, the numbers of Echo Boomers will be insufficient to fill *both* the vacancies created by their parents' retirement *and* the new jobs that will be created by the growth of our economy. For education, training and library occupations, the BLS forecasts that, in addition to the nearly 1.76 million retiring personnel who will have to be replaced over the next 10 years, it will also be necessary to recruit another 1.57 million faculty and staff to fill the new positions created to meet the learning needs of our growing society and economy.

The demographic realities of the next decade and a half will confront education and other labor-intensive components of our economy—health care, construction, consumer services, the military, etc.—with serious, unignorable human resource supply problems.

The Economic Context of Education—2000 to 2010

The BLS forecasts the future size and make-up of the economy by assuming that each additional American will, on the average, consume the same amounts of private- and public-sector goods and services that the average citizen consumes today. This permits the Labor Department's statisticians to extrapolate the probable size and make-up of the US economy on the basis of the Census Bureau's highly reliable population forecasts. Over the past half-century, the BLS's moving 10-year forecasts of the composition of the US economy and job market have proven remarkably accurate.

Figure 2 shows the long-term evolution of the US workforce since 1860, projected through 2010. The coming decade will see the continued growth of Producer Services as the dominant employer in the US economy, with over 55% of all workers engaged in professional, managerial, technical, supervisory or other information-intensive work. The combined numbers of people directly involved in the physical production of food, material, infrastructure and manufactured goods dropped below 20% of the total US workforce for the first time ever during the 1990s, and will continue to decline. Meanwhile, consumer services today employ 25% of US workers for the first time in one hundred years, and their share of total employment is expected to grow.

Because the effective development and use of our human resources are intrinsic to the long-term success of the nation, the federal government publishes detailed, long-range projections of the supply of—and demand for—labor, to help employers, educators and individuals prepare for the future. Forecasts for the specific numbers of positions to be added to—or subtracted from—each type of job in America for the next 10 years are posted at the BLS Web site: www.bls.gov/home.htm. For those occupations that are projected to gain the largest numbers of new positions, the BLS also publishes the median US income for each such job and the typical educational requirements of the position.

Overall, the BLS forecasts that total employment in the United States will rise from 145.6 million in 2000 to 167.8 million in 2010. By comparison, the US workforce is projected to grow from 140.9 million in 2000 to 157.7 million by 2010. This means that the current 4.7 million shortfall of qualified recruits for advertised positions—including many jobs in education—will become a *10 million* worker shortage by 2010! While the labor force will only grow by 12% (16.8 million workers) during the current decade, the number of jobs is projected to grow 15.2% (22.2 million jobs). The BLS forecasts employment in education to rise by 19%, while employment in health care is expected to rise 25%, and by 26% among all other professional, managerial and technical fields. The existing shortage of workers is being met through a variety of expediencies, including overtime, part-time employment, increased workloads, reduced performance standards, and the use of unqualified personnel. But employment experts believe that a doubling of the current labor shortage will almost certainly provoke wage inflation and jeopardize our future economic growth (Francese, 2002).

FIGURE 2 - FOUR SECTORS OF THE US WORKFORCE
1860-2010

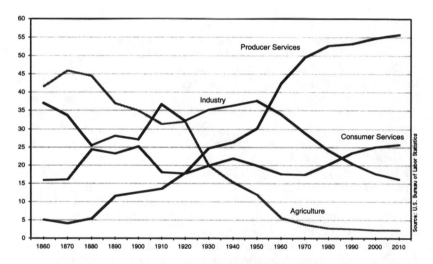

Certainly, a doubling of the current workforce shortfall will jeopardize the future of the current, labor-intensive US system of education. The US Department of Education (DOE) estimates that, as a result of existing shortages of qualified recruits, over one-fourth of recently-hired teachers do not fully meet state certification standards, and are teaching on temporary, provisional or "emergency" licenses. Nearly 28% of all US teachers, according to the DOE, have neither a college major nor minor in the subjects they teach (Perlstein, 1998). The National Commission on Teaching and America's Future reports that more than 12% of all newly-hired teachers—mostly transfers from other occupations—enter the classroom *without any teacher training at all* (Kantrowitz, Wingert, 2000). In many localities, student-teacher ratios substantially exceed national standards, and some large urban school districts began recruiting teachers from Europe, Africa, India and the Philippines. Higher education, meanwhile, has dealt with the instructor shortfall largely by hiring part-time instructors, who now make up over 40% of the faculty at all US post-secondary institutions (Marklein, 1999).

AN UNTENABLE FUTURE!

Together, the two most reliably forecastable realities of the next 10 years—the labor supply and the job market—confront American education with an untenable future. Just to maintain current levels of service, US educational institutions will collectively have to hire 3.4 million replacement and expansion personnel during the coming decade. This means that education will need to hire 20% of the 16.8 million young adults who will enter the labor pool during the next 10 years. BLS projects the supply of K-12 teachers will need to grow 16.6% during the current decade to meet replacement and growth demands, while the numbers of post-secondary faculty will have to increase 23.5%. But the American Association of Colleges of Teacher Education expects the supply of teachers in America to grow by only 3.6% between 1998 and 2004, and by just 1.2% from 2005 through the end of the decade (Kantrowitz, Wingert 2002).

Public sector agencies—including large school districts—have reported an up-turn in recruitment in recent months, fueled by people who say that the 9/11 terrorist attacks made them rethink life and decide to pursue more meaningful careers. Programs throughout the US that help career-changers become teachers have reported 200% to 400% increases in "expressions of interest" (Goodnough, 2002). However, while event-induced changes in marketplace behavior are a well-documented phenomenon, their effect is generally not long-lasting. The fact is that there will be insufficient human resources to meet the projected personnel requirements for our labor-intensive educational institutions. Even raising faculty salaries will not solve the problem, because there will be an absolute shortfall of warm bodies in the labor market to fully staff today's schools and colleges to meet the educational requirements of the coming decade.

Already understaffed, educators must continue to provide their essential services to a steadily growing number of students with the very real prospect of losing more staff to retirement each year than can be fully replaced through new recruits. What's more, the nation's K-12 faculty and administrators are about to be saddled with the unfunded testing provisions of the National Elementary and Secondary Education Act. The relative educational merits of the new national testing regimen aside, most of the substantial resources that will be needed to implement annual testing and meet new academic standards are likely to be diverted from school technology budgets. Ironically, technology offers the principal means by which the nation's schools can purposefully address the educational imperatives implicit in the demographic and economic realities of our knowable future.

The Technological Context of Education—1946 to 2020

New mass-market technology is the third major component of the reliably forecastable future, and during the next two decades, new technology will be the most dynamic and highly leveraged component of the institutional operating environment. From the late 1950s to the end of the 1970s, demographic factors—most notably, the "Baby Boom" and the subsequent "Baby Bust"—were the most powerful forces shaping long-term growth and change in America. Throughout the 1980s to the mid-1990s, economic initiatives—including supply-side tax policies, marketplace deregulation, privatization and free trade, etc.—were the principal forces underlying long-term growth and change. But, in the mid-1990s, new technology became the most potent force for growth and change in America, and is likely to remain so for at least the next two decades. What's more, it is now clear that information technology (IT), in particular, will offer educators the means by which to fulfill all of their basic functions in spite of the challenges posed by our impending demographic and economic circumstances.

Readers will be more than justified in responding skeptically to our assertion of an impending technology-driven transformation of education—or any other institution. It has, after all, been over 56 years since the first computer was switched on, yet our offices are still not paperless and our commerce is still not cashless. And most of us have lived through more failed info-system projects than successful ones. But economic historians tell us that new technologies don't become reliable, affordable and truly productive until they have "matured" for a half-century or so (David, 1990). And in fact, in the mid-1990s, as the computer reached its 50th "birthday," US annual productivity improvement rates doubled, and have remained at that higher rate since, after having stagnated for 20 years. In 1987, the Nobel Laureate economist Robert Solow famously observed, "We can see computers everywhere in today's economy, except in the productivity statistics." But, by March 2000, Prof. Solow reported that "We can now see computers in the productivity statistics" (Uchitelle, 2000).

More importantly, over the past five to 10 years, we have begun to understand exactly how successful early-adopters have employed IT to become substantially more productive than their competitors. A 1995 joint survey by the Harvard and Wharton business schools with the Ernst & Young Center for Business and Innovation reviewed the results of over one hundred studies of business practices and found that, "Economic benefits to companies were greatest when they successfully integrated innovations in management and technology with appropriate employee training and 'empowerment' programs" (Investment, 1995). A similar 2001 survey by the Organization for Economic Cooperation and Development (OECD) concluded that, "Organizational change, understood as the implementation of new work practices such as teamwork, flatter management structures and job rotation, tends to be associated with higher productivity growth. Interestingly, productivity gains of firms that combine new technology with organizational change are considerable, whereas there does not appear to be much economic benefit from implementing new technology alone" (Taylor, 2001).

Based on a five-year study of data gathered from 1,167 large companies in 41 industries, Erik Brynjolfsson (MIT) and Shinkyu Yang (NYU) have found considerable evidence to demonstrate that the direct costs and benefits of computers represent no more than the fractional tip of a "much larger iceberg of complementary organizational, process and strategic changes" (Brynjolfsson, Yang, 2001). Brynjolfsson estimates that, in order to actually reduce labor requirements and increase total factor productivity, for every dollar spent on IT hardware, roughly $10 must be spent on additional investments in employee training, business process re-engineering, systems administration and other producer services (Varian, 2001). (These findings all correspond to co-author Snyder's own experience with IT projects over the past thirty years, including five years as Chief of Information Systems at the US Internal Revenue Service from 1971 to 1975.) While rigorous comparable data are not available regarding total IT-related expenditures in education, a variety of surveys suggest that public K-12 schools typically spend less than $1.00 on training and system change for every dollar they invest on hardware and software (Macavinta, 1997).

NEW SOCIAL TECHNOLOGY

Adding computers to a traditional, authoritarian, hierarchical, compartmentalized bureaucracy is about as productive as adding spark plugs to a steam engine! To fully realize the productive potential of a new physical technology, it is necessary to redesign our existing "social technologies"—i.e., our institutions; either that, or invent entirely new ones. While *physical technologies* are the products of how we organize and apply our physical materials and resources, *social technologies* are the products of how we organize and apply our human, financial, and information resources. Social technologies chiefly take the form of institutions. Insurance, libraries, taxation, hospitals, labor unions, "neighborhood watches," environmental regulations and marriage, etc., are all typical social technologies. In education, books, blackboards and computers are familiar physical technologies, while classroom-based instruction and achievement tests are characteristic social technologies.

Western civilization developed the authoritarian, hierarchical, vertically integrated bureaucracy as an effective social technology for maximizing the productive yield from a succession of new physical technologies: steam power, electric motors and internal combustion engines. In the industrial era, to assure the continuous timely flow of the multiple materials and components required for the mass production of sophisticated goods, manufacturers sought to be *internally self-sufficient*. Henry Ford not only made his own tires, he grew his own rubber. The *Saturday Evening Post* made its own paper. In keeping with this "vertical integration" paradigm, most companies in the 20th century kept their own books, hired and paid their own employees, and owned and operated their own plants and equipment.

While the business press reports the steady spread of purposefully applied IT in a growing number of trades and industries, no single, compelling archetype of postindustrial social technology has emerged yet to complement IT's diverse productivity-enhancing potentialities, and to replace the hierarchical industrial bureaucracy. However, throughout the mature industrial economies today, large, vertically-integrated corporations are disaggregating themselves, disassembling themselves by contracting out big pieces of their operations to other firms. In the industrial era, outsourcing was characteristically employed as a cost-cutting expediency; but in the information-intensive economy, outsourcing has become a strategic necessity.

Outsourcing Information Overload

As IT has made the diverse details of each component of modern enterprise increasingly measurable and linkable to other components of an organization's operations and its environment, the context of every decision has become more complex, more problematic, and much more difficult to optimize. *More* data has made decision makers *less* certain. By the late 1980s, "information overload" began to be a serious problem for a growing number of firms, starting in the electronics and automotive industries (Flaig, 1992). Corporate efforts to improve organizational capacity to deal with modern complexity—including "knowledge management"—have largely proven costly failures. As a consequence, an increasingly common corporate strategy for dealing with information overload has become simply to outsource it.

Instead of self-sufficiency, the essence of enterprise in the information economy will be *collaboration*. By contracting out in-house functions at which they are not particularly adept to outside specialists who are, businesses are able to attain much higher growth rates and profit margins merely by leveraging their non-core expenditures through better-performing partners. Outsourcing non-core competencies also permits firms to devote more of their resources and management attention to those in-house activities whose superior performance gives the organization its competitive marketplace advantage: the activities at which the organization is most competent.

Obviously, the kinds of collegial collaboration between buyer and seller that will be required among the participants in such distributed enterprises are unlikely to arise out of traditional, arms-length, minimum spec/lowest bid procurement contracts. Successful partnerships are negotiated, not dictated. The Nobel Prizes for Economics in both 1996 (Montague, 1996) and 2001 (Hilsenrath, 2001) were awarded for work demonstrating that *symmetrically-informed* marketplace transactions are more productive for the transactors and the economy as a whole than are transactions in which either the buyer or the seller is incompletely informed regarding essential details of the exchange. Clearly, procurement practices will have to be dramatically changed to assure symmetrically-informed contractual relationships become the norm in the distributed enterprises of the information economy.

From Vertical Integration to Virtual Integration

In successful distributed enterprises, the diverse outputs of multiple suppliers are orchestrated—largely via the Internet—into harmonious streams of finished goods and/or services. In the process, "vertically-integrated" industrial era enterprises are transforming themselves into "virtually-integrated" information era enterprises. The working dynamics of these new social technologies are detailed by the authors of two current books: Donald Tapscott in *Digital Capital* and Grady Means and David Schneider in *Meta-Capitalism*. These and other writers argue that productive and profitable businesses today have abandoned self-sufficiency to better compete in the emerging marketplace, where large enterprises will no longer be monolithic corporate entities, but will be embodied in networks of suppliers, service providers, practitioners, producers and customers. These extra-preneurial networks—called "business webs" by Tapscott, and "value-adding communities" by Means and Schneider—are emerging prototypes of *the new social technology that will supplant industrial bureaucracy*.

Grady Means simply asserts, "In the New Economy, the network will be the business!" (Walker, 2000). The evangelists of corporate unbundling are equally certain that this new institutional paradigm applies just as well to public enterprise as it does to private. And, while outsourcing by public institutions is a politically and legally contentious subject, Means is particularly enthusiastic with respect to the performance-enhancing potential of unbundling public agencies. What's more, in 2001, Mr. Means, a senior partner at Pricewater-houseCoopers, took charge of PwC's government consulting services in Washington, DC, where the current administration strongly supports outsourcing—i.e., privatizing—public sector operations in general, *and privatizing public education in particular*. While future political developments cannot be reliably forecast, strong political propensities generally presage future political actions.

Of course, schools at all levels of education have been outsourcing their non-instructional functions for decades—e.g., food services, transportation, security, etc.—as well as some special education. And post-secondary schools commonly engage in a wide range of inter-institutional collaborations, ranging from shared facilities to joint degree programs. But recent disaggregation in the private sector has been much more fundamental. At Volkswagen's new Brazilian assembly plant, 80% of the workforce are employees of Maxion, Cummins, Rockwell, etc.—subcontractors whose suspensions, engines and brakes are going into vehicles that Volkswagen designs and markets. IBM, in an even more radical departure from tradition, began to outsource the assembly of its PCs to its *retail dealers* in 1997! Because most PCs sold in the United States today are equipped and configured to meet each individual buyer's specific requirements, IBM found it was more cost-effective to order the PC components from its suppliers to be shipped directly to its dealers for final assembly, rather than attempting to mass produce custom-tailored machines on their factory assembly lines. The dealer assembly strategy proved so successful for IBM that every major US PC brand except Dell now offers dealer-customized machines.

The VW and IBM examples reflect an emerging pattern in the general restructuring of American enterprise: *the separation of producer services from actual production*. Increasingly, major brand-holders are electing to retain research and development, design and engineering, process management, contracting and marketing as their core competitive competencies, while outsourcing the actual production of their product or service to others. In many service sector markets, the split between producer services and production is reflected by the growth of franchising, in which individual owners operate local outlets of nationally-branded services that are designed, developed and marketed by the corporate brand owner (e.g., Starbucks, Mailboxes, Kinkos, McDonald's, etc.). In many respects, charter schools, home-schooling and some distant learning arrangements reflect an institutional reconfiguration of K-12 education similar to the franchising movement: Individual teachers or independent schools undertake to teach curriculum content and meet achievement standards set by the "branding" institution; i.e., the state or local school system.

Outsourcing Schools

Some proponents of charter schools are working toward a future when all public schools will be outsourced. In their vision for the future of education, the civil authorities will stipulate a core curriculum and physical operating standards, provide capitation-based funding, and test to certify student achievement, while a mixture of contractors—public and private, national chains and local institutions—will actually operate the individual schools. Whether or not such a future is in store for US public education depends upon the unpredictable dynamics of politics. But our understanding of where value is added in manufacturing versus where value is added in education suggests that the restructuring that is working for mass-produced goods and services may not be appropriate for America's public schools.

In the late 1980s, James Quinn and his colleagues at the Tuck School of Business at Dartmouth College published their findings that between 75% and 85% of the value added by the average US manufacturer is attributable to *producer services*: e.g., research and development, product design, quality control, logistics, recruitment, training, marketing and management policies and practices, etc. "The price that a manufactured product can command in the marketplace reflects the product's content of materials and labor *much less* than it reflects the quality, characteristics and availability of the product," all of which are determined by producer services, or management (Quinn et al., 1987). Management's contribution to successful perfor-mance in manufacturing is so highly leveraged that outsourcing the actual assembly of a product involves a relatively modest risk of unacceptable outcomes.

By comparison, findings published by the Educational Testing Service (ETS) in 2000, correlating student performance with three measurements of teacher performance, showed that *the largest effects upon student achievement are associated with the specific classroom practices used by individual teachers*. On average, superior teachers add 70% of a grade level to their students' math test scores, and 40% of a grade level in science tests! The same report found that the second biggest impacts on student achievement were associated with professional teacher development activities that support specific classroom practices. (These net differences remained *after* taking socio-economic factors into account, using data from the year 2000 National Assessment of Educational Progress in eighth grade math and science.) ("Classroom," 2000). Neither IBM nor VW would have outsourced the assembly of their branded products if that much variability in their final products' quality were in the hands of their rank-and-file employees.

The performance of the individual classroom teacher is so substantial a determiner of student achievement in K-12 schools that the proponents of charter schools are entirely justified in their belief that any school anywhere, given adequate resources, sound manage-ment and qualified teachers, should be able to deliver satisfactory levels of student achievement. But the ETS research found a correlation between superior student achievement and *specific classroom practices*, such as "hands-on learning activities" and "an emphasis on higher-order thinking skills." Published accounts of charter schools offer little evidence that such schools typically promote proven best classroom practice (Symonds et al., 2000). There is also little evidence to suggest that outsourced schools have produced improved student achievement (Ascher et al., 1996). To the contrary, after reviewing the 1999-2000 achievement test scores from 376 charter schools in 10 states, the Brown Center for Education Policy at the Brookings Institution concluded that charter school students were anywhere from one-half to one full year behind their public school peers (Toppo, 2002).

Old Schools for the New Century?

While a few US charter schools offer wonderfully innovative curriculum and instructional methods, the great majority are largely indistinguishable in their day-to-day functioning—and classroom content—from the mainstream public schools they are supplanting. The singular common distinction of charter schools is their relative freedom from central office micro-management and, in some cases, union rules. Indeed, it is clear from the educational press that significant numbers of teachers, administrators, parents and members of the general public today believe that, if traditional classroom-based schools could somehow be freed from the pernicious influences of heavy-handed bureaucracy, teachers unions and partisan politics, the same classroom-based schools that we invented to deliver public education at the end of the 19th century would be perfectly satisfactory social technologies for delivering public education in the 21st century.

Techno-economic historians (David, 1990) and contemporary productivity analysts (Johnson, 2002) agree that substantial improvements in economic performance largely arise from the creation of new social technologies that make the fullest use of the productivity-enhancing features of new physical technologies. There is every reason to believe that education, like the other major institutional components of our national enterprise, will ultimately transform itself—or be transformed—in order to fully exploit the instructional potency of our maturing information technologies. Even if some combination of circumstances—or stakeholders—temporarily forestalls the redefinition and redesign of schooling, the combined workforce/workload/workplace realities of the next 10 to 15 years will coerce productivity-enhancing innovations out of America's labor-intensive educational institutions. However, the outsourcing strategy that is working for the mass production of durable goods and franchised consumer services does not appear to be particularly promising for education, at least so long as outsourced education retains the form of our primary industrial-era educational social technology: classroom-based instruction.

The persistent reliance of formal education upon verbal classroom instruction is noteworthy for two reasons:

1. There are, in fact, other proven effective ways to teach/learn, including peer instruction, contextual learning (apprentice-internship), correspondence courses, team learning, games and simulations, etc.

2. Large numbers of students—up to perhaps 70%—are predominantly visual or tactile-kinesthetic learners who do not acquire knowledge effectively in the passive auditory mode of learning that is characteristic of most classroom instruction (Chion-Kenney, 1992). The disconnect between differing instructional and learning styles can be absolute. Researchers at the University of Utah Hospital have used non-invasive magneto-encephalography scans to measure the electromagnetic waves around students' heads as they learn new subject matter. When students who learn visually—as determined beforehand by diagnostic tests—are given visual instruction, the encephalogram reflects high levels of brain activity. When the same students were given solely verbal/auditory instruction, the brain scan was flat (Vuko, 1999).

While most pedagogical research does not produce such startling clinical evidence of a link between teaching techniques and learning styles, over the past 20 years a growing body of literature from studies of human development and brain functioning has given us ample reason to believe that, by establishing only classroom-based, lecture mode teaching systems, industrial era educators seriously disadvantaged millions of people who do not learn effectively in a passive auditory mode. They also ignored both Socrates and Aristotle, who pointedly observed 2,500 years ago that different people learn in different ways. Unfortunately, although the concept of multiple learning styles is now widely acknowledged among educators, and even though there are a variety of effective and accepted non-lecture instructional methods, the adoption rates for these alternative learning processes, while increasing recently, remains quite low.

Outsourcing Classes

One class of alternative learning arrangements with a long history of proven success cannot be easily accommodated within the confines of classroom-based education: contextual learning, including intern and apprenticeship programs, community service learning and cooperative education. While such "experiential" learning is commonly associated with career preparation—e.g., doctors, plumbers, diamond cutters, etc.—the US Department of Defense (DoD) has been using "functional context education" since the 1950s to teach general literacy and math skills to recruits through practical, job-related assignments. A 1987 Ford Foundation study of this program found that individuals experiencing contextualized education had consistently higher test scores and overall improved achievement than individuals completing traditional classroom education. "[Contextual learning] was judged to be more effective than traditional teaching for all levels of aptitude, and unusually effective for lower-aptitude individuals" (Sticht, 1987, cited in Parnell, 2001).

With 1.5 million uniformed personnel in hundreds of locations around the world, the US Defense Department is uniquely able to provide contextual learning assignments for thousands of their own entry-level recruits. But, with 200,000 new enlistees every year, even the DoD can't find enough in-house slots for all those individuals requiring reading and math improvement. Thus, the Army must continue to put recruits through traditional classroom instruction to impart skills which most of them failed to learn in a classroom setting in the first place. Among educational institutions, research universities are able to offer in-house practicum for their technical students, but for most post-secondary institutions, and for all middle and high schools, contextual learning generally requires the involvement of organizations *outside* of the educational institution itself. *Schools must outsource contextual learning!*

The current "disassembly" of America's large, vertically-integrated corporate bureaucracies is being driven by the rationale of "retaining what we do well and outsourcing what we're not particularly good at." If confronted with this choice, the leadership of most educational institutions would presumably elect to retain classroom instruction as one of their core competencies—something that most educators feel they do well. Contextual learning, on the other hand, is something that traditional educational institutions cannot, by and large, provide in-house. In order to afford its students access to the proven benefits of internships, community service projects, cooperative learning, etc., educational institutions will have to enter into ongoing collaborative relationships with private and public sector employers and with community organizations to design and conduct real-world experiential learning processes that will synergize with classroom curriculum.

The demographic realities of the coming decade will provide employers a growing incentive to collaborate with schools in a variety of ways, since the increasing shortage of qualified workers is expected to make all competent labor more valuable—and more costly. This will be an even more pressing reality in Europe and Japan, where the labor force will age even more rapidly than in the US, and where the labor force will grow much more slowly. In an analysis of data from the 1997 National Employer Survey, the Institute for Research on Higher Education at the University of Pennsylvania found that employers who maintain long-term school-to-work initiatives—e.g., mentoring, internships, joint curriculum development, etc.—have a 25% turnover rate among their 18- to 25-year-old employees, while the turnover rate for 18- to 25-year-olds was 50% at firms which did not collaborate with their local high schools (Bronner, 1998). On the face of it, this would appear to be an opportune moment for educators and employers to explore how they might collaborate more purposefully to improve both the productivity of American education and the achievement of its students, while significantly evolving the social technology we call "school" through greater integration of education with employment.

[Authors' Note: A companion piece to this paper, assessing the educational implications of the next three to five years' innovations in mass-market information technology, appears in *On the Horizon*, Vol. 11, No. 2, Spring 2003.]

REFERENCES

"Academic Research and Development: Financial and Personnel Resources, Support for Graduate Education, and Outputs," *Science and Engineering Indicators—2002*, National Science Foundation, 2002, 6-2-15.

Ascher, Carol, Norm Fruchter, and Robert Berne. "Hard Lessons: Public Schools and Privatization," *A Twentieth Century Fund Report*, 1996, 1-2.

Bronner, Ethan. "Benefits of School Business Alliances," *The New York Times*, July 8, 1998.

Brynjolfsson, Erik, and Shinkyu Yang. "Intangible Assets and Growth Accounting: Evidence from Computer Investments," working draft research report from MIT Center for eBusiness (ebusiness.mit.edu/erik), May 17, 2001, 2.

Chion-Kenney, Linda. "The Ways We Learn," *The Washington Post*, April 6, 1992, B5.

"Classroom Techniques Make the Difference," *USA Today*, October 17, 2000, 6D.

Cohen, Linda R., and Roger G. Noll. "Privatizing Public Research," *Scientific American*, September 1994, 73.

David, Paul A. "Computer and Dynamo: The Modern Productivity Paradox in a Not-Too-Distant Mirror," The Center for Economic Policy Research, Stanford University, Stanford, California, 1989, 29-32.

El Nasser, Haya. "Census Predicts Ethnic Face of the Nation in 100 Years," *USA Today*, January 13, 2000, A-3.

"Employment Projections 2000 to 2010," *Occupational Statistics and Employment Projections*, US Bureau of Labor Statistics, December 2001, Tables 1-3.

Flaig, L. Scott. "The 'Virtual Enterprise': Your New Model for Success," *Electronic Business*, March 20, 1992, 153-154.

Francese, Peter. "The American Work Force," *American Demo-

graphics, February 2002, 40-41.

Goodnough, Abby. "More Applicants Answer the Call of Teaching Jobs," *The New York Times*, February 11, 2002, A-1.

Grossman, Ron, and Charles Leroux. "Research Grants Actually Add to Tuition Costs," *The Chicago Tribune*, January 28, 1996, 1-19.

Hayden, Thomas. "Science of Safety," *U.S. News & World Report*, December 31, 2001, 60.

Hilsenrath, Jon E. "Three Americans Win Nobel for Economics," *The Wall Street Journal*, October 12, 2001, 1.

"Investment in Employees Profitable, Researchers Find," *The Register Guard*, Eugene, Oregon, June 6, 1995, B5.

Johnson, Bradford C. "Retail: The Wal-Mart Effect," *The McKinsey Quarterly* (www.mckinseyquarterly.com/home), McKinsey Global Institute, 2002.

Kantrowitz, Barbara, and Pat Wingert. "Teachers Wanted," *Newsweek*, October 2, 2000, 37-39.

Macavinta, Courtney. "Study Tracks School Tech Use," *CNET News.com* (news.cnet.com), November 12, 1997, 1.

Marklein, Mary Beth. "Study Urges Colleges to Boost Standing of Part-Time Faculty," *USA Today*, January 14, 1999, 10-D.

Montague, Bill. "Winners Link Info, Economy," *USA Today*, October 9, 1996, 2B.

Perlstein, Linda. "Schools Cautioned on Hasty Hiring," *The Washington Post*, September 16, 1998, A-12.

Parnell, Dale. *Contextual Teaching Works!* CCI Publishing, Waco, Texas, 2001, 51-76.

Quinn, James Brian, Jordon J. Baruch, and Penny Cushman Paquette. "Technology in Services," *Scientific American*, December 1987, 56.

"Resident Population Projections by Sex and Age," *Statistical Abstract of the United States*, US Census Bureau, 2002, Table 14.

"School Enrollment: 1965 to 2009," *Digest of Education Statistics*, US National Center for Education Statistics, 2002, Table 239.

Symonds, William C. "For Profit Schools," *Business Week*, February 7, 2000, 64-76.

Sticht, Thomas, William Armstrong, Daniel Hickey, and John Caylor. *Cast-off Youth: Policy and Training Methods from the Military Experience* (New York: Praeger Publishers, 1987), 98.

Taylor, Robert. "Bridging the Digital Divide," *Financial Times*, February 23, 2001.

Toppo, Greg. "Study: Charter School Students Score Lower," *The Washington Post*, September 3, 2002, A-7.

Uchitelle, Louis. "Productivity Finally Shows the Impact of Computers," *The New York Times*, March 12, 2000.

Varian, Hal R. "New Economy," *The New York Times*, September 10, 2001.

Vuko, Evelyn Porreca. "Right-Brain, Left-Brain Learning Dance," *The Washington Post*, March 22, 1999, C4.

Walker, Leslie. "The Bigger Boom to Come," *The Washington Post*, July 13, 2000, E1.

Waters, Richard. "Delays in High-Speed Broadband May Cost U.S. Economy $500 Billion," *Financial Times*, July 16, 2001.

Weiss, Rick. "In Recognizing Surprise, Researchers Go From A to B to Discovery," *The Washington Post*, January 26, 1998, A-3.

Zhao, Yilu. "As Endowments Slip at Colleges, Big Tuition Increases Fill the Void," *The New York Times*, February 22, 2002, A-1.

THE QUESTION OF CORPORATE INTEGRITY

IS CORPORATE INTEGRITY POSSIBLE?

by

Marvin T. Brown

From the time we drink our coffee or tea in the morning to when we slip into our bed at night, we live in a world dominated by corporate prices, products, and practices. Some worry that corporations have taken over. As David Korten suggested not so long ago, corporations now rule the world.[1] The September 11 attack on the World Trade Center questioned this assumption. Since then the world seems quite unruly. The attack also raised other questions, including the question of corporate legitimacy. How can we justify their current practices? This paper addresses the question of corporate legitimacy by exploring a smaller question of whether corporate integrity is possible. If corporate integrity is impossible, then we should work at dismantling them; if corporate integrity is possible, then we will know what we should expect from them.

Where we look for corporate integrity, of course, will depend on our notions of corporations and of integrity. Corporations can be defined in different ways, but perhaps the best definition for our purpose of evaluating their integrity is to see corporations as human systems designed for some purpose. Systems are sets of interactive parts that constitute a whole. Some human systems, such as individual persons, are both biological and linguistic systems. Corporations, of course, are not biological. They are, however, constituted by language, or we could say, by ongoing communication patterns. These patterns include both verbal and nonverbal communications. The verbal communication includes mission and policy statements, as well as daily conversations. The nonverbal includes work design, daily schedules, and practical skills. If we look at corporations as ongoing communications, then corporate integrity will depend on the character of these communications.

What communications we should consider and what standards we use to measure integrity depends on how we define integrity. Now if integrity only means "walking the talk," then any organization that achieved consistency in message and action would have integrity. But do we really want to attribute integrity to every group that believes in what it does? What about terrorists or the Klan? They may well act consistently, but do you want to say they have integrity? I think not, because integrity signifies a positive value. Saying that an organization has integrity is a way of praising it, which means that its actions or policies are connected with some goal that is perceived as a good. People may certainly disagree about what is good, but I do not think we can expel it from the meaning of integrity. As we shall see, it actually plays a key role in determining the integrity of corporations.

Marvin T. Brown *is with the Saybrook Graduate School and Research Center, San Francisco, California. He may be contacted at mbrown@workingethics.com.*

So, does consistency *plus* goodness constitute a sufficient definition of corporate integrity? Not completely, because we need to know what should be consistent with what. To be consistent is not the same as to be honest or to tell the truth, although integrity may well entail such behaviors. The consistency that belongs to integrity refers to the relational quality among all the parts of some whole. Integrity means to integrate, "to make whole."[2] So, capturing the full meaning of corporate integrity requires that we know the relevant parts that constitute corporations as well as the part that corporations should play in the larger wholes to which they belong.

See the connection between human systems and integrity? They both see organizations in terms of parts-whole relationships. Describing a corporation as a system, however, does not address the question of what these various part-whole relationships *should be*. The question of integrity does. Still, system thinking invites us to see corporations in their context—in the larger whole to which they belong.

To engage my business ethics students in thinking about the context of corporations, I ask them to imagine starting a business on the moon, and then to list what they would need. They usually list items like a business plan, money, products, markets, and consumers. All are important items for running a business. They have trouble thinking of much else. After a while, someone will mention oxygen or water, and then all the environmental and infrastructural aspects of the business context come to mind. Sometimes, but not always, a student will refer to the need for a government and law enforcement. Only rarely will a student mention the need for a moral community, where people trust one another, keep their promises, and work to continually create and re-create a meaningful life. And yet, all these contextual elements are necessary for successful business practices.

For corporate integrity to exist, corporations must have the capacity to become aware of this multi-layered context and to bring that awareness into their decision-making processes. How could that happen? If we look at corporations as constituted by verbal and nonverbal ongoing communication, as was suggested earlier, then it can happen through the creation of appropriate communication patterns. To more fully understand this possibility we need to see communication from a contextual perspective.

A CONTEXTUAL VIEW OF COMMUNICATION

Viewing communication from a contextual perspective reveals it as something in which we live rather than only as something we use. The drawing illustrates the differences between this contextual model and what can be called the "post office" model of communication.[3]

In the post-office model, one isolated individual has an idea in his head, puts it in some form, and then sends it to another. The other receives the "message," decodes it, and sends back a response.

It is like sending and receiving mail. Communication is a process of "getting one's views across," or "exchanging ideas." In the contextual model of communication, on the other hand, individuals participate *in* communication, and the context is seen as an integral part of the communicative process.[4] The space between persons, which seems like an empty space in the post-office model, becomes laden with meaning in the contextual model. Speakers and listeners are seen as continually relying on, as well as continually maintaining and changing, their context.

FIGURE 1 - MODELS OF COMMUNICATION

Post-Office Model   Contextual Model

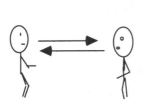

A good example of participating in a communicative context is our participation *in* the English language. As those who have learned a second language know, a particular language is somehow "there," and one learns the language by participating in it. A clear sign of linguistic competence in a second language, in fact, is the ability to think "in" that language.

So to work in a corporation involves participation in its on-going communications. By paying attention to these communications, it is possible to assess and to improve a corporation's integrity. Corporate integrity will depend on how conversations are designed and redesigned, what is talked about within these designs, and how these conversations fit with other conversations in the larger society. The designing of conversations depends largely on a corporation's culture and its assumptions about interpersonal relationships at work. What is talked about revolves around plans to achieve corporate goals. The larger conversations in which corporate conversations must participate include conversations about civic responsibility and the natural environment. This gives us five different dimensions of corporate communication we need to consider, or, in other words, five dimensions of conversational integrity.

FIVE DIMENSIONS OF CONVERSATIONAL INTEGRITY

Just as the appropriate relationships between parts and whole differ in each of these five dimensions, so does the meaning of integrity. The remainder of the paper makes a case for the following connections between each dimension of conversation and integrity. At the cultural dimension, integrity requires openness to differences and disagreements. At the interpersonal dimension, integrity requires relationships of mutual recognition. At the organizational dimension, integrity requires that organizations have some intrinsic pur-pose—they must be up to some good. At the civic dimension, integrity requires that corporations cooperate with cities in achieving the city's mission. And finally, in terms of the natural environment, integrity requires that corporations find their appropriate part in the ongoing conversations about natural prosperity.

FIGURE 2 - FIVE DIMENSIONS OF CONVERSATIONAL INTEGRITY

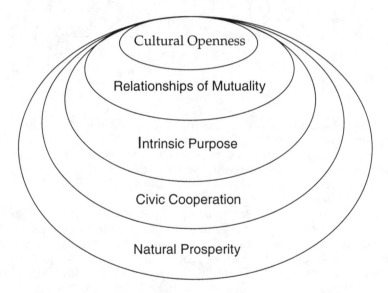

Although all five dimensions belong to conversational integrity, there exists an order among them. Given our pluralistic society, openness to others is a first requirement for conversational integrity. This creates the possibility for relationships of mutuality, which allow for conversations about an organization's purpose, its civic cooperation, and its role in the development of natural prosperity.

Cultural Integrity as Openness

A culture can be seen as providing a coherent worldview. Its stories and rituals maintain and communicate a set of basic assumptions about how things work. Any particular culture is holistic or complete, and yet because we live in a pluralistic society, the larger whole includes more than one culture. People bring different worldviews into the same workplace, and different types of workplaces interact with each other. Encountering differences and disagreements occurs regularly in most work settings today. To acknowledge the complete wholeness in which one lives would require that these differences and disagreements be recognized. The challenge of integrity at this cultural dimension is to determine how to deal with differences and disagreements.

W. Barnett Pearce has developed a typology of four different communicative cultures that gives us a vocabulary to think about cultural differences.[5] His four cultural types are monocultural, ethnocentric, modernistic, and cosmopolitan. Each one's strategy for maintaining coherence has a corresponding response to disagreement. In monocultures, coherence is maintained by tradition. Disagreement is seen as not knowing how things should be done or a lack of common sense. In ethnocentric cultures, which emphasize an "us—them" mentality, disagreement causes defensiveness and aggression. In modernistic cultures, where a thin coherence is maintained by a belief that new is better, disagreement tends to be discounted as resistance to change. In cosmopolitan culture, which is more of an ideal possibility than an everyday reality, coherence is maintained by communicative disciplines such as dialogue. Dialogue can turn disagreement into a resource for mutual learning.

If you look at Table 1, you can probably remember experiences of all four cultural types. Our pluralistic society contains all of them. In many corporations, people bring to work one or another of these responses to disagreement, and the work culture itself may rely more on one communicative type than another. Sometimes the patterns can be quite stubborn. Still, our definition of integrity as wholeness challenges us to design communicative patterns that appreciate differences and disagreements. This comes closest to the cosmopolitan communicative pattern and its emphasis on dialogue. The possibilities for dialogue, however, depend not only on an openness to learning from others, but also on relationships of mutual recognition, the second dimension of conversational integrity.

Interpersonal Integrity as Mutual Recognition

Say you are sitting in a car waiting for someone. Across the street you watch a man and woman encounter each other, exchange packages, and walk away. What is happening here? It depends on how you interpret the relationship between the woman and the man. Are they siblings, drug dealers, co-workers, or all three? You do not know, but that will probably not stop you from imagining some type of encounter. We are like that. We give meanings to events, and the meaning we give (and get) largely depends on the mental models or images we have of interpersonal relationships.

TABLE 1 - COMMUNICATIVE CULTURES

	Coherence	Response to Disagreement
Monoculture	Tradition and Common Sense	Lack of Common Sense
Ethnocentric	"Us vs. Them"	Defensive or Aggressive
Modernistic	Belief in the New	Discounts
Cosmopolitan	Dialogical Conversations	Resource for Mutual Learning

For an interpersonal relationship to have integrity, the meaning it is given—our image of the relationship—must correspond to the desires of persons in the relationship to be recognized as significant parts (partners) of the relationship. (Integrity is all about parts and wholes.) Furthermore, since we all live in multiple relationships, our desire for recognition in any one context, such as the workplace, will be informed by our relational identity in other contexts, such as the family or civic realm. To see what this means for interpersonal relationships at work, we will need to explore different relational images and then see which ones exclude or include family and civic identities. This will allow us to describe the type of relational image that will promote mutual recognition.

Images of Work Relationships. When we turn to images of relationships at work, we find a range of relational images that include master/servant relationships, exchange or market relationships, team relationships, and more recently what could be called entrepreneurial relationships. To understand the differences among these four relational images, we can examine the impact of each one on a standard performance review between a supervisor and her subordinate.

The oldest relational image at work still operative today is the master/servant image. Embedded in the common law tradition and tort law in the United States, this master/servant image provides the institutional background for such laws as "employment at will"—the privilege of employers to terminate employees without due process.[6] A performance review with this image in the background would probably take on a pattern of the supervisor assuming control of the conversation, and the subordinate listening and figuring out how to meet the expectations of her "boss." This pattern may seem familiar, since the master/servant image continues to shape many work conversations.

A second image of work relationships is the image of market relations. Employers and employees see themselves as making exchanges—wages for labor. If this were the image behind the performance review, both parties would be engaged in bargaining for the sake of a best deal possible. This relational image tends to turn people into commodities that can be traded, but it also acknowledges the importance of fair dealing.

A third relational image is that of team members. The team image gives us access to rich resources for learning, for engaging in dialogue, and for discovering new strategies of cooperation. Through the active participation of persons, as Peter Senge has suggested, the organization itself can become a learning organization, or we could also say, a learning community.[7] Performance reviews that share this image would encourage the supervisor and subordinate to work together to develop mutual expectations for future performance. They would also explore how they could improve their interactions for the sake of team performance.

A final relational image is the entrepreneurial, although the emphasis on relationships here is quite weak. It is more an image of instant relationships that individuals learn to use as they move from job to job when corporations merge, downsize, or fold. With the failure of the "new economy" and the "dot-com" world, this entrepreneurial image of relationships has lost some of its luster. Still, one can imagine that performance reviews using this image would be seen as ways of networking and improving one's possibility for either promotions or résumé enhancement.

When we review these different relational images, is one more appropriate than the others? If we remain within the world of work, we cannot say. The world of work, however, is not an independent universe. It belongs to a larger context, which consists of a variety of human relationships, including family and civic relationships. So, we need to reflect on our family and civic relationships before we can select the type of work relationship that corresponds with our desire for recognition.

Images of Family Relationships. In the family sphere, two basic images of relationships are those of nurturing and protecting. Some would say that the nurturing image stresses the feminine side of the family and the protecting image the masculine.[8] In any case, the family provides the context for creating what John Bowlby calls "a secure base," which is constituted by safe and secure relationships with others.[9] Not every family provides this, of course, but at least the family image represents a relational "home" in which all members belong. Although the workplace is not a substitute for the family, I think this image of belonging informs the desire for recognition. People are not like replaceable machines; they are members of human communities.

Images of Civic Relationships. What kind of relational image comes to mind when we think of civic relationship? Benjamin Barber has recommended an image of participation in public conversations, which seems to fit with our contextual perspective.[10] Public conversations recognize each citizen's right to have a say in the development of policies that promote the common good. Citizens influence others not because of their position or wealth, but because of the persuasiveness of their ideas. The image of civic relationship imagines mutual recognition of each person's right to participate in the process of governing. Even though the workplace is not governed through democratic elections, workers do not shed their identity as citizens when they go to work. Relationships between management and workers are relationships between citizens. Given this image of civic participation, plus the family image of belonging, we can now return to select the appropriate images of work relationships.

Appropriate Images of Work Relationships. Before we select the appropriate images of relationships at work, it may be helpful to recount how we got to this point. We started by listing four current relational images that we can find behind current interpersonal relationships in the workplace. We then pointed out that the appropriate work image would include an awareness of family and civic relational life, because these relations provide the context for work relationships. When we looked at family and civic images of relationships, we extracted the relational images of belonging and participation. So now we can use these two relational images to select the appropriate images of relationships at work.

So, to complete our analysis, we can say that the family and civic relational images would reject the master/servant image and the entrepreneurial image. The first violates the civic image of equal participation and the second violates the image of belonging. So we are left with the team and exchange images, which we could bring together as an integrated image of work relationships. This image would then be connected with the family and civic images to give us a more complete image that would match the desire for mutual recognition.

Returning to the example of the performance review, we can see how this composite image of work relationship would inform the meeting. Both supervisor and subordinate would see each other as belonging to the same organization, participating in a common endeavor as a team, based on fair exchanges, with the rights of citizens. With this type of shared relational image, each party should be able to engage in a relationship of mutual recognition.

FIGURE 3 - AN INCLUSIVE IMAGE OF WORK RELATIONSHIPS

Just as we learned from the first dimension of conversational integrity that integrity requires inclusion rather than exclusion, we can now add that the second dimension requires the inclusion of others through the development of relationships of mutual recognition. How the mutual recognition manifests itself will differ in different conversations. We now turn to one type of conversation: conversations about how to achieve an organization's purpose.

ORGANIZATIONAL INTEGRITY AS INTRINSIC PURPOSE

An organization's purpose gives direction and justification for the ongoing conversations that constitute its existence. For conversations about an organization's strategies and policies to have integrity, the organization's purpose itself must have some intrinsic value. Only a good purpose will allow us to know if an organization's actions have integrity.

The notion of purpose requires some clarification. There is a difference between the purpose of agents and the purpose of things or non-agents. For agents, purpose functions as a guide for making decisions. For non-agents, such as affirmative action programs, purpose functions as a guide for design. Both persons and organizations are agents—they use purpose to guide their decisions. The foundation of their purpose, however, is different. A person's purpose arises from desires, intentions, motives, and hopes. An organization's purpose is derived from its function in society. Organizations are designed to fulfill certain functions, and as *human* organizations they are designed to decide how to function. Their purpose, in fact, operates just like the purpose of personal agents—it guides their decision-making. The following graph outlines the basic distinctions:

FIGURE 4 - MULTIPLE MEANINGS OF PURPOSE

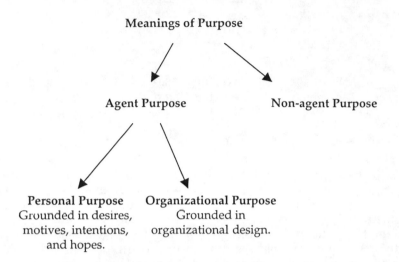

In terms of corporate integrity, not just any organizational purpose will do. Integrity must be reserved for actions that aim for some good. The idea that a corporation must be *for* something *good* may cause some confusion. Are not corporations "for-profit" organizations? We do call them that, but achieving profitability does not ensure integrity. Profit can come from cheating as well as helping. Making a profit certainly has value, but it doe not tell us anything about corporate integrity. So why do we call corporations "for-profits"?

The term "for" has two different meanings. "For" can refer to purpose, as in "He trained for the ministry." In this sense, purpose refers to something a person was aiming at. The term "for" can also refer to desire or intention: "He was eager for fame and fortune." This is the meaning of "for profit." It refers to intentions, not purposes.[11] So when we call a corporation "for-profit" we are referring to the intention of the founder or investor, not to the organization itself. To use the term precisely, we would say that some people start businesses with the intention of profit (some founders may have other motives), but the purpose of the business itself, in distinction to that of the founder, depends on what the business is designed to do—its function.

So, if we look at a corporation at the organizational level, and not at the individual person, then we see that "for-profits" and non-profits are very similar. They are both designed to perform some good function in society. In terms of integrity, whether a hospital is a non-profit or a for-profit, for example, does not make much difference. In either case, its integrity will be determined by whether its actions and policies promote its social function of providing excellent health care.

A corporation's purpose should be determined not only by the "good" product or service it brings on the market, but also by how this product or service fits with the social and environmental context in which it exists. This brings us to the fourth dimension of conversational integrity.

SOCIAL INTEGRITY AS CIVIC COOPERATION

Although corporations can only exist in compatible social and natural environments, this has not always been fully acknowledged. Still, since corporations exist *in* these contexts, their integrity depends on how they relate to them. Remember when we examined interpersonal integrity, we developed three sets of relationships—family, civic and work—and then explored how they overlap in the corporate environment? Some would see these three relational types as references to different social sectors, such as the family, economic, civic. Many would add to this triad another sector: the state or government. In such schemes, corporations usually are relegated to the economic sphere, and therefore their integrity would depend on how they function in this sphere.

Instead of this notion of sectors or spheres separated from each other, a contextual approach examines how each realm or sector provides the context for the others. This view would situate the economic sector inside of the civic, since civic institutions and laws provide the necessary conditions for economic activity. To determine what integrity looks like from this perspective, we will need to explore two different relationships: the relationship between corporations and civil society and the relationship between corporations and city governments.

Corporations and Civil Society. Although people disagree about who belongs to civil society, they tend to agree about its character. The following definition by Robert Post and Nancy Rosenblum seems to reflect this agreement:

> Civil society is a zone of freedom for individuals to associate with others and for groups to shape their norms, articulate their purposes, and determine for themselves the internal structure of group authority and identity.[12]

Given this definition of civil society, it would seem that corporations belong there along with nonprofits and non-government agencies (NGOs). All these organizations are protected by the rule of law and guided by such social institutions as property rights and the value of a good reputation. These different types of organizations do have different coordinating principles, or at least give different weight to different principles of coordination. To see how this works, we can use the three coordination strategies developed by Kenneth Boulding: threat, exchange, and integration.[13]

FIGURE 5 - COORDINATION STRATEGIES

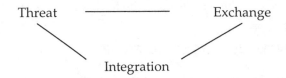

If one were to think in terms of different social sectors, each coordinating strategy could be located in a particular type of organization. The strategy of threat would belong to government agencies since they enforce the laws. Exchange would belong to corporations operating in the market. Non-profits and citizen actions groups would then be left with the integration strategy. Instead of locating the three strategies in different organizations, however, a contextual approach would locate organizational life in the context of the three coordinating strategies.

From a contextual perspective, government agencies may give more weight to the strategy of threat, but also have exchange and integration structures, and the same with corporations and citizen action groups. This means that the integrative context or civil society would be the context for all three types of organizations. This opens the possibility for the development of what Severyn Bruyn calls a civil economy with civil markets. By civil markets, he means a market "based on certain principles of justice and rules of fair competition."[14] Corporations can join in the promotion of this civility by including discussions on justice and fairness in their conversations. In doing so, they will have expanded their communication patterns to include rather than exclude the social context in which they live.

Corporations and City Governments. The relationship with city governments is somewhat more complicated because cities, like corporations, are agents. City governments make collective decisions that are guided by the city's mission. In United States, in the early 20th century, cities were granted the right to "home rule" by the states. This gave them the right to self-governance. How should businesses conduct themselves when in a city's "home"?

The notion of integrity here invites us to explore the relationship between a corporation's purpose and a city's mission. Which one should provide the context for the other? I would argue that when corporations contradict the city's mission they compromise their integrity, because they subvert the achievement of the "whole" that the city's mission symbolizes and "in" which the corporation exists. So, the guideline for corporate conversations here would be to adhere to an obligation not to impede and sometimes to promote the city's mission. Both cities and corporations, of course, must have missions that fit with the natural environment that provides their habitat. This brings us to the fifth dimension of corporate integrity.

ENVIRONMENTAL INTEGRITY AS NATURAL PROSPERITY

Both cities and corporations exist *in* the biosphere: a biosphere that has come under increasing stress. If current trends continue, future generations will not have the resources to enjoy the prosperity that many of us take for granted. Even today, millions suffer from environmental destruction. Since this is the ultimate "whole" in which corporations exist, they must find their appropriate place as a part of this whole if they are to exhibit integrity.

In his book, *From Heresy to Dogma*, Andrew Hoffman argues that the 40 years between 1960 and 1990 witnessed a substantial change in corporate conversations about the environment.[15] As the title of his book indicates, he believes that the topic of the natural environment has moved from being an irritation to businesses to becoming a strategic part of their planning. He offers an example of this chance by examining how people have changed their perceptions of smokestacks:

In the 1950s, prior to the advent of institutionalized environmental norms, it [the smokestack] was viewed favorably, representing jobs, economic progress, and industrial strength. But in the industrial environmentalism period of the 1960s it came to symbolize something less desirable, an ugly and smelly nuisance. In the regulatory environmentalism of the 1970s, it represented the need for government controls. In the social responsibility period of the 1980s it became the source of toxic pollution, hazardous to the health of the community. And finally, in the strategic environmentalism of the 1990s, it has come to symbolize wasted resources.[16]

These changes had a parallel change in corporate involvement in environmental issues, from trying to avoid them to including them as an important element in their strategic management.[17] This change appears to have two meanings. On the one hand, corporations can take on environmental concerns. On the other hand, there is the risk that they will take them over. In other words, instead of participating in conversations where they are one agent among others, they will create their own conversation excluding others. Such a shift would compromise their integrity because even though they belong to the natural environment, they do not possess it.

Current conversations about the natural environment, in which corporations need to find their appropriate place, can be seen as an intertwining of three different conversations that have quite different origins and visions: the United Nations' conversations on sustainability, the Bretton Woods organizations' conversations about global finance and world trade, and conversations about the dynamics and design of nature.

Conversations on Sustainability. The United Nations' first conference on sustainability in 1970 at Stockholm encountered what was to become a key theme for the rest of the 20th century; balancing the need for decreasing environmental damage with the need for economic development. Progress has been made. At the Rio conference in 1992, over 150 nations signed agreements to decrease emission of greenhouse gases, protect biodiversity, and contribute to social development. Later, at the United Nations conference on climate change in Kyoto in 1998, many nations agreed to cut back their emissions even further. The United States, the largest emitter of greenhouse gases, has so far refused to ratify these agreements, so they have not become legally binding for anyone. The Earth Summit in Johannesburg in 2002 continued to work on the theme of climate change, and was able to draw environmental concerns even closer to the concerns for human development. Ensuring a clean water supply and restoring depleted fisheries, for example, are necessary both for a flourishing nature and human communities.

This conversation continues today, and some corporations have become active participants, such as the members of the World Business Council for Sustainable Development (WBCSD).[18] Many international corporations now provide reports on their social and environmental performance, as well as their economic performance. It is estimated that half of the Fortune 500 companies are engaging in some form of triple-line reporting today.[19] Most of these corporations assume that sustainability will only occur through the further development of market economies. Global economics, however, has been guided much less by the United Nations conversation on sustainability than by the conversations originating from the Bretton Wood organizations.

Bretton Woods Conversations on Trade and Finance. During the final days of World War II, representatives from 45 nations met in Bretton Woods, New Hampshire, to restore markets and international finance after the war. The representatives agreed that the dollar would become the dominant global currency, which led to the United States dominating the Bretton Woods institutions: the World Bank, the International Monetary Fund, and the World Trade Organization. In the 1970s, when the United Nations Conference on Trade and Development (UNCTAD) attempted to represent the developing nations' interests in achieving more equality between the North and South, the United States withdrew its support from the UN conference and enlarged the scope of the Bretton Woods organizations, especially in dealing with loans, debts, and, more recently, trade barriers. In 1999, at the WTO meeting in Seattle, the conflict between the WTO and its opponents came to a head, and street demonstrators successfully stopped the WTO from drafting more trade agreements, at least at that meeting. This conversation has created a flood of counter-conversations that now open the way to different perspectives.

As one might suspect, corporations have been deeply involved in the conversations about world trade, especially in terms of promoting the consumption of "stuff." As Buchholz and Rosenthal pointed out several years ago, the world's people have consumed as many goods and services since 1950 as all previous generations put together.[20] The increased consumption is promoted by extensive advertising. In 1986, advertising in United States cost $100 billion. The amount had risen to $231 billion in the year 2000.[21] The promotion of consumption has not "raised all boats" as the neo-liberals predicted, but instead has supported two trends that have their roots in colonialism: the widening gap between the rich and poor and the increase in ethnic hatred. The September 11 attack on the World Trade Center is probably the clearest signal of the volatility of these trends. The wars that have followed these attacks have only increased the urgency of finding a way that corporations can live in a sustainable natural environment. Our third conversation may offer some possibilities.

Conversations about the Dynamics and Design of Nature. Concurrent with the UN conversations on sustainability and the Bretton Woods conversations on world trade, various individuals and groups have developed a multifaceted conversation on ecological systems. This conversation has many more creative voices than we can review here. One can see a trail, however, that begins with Aldo Leopold's land ethic, runs through E.F. Schumacher's notion that small is beautiful, and Arnold Naess's deep ecology, and ends with the understanding of nature as a living system. Throughout this conversation, a key theme is that humans need to find their place in nature rather than using nature to create their place. Or, to put it another way, our quest for sustainable communities should follow nature's design.

> The key to an operational definition of ecological sustainability is the realization that we do not need to invent sustainable human communities from scratch but can model them after nature's ecosystems, which are sustainable communities of plants, animals, and microorganisms.[22]

Paul Hawken has also argued for what he calls "Biomimicry," which means that organizational design would mimic biological design. As Hawken points out, compared to the efficiency of nature, which uses 100% of materials that flow through its systems, the US economy uses only about 6%. The 94% becomes waste.[23] If we could come closer to mimicking nature's patterns, we could become more efficient and cause less harm. This is the idea behind the principles of the Natural Step.

The Natural Step. The Natural Step is an environmental program developed under the leadership of Dr. Karl-Henrick Robert in Sweden. It proposes that corporations design their total operations so that they do not subject nature to: "(1) increasing concentrations of substances extracted from the Earth's crust; (2) increasing concentrations of substances produced by society; (3) increasing degradation by physical means; and (4) that in that society human needs are met worldwide."[24] To meet these conditions, corporations must find new ways to design their resource use, production process, distribution process, and their products so that all "wastes" either become biological resources (biodegradable) or material resources (reusable or recyclable). Several corporations have taken up this challenge to use nature's design as a model for designing their operations. One is the carpet company, Interface Inc.

The Sustainability Program on Interface Inc. Interface Inc., a major carpet manufacturing company in the United States, is one of four corporations highlighted in Nattrass and Altomare's book on the natural step for business. The other three are IKEA, Scandic Hotels, and Collins Pine Company.[25]

As Joseph Desjardins points out in his review of Interface Inc.'s movement toward sustainability, the most impressive thing they have done is reframe how they do business.[26] Instead of a carpet company that produces and sells products, they see themselves as a carpet company that offers floor-covering services. This means that they continue to own the carpet itself, which creates an incentive to produce carpets that are durable, easily replaceable, and recyclable.

The Natural Step, of course, is not the only model for corporate sustainability. Some corporations will be more receptive to the stewardship of natural capital than to a program that imitates nature. In any case, the idea that we can have social prosperity at the expense of nature no longer rings true. The truth seems much closer to the United Nations' 2002 Earth Charter's declaration:

> The resilience of the community of life and the well-being of humanity depend upon preserving a healthy biosphere with all its ecological systems, a rich variety of plants and animals, fertile soils, pure waters, and clean air. The global environment with its finite resources is a common concern of all peoples. The protection of Earth's vitality, diversity, and beauty is a sacred trust.[27]

If corporations are to have integrity, they will need to find an appropriate relationship with nature, a relationship that recognizes nature as a source of life as well as a resource for life. Three guidelines that they could consider to find that relationship are to become clear about their boundaries, to understand that prosperity is always local instead of global, and to see their prosperity connected with the prosperity of nature.

CONCLUSION

Corporations are part of something larger than themselves. They are members of civic and natural communities, and their integrity depends on how they fit into these larger wholes. Finding and securing their appropriate place and function will require contributions from citizen action groups, government agencies, and consumers. They do have a place, a vital place, and we all need to think about what it should be.

Whether corporations can engage in conversations with such groups depends on their cultural openness, which we listed as the first dimension of organizational integrity. The practice of cultural openness, on the other hand, requires relationships of mutual recognition. Without such relationships, people will not engage in a process that can generate the ideas and commitment necessary to find new ways to design organizations so they can practice civic cooperation and encourage natural prosperity. Only from such conversations can participants decide how to formulate a corporation's purpose—a purpose that fits in larger human and natural communities.

Corporations may have to be satisfied with signs of increased integrity, instead of acquiring it all at once. Corporate leaders should not be stifled by the magnitude of the task, but rather look for places to begin the change, or if the change has already begun, for ways to expand upon it. Changes on one dimension of conversational integrity may affect other dimensions as well. If corporations are to have integrity, it will finally depend on whether they are designed so that participants can ask the questions we have been asking, on each of the five dimensions of conversational integrity, and work with each other, as well as other stakeholders, to find the answers.

NOTES

1. D. Korten, *When Corporations Rule the World,* second edition (West Hartford, CT: Kumarian Press, 2001).
2. *Oxford Dictionary of the English Language,* p. 1065.
3. W.B. Pearce, *Communication and the Human Condition* (Carbondale and Edwardsville: Southern Illinois University Press, 1989).
4. Ibid., p. 192.
5. Pearce.
6. K. Orren, *Belated Feudalism: Labor, the Law, and Liberal Development in the United States* (Cambridge, New York: Cambridge University Press, 1991).
7. P.M. Senge, *The Fifth Discipline: The Art and Practice of The Learning Organization* (New York: Doubleday Currency, 1990).
8. G. Lakoff, *Moral Politics: What Conservatives Know That Liberals Don't* (Chicago and London: The University of Chicago Press, 1996).

9. J. Bowlby, *A Secure Base: Parent-Child Attachment and Health Human Development* (Basic Books, 1988).

10. B. Barber, *Strong Democracy: Participatory Politics for a New Age* (Berkeley, Los Angeles, London: University of California Press, 1984).

11. *The American Heritage Dictionary* (1992), p. 715.

12. R. Post and N. Rosenblum, "Introduction" in *Civil Society and Government*, ed. Rosenblum and Post (Princeton and Oxford: Princeton University Press, 2002), p. 3.

13. K. Boulding, *Three Faces of Power* (New York: Sage, 1990).

14. S.T. Bruyn, *A Civil Economy: Transforming the Market in the Twenty-First Century* (Ann Arbor, MI: The University of Michigan Press, 2000), p. 209.

15. A. Hoffman, *From Heresy to Dogma: An Institutional History of Corporate Environmentalism* (San Francisco: The New Lexington Press, 1997).

16. Ibid. p. 148-149.

17. Ibid. p. 183.

18. www.wbcsd.org.

19. R. Lombardi and M. Wilson, "Globalization and Its Discontents: The Arrival of Triple-Bottom-Line Reporting," *Ivey Business Journal* (September/October 2001), taken from Web site: www.pwcglobal.com.servlet.

20. R. Buchholz and S. Rosenthal, "Toward an Ethics of Consumption: Rethinking the Nature of Growth," in *The Business of Consumption: Environmental Ethics and The Global Economy*, ed. L. Westra and P. Werhane (New York: Rowman and Littlefield, 1998), 225-226.

21. *New York Times Almanac* (2002), p. 350.

22. F. Capra, *The Hidden Connections: Integrating the Biological, Cognitive and Social Dimensions of Life into a Science of Sustainability* (New York: Doubleday, 2002), p. 230.

23. Hawken, Lovins and Lovins, p. 14.

24. Nattrass and Altomare, p. 23.

25. Nattrass and Altomare.

26. Desjardins, p. 195.

27. www.earthcharter.org.

BEYOND REGULATION, WHAT?
THE CASE FOR CORPORATE SELF-REFORM

by

Ian Wilson

To say that the past three years have not reflected well on the corporate form of business organization would be an understatement of major proportions. The disasters triggered by Enron, Andersen Consulting, Tyco, WorldCom and Adelphi Communications, to name but a few, have, not surprisingly, created a climate of suspicion and hostility unmatched since the days of the Great Depression.

In the wake of the turmoil caused by these examples of corporate malfeasance and corruption, we have, not surprisingly, experienced a rising tide of punitive legislation, regulation and litigation, as well as widespread public disillusionment at what is seen as a gross betrayal of trust. This reaction was inevitable and largely deserved. But the corrective measures that are currently being proposed (changes in governance and accounting procedures, for example) will, by themselves, almost certainly fail to achieve their ultimate objective of preventing a recurrence of such behavior. They will fail, not so much because they are ill-conceived and hastily drafted, but because they do not deal with the root cause of this behavior—namely, corporations' misperception of their social purpose, and of the changes in governance and accountability that are required to restore public trust and confidence.

In my book, *The New Rules of Corporate Conduct*, I outlined an agenda of corporate reform that would address the full range of issues arising from the current and prospective changes in our social and political environment. These new rules of corporate conduct are:

- *Legitimacy*: To earn and retain social legitimacy, the corporation must define its basic mission in terms of the social purpose it is designed to serve rather than as the maximization of profit.

- *Governance*: The corporation must be thought of, managed and governed more as a community of stakeholders, less as the property of investors.

- *Equity*: The corporation must strive to achieve greater perceived fairness in the distribution of economic wealth and in its treatment of all stakeholders.

- *Environment*: The corporation must integrate the practices of restorative economics and sustainable development into the mainstream of its business strategy.

Ian Wilson *is principal of Wolf Enterprises, San Rafael, California. He may be contacted at jason415xx@aol.com.*

• *Employment*: The corporation must rewrite the social contract of work to reflect the values of the new workforce, and increase both the effectiveness and loyalty of employees and the corporation.

• *Public-Private Sector Relationships*: To ensure the success of the power shift, corporations must work closely with governments for a viable, and publicly accepted, redefinition of the roles and responsibilities of the public and private sectors.

• *Ethics*: The corporation must elevate and monitor the level of ethical performance in all its operations in order to build the trust which is the foundation of sound relations with all stakeholder groups.

Here I want to focus on just two priorities for reform: the need to rethink both the purpose of the corporation, and its system of governance and accountability.

RETHINKING CORPORATE PURPOSE

The need for such a rethinking is nowhere more apparent than in the different ways in which the purposes of corporations and other institutions are perceived. For example, ask anyone what the purpose of, say, a hospital is, and you will be told, "To heal the injured and cure the sick" or (in the modern idiom) "maintain health and wellness." Ask about the purpose of a school or college, and the answers are, "enculture the young," "train the workforce," "increase and transmit knowledge," and "promote self-development and life-long learning." Then ask anyone—entrepreneur or corporate executive, consumer or educator, economist or politician—what the purpose of the corporation is, and, like as not, you will get the terse response: "Profit"—sometimes elaborated as "maximize profitability" or (again in the modern idiom) "create shareowner value."

The contrast between the mind-sets of corporations and other social institutions is startling and dismaying. If business can come up with no better definition of its social purpose than "profit," it is little wonder that it is the object of so much public suspicion and skepticism at best and antipathy and outright hatred at worst. Corporations have always been weak in what Kenneth Boulding used to call "the affective domain": "No one," he was fond of saying, "can love General Electric or the Federal Reserve!" However, I would argue that the corporate response to this question is not merely unsatisfying: It is, quite simply, wrong. It does not reflect the facts of today's business environment.

It is necessity, not sentimentality, that calls for a more acceptable and accurate statement of purpose. The primacy, indeed the exclusiveness, that current statements give to profitability as the *purpose* of the corporation—embraced by advocates and condemned by critics—leaves little or no room for any policy or any action other than those which contribute directly and substantially to that purpose. When there is no other purpose than profit (money), the risk of distortions in corporate values and objectives increases dramatically. As recent events have demonstrated so clearly, absent a strong service orientation, the most perverse objectives and measurements of performance can be pursued, for example:

- The use of "off-balance sheet entities" to hide liabilities and justify the creation of a "new energy trading model" (Enron, Dynegy).

- Manipulation of financial reporting to drive up the price of shares to serve as "currency" for acquisitions (WorldCom, Qwest).

- Using stock grants and options, ostensibly to align management's interests with those of shareowners, but then ignoring the temptation the options create for management to drive up share prices with false promises, take the money, and run.

- Subsidizing the opulent lifestyles of CEOs (Tyco, Adelphi Communications).

Any restatement of the purpose of the corporation must start with recognizing the fact that it is a *social* institution—*not* a social welfare institution, but one designed to serve a social purpose. Its function is economic, but its purpose is social. It exists, like any institution, at the discretion of society, to serve society's needs. On its willingness and ability to serve those needs depends its continuing claim to legitimacy.

Building on that premise, we can come up with a statement that seems to me to encapsulate the true purpose of the corporation:

The corporation is a creation of society whose purpose is the production and distribution of needed goods and services, to the profit of society and itself.

Each element of that definition is needed and important, if the whole is to be an accurate reflection of reality.

The corporation *is* a social institution—a creation of society, not in the sense of being a social welfare entity, but of serving society's needs. It is created by a charter that can be revoked either literally by legal action or figuratively by action of the marketplace. Its principal activity lies in satisfying the *economic* needs of society through the production and distribution of goods and services in all their diversity—coal and chemicals, clothing and food, transportation and entertainment, health care and software. And these goods and services must be *needed*. If they do not meet some individual or communal need, they will not be purchased, and the would-be supplier will have failed to justify its existence.

Finally, if this cycle of events is to be completed successfully—and success is, after all, the aim—*both* the corporation *and* society must profit. This mutuality of interests is important and inescapable. If society benefits, but the business does not make money, then the corporation will go out of business—in the short run. Or if society sees no benefit to itself from a corporation's activities, then in the long run (and the long run is what most corporations plan for) the business will not be profitable.

Of course, the statement of purpose that I have outlined here is generic; it serves only to establish the basic principles and vocabulary of such a statement. Making it specific to a particular corporation requires identifying the precise societal needs it will serve, with what range of products and services, embracing what values, and producing what benefits for stakeholders (not just shareowners).

Critics will object that there is really nothing new in this statement because most executives accept the fact that the corporation has to serve a social purpose in addition to profit making. But the recent disclosures of how, and with what values, executive decisions are made make very clear that such claims are quite superficial and will be suppressed at the first hint of a threat to profitability. So, even if we accept the critics' argument, we can see that CEOs must devote more sustained, sincere and substantial effort to making this claim a reality.

My point, however, goes further and deeper than this. I would argue that *purpose* has everything to do with service to society, and only secondarily to do with profitability. The shareholder value approach is, as John Kay, director of Oxford University's School of Management Studies, noted, "fundamentally instrumental: meeting customer needs is a means not an end." Service on the other hand— service to customers, to employees, to shareowners, to society at large—is more than instrumental: it is fundamental, the raison d'etre for the continued existence of a corporation.

If, then, profit is not the purpose of the corporation, what is its role? In defining my own position, let me start by stating unequivocally that the private corporation must be, in some sense and to some degree, a profit-making organization. Without profit, its existence will be brief and troubled. But this does not require that profit should be its purpose, its reason for existence. *Profit has a vital role to play as means, as motivator, and as measure* of corporate performance, and this role is sufficient to demonstrate its importance in the business equation.

Profit provides the *means*—the resources for investment in research, new product development, plant expansion, and improved equipment. It is not the marginal or profitless corporation that creates new jobs, cleans up the environment, supports education and community activities, or does any other of the socially desirable things that people expect from business—because it can't afford to. Earning a profit and being socially responsible are not incompatible: they can be—indeed, *must* be—bound together.

Profit is also a key *motivator* for the corporation and the entrepreneur alike, to seek out new ventures. It is one of the incentives (not by any means the only one) that spur the application of intellectual creativity and financial resources to the practical needs and problems of society.

And, finally, profit is a *measure* (an important one but, again, not the only one) of the corporation's success or failure in performing its social role of meeting economic needs. In meeting these needs, it is essential that the business earn a profit. More accurately, it is essential that the corporation feels that it *can* earn a profit: the actual realization is the reward of the successful business only.

Rethinking and restating the purpose of the corporation in this way is neither an idle exercise in semantic quibbling nor a public relations gambit. It matters, and it matters profoundly, not just to clarify debate, but more importantly to guide and drive action. It establishes values and priorities, influences strategy and investment, and infuses the whole culture of an organization with a sense of passion and purpose. Jon Katzenbach, in his article "Pride: The Touchstone of Excellence," rightly stresses the powerful motivational force that a sense of service and purpose can exert: it can "build organizational responsiveness, provide strategic advantage, and deliver higher levels of performance."

Conceived in this way, the profit motive can be an efficient and socially desirable means of ensuring that markets work to the greatest good of the greatest number. It is only when profit is viewed as the *purpose*, the raison d'etre for the corporation, that it distorts and corrupts the system.

I am not so naïve as to believe that a simple crafting of a new statement of corporate purpose will change anything. By itself, it could be dismissed as nothing more than a public relations gambit. But it is a necessary starting point for action. It establishes the context, the tone, and the direction for a program of action toward a radical reorientation of corporate culture. This is where the CEO's leadership counts most.

Once crafted, such a statement requires a constant drumbeat of executive leadership and action to underscore the reality and importance of this value shift. Only when managers see that the change is for real will they be inclined to change their own behavior.

In this arena, as in so many, it is leadership by example that counts. Changing the culture from a purely profits orientation to a service orientation requires that the CEO embodies, in action as well as pronouncements, the qualities of this new culture. Consistency and sincerity are, as so often, the essential qualities in this regard. By

204 • Beyond Regulation, What?

word, decisions and unspoken signals, CEOs do more than any other single influence to set the tone for an organization. Arthur Martinez, former CEO of Sears, underscored the importance of this factor when, in the wake of a company-wide scandal, he urged his fellow executives to reexamine their own conduct and ask, "Is what I do, the direction I give, the body language I use, creating an environment when something like this could happen? Is my message 'Make the numbers at any cost'?" Often it is the subtle signals that count for more than the overt pronouncements.

Above all, we must revise the measurement and reward system that guides managerial action. The importance of measurement cannot be overstated. *Organizationally, we become what we measure.* If we measure only profitability, then profit is what we'll get—at any cost, even to our ultimate detriment. If, however, we define purpose more broadly and responsibly, we should devise a measurement system that reflects a corporation's overall performance and responsibility. The "triple bottom line" approach to measurement—focusing on corporate performance against economic, social and environmental parameters—is a step in the right direction.

I know that, even with all these caveats, there will be those who say that this approach is impractical. A friend of mine once said that changing profit from an end to a means was "the corporate equivalent of unilateral disarmament." Corporate executives and apologists such as Milton Friedman and Theodore Levitt have been unequivocal in their argument that "the business of business is making money, not sweet music." "Business, " Levitt once wrote, " will have a much better chance of surviving if there is no nonsense about its goals—that is, if long-run profit maximization is the one dominant objective in practice as well as theory."

My argument, however, is not a plea for "sweet music": Philanthropy and community programs are desirable, but not the issue here. The statement of purpose that I advocate links tightly and inextricably to strategy and strategic objectives—which market segments will be served; with what goods and services; competing with which other suppliers; employing which sources of competitive advantage; aiming at what strategic objectives. In other words, this is not a matter of "unilateral disarmament"; rather, it is a matter of clarifying which "armaments" (strategies) will be used to achieve which objectives.

George Merck, founder of the pharmaceutical firm that bears his name, put it well when he said, "We try never to forget that medicine is for the people. It is not for the profits. The profits follow, and if we have remembered that, they have never failed to appear. The better we have remembered that, the larger they have been." And, speaking for another industry and another age, David Packard, the co-founder of Hewlett-Packard, was equally explicit: "Profit is not the proper end and aim of management—it is what makes all of the proper ends and aims possible."

GOVERNANCE AND ACCOUNTABILITY

A fundamental question that now confronts corporations at this stage is the following: "Under the new rules, for what are managers, and the board of directors, accountable? and to whom are they accountable?" The answer now seems clear that we are moving toward a more pluralistic model of corporate governance. In the Industrial Age paradigm, there was a clear-cut singularity of purpose and responsibility to shareowners for the profitable operation of the company and the creation of shareowner value. The new rules, however, place more emphasis on the plurality of executives' and directors' responsibilities to *all* stakeholders for *all* aspects of corporate performance.

This view, I should point out, is still not widely accepted in the United States. Even in Europe and Japan, where there has, traditionally, been a greater commitment to employees and communities, the impact of corporate restructuring and global competition has had the effect of calling into question the ability of corporations to discharge these responsibilities as fully as they have in the past. In its 1997 *Statement on Corporate Governance*, the Business Roundtable stands by its view that "the paramount duty of management and of boards of directors is to the corporation's stockholders," and adheres to the instrumental view that "the interests of other stakeholders are relevant as a derivative of the duty to stockholders."

However, the new rules insist on recognizing the plurality of stakeholder interests, not as a matter of ideology, but as a matter of fact—a fact that managers have to deal with every day. It seems clear that corporate governance must also face up to the implications of this fact. *Governance, in other words, must be designed to clarify and strengthen the lines of corporate responsibility and accountability to all its stakeholders.*

Does this then mean that, for instance, the composition of the board of directors should be changed to mirror this plurality of interests? All the indicators of the future would seem to give a "Yes—and no" response to this question. No, it is not necessary, and probably impractical, to stipulate in the articles of incorporation that other stakeholders should be directly and specifically represented on the board. But yes, it is important that the board should be composed of directors who, individually and collectively, recognize their responsibility for ensuring that the corporation is managed in the best interests of all stakeholders.

Waiting for governments to act on measures to broaden board representation would be time-consuming, cumbersome and, in the end, probably unproductive. Which stakeholders should be represented on the board? How should they be elected? To whom would they be accountable, and how? A regulatory approach to such governance questions would probably, like most regulations, end up being either meaningless or a straitjacket. It is easy enough to enumerate the standard categories of stakeholders, but the fact remains that they vary in range and importance from one corporation to another. I agree with the Business Roundtable that "good corporate governance is not a 'one size fits all' proposition, and a wide diversity of approaches ... should be expected and is entirely appropriate." Stipulations that some board positions should "belong" to certain constituencies—that, for instance, there should be a consumer representative or an environmental advocate—would be misplaced and divisive. What is really needed is an assurance that directors, collectively, possess all the expertise, experience and perspectives needed to evaluate all the different facets of corporate performance.

A far preferable approach would be for individual corporations to take their own initiatives to ensure that these broader responsibilities are reflected in corporate decision making. As long ago as the early 1970s General Electric picked up the "early warning signals" of this impending change in corporate governance, and in 1972 moved toward a restructuring of its board of directors that, among other things, recognized that the board has a role in addressing issues of corporate responsibility beyond the immediate interests of investors. Because these issues involve the place of the corporation in the larger society and its acceptance in that society, they are very much within the province of the board.

In assessing the utility of such an approach, we should remember that it is only one part of a broader ongoing transformation of the board's role. In the old Industrial Age paradigm, directors played a largely reactive role in monitoring and auditing management's performance: firing CEOs was an almost unheard-of event, and even hiring new ones was often a mere formality of anointing a preselected successor. Under the new paradigm, however, directors are becoming far more active and involved in decision making. It is not a matter of usurping managerial responsibilities, but rather—as more enlightened CEOs are beginning to recognize—of adding value as they bring their experience and differing perspectives to bear on the strategic issues facing the company. In an article in the *Harvard Business Review*, John Pound argued, "Just as a democratic political system cannot work without involved citizens, corporate governance cannot work without the informed involvement of the three critical groups"—directors, managers, and major shareholders. Involving outsiders reduces the danger of insularity in managerial decisions and, he asserted, "can mitigate the behavior problems that cause companies to cling to bad decisions." In such a context, it becomes more feasible to argue that directors have a key role to play in attending to the social responsibilities of the corporation.

Even so, this is not a perfect solution, and certainly it will not satisfy the purists. But it is, I submit, feasible, and preferable to straitjacket regulation. Indeed, to paraphrase Winston Churchill's appraisal of democracy, it may be the worst form of governance "except all those other forms which have been tried from time to time." Such an approach is capable of changing the calculus by which corporate decisions are made, and so of influencing their performance. And it is the realities of performance rather than the niceties of form that weigh most heavily with the public.

There are, however, a number of further conditions that must be satisfied for this approach to be workable, most notably the need to ensure that the board is truly independent, and that there is a clear approach to giving a public accounting of the discharge of their responsibilities.

These and other measures are all aimed at strengthening and opening up the corporate governance system by ensuring that the board is capable of making informed and independent judgments on *all* the key elements of corporate performance. Directors have always had a legal and statutory obligation to the shareowners. They are now being required to assume a de facto (not yet a de jure) responsibility to the public and other stakeholders in the company. It is, of course, not sufficient that directors and corporations recognize this responsibility. It is not even sufficient that they bring performance into line with these new societal expectations. There must also be, and be seen to be, a clear public accounting and auditing of this performance.

Just as the quarterly and annual reports are now published to provide an accounting to shareowners and institutional investors of a company's financial condition, so we are moving toward more detailed and explicit reporting of corporate performance across the whole spectrum of its activities. We sometimes refer to these as "social" or "non-financial" areas, but this terminology misleadingly suggests that they are secondary, less important activities. It masks the fact that activities such as environmental protection, health and safety, equal employment opportunity, employee training, and community relations are now considered integral elements of corporate operations, and can have profound financial implications, both positive and negative.

The fact of the matter is that, under the new rules, society is more and more inclined to judge a company *as a whole*. Certainly, the public places a high value on excellent products, courteous service, satisfying jobs, and increased dividends; but this does not mean that they will be forgiving of toxic pollution, overseas sweatshops, antitrust violations, or ethical lapses. This holistic approach to evaluating a company's behavior is a reflection of a whole array of diverse but related forces. Societal values have become more demanding; regulatory requirements have broadened; and public interest groups have grown in number and influence.

A central factor in this new Information Age is, of course, that information, on almost any topic, becomes, almost instantly, widely and freely available. Attempts to stem this flow, whether from Tiananmen Square, the Pentagon or the tobacco companies, have universally failed. This is a fact of life with which corporations are now having to grapple. Where a repressive communist government has failed, there is little chance that corporations, with their looser discipline and more porous boundaries, will succeed. Whether from internal whistle-blowers or from governments, the press or institutional investors, auditors or interest groups, information will out.

What is emerging, slowly but surely, is a system of corporate disclosure and accountability that will eventually be:

• *Comprehensive*: It will be designed to cover both financial and competitive performance and what we now term the "social aspects of business."

• *Understandable*: It must be phrased in terms that are both interesting and intelligible to the concerned layperson. One of the lessons from the failed experiments in social audits is that, quite apart from the difficulty of placing a financial evaluation on these social activities, ordinary prose is more appropriate—and more descriptive—than financial calculations for such a report.

• *Standardized*: Although uniformity of reporting is an elusive, probably unattainable, goal, some measure of standardization is desirable. Just as financial accounting has developed its conventions as to how expenses, depreciation and revenues should be reported, so social accounting will have to establish some commonly accepted ground rules governing reports of other corporate domains.

• *Audited*: For this accounting to earn broad credibility, it must be reviewed and certified by an independent professional body in the same way that financial accounts are at present.

• *Available*: The results of the audit must be publicly available and accessible to any concerned stakeholder. Since it is clearly impossible to maintain a register of all stakeholders in the same way that there is a register of shareowners, there cannot be a routine distribution of these reports, but their availability, including online, must be publicized and well known.

All of these efforts fall short of the complete disclosure and accountability system outlined above, but they are all steps taken in the same general direction. And the movement is likely to gain increasing momentum, not from government regulations as in the past, but from millions of consumers and concerned citizens worldwide who will come to expect compliance with such standards, and who will demand information on which to base their judgments.

"Sunlight," Justice Louis Brandeis once wrote, "is the best disinfectant." In an increasingly democratic society—and that is the direction in which most societies are currently moving—"sunlight," in the form of public access to information on the workings of all societal institutions, is the most direct, least intrusive route to ensuring accountability and the alignment of institutional goals with societal values. This is a truth that corporations must learn to accept. In the past, the emphasis was on minimum disclosure and the *privacy* of the private corporation. In a more open future, one in which their performance is more widely and critically appraised, corporations will have to recognize that increased disclosure is not only the price they must pay for reduced regulatory oversight. It is also, and more positively, a way in which they can build more trusting relationships with the multiple stakeholders on whom their success will depend.

ETHICAL VALUES

NEW FUTURES AND THE ETERNAL STRUGGLE BETWEEN GOOD AND EVIL

by

Wendell Bell

PROLOGUE: OCTOBER 28, 2002

I wrote the following article during the summer of 2000, more than a year before the deaths and destruction of the attacks of 11 September 2001 on the World Trade Center, the Pentagon, and the airliner that crashed in Pennsylvania.

With sadness, I note that this article has turned out to be prophetic. The ancient concept of "evil" has been prominently thrust into our daily lives. Our leaders and media pundits have bombarded us with the rhetoric of evil to interpret the events of 9/11 and the motives of the perpetrators. "This is a new kind of evil," President George W. Bush said, "and we will rid the world of evil-doers." And he identified an "evil axis" of countries. The enemies have been defined and they are evil terrorists.

We are victims of evil demons, a chorus of Americans repeated, and we will punish them. Vengeance will be ours. In all sincerity and righteousness, we Americans view our own recent aggressions as justifiable, perfectly understandable, and rational acts designed to destroy evil. But in our efforts to destroy members of al Qaeda and the Taliban regime in Afghanistan, we also killed and injured civilians, demolished homes and places of work and worship, and created still more innocent victims of primordial beliefs. "Regrettable collateral damage," we said.

And what of Osama bin Laden, his al Qaeda followers, and other violence-prone Islamic fundamentalists? Do they see themselves, as we have defined them, as evil incarnate? No, they do not. They, too, see themselves, just as we see ourselves, as righteous, moral, and sincere as they try to destroy what *they* regard as evil in the world. They claim to believe that they are following the bidding of their God, willing to become martyrs in the struggle against evil. Thus, they, too, are victims of the tragic rhetoric of evil. They are, if you can for a moment suspend disbelief and think an unthinkable, horrifying thought, mirror images of us Americans as we now act to destroy evil in the world.

As you read this paper, can you see how the following process applies equally to opposing sides in a conflict?

• Feeling victimized by the harmful acts of some perpetrators, an Other

---

Wendell Bell *is professor emeritus of sociology and senior research scientist, Center for Comparative Research, Yale University. He may be contacted at wendell.bell@yale.edu.*

• Exaggerating the harm done to us by these acts

• Failing to understand the true and sincere motives of these perpetrators

• Defining their acts as incomprehensible except as acts of pure evil

• Demonizing the Other as inhuman monsters

• Retaliating against the Other by the use of violence and deadly force

• Defining our use of such violence and force as the righteous and understandable acts of justice somehow proportional to the original harmful acts against us.

Can you see, further, how victims become perpetrators and how perpetrators, when retaliatory harmful acts are taken against them, turn themselves into victims in their own eyes and see their former "victims" as the "perpetrators"?

Can you see how the harmful acts and retaliatory harmful acts can easily become a never-ending, vicious circle of violence and escalating counterviolence?

Can you see how the rage and hate produced by these harmful acts are used to dehumanize the Other, turning the Other into legitimate targets of terrifying acts of violence?

Can you think of any effective ways of interceding in the process and preventing further violence? (The destruction we have brought to the people of Afghanistan and the fall of the Taliban regime have not achieved our purposes. For example, we are told that al Qaeda cells and the threat of their terrorist acts continue to exist.)

From the research that I have done on the topic of evil and from the principles of futures studies, I give in the paper that follows some possible ways to restrain evil.

What seems clear is that the peaceful resolution of conflicts requires that we go beyond the limitations of the rhetoric of evil as the interpretation of conflict. This is not to say that there is no evil in the world. There certainly is.

But if we wish to promote peace and not to perpetuate harmful acts, we ought to try to understand the Other. We ought to look at the world through the eyes of our enemies, recognize their point of view, and respect the sincerity of their beliefs, no matter how wrong we think they are and no matter how they have injured us. And we ought to attempt to engage the Other in honest discourse and negotiations.

Also, we Americans ought to cooperate with other nations to capture the guilty criminals of harmful acts and bring them to justice within the law and international legal institutions. And we ought to do so without doing additional harm ourselves by demonizing entire groups, nations, or religions.

Finally, we must not believe that we are always good and morally right and that our enemies—the Other—are totally and unredeemably evil. For that is a belief that serves neither truth nor justice. It is an oversimplification that has no place in a world of reason and often results in a tragic and senseless continuation of death and destruction.

INTRODUCTION

In 1970, when he published *Future Shock*, Toffler told his readers that they were in danger of being buried by ever-accelerating social changes. Changes, he said, had become electrifyingly fast, outstripping people's images of the future and their abilities to adapt to them, much less to control them. People were being shocked and surprised by change, by unwanted and unanticipated consequences of their actions, and by untamed forces beyond their understanding and control. Toffler argued, as had H.G. Wells decades earlier, that people must start thinking about and anticipating the future. Despite the rise of a field of futures studies, despite the spread of futures thinking in both government and corporations, despite the increased consciousness of threats to the environment and many local and international efforts aimed at conservation, despite the growing consensus about the need for sustainable development, and despite the hundreds of articles and books about a variety of technological revolutions—despite all these things—Toffler's warning not only remains true more than thirty years later, but is, perhaps, more urgent than ever.

Recent technological and social changes have many people reeling. Current developments in biotechnology and genetic engineering, information technology, communications, e-commerce, Internet dot-coms, robotics, nanotechnologies or moletronics (molecular electronics), globalization, medical diagnosis and treatment, human potential, energy technologies, and knowledge of the universe would have been, and often were, the stuff of fantasy not many decades ago. These—and a thousand other developments, both large and small—are changing our lives. They threaten many people, not least of all because they bring uncertainties and unknowns, making people feel that the world is becoming chaotic and that they are losing control of their lives.

Yet there are other changes that are not occurring fast enough for some of us. I refer to such things as achieving environmental sustainability; lowering birthrates in some places and reducing the increase in per capita consumption in others; spreading democratic participation and public liberties; generally accepting the principles of human rights and responsibilities for both men and women, including freeing women more fully so that they may have lives of their own choosing; providing basic sanitation and fresh water to people everywhere; reducing illiteracy and extreme socioeconomic inequalities; adopting a global ethic and creating a world community of concern for other people; preventing aggression and violence and constructing a world at peace; building a win-win world in which there is respect for the freedom, well-being, and dignity of every individual; and encouraging a self-identity among peoples every-where that, without replacing local identities, includes a sense of being a member of the human species (Bell, 1999).

Of course, for many people these changes—or potential chang-es—are just as threatening, sometimes more threatening, than rapid technological changes. For they not only disturb comfortable routines, they also challenge traditional beliefs and values and bring into question the very purposes and meanings of people's lives.

PURPOSES

In this paper, I discuss some of those traditional beliefs that still remain with us after centuries, indeed after millennia, of human existence and that still are influencing the future of the human community. I discuss a set of beliefs known as millennialism, focusing specifically on a major component of it, the problem of evil. Although the idea of evil may be of doubtful utility as an analytic concept for the social sciences, it is of great—perhaps major—impor-tance in understanding how, even today with all our science and technology, most people nearly everywhere interpret their world and how they act in it.

Stimulated by some recent writings of the social psychologist, Roy F. Baumeister (1997), I explore four related topics:

1. millennial myths and how they relate to beliefs about evil;

2. the nature of evil;

3. how evildoing can be reduced, if not entirely prevented; and

4. how futures thinking can help to restrain evildoing.

MILLENNIAL BELIEFS

Millennialism, in its most limited meaning, refers to a belief that the Millennium, as described in the Book of Revelation, the last book of the New Testament, is coming. "This text, otherwise known as the Book of the Apocalypse ... consists of a series of fantastic visions of the End of Time in which the forces of Christ and Satan do battle." "The Millennium" refers to the thousand-year period during which the battle ceases, Satan is caged, while Christ and his saints reign on

Earth. "Millenarians" in the strict sense, thus, are people who expect "this thousand-year paradise to dawn at any moment" and who also believe that "only they will witness, and *survive*, the End" (Thompson, 1998: xi-xiii).

Although specific details differ, millennial beliefs wherever they occur contain a core of similar ideas. They exist in almost all religions, both in those that are well established such as Judaism, Christianity, and Islam as well as in the eschatological expectations of sects and extremist cults. Moreover, this core of similar ideas may go back to the dawn of human existence. We have evidence that they existed at least 7,000 years ago among the ancient Egyptians. They existed, also before Christ, among the Mesopotamians, Vedic Indians, Sumerians, Babylonians, Indo-Iranians, Canaanites, and Zoroastrians, as well as many other groups

One of the common themes of millennialism is the conviction that a supernatural world exists alongside the natural world of everyday human life. From the earliest times, the stories of how the world is and how it came to be are filled with supernatural beings. There are gods—or in later times at least *a* God—and a variety of spirits (sometimes of ancestors), angels, demons, devils, and monsters that are viewed as influencing human behavior and events in this Earthly world.

Another view that is central to millennial beliefs is the conception that both the supernatural and natural worlds are dominated by a mighty, continuous struggle between the forces of good and evil, a struggle sometimes described with "scenes of stomach-churning violence and cruelty" (Thompson, 1998: xi). Evil spirits and their human allies are viewed as a constant threat to order and security.

Also, among otherwise diverse religious beliefs there is a striking agreement about how good and evil are defined. The good usually includes, among other values, order, justice, fertility, abundance, bodily nourishment, industriousness, generosity, knowledge, wisdom, truth, incorruptibility, fulfilling one's obligations to others, courage, cooperation, and the importance of human life itself. Their opposites—from chaos to death—are evil. Many such values, as I have tried to show elsewhere (Bell, 1997, Vol. 2), can be objectively justified as being the right values by which humans ought to live, now and in the future.

Millennial beliefs also include a belief in prophecy itself, a belief that foreknowledge of what will happen in the future and when it will happen is possible, often through some omen or a message, either from a supernatural being or its human spokesperson.

Additionally, these millennial prophecies include a belief in some coming End of Time, Final Judgment Day, or the Return of the Messiah. Moreover, it is coming soon. People are told to prepare for an apocalyptic upheaval, some sudden—often violent—change, a final confrontation between good and evil in which, at long last and forevermore, the good will be victorious.

Included in these prophecies, additionally, is the belief that, when this End of Time comes, people will be judged on how they have lived their lives; they will be sorted and divided into evildoers who have sinned and the righteous who have lived morally upright lives. The evildoers will be condemned and punished, horribly tormented, and destroyed. The righteous, to the contrary, will be rewarded by eternal life in some terrestrial or celestial afterlife utopia (Boyer, 1995; Thompson, 1998). For the people who live their lives rightly, there is the promise of salvation and often of immortality.

These stories are familiar to us all. In one form or another and with one cast of characters or another, most of us grew up with them. Even in homes where they were not taught to us directly as received truth, we learned about them from the popular culture around us. But what do these beliefs, except as artifacts for our objective research, have to do with us modern people today?

Indeed, modernity means scientific thinking and, more generally, rationality. We have been told that it leads to the dissolution of traditional mythic worldviews and the weakening of the authority of the world's religions (Habermas, 1987). Educated, modern people are expected to be enlightened, to be devoted to discovering or formulating the facts of the natural and social worlds through empirical observation and to be free of such supernatural nonsense. The occasional odd physicist who embraces a new cosmotheology after deciding that he has discovered God in some physical theory of the universe is certainly the exception (Harrison and Dick, 2000). Surely, these chiliastic worldviews have relatively little influence on human actions today and will have less in the future.

Although I wish that this were the case, the truth is that, despite the rationalization of many spheres of modern life, many, if not most, people in the world believe in these chiliastic expectations. Most of all, they believe in a world of good and evil.

With the exception of the belief in a supernatural world, many thoroughly secularized people, including many members of the academy, believe in comparable propositions. Millennial themes, for example, have their counterparts in many ideologies of political and social movements, including Marxism, modern nationalism, environmentalism, and the peace movement—to mention only a few examples. The ideologies of such movements identify an existing world in which certain things are wrong, unjust, harmful, or evil (such as the exploitation of the working class, the political oppression of a colonial people, air and water pollution, or organized aggression and violence against others). Although beliefs in the supernatural are not part of them (even though a New Age spiritualism may be), these ideological convictions may be held with all the fervor and emotion—even fanaticism—that devout people express for their religious faith. Although the evils that such secular ideologies identify are presumed to exist in this one everyday real world, they are nonetheless evils.

These secular ideologies also contain a vision of some kind of a coming upheaval or significant change in the old order, although not necessarily violent, and a impending future renewal, largely occurring through the actions of true believers of the ideological movement and with the participation of their enlightened followers. They contain, additionally, an image of a new world of social justice and order, individual freedom and equality of citizenship, a sustainable life-supporting Earth free of pollution, peace and harmony—a terrestrial, this worldly, even scientific, utopia where all that was evil in the old order will be gone. Thus, in the broadest sense, millennialism can refer to any belief that the end of some aspect of the present, evil world is—and ought to be—coming and that the changes will produce a better, if not perfect, world that will exist in some other place or in this place at some future time.

THE NATURE OF EVIL

As we have seen, a core element of millennial beliefs and a major force in motivating and shaping human action is the pervasive view of the world as a struggle between good and evil. Among intellectuals and academics, such as ourselves, this idea may appear to be much too simple, too utterly devoid of sophistication, too lacking in intricate theorizing, and too bare of polysyllabic conceptualizing to carry any significant explanatory power for our understanding of human behavior. Although it, indeed, may be simple, it is also one of the most powerful of all underlying folk beliefs shaping human behavior. In every society on every continent on Earth, political, religious, educational, and other leaders urge people to seek the good and to oppose the evil. Everywhere, judgments of what is good and what is bad are the most important judgments that people make and the most central to their lives (Osgood et al., 1975). Moreover, this overall view of the world as a mighty struggle between good and evil encourages people to believe in the evil of others.

But what is evil? In seeking an answer, I rely heavily on Baumeister (1997), although I will indicate a few minor disagreements with his view. His book on *Evil* rests upon his integrative study of the relevant literature, including the findings of empirical social research. Although it is less complex and comprehensive than his masterpiece, *Meanings of Life* (1991), it is a reliable, scholarly work.

For the sake of this discussion, I will define evil as human actions or inactions that harm other people. Although such harm often prominently includes violence and physical harm, it can also include other forms of cruelty that cause suffering in others, such things as stealing, treating others unfairly, humiliating others, betraying or threatening others, oppressing others psychologically, lying, and so forth. It does not include all forms of pain inflicted on people, however. For example, a dentist or a doctor may have to hurt his patient in the course of providing treatment, but his purpose—and, if he is competent, the result—is beneficial for the patient's health.

Contrary to what Baumeister (1997: 8) says at one point, I don't define evil as necessarily the result of an intentional act to harm others. Of course, people often impute evil intentions when people harm them, even when no harm is intended. I include unintentional harm in the definition of evil, however, not for that reason, but rather because people ought to be held accountable when their irresponsible or incompetent acts harm other people, even if they do not intend to do harm, as in the case of a person who causes the death of another person in an automobile accident because he was talking on his cell phone while driving. I add "inaction" to the definition because there are times when the choice not to act—as in the case of a bystander who witnesses an evil act and does not come to the aid of the victim—may also cause harm to others.

Think of evil as a continuum, ranging from those acts that are horribly grotesque and monstrous in the harm and suffering that they cause to those that are relatively minor. Think of evil, too, as a choice that people make, even though the choice is frequently situated within a context of group pressures and social conventions.

Thus, evil involves the infliction of harm, sometimes intentional, on people. But its causes have been obscured by the myth of pure evil. Evil is not generally driven by some force or person relentlessly seeking "to inflict harm, with no positive or comprehensible motive, deriving enjoyment from the suffering of others." It is not the seeking out of "unsuspecting, innocent victims from among the good people of the world." Nor is the victim always completely innocent. Nor is evil some eternal other seeking to throw the world into chaos (Baumeister, 1997: 75). Rather, evil is often the result of understandable acts of well-meaning, decent people, such as you and me.

This is the most important point: The production of evil is for the most part the result of the behavior of ordinary people. Only "a tiny proportion of this century's massive killings are attributable to the actions of those people we call criminals, or crazy people, or socially alienated, or even, people we identify as evil people. The vast majority of killings were actually carried out by plain folk in the population" (Katz, 1993: 10). The most terrible deeds are often done while people are engaged in the mundane tasks of everyday life. For example, this was Hannah Arendt's judgment in her famous study of Adolf Eichmann. During his trial in Jerusalem, Eichmann was depicted as a monster, the very embodiment of evil, for his role in the Nazi extermination program. Yet Arendt (1964) concluded that even the horrendous evil that he did was banal. Looking at the details of his life and his unspeakable crimes, she reached a crucial insight: Eichmann was not some perverted crackpot or demonic monster. He was, rather, the most ordinary of human beings.

Thus, the idea of evil as fun and of hurting other people as a source of joy for the evildoer, contrary to popular conceptions, does not account for many evil acts. Baumeister (1997: 205) concludes, for example, that although sadistic pleasure exists it is relatively rare, acquired gradually, "and responsible for only a minority of evil."

INSTRUMENTAL EVIL

Two other types of evil are more prevalent. One is instrumental evil. It is the use of harmful acts as a means of achieving some goal. The goal itself might be perfectly acceptable—such as getting money, property, political advantage, a passing grade on a test, and so forth. Thus, if acceptable means were used to achieve such goals, the behavior would not be considered evil. But, under normal circumstances, when people engage in lying, stealing, political tyranny and torture, assassination, warfare, murder, and other harmful acts to achieve their goals—even socially approved goals—then they are committing immoral, evil acts.

Why do people use harmful acts to achieve their goals? Because people often view such acts as being easier, more readily accessible, or quicker than using legitimate means. They view deception, bribes, threats, or the use of violence as requiring little skill, patience, institutional credentials, or long-term planning compared to acceptable ways of doing things. Generally, people would prefer to use legitimate rather than illegitimate or illegal means. But when they view acceptable means as being too difficult, too slow, or impossible for themselves, they reluctantly turn to harmful means.

In general, evil is not very effective as a means of fulfilling long-range objectives (Baumeister, 1997: 109). The exception is that evil is effective at making people suffer and sometimes in establishing dominance over them; i.e., to gain and maintain power. Thus, although many aggressor nations, armed rebels, and revolutionaries have been defeated, others have succeeded in acquiring land or establishing states and governments, some of which remain in existence today. An example is the Revolutionary War that helped establish the United States of America. But the "successes," as we all know, have often been as costly in death and destruction for the victors as they have been for the vanquished. Surely, the human community would have been better off without the suffering and death, the tortures, the savage brutalities, the genocides, the rapes, the starvations, the dislocations, and the other miseries that occurred during the 20th century alone.

IDEALISTIC EVIL

Also accounting for a sizeable proportion of evil acts is idealism. Idealistic evil allows people not only to do violence against others, but also to believe that they are, in fact, doing the right thing. True believers define themselves and their causes as just and good. They define individuals and groups who oppose them as their enemies. They tend to marginalize, dehumanize, and demonize them. As a result, they deprive their enemies of having any truth, decency, or legitimacy (Doob, 1978). Looking through the lens of the myth of pure evil, they see them as having no valid, comprehensible reason for their evil acts. In such a perspective, the "ordinary restraints that apply even to severe conflicts may be waived" (Baumeister, 1997: 186) and it may become one's sacred or patriotic duty to destroy the evil Other.

This process of thinking can lead morally conscious and ethical people to commit hideous deeds against others, while believing that they are doing God's or Allah's or some secular ideology's righteous work. In idealistic evil, thus, the very traits that ordinarily contribute to making a person a good and decent member of the community, such as having a conscience and strength of character, "operate to spur the perpetrator on to more severe and intense deeds" (Baumeister, 1997; 170).

The Christian Crusades of the 11th, 12th, and 13th centuries are examples. In their efforts to regain the Holy Lands from the Muslims, the Christians killed, maimed, tortured, and committed unspeakable acts of cruelty, all in the belief that their brutal violence was divinely sanctioned. They were, according to their view at the time, behaving in an exemplary fashion, fulfilling their sacred obligation.

The same can be said of most of the ethnic and political conflicts throughout the world. From Bosnia, Croatia, Kosovo, and the Basques of Spain to Cambodia, West Timor, Chechnya, and the Kurds of Turkey and Iraq to the Palestinians and Israelis, Angola, Sudan, Rwanda, Somalia, Sierra Leone, and the ultra-right paramilitaries and the Marxist guerrillas in Colombia, to mention only a few of the violent confrontations that have occurred in recent years, each side believes itself to be in the right and the other side in the wrong. Each side sees itself as good and the other side as evil. Extremists on each side feel justified in doing the most horrendous harm to their enemies, including rape, hacking off hands and feet, bombing of public places, and wanton killing of combatants and noncombatants alike. Righteousness leads to menace, malice, and mutual carnage.

In many parts of the world, Hitler and other leaders of Nazi Germany remain in people's memories as prime candidates for recent history's worst devils. Many people believe that there was no punishment too dreadful for them because of their crimes against humanity. The ghost of Hitler appeared again during the 1999 NATO bombing of Yugoslavia. For example, I received an e-mail message from Slobodan Vukovic, president of the Serbian Sociological Association, in which he compared the NATO attack to 1941 when "Hitler's Germany bombed Serbian towns and spread death" and to World War II, more generally, when 1.1 million Serbs were killed. He protested the bombing, calling it, among other things, an act of "barbarism" and a "genocidal campaign against the Serbian people." He accused NATO of using prohibited weapons, killing close to 10,000 civilian victims, and bombing schools and hospitals. He attacked US President Bill Clinton, Secretary of State Madeleine Albright, and other Western politicians.

Such demonization was a mirror image of how NATO countries were depicting the Serbs at the same time. The media in Europe and the United States demonized Yugoslavian President Slobodan Milosevic and the Serbs, labeling Milosevic as another Hitler for his dictatorial and oppressive actions and calling him "the butcher of Belgrade," while referring to the Serbs as monsters for their ethnic cleansings, rapes, and mass murders of Muslims in Bosnia and of ethnic Albanians in Kosovo. The NATO countries and the Serbs demonized each other, each side tragically playing out yet again the ancient drama of the eternal struggle between good and evil.

VICTIMS, PERPETRATORS, AND THE ESCALATION OF EVIL

Although Baumeister (1997: 128-168) may be correct in classifying revenge as a distinct form of evil, I see it more as idealistic evil. Revenge, after all, is an act of response. Victims retaliate in order to right a wrong. They want to even the score, to restore justice by punishing the perpetrator for the harm he or she has done to them. Moreover, the principle of revenge may enter into the relationship between perpetrator and victim, no matter what the motivation for the initial harmful act. Acts of instrumental evil, for example, can inspire its victims to retaliate against the evildoer.

Let's consider some of the factors at work. First, perpetrators tend to minimize the harm that they do to others, while victims tend to exaggerate the harm that is done to them. Baumeister (1997: 294) calls this the "magnitude gap" between perpetrators and victims. As a result of this magnitude gap, when victims retaliate, they often do so with a harmful act that is more severe than the perpetrator's was in the first place.

When revenge is taken, roles are reversed. The victimizer now sees himself as the victim. He, in turn, tends to exaggerate the harm done to him by the original victim, to be affronted by its unwarranted excess, and to strike back, raising the level of harm still more. "Just when one side thinks things are even, the other side thinks it has been the victim of an outrage that cries out for retaliation" (Baumeister, 1997: 294).

Second, as we have seen, victims tend to see harmful acts against them as arbitrary, unwarranted, and deliberately malicious. Perpetrators, to the contrary, often see their acts not only as minor but also as quite reasonable and perfectly understandable.

Third, perpetrators use a short time span, while victims tend to use a long time span to justify their sense of victimization and to justify their response. Perpetrators say, "Let bygones be bygones." Victims say, "Never forget." For example, Serbs who committed atrocities in Bosnia in the late 20th century justified their actions by portraying themselves as victims going back to Turkish atrocities against the Serbs in 1389. Their present-day Muslim victims were mystified, wondering what that distant past had to do with them.

Fourth, a time perspective also enters into harmful acts against others in another way. The use of cruelty and violence to solve a problem or to resolve a dispute is often a victory of the present over the future. People who cannot think ahead beyond the immediate present are most likely to view an evil action as rational. Yet other people who stop and evaluate the consequences of their actions for their own future, even for tomorrow or next week as well as for the rest of their lives, are more likely to refrain from harmful acts against others (Baumeister, 1997: 123). Of course, people who think too far into the future—say hundreds of years—may not be restrained by the future, because, by then, they imagine themselves dead and beyond caring.

Fifth, whatever the perceived underlying cause or the justification of harmful acts against others may be, the proximate cause frequently is a loss of self-control (Baumeister, 1997). Emotional distress breaks down self-control and tends to wipe out any thought of future consequences. It is a flashpoint of instant action. A person's entire body chemistry may change. No doubt, during the long period of human development, such momentary disregard for the future must have been of survival value for human groups. Rage, for example, blinds people to their own vulnerability and to a normal concern for their own safety, allowing them to ferociously enter combat against opponents. In today's world of large-scale, complex society, however, rage is almost always dysfunctional. Alcohol consumption sometimes leads to aggressive acts precisely because alcohol reduces self-restraint and the ability to think through the future implications of one's actions.

Sixth, aggressive acts often escalate if the aggressor is allowed to get away with his harmful acts. A perpetrator—whether an individual or a repressive government—can grow more violent unless some intervention is made to stop his aggression. For example, after reviewing the work of experimental social psychologists on bargaining games, Hornstein et al. (1971: 538) conclude that "subjects who are exposed to a non-violent other will consistently exploit the other's non-violence." This creates a dilemma in that on the one hand the victim must respond in order to stop being harmed but on the other hand must not respond so vigorously as to set in motion the escalating and potentially endless cycle of retribution. Clearly, there is a judicious balance between the two, letting the perpetrator know that he has done a wrong, harmful act but keeping a counter harmful act to a minimum.

Seventh, and finally, the structuring of society into collectivities (e.g., corporations, states, government agencies, military units, schools, churches, hospitals, art centers, universities, and thousands of other complex organizations) which, as a sociologist, I regard as the *sine qua non* of many achievements of human civilizations, nonetheless also contributes to the production of evil. It does so through the diffusion of responsibility and the isolation of top decision makers from face-to-face contact with the harmful actions they may foster. The division of labor in large organizations, for example, divides and obscures responsibilities, making it sometimes difficult to know who exactly is responsible for what. Also, the separation of the decision makers from the persons carrying out harmful acts in many organizations allows the blame for wrongful acts to be diluted and shifted to others.

At the other extreme, the people who personally do the harm in organizations are only following orders, and following orders, it must be remembered, is ordinarily a positive value embodying both trust and loyalty (Baumeister, 1997). Also, taking part in an evil act as a member of an organization, such as American soldiers at My Lai in Vietnam or ordinary Germans during the Holocaust, tends to suppress individual and private doubts. Even transient groups such as street crowds contribute to the diffusion of responsibility. Although a bystander who is alone may come to the aid of a victim, the exact same person as part of a large crowd of bystanders may not act.

SOME IMPLICATIONS FOR THE RESTRAINT OF EVIL

Must we simply accept evil as an inevitable product of human nature and an unavoidable cost of organized social life or can we hope to take some positive actions to reduce the number of evil acts in the world? Can we, both as individuals and members of groups, do anything to effectively suppress the escalating cycle of vengeance and counter vengeance?

The answers, of course, are no, we must not accept evil as inevitable and unavoidable. And yes, we can act effectively to suppress acts of vengeance.

It is true that collective solutions at the international level may be implemented only slowly and too late to prevent hundreds of thousands, if not millions, of needless deaths and much suffering in the coming century (Singer and Wildavsky, 1993). We are dealing, after all, with human predispositions and maxims of behavior that come from eons of biological evolution of the human species and from millennia of the social evolution of human groups. Obviously, many human adaptations were successful or we humans would not be here now. But they are retentions of what worked in a past world different from today and even more different from the coming future. Some old solutions, the insights and learning of human experience, may be as useful as ever. Others may be dysfunctional in today's world, such as the continued value placed on high reproductive rates in some parts of the world and the reliance on aggression and the use of force to resolve conflicts. In order to reduce evil, people may have to invent new social mechanisms and ethical systems.

We can hope that we humans can do so. The foundation for such hope is found in the knowledge that evil is, as we have seen, largely the result of the behavior of ordinary people. Thus, we can try to reduce evil acts by focusing our efforts on the average person and the mundane. People can learn to turn away from evil just as they can learn other things. They can learn self-restraint. Remember that no "alien powers are at work in evil, merely human beings responding to the context in which they find themselves and making decisions on their own. This knowledge can empower us to take charge of our lives in realms of evil, just as we do in other realms" (Katz, 1993: 126).

On the level of supraregional and global cooperation, hundreds, if not thousands, of treaties and agreements have been written and ratified, dealing with everything from peace and disarmament to protecting the environment. Also, although they are by no means fully adequate, the many agencies of the United Nations and other international institutions, including nongovernmental organizations, are a promising beginning. They provide a variety of forums for planning action concerning common problems and the resolution of conflicts. One important achievement that these developments share is the fact that people are talking to each other—people of different countries, languages, religions, and cultures—and issues of disagreement are being clarified just as many mutual understandings are being reached.

THREE FUTURIST PRINCIPLES FOR RESTRAINING EVIL

There are at least three major concerns of futures studies that may be of use in reducing evil. They are the principles of foresight, the principles of a universal and inclusive ethic, and a theory of knowledge that emphasizes the uncertainty of knowledge.

First, people can be taught to forecast the future consequences of their actions and, if they do, evil acts may be reduced. But a proviso must be added. People have to be reasonably accurate in foreseeing such consequences. If they have totally unrealistic images of the future consequences of their contemplated actions, then they may harm others simply because of their erroneous forecasts, the way doctors sometimes used to damage their patients by bleeding them under the false belief that such treatment would cure them. Also, if people can foresee no outcomes to their actions that will affect them and people they care about, then they have nothing to evaluate and make judgments about. To make intelligent decisions about how to act, people first need to foresee with some accuracy what will happen as a result of their actions.

Second, to make the right choices and decisions to act, people need not only foresight but also an objective basis for moral judgment that includes a concern for the well-being of other people. They need to be able to assess the consequences of their actions toward others as good or bad within an ethical system that defines every member of the human race as worthy of equal consideration. No matter what they have done, other people ought to be regarded as human beings like yourself.

Although some of our judgmental responses to the world around us may be biologically based—as a baby knows that it is better to be fed and warm than hungry and cold—in most cases the "distinction between good and evil has to be learned and continually reinforced" (Doob, 1978: 120). Existing institutions of socialization—the family, the neighborhood, the school, the church or temple or mosque, etc.—will continue to be important in such learning and reinforcement, although their teachings may have to be enlarged so that the scale of application of morality expands to include everyone, not simply members of their own groups. International organizations and the growing global discourse on ethics that some of them have initiated may have an important role to play in promoting this enlargement of caring.

The physical and social sciences, during the past fifty years or so, have largely abdicated their responsibility for investigating the nature and function of morality. At least in part this has been because of the dominance of the false belief that moral questions have no objective answer. It is time for this dogma to go. The fact is that we do know how to ground morality in reason—in empirical fact and logical analysis. Moreover, futurists, given their concerns about preferable futures, are playing a role in spurring an interest in examining value judgments objectively. Many universal and near-universal human values, for example, can be shown to have their origins in the biological-psychological nature of human beings, in the preconditions of social life, or in the human interaction with the physical environment. Also, there are methods of analysis, such as Keekok Lee's (1985) epistemic implication, that allow objective testing of moral propositions by examining the reasons given to justify them. I discuss this at length elsewhere (Bell, 1997, Vol. 2) and suggest some modifications in Lee's method to adapt it to a future-oriented, decision-making perspective, so I won't elaborate on it here.

Before leaving the topic of moral judgment, a final word needs to be said about the obligations of bystanders. In today's globalizing society, where electronic communications link hundreds of millions of people from distant parts of the Earth into information-sharing networks, more and more of us are becoming bystanders, watching as perpetrators harm their victims in this or that distant place. It is, thus, increasingly important that the international community expand its role to try to prevent local violence and cruelty, because inaction of bystanders when faced with scenes of organized violence can imply moral approval.

Third, in addition to foresight and an inclusive morality, people, ought to be skeptical about their own beliefs. As Confucius taught us, people should tell themselves the truth. That is not always an easy thing to do. It requires that they question their own convictions. Of course, science in general rests upon such skepticism, but, as we all know, positivistic science as carried out by imperfect human beings has sometimes been arrogant and itself a purveyor of unwarranted certitude.

Elsewhere (Bell, 1997, Vol. 1), I have proposed a post-Kuhnian theory of knowledge, known as critical realism, that emphasizes the uncertainty and corrigibility of knowledge and the importance of discourse in arriving at warranted assertions. Critical realists give reasons for their beliefs and they make serious efforts to refute them. Following Karl Popper's fallibilism, they accept beliefs as warranted only if the evidence supporting them remains unrefuted and they rely on public and open examination of the evidence (Musgrave, 1993). Of course, this means that only serious, naturalistic evidence is admitted. "God told me" cannot be refuted or confirmed. Thus, it cannot be offered as evidence in critical realism.

Critical realists are dedicated to the principle that they really do want to know that they are wrong if what they believe is, indeed, wrong. Moreover, they believe that knowledge is conjectural and they allow for the possibility that it may turn out to be false. Thus, they avoid absolutist claims.

Can we teach people the principles of critical realism and encourage them to apply them to their life's circumstances and decisions? If we can, then we can contribute to the reduction of evil in the world. Critical realism encourages people to hold their own beliefs tentatively and contingently. Most important, it encourages them to question their own beliefs and actions, to ask, for example, "Am I really certain that what I believe is true?" When people are dealing with others, for example, it leads them to question whether they or members of their group themselves are guilty of harmful acts against others. Critical realism reminds you that you may be in the wrong.

Restraining evil in ourselves may require something more than foresight, an inclusive ethic, and critical realism. It may also require understanding and empathy for our opponents, trying to see the situation from their point of view and giving them the benefit of the doubt (Pybus, 1991). We need some feeling for the plight of others, some understanding of the full, human consequences of others' joy or suffering that follows from our acts. For all of us to try to understand others is civil, decent, and fair. It may also redound to our own benefit. At least from the limited evidence of laboratory studies, there is reason to believe that nice strategies win out over mean strategies in producing cooperation in others and that nicer strategies do even better (Axelrod, 1984).

Finally, although you ought to remember the past, be prepared to forgive those who have harmed you. Do not hold grudges and do not seek revenge. For, as Archbishop Desmond Tutu (1999) has said, focusing on future goods rather than past wrongs can help break the vicious circle of retribution and counter-retribution. In his account of the Truth and Reconciliation Commission in South Africa, he shows how South Africans, by embracing forgiveness and focusing on a desirable future, have given themselves a chance to break the vicious circle of mutual violence. Although it may be too early to tell if it will be successful or not, it is a noble experiment soundly based on our present knowledge of how to create a desirable future. The alternative would have South Africa already lying in ashes.

CONCLUSION

Let me conclude by saying that I consider myself to be a scientist. I have spent much of my career doing empirical social research on social change in American cities and in the new states of the Caribbean. Although I believe that knowledge is conjectural, I also believe that some things are true and some things are false and that we can often determine which is which. Although there is a place in science for creativity, imagination, intuition, and insight, in the end we can rely only on those truth propositions that are testable and that have survived efforts to falsify them. Within the limits of the human senses and their application to the realities of the natural and social worlds, I believe that warranted assertibility is possible. Moreover, I believe that we each have but one life to live in this one natural world.

As a futurist, I believed for a long time that, except for the passing moment of the present, all human life is composed only of memory and anticipation. Although I still think that there is much truth in that contention, it is not complete. Except for images of the future, it fails to sufficiently emphasize the human ability to create imaginary worlds—sometimes fantastic, irrational, and counter-factual worlds that never did and never will exist. Even the most normal people can imagine these fantasy worlds (whether supernatural, science fiction, political pseudo-realistic, or whatever). Such daydreams and illusions have a kind of reality for some people, are sometimes organized as stories and shared with others, provide frames of reference that people use to make sense of their lives, and sometimes influence the way they behave. Such illusions mix with, and sometimes replace, memories of actual past events just as they insinuate themselves and mingle with real-world anticipations, hopes and fears.

One of the most universal of such beliefs is the myth of pure evil. It includes the beliefs that most of the evil in the world is committed by malevolent monsters or demented individuals who are intent upon doing evil things to their innocent victims largely for the pleasure of having power and creating suffering. This myth itself is part of a larger cluster of millennial beliefs about the existence of a supernatural world, an eternal struggle of good and evil, the threat of social chaos, a coming apocalyptic upheaval in which good will triumph over evil, and, finally, an aftermath in which evildoers will be punished and the righteous will be redeemed. Although these beliefs are millennia-old, they continue to exist, in one form or another and in both sacred and secular versions, in nearly every country of the world.

These millennial beliefs are not benign. Despite the many positive values that they may promote through religious and political teachings—from justice to generosity and from industriousness to honesty—they tend to create true believers whose absolutism in the rightness of their beliefs leads them to clash with people who have different views. On the one hand, millennial beliefs blind people to the fact that ordinary people, including themselves, commit most of the evil acts of the world. On the other hand, they foster the demonization of other people, encouraging retaliation and an escalation of harm between people. Millennial views allow plain and decent people to feel justified in carrying out the most hideous crimes against others whom they see as evil, subhuman monsters.

Given the long history and present spread of such millennial beliefs, the task confronting anyone who tries to intervene and to break the cycle of evil seems overwhelming. But it may not be impossible. We can take heart from the knowledge that evil is banal. In fact, no alien powers are at work, only ordinary people carrying out largely innocuous tasks. Ordinary people can learn that the idea of pure evil is a myth. They can learn self-restraint and not to harm others. They can learn empathy and fairness. Although the lessons may have to be taught from an early age and continually reinforced, people can learn to exercise foresight, to care for the freedom and well-being of all members of the human species, and to be skeptical about their own beliefs, just as they can learn anything else.

Also, consider that each of us is the world—even if only some small slice of it—for those people with whom we share our lives, from family members, friends, neighbors, and co-workers to others with whom we have but fleeting contact. Although we cannot control the actions of nations and multinational corporations or the momentous events of history, we can control ourselves. Sometimes, it takes courage to do so, because we may have to stand against the views of our own groups. But it can be done. Thus, it is within our power to create a new future of self-restraint, empathy, understanding, and generosity for each person with whom we are interacting. Within the narrow band of the lives of others that we constitute, each of us can create the good society that we hope will become the future. Such behavior on our part is not mere selfless altruism, because what goes around comes around. As we act, we create the world, not only for others but also for ourselves.

[Author's Note: This paper is a revision of an article that was first published in the *Journal of Futures Studies*, Vol. 5, No, 2 (2000), 1-20 (Tamkang University, Taiwan). It appears here with the kind permission of the editors of *JFS*.]

REFERENCES

Arendt, H. *Eichmann in Jerusalem: A Report on the Banality of Evil* (New York: Penguin Books, 1964).

Axelrod, R. *The Evolution of Cooperation* (New York: Basic Books, 1984).

Baumeister, R.F. *Evil: Inside Human Cruelty and Violence* (New York: W.H. Freeman and Company, 1997).

Baumeister, R.F. *Meanings of Life* (New York: The Guilford Press, 1991).

Bell, W. "Images of the Future for Our Time," *Transactions* 56 (New Haven, CT: The Connecticut Academy of Arts and Sciences, 1999), 45-89.

Bell, W. *Foundations of Futures Studies*. Two volumes (New Brunswick, NJ: Transaction Publishers, 1997).

Boyer, P. *When Time Shall Be No More: Prophecy Belief in Modern American Culture* (Cambridge, MA: The Belknap Press of Harvard University Press, 1995; 1992).

Doob, L.W. *Panorama of Evil: Insights from the Behavioral Sciences* (Westport, CT: Greenwood Press, 1978).

Habermas, J. *The Philosophical Discourse of Modernity: Twelve Lectures* (Cambridge, MA: MIT Press, 1987).

Harrison, A.A., and S.J. Dick. "Contact: Long-Term Implications for Humanity," ed. A. Tough, *When SETI Succeeds: The Impact of High-Information Contact* (Bellevue, WA: Foundation For the Future, 2000).

Hornstein, H.A., B.B. Bunker, W.W. Burke, M. Gindes, and R.J. Lewicki, eds. *Social Intervention: A Behavioral Science Approach* (New York: Free Press, 1971).

Katz, F.E. *Ordinary People and Extraordinary Evil* (Albany, NY: State University of New York Press, 1993).

Lee, K. *A New Basis for Moral Philosophy* (London: Routledge & Kegan Paul, 1985).

Musgrave, A. *Common Sense, Science and Scepticism* (Cambridge: Cambridge University Press, 1993).

Osgood, C.E., W.H. May, and M.S. Miron. *Cross-Cultural Universals of Affective Meaning* (Urbana, IL: University of Illinois Press, 1975).

Pybus, E. *Human Goodness: Generosity and Courage* (Hertfordshire, UK: Harvester Wheatsheaf, 1991).

Rummel, R.J. "Democracy, Power, Genocide, and Mass Murder," *The Journal of Conflict Resolution*, Vol. 39, No. 1 (1995), 3-25.

Singer, M., and A. Wildavsky. *The Real World Order: Zones of Peace/Zones of Turmoil* (Chatham, NJ: Chatham, 1993).

Thompson, D. *The End of Time: Faith and Fear in the Shadow of the Millennium* (Hanover, NH: University Press of New England, 1998, 1996).

Toffler, A. *Future Shock* (New York: Random House, 1970).

Tutu, D.M. *No Future without Forgiveness* (New York: Doubleday, 1999).

COGNITIVE ENHANCEMENT AND COGNITIVE LIBERTY: COMMENTS TO THE PRESIDENT'S COUNCIL ON BIOETHICS

by

Wrye Sententia

[Author's Note: The President's Council on Bioethics was created by executive order (No. 13237) in November 2001 for the purpose of advising the president on bioethical issues that may emerge as a consequence of progress in biomedical science and technology. The Council is charged with keeping the president and the nation apprised of new developments, and providing a forum for discussion and evaluation of these profound issues. Beginning in the year 2002, 17 leading scientists, doctors, ethicists, social scientists, lawyers, and theologians named by President George W. Bush to serve on this Council, began a series of discussions in Washington, D.C. that continues today (visit: www.bioethics.gov/).]

When a conservative creationist meets a radical transhumanist, or a neuroscientist talks to a spiritual philosopher about enhancing cognition, it is more than likely that their ideas of what is possible, or even desirable, will be at polarized odds. Biotechnologies have received widespread media attention and spawned heated interest in their perceived social implications. Now, with the rapidly expanding purview of neuroscience and a growing array of technologies capable of affecting or monitoring cognition, the emerging field of neuroethics is calling for a consideration of the social and ethical implications of neuroscientific discoveries and trends.

To negotiate the complex ethical issues at stake in new and emerging technologies for improving human cognition, we need to overcome political, disciplinary, and religious sectarianism. Yet, the complexity of our social fabric, with its diversity of interests, identities, and cultures, conspires to make any assignation of transcendent value difficult, particularly when, as is the case with bio- or neuroethics, the issues may turn upon deeply rooted religious, political, or scientific world views. The complexity of many of these issues, and in particular those involving brain enhancement and monitoring, are not easily resolvable.

We need analytical models that will protect values of personhood at the heart of a functional democracy—values that will allow, as much as possible, for individual decision making, despite differences of opinion on the implications of transformations in our understanding and ability to control, monitor and manipulate cognitive processes. By addressing cognitive enhancement from those individual rights embedded in our democratic constitution, the legal and ethical notion of "cognitive liberty" provides a powerful tool for

Wrye Sententia *is co-director of the Center for Cognitive Liberty & Ethics (CCLE) in Davis, California. She may be contacted at wrye@cognitiveliberty.org.*

assessing and encouraging developments in cognitive enhancement.

Cognitive liberty is a term that updates notions of "freedom of thought" for the 21st century by taking into account the power we now have, and increasingly will have, to monitor and manipulate cognitive function. Cognitive liberty is every person's fundamental right to think independently, to use the full spectrum of his or her mind, and to have autonomy over his or her own brain chemistry. Cognitive liberty concerns the ethics and legality of safeguarding one's own thought processes, and by necessity, one's electrochemical brain states.

Potential applications in areas of cognitive enhancement can move forward by safeguarding individual rights of mind, and cognitive liberty provides a starting point for negotiating the needs and demands of diversely opinioned constituencies. As the central organ concerned with human decision making, the brain and its higher cognitive processes demand unique ethical consideration. In light of a growing body of information about brain function, and in anticipation of even greater precision in understanding and manipulating higher cognitive processes, it is incumbent upon us as a society to anticipate individual rights in relation to these developments. Only by protecting our very ability to think as individuals can we hope to reconcile our widely diverse viewpoints and, through the democratic process, parse out the thorny ethics of a spectrum of social issues that will face us as we negotiate the future.

As exciting advances in bioscience, neuroscience, neurotechnology and nanotechnology further raise ethical issues concerning manipulation of the human body and brain, the question of whose ethics will be adopted will become increasingly strained. We must collectively come to terms with the advantages of human enhancement, while staying off applications that are potentially destructive of democratic values.

In October 2002, I presented the following comments to the President's Council on Bioethics in Washington, D.C. With them, I raised the issue of cognitive liberty and individual choice in relation to drugs and technologies of brain enhancement, a topic then under scrutiny by the Council. The written comments I provided the Council follow:

- The Center for Cognitive Liberty & Ethics (CCLE) is a non-profit education, law, and policy center working in the public interest to foster cognitive liberty. The CCLE defines cognitive liberty as the right of each individual to think independently and autonomously, to use the full spectrum of his or her mind, and to engage in multiple modes of thought. The CCLE works to protect the full potential of the human intellect.

- The CCLE's comments before this Council center on those pharmacological and technological interventions that directly affect the mind, and consequently implicate cognitive liberty. The CCLE is concerned with the ethics of treating or manipulating the mind, or as some are now calling it, "neuroethics." Our focus is on those uses of drugs or other technologies and their attendant social policies that encroach upon individual rights to cognitive liberty and its logical corollary, cognitive autonomy—two faces of the same coin.

Cognitive liberty is an essential human right. The United Nations' Universal Declaration of Human Rights and the US Constitution's Bill of Rights both support a basic human right to cognitive liberty, or freedom of thought.[1] Yet "freedom" is the sort of preeminent democratic value that is often the subject of political hair-splicing and posturing. The complexity of our social fabric (with its diversity of interests, identities, and cultures) conspires to make any assignation of transcendent value difficult, particularly when, as is the case with bio- or neuroethics, the issues span such elementary, yet increasingly malleable values as individual and collective quality of life. The CCLE recognizes, as does this Council, that the complexity of many of the issues involving brain enhancement are not easily resolvable. However, we hope that by interjecting the principle of cognitive liberty into the discussion, the Council will find useful distinctions in drafting its recommendations.

To the CCLE and our supporters, the question of mind enhancement is fundamentally a question of cognitive self-determination interwoven with an ethics of reciprocal autonomy. While etymologically, autonomy means "establishing one's own laws," reciprocal autonomy is interactive. Reciprocal autonomy is not a question of arbitrary legislation, created for oneself, but rather of laws that permit, whenever possible, successful interaction with others based on respect and tolerance for each other's core values and freedoms. As Dr. J.F. Malherbe, professor of social work at the Université du Québec at Montréal, and author of *The Contribution of Ethics in Defining Guiding Principles for a Public Drug Policy*, has written, "Every unjustified restriction, which adds to the already heavy burden of civilized individuals, can only increase their sense of being the object of some form of totalitarianism, rather than the subject of their own destiny."[2]

Decisions about as intimate a freedom as cognitive liberty should be allocated to the individual rather than the government. The CCLE works from the premise that the role of the state, criminal law, science and ethics, should be guided by principles that maximize opportunities for each individual to self-actualize. Public policy decisions should be framed by principles of legal liberalism, rather than moralism, or paternalism. This is not to say that morals or safety precautions have no place in determining appropriate uses of drugs or other technologies, but that the role of the state should not be to determine what is or isn't moral, what are or are not acceptable personal risks. In our opinion, public policy for psychotropic drugs and/or brain technologies should stem from our democratic government's responsibility for preserving individual autonomy and choice to the maximum extent possible.

While neuroethical issues are complex and often deeply philosophical, the CCLE maintains that a solid starting point for practical discussion and analysis begins with two fundamental recognitions that may seem axiomatic:

• As long as their behavior doesn't endanger others, individuals should not be compelled against their will to use technologies that directly interact with the brain, or be forced to take certain psychoactive drugs.

• As long as they do not subsequently engage in behavior that harms others, individuals should not be prohibited from, or criminalized for, using new mind-enhancing drugs and technologies.

Simply put, the right and freedom to control one's own consciousness and electrochemical thought processes, is the necessary substrate for virtually every other freedom.

As long as their behavior doesn't endanger others, individuals should not be compelled against their will to use technologies that interact with the brain, or be forced to take certain drugs.

The development of psychopharmaceuticals and electronic technologies in use now, or, on the cusp of interfacing directly with brain function, raises numerous cognitive liberty concerns. The individual, not corporate or government interests, should have sole jurisdiction over the control and/or modulation of his or her brain states and mental processes.[3] While the development of psychopharmaceuticals can be applauded for their potential to aid millions of suffering Americans who *voluntarily* take them, the application of such drugs, in mandatory government contexts, raises the chillingly dark prospect of the government *forcibly* administering these new drugs to chemically alter the way that certain people think. Likewise, while electronic technologies that interface with the brain have positive applications, issues of mental privacy and coercion come into play when corporate or government policies mandate use.

One pressing concern of the CCLE is that of government-mandated drugging using psychotropic drugs.[4] At least two instances in the recent news suggest that this may be something that the US government considers to be within the purview of its power. The first concerns a proposal discussed by the FBI as a potential measure to administer mind-altering drugs to terrorist detainees (not those convicted of terrorism, merely suspect detainees) in order to elicit information. Fortunately, torture—which includes the forced use of mind-altering drugs—is banned by international conventions to which the US is a party, and therefore is not yet an option within the United States (although there was some talk of deporting the suspects to countries where mind-drugging torture would be allowed, an action which also violates US signatory agreements).[5]

The second instance concerns a recent federal court case currently being considered by the US Supreme Court.[6] In this case, the US government is seeking to forcibly inject a St. Louis dentist, Dr. Charles Sell, with a mind-altering drug against his will for the purpose of making him "competent" to stand trial on fraud charges. The CCLE is an *amicus curiae* party to this case in support of Dr. Sell. While the government may control the behavior of those in custody of the state, the Sell case concerns an explicitly declared non-dangerous pre-trial detainee and a government effort to chemically alter his thinking process. In the context of the ever-increasing ability to pharmacologically intervene in the minds of Americans, the Dr. Sell case presents the Supreme Court with the timely and extremely important opportunity to articulate some unequivocal rules that respect freedom of thought and cognitive liberty.

The state cannot, consistent with the First Amendment of the Constitution, forcibly manipulate the *mental states* of individuals. Pre-emptive control of thoughts by the government via drugs or technologies should be strictly prohibited. The US Joint Non-Lethal Weapons Directorate (JNLWD) is reportedly pursuing the development of neurochemical weapons aimed at combatting unruly mental states that may precede disruptive behaviors. In an October 2000 report prepared for the JNLWD by the Institute for Emerging Defense Technologies (a subunit of the Applied Research Laboratory at Pennsylvania State University), research was undertaken to examine the viability of using psychopharmaceutical agents, or "calmatives," as "non-lethal techniques" of military and civil intervention; listing, among other possible applications, crowd control.[7] Different environments, the report explains, require tailored means of drug administration: "In many cases the choice of administration route, whether application to drinking water, topical administration to the skin, an aerosol spray inhalation route, or a drug-filled rubber bullet, among others, will depend on the environment."[8] Examples of environments include "a group of hungry refugees that are excited over the distribution of food and unwilling to wait patiently," "a prison setting," an "agitated population," and "hostage situations."[9]

As with emergent drugs, a number of electronic technologies that interact with the brain could promise benefit or peril. Some applications of neurotechnologies, while still in their infancy, are already being used to monitor thought processes for control measures. While something like transcranial magnetic stimulation (technology which uses noninvasive magnets placed around the brain to alter electronic impulses, and thereby enhance mood) may be valuable as a form of depression therapy, the prospect of its perfected or future application to alter "improper" or dissident thinking is daunting.[10] The Human Brain Project, an internationally orchestrated research project sponsored by the National Institute of Mental Health, is seeking to, among other things, provide a blueprint of so-called "normal" brain activity.[11] From brain scanning to brain implants, these kinds of technologies draw attention to questions of mental privacy and should alert us to the real need for protections of mental autonomy.

Scientists are now using Functional Magnetic Resonance Imaging (FMRI), a brain imaging technique, to detect differences in brain blood flow activity between intentionally deceptive and truthful statements.[12] Similarly, what is being called "Brain Fingerprinting" (a method currently debated in terms of its efficacy) uses electro-encephalographic (EEG) recordings of a subject's brain waves in relation to his or her memory of events as an improved polygraph, which claims to distinguish a person's "guilty" thoughts. Proponents of "Brain Fingerprinting" have been working on corporate and government applications, including airport brain-scan security checks.[13]

These examples all underscore the need to set bright line rules that protect individuals from being compelled or unwittingly subjected to mind-changing drugs or technologies. Compelled use of (legal or illegal) psychotropic drugs or technologies should be considered abusive, and can be strictly discouraged by drafting policies that respect the integrity of an individual's fundamental right to cognitive liberty.

As long as they do not subsequently engage in behavior that harms others, individuals should not be prohibited from, or criminal-ized for, using new mind-enhancing drugs and technologies.

For millennia, humans have used various plants and psychoactive substances to occasion states of mind conducive to personal and interpersonal healing, spiritual or religious states, philosophical exploration, or creativity boosting.[14] Some researchers and scholars have concluded that the occasioning of alternative states of con-sciousness is nothing less than a fundamental human drive, akin to the sexual drive or the drive to sustain life.[15] William James (1842-1910), one of America's preeminent philosophical thinkers on the nature of consciousness, experimented with psychoactive drugs in his pursuit of knowledge, and gave philosophical credence to the role of alternative states of consciousness in evolving conceptions of the self and society.[16]

This touches on a thorny issue raised by Dr. Krauthammer in the Council's inaugural meeting on the topic of "Enhancement." Dr. Krauthammer pointed out the difficulty in distinguishing "enhance-ment" aided by new legal psychopharmaceuticals from the decades-long debates over "illicit" substances in the war on drugs.[17] Distin-guishing "recreational" use from mind-enhancement purposes appears as fraught as attempts to distinguish therapeutic uses from enhancement—one person's mental recreation is another's consciousness tool for self-improvement. Under a liberal democracy, we must recognize that what goes on inside a person's head is entitled to privacy and autonomy. We should police dangerous conduct, not different thoughts. We must also not confuse a possibility of personal risk with social harm. Indeed, the CCLE would assert that making people criminals simply for using a particular psychoactive drug violates the fundamental right to cognitive liberty, oversteps the government's legitimate powers, and, further, has been ineffective in eradicating illicit drug use, while eroding citizens' confidence in government information about drugs.[18]

Despite the lessons that should have been learned after the failure of alcohol prohibition, the US government is currently leading an international war on drugs, budgeting in 2002 roughly $19 billion to police the criminal laws aimed at prohibiting the use of illegal drugs. Inasmuch as this is a real and present instance of government policy with respect to mind-altering drugs, the CCLE believes it presents a glaring example of a failed policy—one that this Council should guard against repeating, or using as precedent, for crafting future policies with respect to mind enhancement.

CCLE RECOMMENDATIONS

The CCLE suggests that a declarative statement of the individual's right to self-determination over his or her mental states incorporated in the language of national policy directives would deter abuses of power while still respecting individual choice.

Discrimination on the basis of what psychotropic drugs or technologies one does, or does not use should be strictly prohibited. The wording of existing discrimination policies could be adapted to incorporate a cognitive liberty clause, protecting against surreptitious technological or pharmaceutical interventions.

Additionally, "drug testing" as an employment screening policy for the purposes of assessing one's mental state, rather than one's performance, should be curtailed.

Again, the CCLE maintains that a solid starting point for practical discussion and analysis begins with these two fundamental recognitions:

1. As long as their behavior doesn't endanger others, individuals should not be compelled against their will to use technologies that directly interact with the brain, or be forced to take certain drugs.

2. As long as they do not subsequently engage in behavior that harms others, individuals should not be prohibited from, or criminalized for, using new mind-enhancing drugs and technologies.

The CCLE respectfully urges that any regulatory recommendations arrived at by the Council take these two principles as bright-line rules.

NOTES

1. UN Universal Declaration of Human Rights, Article 18: "Everyone has the right to freedom of thought ..."; *Abood v. Detroit Board of Education*, 431 US 209 (1977) ["[A]t the heart of the First Amendment, is the notion that an individual should be free to believe as he will, and that in a free society one's beliefs should be shaped by his mind and his conscience rather than coerced by the State ..."]; *Palko v. Connecticut*, 302 US 319, 326-327 (1937) ["... freedom of thought ... one may say ... is the matrix, the indispensable condition of nearly every other form of freedom. With rare aberrations a pervasive recognition of that truth can be traced in our history, political and legal."]

2. Ch. 3, *Canadian Senate's Special Committee on Illegal Drugs*, "Final Report: Cannabis: Our Position For a Canadian Public Policy" (September 2002). Report summary available online at: www.cognitiveliberty.org/pdf/Canadian_MJ_Rpt.pdf.

3. The sale of Prozac™ and similar antidepressant drugs is currently one of the most profitable segments of the pharmaceutical drug industry. According to IMS Health, a 50-year-old company specializing in pharmaceutical market intelligence and analyses, "antidepressants, the #3-ranked therapy class worldwide, experienced 18% sales growth in 2000, to $13.4 billion or 4.2% of all audited global pharmaceutical sales." (IMS Health, *Antidepressants*, online at: www.ims health.com/public/structure/navcontent/1,3272,1034-1034-0,00.html) Sales of "antipsychotic" drugs are currently the eighth largest therapy class of drugs with worldwide sales of $6 billion in the year 2000, a 22% increase in sales over the previous year. (See IMS Health, *Antipsychotics*, a summary of which is available online at: www.ims health.com/public/structure/navcontent/1,3272,1035-1035-0,00.html.) A report published by the Lewin Group in January 2000 found that in 1998 antidepressants and antipsychotics accounted for 9% of Medicaid prescriptions. The same report found that within the Medicaid program alone, "Antidepressant prescriptions totaled 19 million in 1998 ... [and] [a]ntipsychotic prescriptions totaled 11 million in 1998." (Lewin Group, Access and Utilization of New Antidepressant and Antipsychotic Medications, January 2000, prepared under contract for the Office of Health Policy, Office of the Assistant Secretary for Planning and Evaluation, and The National Institute for Mental Health, Department of Health and Health Services. Available online at: aspe.hhs.gov/health/reports/Psychmed access/.) According to Datamonitor, "Antidepressants have become

a key focus for pharmaceutical manufacturers due to the huge growth in the market instigated by the launch of Prozac™ in the 1980s. Due to their expansion into new markets away from depression, the therapy class is now valued at $14 billion and is set to continue expanding despite the upcoming patent loss of numerous key products." Datamonitor, Market Dynamics 2001: Antidepressants, Report-DMHC1725 (December 21, 2001). Datamonitor forecasts that the demand for antidepressants will continue to grow and estimates the market value to reach $18.3 billion by 2008. (Ibid.)

4. The former Soviet Union had no First Amendment equivalent. It was not uncommon for prison psychiatrists to forcibly drug political dissidents after labeling them "mentally ill." See Sidney Bloch and Peter Reddaway, *Psychiatric Terror: How Soviet Psychiatry Is Used to Suppress Dissent* (1977); Clarity, "A Freed Dissident Says Soviet Doctors Sought to Break His Political Beliefs," *The New York Times* (February 4, 1976), A1, 8.

5. Walter Pincus, "Silence of 4 Terror Probe Suspects Poses Dilemma," *Washington Post*, October 21, 2001. For CCLE commentary and resources, see: "Drugging or Torture of 9-11 Suspects Breaks Constitution, Law, and Treaties," www.cognitiveliberty.org/news/narcointerrogation1.htm.

6. *United States v. Sell* 282 F.3d560 (2002), US Supreme Court, No. 02-5664. Oral arguments in the case began March 3, 2003. *Amicus Curiae* brief online at: www.cognitiveliberty.org/dll/sell_index.htm.

7. Calmatives are defined in this report as "compounds known to depress or inhibit the function of the central nervous system," with an emphasis on those drugs that "can be tailored to be highly selective and specific for known receptor (protein) targets in the nervous system with unique profiles of biological effects on consciousness, motor activity and psychiatric impact." Dr. Joan M. Lakoski, Dr. W. Bosseau Murray, Dr. John M. Kenny, "The Advantages and Limitations of Calmatives for Use as a Non-Lethal Technique," University of Pennsylvania (October 3, 2000), p. 2, 3. Online at: www.sunshine-project.org.

8. Ibid.

9. Ibid., p. 10.

10. "Magnets That Move Moods," *Newsweek* (June 24, 2002), 57.

11. Human Brain Project, online at: www.nimh.nih.gov/neuroinformatics/index.cfm. For an informative article on the Human Brain Project, see Jennifer Kahn's "Let's Make Your Head Interactive," *Wired* (9.08 August 2001), 106-115. Online at: www.wired.com/wired/archive/9.08/brain.html.

12. See briefing paper from Society for Neuroscience on Brain Wave Deception Research 2001; web.sfn.org/content/Publications/Brain Waves/PastIssues/2002spring/index.html.

13. On proponents pushing to use this technique as anti-terrorist screening device, see: Lawrence Farwell, "Brain Fingerprinting as Counter-Terrorist System." www.brainwavescience.com/counter-terrorism; Steve Kirsch, "Identifying Terrorists Using Brain Finger-printing," www.skirsch.com/politics/plane/ultimate.htm. For two critiques of Brain Fingerprinting, see: Wrye Sententia, "Brain Fingerprinting: Databodies to Databrains," *Journal of Cognitive Liberties*, Vol. II, No. 3, 31-46 (online at: www.cognitiveliberty.org/6jcl /6JCL31.htm); US General Accounting Office Report (October 2001), "Federal Agency Views on the Potential Application of 'Brain Fingerprinting'" (online at: www.cognitiveliberty.org/issues/mental_surveillance.htm#Reports).

14. P.T. Furst, *Hallucinogens and Culture* (Novato, CA: Chandler and Sharp, 1976); R.E. Shultes and A. Hofmann, *Plants of the Gods: Origins of Hallucinogenic Use* (New York: McGraw-Hill, 1979).

15. Ronald K. Siegel, *Intoxication: Life in Pursuit of Artificial Paradise* (New York: Dutton, 1989).

16. Dimitri Tymoczko, "William James the Nitrous Oxide Philoso-pher," *The Atlantic Monthly* (May 1996; Vol. 277, No. 5), 93-101. Online at: www.theatlantic.com/issues/96may/nitrous/nitrous.htm. Additional references and resources available at: www.cognitiveliber ty.org/proj_willjames.html.

17. "But fundamentally, I am [sic] yet to see how our debate about enhancement and all the issues that we have raised differ from the debate that people have about whether or not people ought to be able to use stuff that makes them feel better, and whether that should be legal or not." Charles Krauthammer, M.D., in President's Council on Bioethics, Session 5: Enhancement 1: Therapy vs. Enhancement (April 26, 2002); Transcript available online at: www.bioethics.gov/april26full.html#five.

18. According to the US government's 2001 National Household Survey on Drug Abuse, 15.9 million Americans age 12 and older used an illicit drug in the month immediately prior to the survey interview. This represents an estimated 7.1 percent of the population in 2001, compared to an estimated 6.3 percent the previous year. Additionally, the Survey found that 1.9 million persons used Ecstasy (MDMA) for the first time last year, and that an estimated 8.1 million persons have tried MDMA at least once in their lifetime. In other findings the Household Survey found that: 1.3 million (0.6 percent) of the population aged 12 or older were current users of "hallu-cinogens," meaning that they had used LSD, PCP, peyote, mescaline,

mushrooms, or MDMA (Ecstasy) during the month prior to the interview. Marijuana remains the most commonly used illicit drug. Most drug users were employed. Of the 13.4 million illicit drug users aged 18 or older in 2001, 10.2 million (76.4 percent) were employed either full or part time. An estimated 66.5 million Americans 12 years or older reported current use of a tobacco product in 2001. This number represents 29.5 percent of the population. Almost half of Americans aged 12 or older reported being current drinkers of alcohol in the 2001 survey (48.3 percent). This translates to an estimated 109 million people. (Substance Abuse and Mental Health Services Administration, 2002). *Results from the 2001 National Household Survey on Drug Abuse: Summary of National Findings* (Office of Applied Studies, NHSDA Series H-17, DHHS Publication No. SMA 02-3758, Rockville, MD.) Entire report available online at: www. samhsa.gov/oas/nhsda.htm#NHSDAinfo.

ON THE HORIZON

NATIONAL GOVERNMENTS ARE MOVING INTO A NEW STAGE IN ELECTRONIC GOVERNMENT: HOW FAST WILL THEY EVOLVE?

by

Francis A. McDonough

WHY DO WE WANT TO KNOW WHAT THEY ARE DOING IN OTHER GOVERNMENTS?

As government information managers, we often know only the system for which we are responsible. We plan and make decisions and choose directions based on many inputs, including past experience, perspectives from other government-wide officials, conferences, and media reports. But if we have the opportunity to learn about the experiences of colleagues in other national governments, we can confirm our decisions and obtain ideas that we might not have had otherwise.

For these reasons, I have been active internationally for 15 years; and, in recent years, I have analyzed country reports to compare and contrast directions and trends in some two dozen nations.

In all developed countries there is good progress in e-Gov. Yet, there are barriers. Officials with government-wide responsibilities are aware that e-Gov is new. There are no models of success to reference and to copy. Government-wide e-Gov leaders do not show it but they have the occasional uncertainty. Normal, unspoken questions include the following:

Are we making the right decisions? Are we spending resources on the proper priorities? If we stay on this road for 10 more years, will there be success at the end of the road? Answers to these questions are not easy to find. One way to find answers is to study the results in other national governments.

The majority of the information in this report is based on detailed analyses of the ICA[1] country reports provided at the most recent annual conference. This was held in October 2002 in Singapore at the invitation of the national government. The opportunity to meet with delegates of 26 nations in open and frank discussions is a special event regretfully open to the few. The insights obtained allow one to find answers to the following questions and to have confidence in the use one is making of scarce resources.

Are we doing the same things in e-Gov as other national governments? Have others solved problems and eliminated barriers that we are still dealing with? Should our government be highly rated as an advanced electronic government? How do we compare? What new issues are surfacing as e-Gov progresses in national governments? Is the public rushing to accept the online e-Gov services offered by

Francis A. McDonough *heads the Office of Intergovernmental Solutions in the General Services Administration, Washington, D.C. He may be contacted at* frank.mcdonough@gsa.gov.

governments?

There are many questions about e-Gov because it is slowly revealing itself to us. And, with the greater understanding that derives from the experiences of other national governments, we develop still further respect for the possibilities as well as the complexities.

ELECTRONIC GOVERNMENT SINCE 1987

E-Government, or e-Gov as it is most often called, is slowly revealing itself to the world. We understand it better today than last year and much better than we did several years ago.

Fifteen years have passed since member nations first discussed providing better service to the citizens at an ICA conference in Estoril, Portugal. Eleven years have passed since Internet browser capability became available, and it was used almost immediately to provide information to the public. Even in the early years, however, Internet was envisioned as a tool that would, one day, provide integrated transactions and better service to the citizens.

Nine years have passed since we invented the term "electronic government," now known as "e-Gov." Much has been accomplished in building portals, linking communities of interest such as students and seniors, and providing online information and forms. Yet, as we begin to grow familiar with e-Gov in its emerging big picture, we have a sense that we have been doing the easy work in electronic government. There is now recognition that the low hanging fruit has been picked.

ELECTRONIC GOVERNMENT TODAY

As we enter 2003, Canada is rated number one in the world in the delivery of electronic services to citizens by Accenture and Booz Allen. Sweden and the United States are close behind in these surveys. Finland's public procurement company, Hansel, is rated as the most advanced by the European Union for its electronic end-to-end procurement system. Every country is building e-Gov systems. Noteworthy is Singapore, which has 1,600 e-services available electronically with 1,300 at the "interact and transact" levels. Singapore is quick to point out that citizen "takeup" takes time, often several years. In some cases, incentives are required to encourage initial use of online services by the public.

Paying taxes, obtaining licenses and permits, applying for benefits and loans are online services that are already available to the public in many ICA member countries. The next phase of e-Gov will provide integrated services to the public. One study in a leading country concluded that 516 programs work fairly independently in environmental protection activities. In advanced e-Gov, these initiatives would be integrated to allow the public to obtain a single response to an inquiry instead of making and receiving separate responses to dozens of inquiries to each relevant program.

ICA nations have somewhat different e-Gov goals. Some invest in e-Gov to connect their nation. Others emphasize economic development; and there are many other diverse goals as well. What is important, however, is that most nations are doing similar things and taking the same road even though their objectives differ at the highest level.

There are impressive programs in ICA member nations. Canada, especially, is receiving broad recognition for its work in delivering services to the public. Others are close behind. Nations can and do learn from each other and adopt useful practices to leverage their own scarce resources.

Today, e-Gov can be viewed as having two phases: the "Low Hanging Fruit" phase and the "Way Up There" phase. Today, the Low Hanging Fruit phase is ending. E-Gov has been productive by providing information, forms, and simple transactions to the public. These have been fairly easy tasks. Now the job is getting tougher.

E-GOV IN THE NEXT FEW YEARS

In the current ICA country reports, governments are reporting that the next stage of e-Gov (integrated government transactions) is different and more complex than the information delivery phase, now in maturity. The good news is that planning to integrate services causes a "whole of government" view to be taken. At the same time, most governments of size and complexity are organized in the post World War II model, which we call stovepipe government. Integrating services and managing across vertical programs is proving to be the major challenge facing e-Gov. Many officials say "the problem is not with the technology, it is with organizational barriers and cultural issues."

A few years ago, many thought that governments needed to reorganize to allow horizontal, cross-government management as opposed to the traditional, vertical management of the past 55 years. Others felt that the growth of special interests would make it too risky to open up entire governments to broad reorganizations. As a result, it is the rare government that chooses to reorganize to address e-Gov.

Yet, progress is being made in cross-government management, and it can be observed in many governments. While progress in e-Gov is not as rapid as it would be if we could begin from scratch to organize government, there is progress. The steady evolutionary progress toward integrated government can be seen in the discussions and country reports provided year by year at ICA's annual conferences. These provide a composite of the most advanced thinking and progress from around the world.

Advanced e-Gov is integrated government. Later on, it will mean the harmonization of business processes. Several themes provide a hint of the dimension of advanced e-Gov:

- A whole of government approach

- Connecting all in society

- There is no wrong door in service delivery

- Building once using many times.

These themes of "whole, all, multiple doors, and multiple uses" fall easily into the vocabulary of e-Gov managers in ICA member countries. The trouble is that in the history of Information Technology, success has come from bite size pieces called pilot programs. Grand Designs taking the "whole of" or "all of" approach have failed with regularity over the years.

Here at the beginning of the advanced e-Gov phase as we climb higher in the tree, there are some victories within our grasp. At the same time, other goals will take longer. National portals have been successful. With experience, new ideas have surfaced. Many national portals have been revised once or twice. Some portals are now in release three. New functions are now being assigned to portals as our understanding of what portals can do increases. As one example, a few countries are working to provide personalized services for the public on their nationalized portal.

Echoing the "no wrong door" concept, organizations that manage the portal are being merged with organizations that manage other service delivery channels, such as call centers, kiosks, digital TV, and ATM networks. Converging several service delivery channels is under way in many countries. This work will provide a "common look, common feel" for the citizen accessing any of the formerly independent service delivery channels.

Another victory within reach is the new "national gateway" concept. These government-wide entry points will provide common services to all ministry or agency sites in a government. Examples include the payment of bills and services for all government organizations, and the authentication of the person initiating the transaction. While the relationship of gateways to national portals is uncertain at this time, it is clear that they will be important in the future in ICA governments.

At the same time, other advanced e-Gov initiatives will take longer to achieve. Climbing higher into the fruit tree requires more planning and preparation. While Government Without Boundaries (GWoB) initiatives are the essence of advanced e-Gov, most governments have some early experience with these complex programs. Remarkably, governments are finding ways to transform themselves without exposing themselves to the risk they would face from special interest organizations if reorganizations were considered to advance e-Gov. They are doing this by initiating GWoB initiatives that require agencies doing related work to collaborate and share the funding requirements.

In addition to stovepipe organizational structures and funding deficiencies, there are additional challenges that must be overcome before important progress can be made. While significant work is being done in many nations in the following areas, no country has a nationwide solution in operation for the following obstacles:

- The ability to authenticate the person on the other end of an electronic transaction remains in the pilot program stage in most governments.

- Placing government wide architectures and standards in operation has yet to be accomplished.

- Implementation of balanced security and privacy procedures are needed to assure the public that their personal information, if supplied, will be secure and private.

- In a different type of advanced e-Gov barrier, few nations are awake to the need to train their managers and policy officials to think and act intergovernmentally.

NEW QUESTIONS ARE BEING RAISED ABOUT E-GOV INITIATIVES

For several years, e-Gov investments were made based on intuition. Government officials pushed ahead based on their "feeling" that the public would want the online service they contemplated. This continues the "top down" approach that has been problematic throughout the 40-year history of general purpose computing.

Today, there are early signs that more rigor is needed before investments are made. In some countries, there is a low uptake of the new online services. Internal auditing groups in governments are asking questions about the use of these new services by the public.

Measurement, marketing, and outreach programs are being initiated to provide better understanding about the public's uptake of the new services. Measuring the results of e-Gov investments is going to be a high priority in 2004. The United States is completing a report on this subject that will be useful to all governments newly engaging the question of e-Gov payoff.

The remainder of this report describes four of the 16 building blocks required to build a strong e-Gov program in a nation. These are singled out because they are holding back faster progress in all nations.

AUTHENTICATING THE PERSON INITIATING THE ELECTRONIC TRANSACTION

There are many authentication initiatives in ICA member countries. Governments need to know the identity of the person on the other end of an electronic transaction. While there are many different authentication initiatives, what seems to be evolving is a central solution to be used by all government systems in a nation. One reason is cost effectiveness. Finland points out that in most cases it is not cost effective to build a user ID, password system, for a single service.

Australia is working on authentication guidelines to be used by all jurisdictions. Finland and Australia are working with commercial banks to provide authentication services.

Estonia is using the private sector to provide authentication using Public Key Infrastructure and an identify card. Germany is using e-signature and smart cards.

Germany is also organizing a project group to study biometrics. United States federal managers indicate that biometrics in their environment are not needed to provide authentication in an electronic transaction.

Denmark is developing a common standard for the government. One or more vendors will implement it. In Mexico, 156,000 middle and senior managers in the federal government use digital signatures to report income and asset statements.

• Free digital signature capability was issued to 200,000 citizens and companies. (Denmark)

• A committee is looking at a "whole of government" solution for digital signature and PKI. (Norway)

• Authentication is easier with businesses than citizens due to trust issues. (Australia)

• The smart card pilot will allow transactions to be signed electronically. (Israel)

• The Bridge authority allows different PKI implementations to decide whether to trust each other. (United States)

In the United States, 700,000 ID thefts are delaying uptake of e-Gov. Private groups in the United States have created a special task force on identification. The goal is to strengthen security of the drivers' licenses (issued by state governments). According to the group, the drivers' license has become the "de facto" national ID card in the United States.

Several countries have pilot projects with compulsory ID cards

(Estonia, Finland, Israel). In other countries, e.g., Australia, any discussion of a national ID card would bring the government down.

BUILDING THE GOVERNMENT-WIDE ARCHITECTURE

Government-wide architecture has become a major priority in ICA member countries. To date, though, national solutions are not yet in operation. There is a lot of activity.

A single standard will not do the job as we thought in earlier years. Today there are as many as seven different architectures in areas such as:

- Standard business lines
- Standard performance measures
- Standard technologies, etc.

Canada plans three architectures:

- Technical
- Information, and
- Business architectures.

The Interoperability Framework sets architecture, XML standards, and meta tags mandatory for legacy systems and all interactions horizontally and vertically. (United Kingdom)

The United States has five architectural reference models, including two that have been released: Business Reference Model, and the Performance Reference.

- Fifty-four departments use the common database to share information without exhaustive prior agreements. (Malta)

- XML is the standard for document formats to make interoperability possible without exhaustive reviews freezing innovation. (Austria)

The European Union "interchange of data" program influences many nations.

Singapore has put in place the *"Public Services Infrastructure."* This provides a standards based infrastructure, applications services, and supporting procedures to facilitate e-services delivery.

ACHIEVING SECURITY IN THE GOVERNMENT AND PRIVACY FOR THE INDIVIDUAL

Information security is a top priority at this time. Some national plans are being developed (Australia). Secure government-wide networks are being built in Australia, Canada, Korea, and elsewhere.

Special security organizations are being established. Canada reports that concerns by the public over information security are lessening.

Privacy impact assessments are required in Canada and the United States. There is a suggestion however, that the requirement is not always effective in the United States.

Security within e-Government is being given as much attention as e-Government itself. Large, well-rounded security organizations with significant resources are being established. These are often responsible for laws, policies, milestones, and operational implementation.

A special word about the use of smart card technology in the United States is warranted because its difficulties with the technology may be due to the size and complexity of the government. Although the United States has about eight years of experience with some 62 pilot programs in place, smart cards are not widely used. A recent report by the US General Accounting Office, *Progress in Promoting Adoption of Smart Card Technology*, indicates that the technology remains difficult to implement and is gaining traction slowly. The report mentions several reasons for the slow uptake, including inability to maintain high level support over time, lack of understanding of the true costs involved in deployment of smart cards beyond a pilot stage, and inability to maintain security of the card and the privacy of personal information.

SYNOPSIS AND PREDICTIONS

Governments have done about as much as they need to do in setting the stage for integrated e-Gov. Prime ministers and presidents are generally involved. Detailed strategic plans are in place. Organizations have been created. Laws, regulations, and policies have been created or changed to create a good environment for e-Gov. Now it is up to the e-Gov leaders to deliver. However, there are several problems (barriers) facing them.

In the short term, over the next two to three years, we will see steady but slow progress toward an integrated e-government. Government officials, in general, do not have a "whole of government" view, and they instinctively reject government-wide solutions that could affect their program. On the other hand, more powerful forces will require the stovepipe outlooks to change.

Perfect storm conditions are converging. These may affect any predictions. Poor economies lead to deficit government. Integrated government can save a lot of money. This will be a stimulus for change. The second force is that integrated government allows the sharing of information necessary in modern societies to thwart terrorism and other domestic crises. Homeland security requirements may drive integrated government in ways not possible in relaxed periods in a society. These may accelerate solutions to issues that are holding e-Gov back at this time. On the other hand, it takes nine months to produce a baby, no matter how much money and how many mothers are assigned to the goal.

The next few years will see progress in three of the easier tasks in advanced e-Gov. These are the implementation of applications in portals, gateways providing services for all sub portals, and the convergence of service delivery channels.

Lack of steady sources of funds and difficulties in measuring the payoff from electronic government investments will retard the progress of other advanced e-Gov applications. In addition, there are several intractable problems. The lack of authentication procedures to identify the person initiating the electronic transactions is a big problem. Governments recognize this, as indicated by the many pilot projects under way in ICA member nations.

Another big problem is the lack of operational government-wide architectures to allow the sharing of information across related systems. Almost every government has programs under way to address this problem.

The third barrier is the lack of believable security procedures to guarantee the safety of information supplied by the public. Finally, privacy procedures are being implemented in a spotty manner, causing distrust in some societies.

These are not new problems. That they have been recognized and discussed for years is an indication of the difficulty they present to those attempting national solutions. It would seem, therefore, that broad solutions to these four problems will occur only marginally in the next three years. If true, this means that the advanced phase (integrated) of e-Gov will not be fully implemented in this period.

These problems will limit the progress in Government Without Boundaries type systems. However, a lot of progress will be made behind the scenes in the systems that are one level down from government-wide solutions. Progress will be made in systems that emphasize communities of interest, such as citizens, seniors, and students. Later, when authentication procedures, architectures, security, and privacy solutions are in place, these GWoB systems will be implemented quickly.

In summary, some measured progress will be made in all of the building blocks of e-Gov in the next few years, setting the stage for accelerated growth when operational solutions are in place for authentication, architectures, security, and privacy. These solutions, however, will probably not occur fully in most governments in the next few years.

NOTES

1. The International Council for Information Technology in Government Administration (ICA) is a 33-year-old organization headquartered in London. Its member countries represent Asia, Europe, the Middle East, and North America.

CONSIDERING THE SINGULARITY: A COMING WORLD OF AUTONOMOUS INTELLIGENCE (A.I.)

by

John Smart

WHAT IS THE SINGULARITY?

Some 20 to 140 years from now—depending on which evolutionary theorist, systems theorist, computer scientist, technology studies scholar, or futurist you happen to agree with—the ever-increasing rate of technological change in our local environment will undergo a "singularity," becoming effectively instantaneous from the perspective of current biological humanity. It has been postulated that events after this point must also be "future-incomprehensible" to existing humanity, though we disagree.

Our nonprofit organization, the Institute for Accelerating Change (IAC) (Accelerating.org and SingularityWatch.com) is dedicated to analysis, informed speculation, and promoting activist agendas in understanding and managing accelerating change. We are an independent community of 1,200 scholars, professionals and lay futurists systematically exploring science, technology, business, and humanist dialogues in accelerating change. Please join us in considering, critiquing, and prioritizing what may be the single most important issue of the human era.

With increasing anxiety, many of our best thinkers have seen a looming "Prediction Wall" emerge in recent decades. There is a growing inability of human minds to credibly imagine our onrushing future, a future that must apparently include greater-than-human technological sophistication and intelligence. At the same time, we now admit to living in a present populated by growing numbers of interconnected technological systems that no one human being understands. We have awakened to find ourselves in a world of complex and yet amazingly stable technological systems, erected like vast beehives, systems tended to by large swarms of only partially aware human beings, each of which has only a very limited conceptualization of the new technological environment that we have constructed.

Business leaders face the prediction wall acutely in technologically dependent fields (and what enterprise isn't technologically dependent these days?), where the ten-year business plans of the 1950s have been replaced with ten-week (quarterly) plans of the 2000s, and where planning beyond two years in some fields may often be unwise speculation. But perhaps most astonishingly, we are coming to realize that even our traditional seers, the authors of speculative fiction, have failed us in recent decades. In *Science Fiction Without the Future* (2001), Judith Berman notes that the vast majority

---

John Smart *is the director of the Institute for Accelerating Change in Los Angeles, California. He may be contacted at john.smart@cox.net.*

of current efforts in this genre have abandoned both foresighted technological critique and any realistic attempt to portray the hyper-accelerated technological world of fifty years hence. It's as if many of our best minds are giving up and turning to nostalgia as they see the wall of their own conceptualizing limitations rising before them.

To some, exponential growth in technological change appears to be an unstoppable force, driven by stunning and continuous advances in computer and communications industries. Technology appears to be rapidly pushing us toward, in John von Neumann's phrase, "some essential singularity," an environment where the dominant variety of local computation must be some form of post-biological intelligence.

INCREASINGLY AUTONOMOUS TECHNOLOGICAL EVOLUTIONARY DEVELOPMENT WILL LEAD TO THE SINGULARITY

Increasing technological autonomy, however we choose to measure it, is one key assumption behind the singularity hypothesis. Were it to be proven incorrect in coming years, singularity models would have to be fundamentally revised. However, data to date give every indication that autonomy is dramatically increasing every year. Writers on the singularity topic now suggest that progressively more human-independent computer evolution must eventually transition to a "runaway positive feedback loop" in high-level machine computation, from our perspective.

We are well on the way down the autonomy path within the computer hardware domain. Since the 1950s, every new generation of computer chip (integrated circuit) has been designed to a greater and greater degree not by human beings but by computer software. In other words, an ever-decreasing fraction of human (vs. machine) effort is involved in the hardware design process every year, to produce any *fixed* amount of computer complexity, however we choose to define that complexity.

In fact, 1978 was the last time entirely human designed (non-software aided) chips were routinely attempted. The 1980s saw the rise of powerful chip design software, the 1990s the emergence of electronic design automation (EDA) software, and recently, evolvable hardware approaches have produced a few specialized chips that are "grown" entirely *in silico*, without any human intervention whatsoever, beyond initial configuration of the design space. Such systems discover useful algorithms that are often incomprehensible to human designers. Self-replicating robots, while also still quite primitive, have recently passed the proof-of-concept stage, and are now benefiting from powerful advances in simulation and rapid prototyping technologies.

It is now well known that software follows a slower complexity/performance doubling rate than the hardware substrate. Commonly cited measures are six years, vs. 18 months, for a doubling in price performance, a figure that must vary widely with algorithm, development approach, and software class. But even here, we have seen surprising autonomy advances in recent years. In an accelerating emergence since the 1980s, we have seen several new sciences of emergent, evolutionary, and "biologically-inspired" computation, such as artificial life, genetic algorithms, evolutionary programming, neural nets, parallel distributed processing, and connectionist modeling. These new computer sciences, though still limited, have created a range of useful commercial applications, from pattern recognition networks in astronomy that seek out supernovas, to credit card fraud-detection algorithms which substantially outperform classical programs. These industries, while still underdeveloped and of limited scalability, now employ tens of thousands of programmers in a new, primarily bottom up (self-guiding), and only secondarily top down (human coded) approach to software design.

Perhaps even more importantly, biologically-inspired approaches have demonstrated that they can increase their own adaptive complexity in real-world environments entirely independent of human aid, when given adequate hardware evolutionary space. And it is clear that the hardware space, or "digital soil," for growing these new systems will become exponentially cheaper and more plentiful in coming decades.

Both Ray Kurzweil (*The Age of Spiritual Machines*) and Hans Moravec (*Robot*) have recently proposed that perhaps even as early as 2020 to 2030 we will have sufficient hardware complexity, as well as sufficient insights from cognitive neuroscience (reverse engineering salient neural structure of the mammalian brain), to create silicon evolutionary spaces that will develop higher-level intelligence.

But in what may be the most interesting and profound observation, there is now good evidence that technological systems enjoy a *multi-millionfold increase* in their speeds of replication, variation, operation (interaction/selection), and evolutionary development by comparison to their biological progenitors. Many of these speedup factors appear to range between 1 million and 30 million for higher order processes, with a proposed "average" of 10 million (electrochemical vs. electronic communication speeds).

Therefore, if it is true that accelerating autonomy is an intrinsic feature of any learning system, as some systems theorists have proposed, and if it is also true that today's technological systems are learning on average *ten million times* faster than the genetic systems which preceded them, and *thousands of times* faster than the human beings who catalyze them, then we can expect substantial increases in machine autonomy in coming years. This speed differential has been measured by a number of different approaches, and it is not yet clear which is the most important learning metric. Commonly used genetic-technologic comparisons are data input rates, output rates, communication speed, computation speed at the logic gate and in the entire system, memory storage and erasure speed, and cognitive architectural replication speed, among others.

If this multi-millionfold learning differential truly exists, and if today's most complex computers are roughly as intelligent as differentiated cells or simple insects, each of which emerged 400-600 million years ago, this implies that the evolutionary computational systems of coming decades may be engaged in rediscovering the entire metazoan evolutionary developmental learning curve within a period of perhaps 40-60 years. That idea alone is breathtaking to contemplate.

Even the evolutionary developmental history which allowed *Australopithecus* to advance very quickly, in evolutionary timescales, through *Homo habilis* and *Homo erectus* to modern *Homo sapiens,* over a span of 8-10 million years, represents less than one year in the hyper-accelerated technologic evolutionary developmental time. We begin to suspect, incredibly, that even this type of high-level "discovered complexity" will be recapitulated within the coming machine substrate in one very interesting year of development only a few decades from the present date (2041? 2061?).

So it is that many sober and skeptical thinkers now expect that the semi-intelligent systems of the 21st century, as they become *truly* self-improving and evolutionary, will rapidly reinvent within the technologic substrate at first all of the lower functions of autonomy and intelligence, and in one final brief burst, even the higher functions of the human species. Thus even such functions as high-level language, self-awareness, rational-emotive insight, ethics, and consciousness, complex and carefully-tuned processes that we consider the essence of higher humanity, are likely to become fully accessible to tomorrow's technologic systems. What happens after this occurs must be even more dramatic, as you can well imagine.

SELF-ORGANIZING AND SELF-REPLICATING PATHS TO AUTONOMOUS INTELLIGENCE (A.I.)

The better we come to understand the way intelligence develops in complex systems in the universe, the more clearly we'll perceive our own role and limits in fostering technological evolutionary development. Top-down A.I. designers assume that human minds must furnish the most important goals to our A.I. systems as they develop. Certainly some such goal-assignment must occur, but it is becoming increasingly likely that this strategy has rapidly diminishing marginal returns. Evolutionary developmental computation (in both biological and technological systems) generally creates and discovers *its own* goals and encodes learned information in *its own* bottom-up, incremental, and context-dependent fashion, in a manner only partially accessible to our rational analysis. Ask yourself, for example, how much of your own mental learning has been due to inductive, trial-and-error internalization of experience, and how much was a deductive, architected, rationally-directed process. This topic, the self-organization of intelligence, is observed in all complex systems to the extent that each system's physics allows, from molecules to minds.

In line with the new paradigm of evolutionary development of complex systems, we are learning that tomorrow's most successful technological systems must be organic in nature. Self-organization emerges *only* through a process of cyclic development with limited evolution/variation within each cycle, a self-replicating development that becomes *incrementally tuned* for progressively greater self-assembly, self-repair, and self-reorganization, particularly at the lowest component levels. At the same time, progressive self-awareness (self-modeling) and general intelligence (environmental modeling) are emergent features of such systems.

Most of today's technological systems are a long way from having these capacities. They are rigidly modular, and do not adapt to or interdepend with each other or their environment. They engage not in self-assembly, but are mostly externally constructed. In discussing proteins, Michael Denton reminds us of how far our technological systems have to go toward this ideal. Living molecular systems engage extensively in the features listed above. A protein's three-dimensional shape is a result of a *network* of local and non-local physical interdependences (e.g., covalent, electrostatic, electrodynamic, steric, and solvent interactions). Both its assembly and its final form are a developmentally computed emergent feature of that interdependent network. A protein taken out of its interdependent milieu soon becomes nonfunctional, as its features are a convergent property of the interdependent system.

Today's artificial neural networks, genetic algorithms, and evolutionary programs are promising examples of systems that demonstrate an already surprising degree of self-replication, self-assembly, self-repair, and self-reorganization, even at the component level. Implementing a hardware description language genotype, which in turn specifies a hardware-deployed neural net phenotype, and allowing this genotype-phenotype system to tune for ever more complex, modular, and interdependent neural net emergence is one future path likely to take us a lot further toward technological autonomy. At the same time, as Kurzweil has argued, advances in human brain scanning will allow us to instantiate ever more interdependent computational architectures directly into the technological substrate, architectures that the human mind will have less and less ability to model as we engage in the construction process. In this latter example, human beings are again acting as a decreasingly central part of the replication and variation loop for the continually improving technological substrate.

Collective or "swarm" computation is also a critical element of evolutionary development of complexity, and thus facilitating the emergence of systems we only partially understand, but collectively utilize (agents, distributed computation, biologically inspired computation), will be very important to achieving the emergences we desire. Linking physically-based self-replicating systems (SRSs) to the emerging biologically inspired computational systems (neural networks, genetic algorithms, evolutionary systems) which are their current predecessors will be another important bottom up method, as first envisioned by John von Neumann in the 1950s.

Physical SRSs, like today's primitive self-replicating robots, provide an emerging body for the emerging mind of the coming machine intelligence, a way for it to learn, from the bottom up, the myriad lessons of "common sense" interaction in the physical world (e.g., *sensorimotor* before *instinctual* before *linguistic* learning). As our simulation capacity, solid state physics, and fabrication systems allow us to develop ever more functional micro, meso and nano computational evolutionary hardware and evolutionary robotic SRSs in coming decades (these will be functionally restricted versions of the "general assembler" goal in nanotechnology) we may come to view our technological systems simulation and fabrication capacity as their "DNA-guided protein synthesis," their evolutionary hardware and software as their emerging "nervous system" and evolutionary robotics as the "body" of their emergent autonomous intelligence.

At best, we conscious humans may create selection pressures which reward for certain types of emergent complexity within the biologically inspired computation/SRS environment. At the same time, all our rational striving for a top down design and understanding of the A.I. we are now engaged in creating will remain an important (though ever decreasing) part of the process. Thus at this still-primitive stage of evolution of the coming autonomous technologic substrate, a variety of differentiated, not-yet-convergent approaches to A.I. are to be expected. Comparing and contrasting the various paths available to us and choosing carefully how to allocate our resources will be an essential part of humanity's role as meme-driven catalysts in the coming transition.

In this spirit, let me now point out that on close inspection of the present state of A.I. research, one finds that there are very few investigators remaining who do not acknowledge the fundamental utility of evolution as a creative component in future A.I. systems. Those nonevolutionary, top-down A.I. approaches which still remain in vogue (whether classical symbolic or one of the many historical derivatives of this) are now few in number, and despite decades of iterative refinement, have consistently demonstrated only minor incremental improvements in performance and functional adaptation. To me, this is a strong indication that human-centric, human-envisioned design has reached a "saturation phase" in its attempt to add incremental complexity to technologic systems. We humans simply aren't that smart, and the universe is showing us a much more powerful way to create complexity than by trying to develop or deduce it from logical first principles.

Thus we should not be surprised that on a human scale the handful of researchers working on systems to encode some kind of "general intelligence" in A.I., after a surge of early and uneconomical attempts in the 1950s to 1970s, now pale in comparison to the 50,000 or so computer scientists who are investigating various forms of evolutionary computation. Over the last decade we have seen a growing number of real theoretical *and* commercial successes with genetic algorithms, genetic programming, evolutionary strategies, evolutionary programming, and other intrinsically chaotic and interdependent evolutionary computational approaches, even given their current *primitive* encapsulation of the critical evolutionary developmental aspects of genetic and neural computational systems and their currently severe hardware and software complexity limitations.

We may therefore expect that the numbers of those funded investigators who currently engage in this new evolutionary developmental paradigm will continue to swell exponentially in coming decades, as they are following what appears to be the most practical path to increasing adaptive computational complexity.

In coming years, in concert with much larger and more traditional futures organizations like the World Future Society, our own organization, the Institute for Accelerating Change (at Accelerating.org), will do its own part to improve multidisciplinary dialog on the understanding and management of increasingly autonomous technological change. Ours is apparently the first human generation to be definitively surpassed, in computational complexity, by evolutionary developmental technological systems initially constructed by human invention.

What is perhaps even more interesting is that this appears to be a natural, universally-permissive process, facilitated by the special structure of the physics of the microcosm (small scales of matter, energy, space, and time). Join us in an ongoing critical dialog on what may be the single most important issue of the human era.

What an amazing time to be alive.

TRANSITION PATHS TO SUSTAINABILITY: INFORMATION, ENERGY AND MATTER

by

Hazel Henderson

The transition of industrial societies toward ecological and social sustainability is under way amid widespread disarray. Cognitive dissonance and confusion over definitions, criteria, political and economic decisions—not to mention moral and cultural stances—are part of all paradigm shifts. The paradigm shifts that "sustainability" implies are unprecedented. Sustainable development is commonly defined as development which meets the needs of the present without compromising the ability of future generations to meet their own needs. For such a paradigm shift to occur, whole cultures and societies will need to embrace a planetary and biospheric view—beyond their anthropocentrism. Further, as explored by Robert Wright in *Moral Man* (1994) and Mauro Torres, M.D., in *A Modern Conception of Universal History* (TM Editores, Bogotá, Colombia, 1998), humans will need to reexamine their biological and cultural evolution as a continuum.

Today, we in all societies need to extend such concepts to political democracy, social equity, economic efficiency, environmental preservation and cultural diversity. I claim that standards of sustainability must include the extension of domains of non-zero-sum human interactions, i.e., win-win games and the evolution of human cooperation. Thus, game theory is a more useful framework than today's prevalence of economics, which emphasizes competition.

Both competition and cooperation are essential in human societies, but their content and modes are changing in today's shift toward global interdependence. As ecological and social niches are filled, competitive, win-lose strategies—which were ideal for lower population densities and unexploited environments—begin to fail. Thus, today's globalization of markets and technologies rooted in such competitive economics often becomes "lose-lose," cutthroat competition—which leads to the kind of corporate crime wave we see in the US, or leads to "winner-take-all" election outcomes. Other effects include destructively overefficient fishing boats, which collectively have led to collapses of fisheries, not to mention the marginalizing of whole countries, bypassed by information and financial networks (Henderson, 1995; 1996; 1999).

Within one generation, according to the Living Planet Index assembled by the World Wide Fund for Nature and the London-based New Economics Foundation, around 30% of nature's productive capacity has been lost. A new report, *Pure Profit* from the World Resources Institute, focuses on ecosystem risks overhanging the balance sheets of many companies, for example in the energy, chemi-

Hazel Henderson *is a futurist, economist, author and partner, Calvert-Henderson Quality of Life Indicators (www.calvert-henderson.com).*

cal, pulp and paper industries, all part of the early industrialization process.

Today's globalization of economies, finance, markets and trade is driven by two mainsprings. The first is technology, which has accelerated innovation in telematics, computers, fiber optics, satellite and other communications; their convergence with television, global multimedia, electronic bourses for trading stocks, bonds, currency, commodities, futures options and other derivatives; and the global explosion of e-commerce and the Internet. All of this was described by markets and media as the "new economy." The second is the 15-year wave of deregulation, privatization, liberalization of capital flows, opening of national economies, extension of global trade and the export-led growth policies that followed the collapse of the Bretton Woods fixed currency-exchange regime in the early 1970s. This kind of globalization is unsustainable and increases poverty gaps, social exclusion, pollution and depletion of resources. All this became known as "The Washington Consensus," and it was rooted in the economic paradigms of the now receding Industrial Age and its fossil-fueled, heavy-machinery sectors of the Old Economy.

Some economic historians have pointed to earlier thrusts toward globalization: from the 15th century explorers of the Americas and the East Indies[1] to the open trade regimes in this century, which collapsed in the Great Depression of the 1930s and contributed to igniting World War II. Yet today, the evidence is in. Today's globalizations are new and are leading to the radical restructuring of national economies and societies—creating the rapid bifurcation between traditional cultures and earlier industrial economies vis-à-vis the new networked societies and e-commerce cultures. Not surprisingly, globalization has unwittingly strengthened social movements, such as libertarianism, human rights, feminism and environmentalism. All joined forces with labor unions in opposing the World Trade Organization (WTO). Reactions to globalization, and to "western" technologies and ideas have included rising fundamentalism (Christian in the United States, Muslim in many countries) and new searches for identity in ethnicity or nationalism—and the conflicts these often engender. These tensions were exploited by al Qaeda and other Islamist groups opposed to US policies in the Middle East, driven by oil-dependency.

Diverse traditional values, cultures, and institutions, which form the "cultural DNA codes" of different societies, have been steam-rollered by corporate economic and technological globalization. Lower prices on the Internet are promoted as a boon to consumers, while the costs pile up elsewhere, unnoticed, or get paid by someone else—or get passed on to future generations in ecosystem losses. Finance, which is supposed to serve the world's real production and exchange processes, has decoupled from the "bricks and mortar" of real economies of local places and communities. Commodities are undervalued today, not only due to unequal terms of trade, but also due to the "dematerializing" of the Internet and e-commerce. Today, globalizing electronic markets offer a "fast-forward" view of what we can expect—even after the collapse of so many of these companies after 2000 in the aftermath of the Wall Street "bubble." Over half of *Business Week*'s 100 biggest global corporations in 1999 were in information and financial services. They unwittingly accelerated the "digital divide" in their competition for market share. The dominance of the below-full-cost price system (today's prices still do not include social and environmental costs) still expands financial markets—as does Metcalfe's law. Most large corporations in the "smokestack" industrial sectors bought electronic technologies and software to increase their energy and materials efficiency.

Today's world trade accounts for less than 10% of the 24-hour global currency trading of $1.5 trillion every day—another bubble de-linked from the economies of "Main Street." The "digital divide" begins with offshore tax havens: Switzerland, the Cayman Islands, the British Virgin Islands, Cyprus, Antigua, Liechtenstein, Panama, the Netherlands Antilles, the Bahamas, Luxembourg, and the Channel Islands. More than 20,000 corporations are chartered in the Cayman Islands, and the deposits in its 575-chartered banks now total some $500 billion. Only 106 of these banks have a physical presence in Cayman, and an estimated 1.5 million of such corporations now operate "offshore" in secrecy—up from 200,000 in the late 1980s. US citizens account for some 40% of these assets.[2] In 1999, former Treasury Secretary Larry Summers, together with the G-7 and the OECD, began to crack down on money laundering, drug kingpins and tried to shut down tax havens.[3] Before the terrorist attacks of September 11, 2001, President George W. Bush had opposed this crackdown, but soon changed his mind—to pursue al Qaeda financing. The corruption and disordering of the world's money systems make barter and countertrade, payments unions, such as existed in the former COMECON countries more attractive. Some 25% of world trade is conducted in barter today, and electronic barter companies are flourishing.

Luckily, more humans, particularly in our wired and networked world, have access to this kind of whole systems information and are adept at creating new feedback mechanisms, such as the World Social Forum, which challenges the "Davos" worldview with the theme "Another World is Possible." Even with little or distorted mainstream media coverage, they organized and clarified their response via the Internet. However, industrial structures accreted over three centuries represent large intellectual social and financial investments and result in powerful interest groups. They range from US and other OECD governments to OPEC, whose member countries control 65% of the world's proven petroleum reserves and global corporations to the emergence of global civil society. Clearly, definitions, standards, criteria and performance monitoring of "sustainability" are all works in progress. Further, these social tools must be applied differentially at many levels from global to local. I have suggested at least seven such levels in my *Beyond Globalization* (1999) and in the following box "Toward Reshaping the Global Economy."

TOWARD RESHAPING THE GLOBAL ECONOMY

Level One: *The Global System*, human societies beyond the borders of nations, and their planetary ecosystem effects.

Level Two: *The International System*, including evolving treaties, agreements and unions between nations—beyond the Westphalian system.

Level Three: *The Nation-State*, sovereignty and domestic economic domains.

Level Four: *The Corporate System*, global corporations, charters, and governance.

Level Five: *The Provincial and Local Systems*, small business, local governments, community organizations.

Level Six: *The Civic Society*, voluntary, nonprofit groups, the civil sectors from local to global.

Level Seven: *The Family-Individual*, patterns of culture, organization, and behavior.

Human societies are experiencing an uneven, often traumatic global transition from 300 years of industrialism based on fossil fuels to economies based on accelerating information flows and de-materializing of OECD countries' GDPs toward services. Such epochal shifts require paradigm shifts, evidenced by the crisis within economics, which is slowly moving away from equilibrium theories, simple, static models of human behavior and its pseudo-scientific misuse of mathematics. Today, the growing "hyphenated" societies of ecological-economics, social-economics, political-economics and evolutionary-economics attest to their broadening focus.

Similarly, development models are in disarray. My own model sees development as the evolution of human societies' understanding of three basic resources: matter, energy and information and the substitution patterns toward greater thermodynamic[4] (not economic) efficiency. Thus, a society's key resource is information and the extent to which its culture educates and nurtures its human and social capital, and applies its knowledge base to managing its material and energy resources. An example is the evolution of fossil-fuel technologies since 1850 from solids and liquids to gases. This transition is still dominated by the transnational corporations dominating energy systems, fossil fuels, nuclear power, high-tech weapons systems, industrialization, agribusiness and genetic engineering of living organisms, chemicals, pharmaceuticals, transportation and communications technologies, mass media and networks. As David Korten has described in *When Corporations Rule the World* (1995), today's forms of globalization have been designed by transnational corporations (TNCs), with support of the government bodies—local, national, regional and international—over which TNCs exert major influences.

As I have described (Henderson, 1996; 1999), the powerful academic and institutional apparatus of neoclassical economics steered and legitimized this form of globalization. Biases within traditional economics were transmitted to policies of both private and public sector financial institutions and other government decision makers. Examples of these paradigm problems include the recent narrow-gauge approaches of the IMF, the WTO, and other institutions to regulation and reform of international financial architecture. At an even deeper level, the myopia of "Washington Consensus" policies of development has blinded a generation of public and private decision makers—however well intentioned and democratically inclined. Such tragic myopia and even psychological states of denial within academic economics—particularly in the United States and the United Kingdom surprised me (Henderson, 1978; 1991; 1995). I also examined (Henderson 1981; 1988) the social processes whereby this discipline (economics is not a science) came to bestride public policy worldwide, crowding out many other relevant disciplines, from sociology, psychology and anthropology to game theory, thermodynamics, chaos theory and ecology.

Now that globalization of markets has followed the erroneous dictates of such faulty economic paradigms targeted toward per-capita averaged GDP growth, we are dealing with their growing "externalities." These include the costs in wider poverty gaps and social exclusion, but also in continued erosion of non-money-based local livelihoods and cultures—as well as the extinction of other species and ecosystems disruption. Expanding micro-credit can usefully bring millions of traditional small entrepreneurs into money-based economies. Unfortunately, these money-based systems, now globally linked and highly unstable, must be overhauled to prevent the massive epidemics of new and exacerbated poverty they can precipitate. We witnessed such impoverishing of millions in Thailand, Indonesia and the other "tiger economies" during the Asian meltdown, as well as most recently in Argentina.

Too often, luring people from their traditional ways and communities into monetarized urban areas—where there are promises of "development" and the advertised "good life"—has proved unsustainable and led to such human tragedies. Public relations efforts of governments, TNCs and financial players in today's global markets blame domestic causes for these national meltdowns—from cronyism, lack of oversight, transparency and institutional structures to faulty macro-economic policies. The usual remedies included "market discipline" of governments via floating currency regimes or pegs, even dollarization, and ever-wider opening of their markets to "free" trade. An example of this "market discipline" and how finance threatens democracy was the statement of George Soros—amplified by mass media—warning that the *real* (Brazil's currency) would fall if Lula de Silva were elected. As Harvard economist Dani Rodrik documents in "Trading Illusions" (*Foreign Policy*, March-April 2001, pp. 55-62), this "incessantly repeated openness mantra," echoed by officials of the IMF, the World Bank and other international financial agencies, has perverted development priorities in many developing countries. Like Rodrik, I have also stressed the need to build homegrown economies without falling into the longer-term traps of import-substitutions, excessive tariffs, etc. In any case, global foreign direct investment (FDI) flows are shrinking from $1.1 trillion in 2000 to probably less than $800 billion in 2005. The share going to developing countries is estimated to remain around $200 billion, still only 29% of the total.[5] Today, with the global sharing of experiences, more pragmatic development can be country-specific, employing multiple strategies more fitted to culture, knowledge, geography, ecological and social assets.

The 2002 corporate crime wave in the United States has brought to light the erosion of values and ethics underlying US-style capitalism and markets—even business journals, including *Business Week* and *Fortune*, reject the notion that a few CEOs were "bad apples" and point to the wider systemic breakdown of ethical behavior needed to operate capital markets: honesty, transparency, accountability and contractual fidelity. Excessive greed, fraud, accounting tricks, conflicts of interest of security analysts, investment bankers, commercial banks, cash contributions to politicians in exchange for regulatory favors and the "bull market" hype of the financial media further inflated the Wall Street bubble.[6]

All these crises have shattered investor confidence and exacerbated fears—now amplified by the Bush administration's unilateralism and global war policies. President George W. Bush, contrary to his pre-election promises, sees the United States as the "world's policeman." His former top economic adviser Lawrence Lindsay, estimated that the war on Iraq would cost a "manageable" additional $200 billion. Meanwhile, $7 trillion of nominal equity wealth has evaporated, and the United States has gone from the surpluses of 1999-2000 to an approximate $200 billion deficit in FY2002, with further deficits as far as the eye can see. Unemployment has risen from 4% in 2000 to between 5.6% and 5.9% in 2002, with 1.5 million jobs lost in the private sector. Public sector jobs in homeland security and the defense sectors have increased, as the US economy has taken on the global war effort.

Meanwhile, not surprisingly, the dollar has fallen 25% against the euro—a stabilizing factor for the world. The US trade deficit is at historic highs, as are corporate and personal bankruptcies. Many countries are now wisely diversifying their currency reserves with more euros, as they fear that the United States is no longer the locomotive of global GNP growth. The United States is still addicted to wasteful automobiles and infrastructure and still importing over 50% of its oil from OPEC—a dependency that underlies US polices in the Middle East region. China has already become the locomotive of the Asia-Pacific region and is seeking closer ties with Brazil.

As I have editorialized (see www.hazelhenderson.com and click on Editorials). The majority of the US public (65-70%) does not want the United States to be the world's policeman. A September 25, 2002, survey (PIPA— Knowledge Networks—University of Maryland) found 64% agreeing that the United States should only invade Iraq with UN approval and the support of allies, and 62% agreed that "The UN should first try to disarm Iraq peacefully and see if that proves to be effective or not." Yet, the Bush warnings and cam-paigning—amplified in all mass media took public attention away from the economy. In early 2003, 47% agreed that "resolving the problem of Iraq" was very urgent although a similar percentage believed that the economy was more urgent as unemployment neared 6%.

Today, the world stands at a significant choice point: Either

1. A continuation of the Westphalian, competitive nation-state system of sovereignty and national interest-based policies—and a US-led open-ended global war on terrorism, backed by TNCs and other private-sector interests, or

2. A continuation of the UN-based 57 years of building multi-lateral, cooperative, legal regimes to address global issues that cannot be solved by any nation acting alone: globalized epidem-ics, terrorism, crime, money-laundering, financial meltdowns and instability, increasing poverty and information gaps within and between countries—exacerbated by "Washington Consen-sus" policies, climate and ecological disruption, species extinc-tion, loss of forests and biodiversity and peace-keeping in a world of increasing non-state actors.

These two radically different paradigms and approaches to international relations and governance will drive our strategies for shaping globalization and the values, goals, ethical norms, standards and regulations to steer humanity toward more equitable, ecological and socially-sustainable human development, as I outlined in *Building A Win-Win World* (1996).

I welcome the recent honesty of defectors from "old-time religion" orthodoxies, including Joseph Stiglitz, Jeffrey Sachs, Amartya Sen, George Soros and the more cautious Paul Krugman and Lester Thurow—to cite those who are well known. I hope they are helping expand the horizons of the economics profession toward a more humble, interdisciplinary stance—rather than the usual conceptual imperialism of economics. London's *The Economist*, for example, has been claiming the territory and contributions of game theorists, psychologists, ecologists, etc., all as part of economics. This kind of intellectual inflation is understandable, because circulation, consulting fees and textbook sales are at stake!

I will now focus on two approaches and three practical initiatives to reducing poverty gaps and inequality that stem from my "outside the economics box" analyses. I consider them key tools to apply at global "acupuncture points" where focused interventions can produce beneficial results:

1. Reforming the world's money systems, particularly currency exchanges. Such reforms must also include macro policy and banking reforms I have advocated (Henderson, 1999) to address structural inequities and to expand today's narrow indicators of "wealth" and progress. Conventional policies and paradigms promoted by powerful special interests that have led societies off course—in the pursuit of per-capita averaged, money-denominated GDP-growth—will be difficult to change, but not impossible.

2. Building out electronic platforms from global to local for extending barter, countertrade and other money-free, pure information-based trading systems. This task is much easier, since it builds on age-old cultural knowledge, rests on powerful incentives, makes use of the Internet and is growing via private sector and technological initiatives involving civic society and local governments.

I must disclose both intellectual and financial interests in both areas since I have crafted with colleagues three interventions, or social innovations, targeted to these two global acupuncture points:

1. I am a patent holder in the Foreign Exchange Transaction Reporting System (FXTRS℠) now under consideration by several central banks to create "best practice," transparent, well-regulated, fee-based currency exchanges. I and my co-patent holder, Alan F. Kay, founder and CEO of AutEx, Inc., in 1969 (the first e-commerce company) have pledged our royalties to the United Nations—because our country still owes the UN some $500

million back dues.

2. I co-created with the Calvert Group, Inc., of Bethesda, Maryland, a socially-responsible mutual fund manager with some $7.5 billion under management, the *Calvert-Henderson Quality of Life Indicators*, a wider view of "wealth" and progress in the United States: www.calvert-henderson.com (click on FOREWORD for my May 2003 update). Overhauling national accounts toward such broader measures can capture and value a country's social capital and ecological assets—as well as its infrastructure. This can better account and thereby reduce its public debt, since the public infrastructure created thereby should be amortized over the long lifetimes of such roads, bridges, dams, airports, etc.

3. I am an investor and advisor to several electronic barter start-ups and have long been an advisor on barter systems and local scrip and similar trading systems to clear local markets. Indeed, I consider the proliferation of these information-based trading and credit systems as leading indicators of the underperformance of monetary authorities, banking systems and macro-economic management.

Before I describe the FXTRS and my approaches to barter, a little context is necessary. We are well into the Information Age—whose technologies have changed and will continue to change our economic landscapes on the planet. The world is already off the gold standard and on the information-standard; i.e., information is the world's new currency (either on paper or as bits in electronic telecommunications) and most importantly, information, unlike money, is not scarce.[7] This represents a major paradigm shift.

All traditional economic models are money-based and rooted in concepts of materialism, scarcity and therefore competition. Information, on the other hand, is abundant and non-exclusionary. If you give me information, you still have it as well. Sharing information creates synergy, innovation and abundance. This is why bartering, formerly a local phenomenon of traditional societies (and still used by some 2 billion people who are marginal to the world's money economies), is now going high tech.

There are two ways that humans transact: (1) via money systems and currencies, which are still creating artificial scarcity and reinforcing competition (e.g., via the rationing and steering of credit and restrictive monetary policies, high interest rates, etc.); and (2) via all forms of barter, from local to corporate barter, countertrade, payments unions (familiar to Eastern Europeans) and estimated annually as between 10% and 25% of all world trade. Therefore, as we devise reforms for the international financial architecture, banking and money systems, we must keep in mind that today, high-tech barter and freestanding electronic platforms are bypassing malfunctioning money systems, as I will describe. Meanwhile, I now turn to one discrete tool to reform traditional currency trading.

STABILIZING CURRENCY MARKETS USING FXTRS^{SM}: BRIDGING THE PUBLIC-PRIVATE GAP

The Foreign Exchange Transaction Reporting System (FXTRS^{SM})[8] is targeted precisely at making foreign exchange trading more efficient and transparent. Once it is adopted by one or two important central banks in OECD or developing countries, it will probably become a global technological standard as others follow suit. Private market players can adopt interfaces in spite of the very small trading fees—simply because the system provides the information they lack and is more efficient. This can also reduce the money-laundering, tax-evasion and criminality that exist in today's unregulated global casino. Such systems must handle many currency market functions and reduce the likelihood, scope, and force of a massive bear raid attack on a weak currency. Such attacks have sometimes played a role in crippling the economy of the target currency. Nevertheless, at times and to some degree they are inevitable. FXTRS^{SM} systems will not eliminate them, but greatly reduce their likelihood and their severity.

Private sector FX traders, per se, are not the cause of the problem; they do not make the rules. On the contrary, traders provide liquidity, with generally razor thin bid-offer spreads and very low transaction costs, which are essential to the satisfactory operation of the $1.5 trillion global FX market. This is only possible because trader activities, including speculation, produce a market of such enormous size that it is economically possible for both high liquidity and thin margins to coexist. Bear raids on weak currencies are examples of herd behavior and can be viewed as battles. On the public side are the central banks, whose task is to help manage their domestic currency and economy. They are the only market players ready, if necessary, to sell low and buy high to protect their national economies. On the other side are all others, individuals, banks and all other financial institutions. This includes not just speculators and hedge funds, but anyone who is ready to jump into the fray at some point in hopes of buying low and selling high.

When an economy is weak, there is no doubt that to some extent its currency price should fall. Yet whether a bear raid succeeds does not primarily depend on how overvalued the currency is, but more on how much capital can be brought into the attack and how much capital is fleeing the country. Even sound currencies can succumb to a large enough raid. A bear raid will succeed because of the size of the traders' at-risk war chests. Even groups of central banks in concert cannot defend against today's huge leveraged hoards of cash. The bear raid forces an excessive measure of so-called "market discipline" onto countries—even those whose "fundamentals" are sound. Bear raids were prevalent prior to the US 1929 crash. In 1934, the newly created Securities and Exchange Commission (SEC) introduced a number of changes in the transaction process itself. One was the "uptick" rule, which prevented a broker from selling "short" if the last sale price of a listed stock was lower than the previous transaction price. This slowed the momentum of bear raids and they largely disappeared. Note that this rule utilized "ticker tape" action. "Tickers," now electronic, are based on transaction reporting, at the heart of FXTRS℠ systems.

Today, with screen-based technology undreamt of in the 1930s, a much smoother process handles the more active global currency markets. Technological designs in the FXTRS℠ will enable the recording of purposes of trades and counter-parties and help the relevant standards body to curb bear raids without impairing the functioning of the market in normal times and without depriving or slowing the execution of any transaction desired by willing buyers and sellers at a mutually agreeable price. These systems would fulfill some of the needs cited by central bankers and finance ministers for "a new global financial architecture." The system can be set up to be acceptable both politically and financially to central banks, financial firms and other users, vendors (Reuters, Bloomberg, etc.), foreign exchange brokers and dealers, as well as to national political leaders and the public. The participating central banks can assure that all transactions will be promptly reported to the system on a "ticker tape." Trade reporting itself in existing markets generally helps stabilize the market. When a market lacks information, participants must pay for extra research and are still sometimes scared or too easily vacillate between over-caution and recklessness, characteristics exhibited by the global currency markets and their recent volatility, overshooting and undershooting.

Trade reporting will help smooth currency markets, but further stabilizing mechanisms are still needed. The transaction fees of 0.001% are assumed on all trades of $1 million equivalent, amounting to $10 to the buyer of dollars on a baseline trade (or whatever 0.001% equals in a baseline trade for the buyer of another currency). That amount is slight compared to other costs and benefits perceived by both parties to any trade. It is reasonable to assume that a charge this small would not derail any trade, or normally even be noticed. However, the basic fee revenue for the system would then be $10 million per day or about $3 billion per year if and when all major currency countries were participating. The fuller patent description of the financial architecture FXTRS℠ is available from the authors.

National policies are also needed, including tightening oversight and regulation of capital flows, domestic banking and corporations' borrowing and central bank supervision. Chile has provided the world with useful models in these areas. Since Argentina's default, proposals for debt workouts, bailing in investors and country bankruptcy procedures are gaining a hearing. I have advocated that bankruptcy procedures should be modeled on Chapter 9 (not chapter 11) of the US Bankruptcy Code, which covers municipal defaults and allows for continuation of all public social services (see my "Revolution Required in Global Finance," PriceWaterhouseCoopers, May 2002). Currency markets can use fully transparent "best practices" trade reporting, such as the FXTRS^{SM}. Such independent, "virtuous circle" regulating is understood better by game theorists than economists. For example, in the United States in 1910 the state of Kansas bucked the lawless trend of lax corporate charters. Yet in two years, 24 other states followed Kansas's lead with modern, accountable charter laws, which restored investors' confidence.

Many countries will continue setting their own domestic rules and financial institutions' frameworks according to their own cultures and domestic concerns. This is especially so since the bouncebacks of Korea, Malaysia, Thailand, and the Philippines, which flouted much IMF advice and used Keynesian deficit-spending to stimulate their recoveries. Japan is still trying to restructure its economy, with much conventional economic advice about "opening up" that misunderstands Japanese culture and goals of social stability and full employment. National governments have wide latitude to act creatively, without waiting for international agreements or bowing to the dictates of the IMF or currency traders and corporations.

Indeed, public, private and civic society interventions are needed at all levels, from global to local, to shape a sustainable global economy. The tasks include designing, at all levels, additional dimensions of globalization so as to include more accurate accounting; global monitoring and feedback; higher standards; criteria; better rules; regulations and codes of conduct and principles—embracing human rights, equity, and Earth Ethics. All these must embody better science and information based on new biological knowledge of our relationship to nature.

FACILITATING MONEY-FREE BARTER TRADING FROM LOCAL TO GLOBAL

As mentioned, barter has been the province of the 2 billion humans not fully part of monetarized and urbanized sectors. Countries use payments unions, such as the Soviet Union's COMECON system prior to its collapse in 1991, while corporations routinely exchange an estimated $1 trillion worth of goods and services annually, both domestically and internationally. Because all these barter exchanges are made by agreements, contracts, letters of credit and local scrip currencies, etc., i.e. information, their value is not tracked well in conventional monetary statistics. Even the use of reference currencies is not necessary. Many of these barter exchanges involve two, three, four-way or more commodity transactions. Barter is a bedrock of sustainability because it more fully utilizes all resources, through second-hand use, sharing and matching unemployed people with local resources and services as Gov. Jaime Lerner demonstrated in Curitiba.

Barter in wider areas was inefficient—and cumbersome—prior to computers and the Internet. Today, it's a snap—and barter has several advantages over currency-based trading. Firstly, barter enables resource and commodity based economies to trade directly with each other—without first needing to earn or hold foreign exchange in key currencies. For example OPEC, which dollarized its oil 40 years ago, is now whipsawed in today's $1.5 trillion daily global casino. While OPEC still has considerable pricing power (OPEC controls 65% of all the world's proven oil reserves) and the world is still gulping its products, many of OPEC's member states are still developing and short of foreign exchange or in debt. Direct barter (or very low interest rate loans, which can also be repaid in goods and services) open their trading options and opportunities enormously.

For non-OPEC developing countries, barter deals allow them to avoid high dollarized oil prices (currently at $25 per barrel) and obtain the oil they need by trading their undervalued commodities in exchange. Similarly, governments can procure needed capital goods, infrastructure components, etc., by bartering with each other—just as corporations barter media time, bandwidth, airline seats, hotel rooms, equipment and a host of other goods and services. All this can be facilitated with robust computer software that can handle different countries' tax regimes, and all the requisite back-office clearing and settlement systems for this type of information-based, credit-trading.

As the volume of real commodities on such systems grows, today's fiat currencies will tend to float against these "baskets of commodities" (e.g., oil, generators, machinery, agricultural com-modities, etc.) whose prices in currencies are often tracked. We must remember that currencies, money *per se*, has no value, but performs as a tracking and scoring system—and, when properly managed, a store of value. As we see for example, in the case of oil: This "black gold" is more liquid, valuable—and fungible than most fiat curren-cies. Furthermore, oil is the essential energy source that still drives most of the world's transportation systems. Venezuela, the country that invented OPEC, understands all this, and President Hugo Chavez has taken leadership in signing 12 new oil agreements with Latin and Central American countries to provide their oil needs under innovative concessionary, exchange terms. Bankers and their economists, still trying to re-impose scarcity on the Internet (via encryption, cyber cash, secured credit cards, etc.), are horrified. The Bush administration's efforts to help destabilize President Chavez failed, but continues to oppose his bilateral deal with Cuba: oil in exchange for Cuban doctors and paramedics who are setting up public health clinics in rural Venezuela. The paradigm clash between money and barter is evident in this case.

Economists tend to dismiss barter as "primitive" as their textbooks teach—but it will be Internet barter companies and real traders in real commodities that will prove those textbooks obsolete (see for example, *Barter News*, an industry journal in Mission Viejo, California). How can barter be facilitated among the world's 2 billion people largely outside money systems? They are not "poor" (which is what economists call people without currencies). These 2 billion people are richly resourceful, often living sustainable lives. Today, off-grid, solar-powered microgenerators, such as those being supplied to rural villages in Africa and Asia—by Equal Access, Solaria, Inc., SELCO, Hewlett-Packard and other companies—provide connectivity. Barter menus, from global to local, can be accessed via cheap hand-held devices. Villagers may find a local menu of barter partners and little need to make a long trip to a market town with no assurance of selling their produce. For example, in Laos, the new Linux-based mini PCs of the Jhai Foundation powered by car batteries charged with bicycle cranks are connected by solar-powered relay stations to the Internet to allow farmers to check produce prices in markets in Phon Hong, 30 km away.[9]

All countries have the sovereign public power to coin their own currency and benefit from the seigniorage this confers. Countries can also make public works loans directly as opposed to the practice (often caused by political pressures from private banks) of loaning the federal funds directly to private banks that then lend on to consumers at market rates of interest. This fractional-reserve banking system term has become the norm in the United States and many countries. Many believe that the sovereign power of creating a nation's money should not have been ceded to private banks, who can lend it out at interest while only retaining a fraction (usually 8% under BIS current rules) in reserves. Other essential strategies for local control and building thriving, home-grown economies include local credit-unions, micro-credit, small banks devoted to local lending (mandated in the United States by the Community Reinvestment Act), local business development groups, and networks of local venture funders.

However, many civic society organizations (CSOs) are now challenging the practice of bringing money into creation as debt to private banks. For example, in the United States, the Chicago-based Sovereignty Project, a coalition of local development advocates, has introduced a bill in the US Congress which would allow the US Treasury to lend directly to cities, interest-free, for democratically approved, public works projects, ecologically sound development, new schools, etc. Rather than floating high-interest bond issues, which burden future generations, such municipal sovereignty debts would be repaid back to the US Treasury directly. This was the practice with Canada's central bank until the 1950s. Direct lending to municipalities and states for approved public infrastructure projects will become even more necessary if tax-free municipal bonds become disadvantaged by repeal of taxes on dividends.

Local barter networks and various forms of local currencies and scrip are as old as human communities, and those used in Curitiba and recently Argentina are used widely in traditional societies and informal sectors worldwide. Western adaptations include Cincinnati's Time Store, a typical "bring and buy, skills and labor exchange" café operating in the late 1890s, and Ralph Borsodi's commodity-backed currency "the constant," which circulated in Exeter, New Hampshire, in the 1970s. Indeed, such local currencies in every state and most cities in the United States during the Great Depression helped local communities survive, as documented in Mitchell and Shafer, *Depression Scrip of the United States* (1984).[10]

Today, we relearn that any person, business, CSO or country short of official national, or hard currencies can engage in as much barter as necessary. Today, these include high-tech exchanges using personal computers, local exchange trading systems (LETS) and the many kinds of local scrip currencies now circulating in hundreds of towns in the United States, Europe, and other OECD countries. Today in Argentina, millions of people meet their basic needs for goods and services through barter clubs, many electronic, local bazaars and currencies they trust more than the official Argentina peso. In a perfect example of the clash of paradigms, the government, the IMF and orthodox economists insist these barter networks and local currencies be made illegal. The most successful Internet second-hand auction company, eBay is based on the same model. These tools can complement scarce national currencies, overvalued US dollars, or where monetary policy is ill conceived or too restrictive so as to help clear local markets, employ local people, and provide them with an alternative local, purchasing power. In short, no poverty-reduction strategy will be complete without barter.

The globalizing of information and communications technologies and the networks they create, are well described by Professor Manuel Castells. I agree that they represent a new stage of human societies —even though I would say they are still governed by industrial zero-sum thinking. This is at odds with their fundamental win-win logic, based on the non-competitive, non-exclusionary nature of information. While some attention is now focused on the digital divide of info-rich and info-poor thus created, many Silicon Valley "cyber-libertarians" have revived a new form of social Darwinism. Washington policy makers adopt the rhetoric of *laissez-faire*, to justify non-intervention in the Internet sector. The reality is a new form of industrial policy (condemned in others) of subsidizing this "infant industry." The Internet was developed as a public good with US taxpayers' funds—and enjoys subsidized access to telephone networks, and a continuing tax holiday. All these subsidies, as well as active US foreign policy to discourage other countries from taxing the Internet, account for much of its rapid growth.

Information and energy management are two fundamental technologies of human social development. Both must now be measured
in terms of ecological and social sustainability (which require equity
and justice, as well as efficiency). This means that investments cannot
be measured using traditional capital asset pricing models (CAPMs),
because they omit social and environmental costs. Crucial to steering
our societies toward sustainability, will be new scorecards, beyond
GNP/GDP and other over-aggregated macro-economic measures of
wealth and progress that measure energy-efficiency, education,
health, infrastructure and other social domains.

Let us take some current examples of transition paths to sustainability, in energy and information. In *The Politics of the Solar Age*
(1981; 1988) I traced the history of the fossil-fuelled Industrial
Revolution and the evolution of positivist science and classical and
neo-classical economics in the United Kingdom and Europe. I
showed how economic theories of value changed over this period—leading to the Keynesian revolution from the late 1930s through
the 1970s. I showed the lag in economic theories in properly
evaluating the role of factors of production—particularly the special
role of energy and knowledge (which were subsumed under
"capital," "land and labor"). I showed how this error had lulled
industrial societies into under-pricing and overuse of energy, while
under-investing in education. This, together with Europe and the
United States' growing political, corporate and military power had
contributed to their addiction to petroleum. I viewed OPEC's
quadrupling of the price of oil in 1973 as a necessary correction
toward full-cost pricing (even though environmental damage and
other externalities were still not included). The imbalances in world
energy consumption continued to become more ex-
treme—exacerbated by the global hegemony of the US dollar.

My service from 1974 until 1980 as a member of the Technology
Assessment Advisory Council of the US Office of Technology
Assessment (OTA) led to my research into more benign, diverse,
decentralized forms of solar, wind, tidal, wave and biomass sources
of energy and the huge unexploited opportunities for energy-
efficiency improvements. At that time, the powerful trade associations and lobbyists for the coal, oil and nuclear energy sectors had
influenced the US Congress to subsidize them to the tune of some
$150 billion. The fledgling renewables sectors were left to compete
unaided on this unfair, tilted playing field. The Carter administration
accepted the many reports from the OTA on the need to increase
efficiency of all energy uses: in machinery, agriculture, construction,
transportation and the household sectors (available on CD-ROM from
the US Government Printing Office, Washington, D.C., stock number:
052-003-01457-2, phone: 202/512-1800, $23). Many small programs
were pushed through a resistant Congress, from insulating houses
and rating appliances, increasing automobile mileage to setting up
the Solar Energy Research Institute in Golden, Colorado. During this

period, energy consumption was de-linked from US GDP-growth due to efficiency gains.

By 1992, this new information led to a new "supply" of "conserved" energy representing 24.3% of US consumption (27.9 quads) and almost equaling the 29.4% of petroleum (33.7 quads)—with renewables at 5.6% (6.4 quads). The balance was in natural gas at 18.1% (20.8 quads), coal at 16.9% (19.4 quads) and nuclear at 5.7% (6.5 quads). By 1998, efficiency gains were the largest "source," 28% bigger than oil and six times bigger than nuclear power, and total consumption was 94.7 quads.[11]

Thus, in the United States, despite our massive energy consumption, population growth and the doubling of automobiles on our highways, the US energy-to-GDP ratio (E/GDP) has steadily declined. From the E/GDP of 1 (i.e., a one-to-one ratio) in 1960, to an E/GDP of 0.64 by 1998 (i.e., the energy intensity of our economy had almost been cut by half). The OPEC price increases clearly contributed to this change, together with price volatility and fears of supply disruptions.[12]

Demand-side management (DSM), consisting of information technologies of conservation options, became a lucrative, competitive service.

The recent petroleum price increases have led to scapegoating of OPEC. Even with mid-2000 prices of $25-30 per barrel, in inflation-adjusted terms, these prices are really half of what they were in 1975. Furthermore, OPEC's share of the prices consumers pay in North America and the European Union for gasoline are only between one-fifth and one-third of the total, due to local taxes and refinery mark-ups. Many US interests, particularly small producers and investors in costly exploration, actually want oil prices to remain high. US politicians criticize the big oil refiners for high US gasoline prices and have called for a US anti-trust investigation. President Hugo Chavez has focused on OPEC, founded by Venezuela, and the need to re-think World Trends and the Future of Oil and Energy, the title of the international seminar he hosted (in which I participated) to enrich the mix of options discussed at OPEC's Second Summit held in Caracas, September 2000.

Turning to information technology, between 1998 and 2000, the acceleration of technological changes and the growth of the e-commerce sector has speeded up the growth of the energy-efficiency ratio and led to an overall increase in US productivity. However, much research is needed to systemically verify these pathways of substitution. Energy economist John A. Laitner's review of these issues and his preliminary estimate of their effects might additionally conserve 5 quads in the United States, reducing current energy forecasts for 2010 and lowering carbon emissions by 80 million metric tons.[13] These shifts will require policy reassessments as these new trade-offs occur between information, energy and materials-use in many other countries, including energy-self-sufficient Brazil.

The continuing US stock market shakeout of the electronics sector is similar to that which occurred in earlier stages of technological evolution, from railroads and electricity to telephony and automobiles. Each of these waves of technological innovation produced thousands of start-up enterprises. This ended with the consolidation of these sectors under three or four giant producers—or, as in the case of electric utilities and telephony, government-regulated monopolies. Both telephony and electric utilities were de-regulated and over-invested—leading to the wave of telecom bankruptcies. The Houston-based energy giant, Enron, saw itself as a trading platform and electronic-marketplace for energy futures and water futures. Investors were duped by this business model and Arthur Andersen's accounting until Enron's bankruptcy revealed its widespread fraud and criminality. The now-consolidating oil "super-majors" (e.g., Shell and BP Amoco) are increasingly investing in solar and hydrogen. A venture capital boom is beginning in decentralized, renewable energy (solar, wind, fuel cells) as I had predicted in the 1980s. As traditional economic analyses were broadened, large central generating plants incurring huge transmission losses are at last seen as un-economical (*The Economist*, Aug. 5, 2000, pg. 27).

Of course, most of the United States' energy demand is still met by fossil fuels (petroleum 39.4%, natural gas 23.2% and coal 23%) with the balance of 14.7% equally met by renewables and nuclear. However, with rising public concern for the environment and climate change, the fossil fuel component will decline, with natural gas becoming the cleanest fuel of choice in the mix. Meanwhile, public pressure on automobile companies and California's "zero-emission" standards are now paying off in electric and hybrid vehicles. They compete with the new Toyota and Honda hybrids (with approximately 50-70 miles per gallon performance) now in US showrooms. The good news is that these technological advances, together with e-commerce, are peaceful paths toward reducing oil dependence. The bad news is that US military intervention to assure oil supplies is still the policy of the George W. Bush administration. Brazil has the opportunity to assure that future automobile plants produce lower and zero-emission cars to serve its own and export markets.

Climate change was added to the policy mix by 1994. All these changes have caused OPEC countries to steadily lose market share to the "super-majors" and non-OPEC producers. Additional challenges for all oil-producing and consuming countries include the increasing uncertainty of most energy forecasts with widely-divergent estimates of the world supply/demand balance and the need for OPEC oil. These forecasts, according to Dr. Fadhil J. Chalabi, executive director of the London-based Centre for Global Energy Studies, are based on assumptions of market conditions at the time they are made. These are bound to change with economic, political and technological developments—rendering them worthless. In addition, US dollar-denominated prices for petroleum have proved a double-edged sword. Focus on the price (in whatever currency) has meant loss of control in today's unregulated electronic currency markets.

These turbulent currency markets are dominated by the US dollar, formerly the de-facto global reserve currency and now challenged by the parity of the euro. Countries still play into the hands of US policy makers and financial markets by holding too many dollars in their currency reserves. This continues to allow US dollar-holders to purchase assets at below fair value. As an advisor to the South Commission in 1988-1989, I urged the countries of the South Commission to set up a jointly-operated computerized barter-trading system for all South countries' major commodities, including oil.

The need to expand into renewable resources, "green" energy technologies and environmental protection and restoration is now on the radar screens of governments and venture capitalists, as well as the oil "super-majors." The market for "green" products of all kinds in the United States is now $230 billion (LOHAS, Vol. 3, No. 3, Fall 2002, Boulder, CO, USA). All oil companies and OPEC will also need to get on this renewable technology train before it leaves the station. Today's faulty accounting and CAPM models still makes it easier to follow the herd than to look at the underlying deep processes at work and find really cutting-edge new businesses. Similarly, today's forms of globalization look good because traditional accounting disenfranchises a significant minority, ignores the running down of natural resources, and discounts future risks. Meanwhile, visionary enterprises and business plans are beginning to underpin the great transition now under way from the Industrial Age to the information-rich "Age of Light." The sustainability debate and higher oil prices are kick-starting the wave of new business opportunities in hydrogen, fuel cells, solar, wind, wave and biomass companies. Much financing goes into continuous improvements in resource-utilization, energy storage and efficiency gains, i.e., information technologies.

In many developing countries, off-grid solar electricity is needed to access the Internet and better the lives of rural people and prevent in-migration to cities. Why should resource-rich developing countries feed the United States' energy and materials addiction at knock-down prices when so many of these countries need investments in longer-term, more sustainable, renewable energy and e-commerce "info-structure"? US citizens *don't own* most of the world's oil, natural resources and biodiversity. Many agree with the thesis that the productivity gains of the new economy were largely the effect of cheap oil.[14] Even though cyber-libertarians, Internet entrepreneurs and electronic currency traders do not like earthbound constraints, the laws of thermodynamics still operate. One cannot fill a car's gas tank with a "virtual gallon of gasoline" or drive across the "flow of services" of a bridge. All this was pointed out by Nicholas Georgescu-Roegen in his *The Entropy Law and the Economic Process* in

1971.[15]

Although improvements in communications and materials sciences have led to a profound de-materializing of OECD economies, today's debates involve the extent to which, this process—which futurist Buckminster Fuller called "ephemeralization"—can continue substituting services, knowledge, communications, recycling and renewables for virgin natural resources. Between four-fold and ten-fold efficiency increases in energy and materials use are possible. Here is where investments in people and social infrastructure are key. Societies cannot continue de-materializing their economies without investing in education, health and maintaining infrastructure, social architecture and human capital for further advances in research.[16] Knowledge, human capital, trust, cohesive values and sound management of the planet's biodiversity and natural resources are now the key factors of production. All must be carried as assets in expanded national accounts rather than being written off, as such public investments in education, health and infrastructure still are today in many countries. Brazil and all newly-industrialized countries can benefit from older industrial societies' mistakes and leapfrog into the decentralizing technologies and distribute intelligence of the emerging Age of Light.

Yet, today, government and private investors cannot ignore that ever more problems and issues have become global—beyond the reach of national governments—from climate change, cross-border pollution, desertification and loss of biodiversity to space junk. Proliferating weapons-trafficking, drugs trading and unregulated currencies favor the business of organized crime. Nuclear and toxic wastes must be contained. Epidemics spread by air travel, as well as global terrorism, cannot be addressed by any nation acting alone. We cannot avert our gaze in the globally interdependent world we have helped create. Powerful new biotechnologies such as cloning and genetically-modified organisms require international safety-testing, labeling and standards. Socially-responsible companies and investors can support and even capitalize on global standards that raise the ethical floor under the global marketplace. Meanwhile, dealing with the continued growth of mega-cities while maintaining safety-nets requires massive public and private investments. This is why all national accounts (GDP) must now include an asset side to properly value these infrastructure investments and balance their public debt. The United States instituted this change in January 1996 (which reduced its deficit by one-third). Canada followed suit in 1999 and went from deficits to a $50 billion surplus.

Nations face all these problems of sovereignty in an era of global financial flows at the same time that their tax revenues are eroding and diverted into tax havens or Swiss banks. Powerful special interests lobby in most countries for tax favors—undermining the redistributive role of taxation and exacerbating the digital divide. The tax bases of municipalities and local governments are also eroding in the United States due to the subsidized explosive growth of Internet e-commerce.

Money itself has morphed into information, as debit cards, credit cards and trillions of digitized bits flow between millions of computers, and escape money-supply regulators at central banks. All these new problems and issues are driving national governments into pooling or sharing their sovereignty to set up or strengthen international agencies, rule-making bodies and global standards. OPEC's raison d'etre involved such sovereignty issues[17]—all of which need re-thinking and re-strategizing for today's challenges. Money has become the curse of democratic political processes in many OECD and developing countries aspiring to become more democratic.[18] For example, London-based *The Economist* reported (February 1, 1997, pg. 25) that in 1991 Portugal paid Auto Europa, Ford and Volkswagen $254,000 per job created, while the state of Alabama, "bribed" Mercedes-Benz with $167,000 per job created. Such subsidies have propped up the fossil-fuels sectors and stifled innovations of clean, zero-emission cars. The US farm and steel subsidies enacted by the Bush administration are at odds with its "free trade" rhetoric. Few such subsidies finance the small companies building the new sustainable "green," clean energy sectors. There is still time for newly-industrializing countries to avoid huge infrastructure costs by shifting to off-grid solar photovoltaics, wind and biomass energy—as well as wireless telephony and accessing the Internet directly with Palm Pilots and solar-powered radio, computerized with modems.[19]

The new mechanisms of the Kyoto Accords on Climate Change (1998) can also be used to advantage. These include the Clean Development Mechanism (CDM), Joint Implementation (encouraging cross-country partnerships in "green" technology) in which Brazil played an innovative role. Emissions Trading (ET), which has commenced in Chicago and on other futures exchanges to trade "credits" in SO_2 and CO_2 (sulfur oxides and carbon dioxide), is still inequitable. ET subsidizes dirty companies and technologies while punishing renewable and sustainable ones. Worse, the credits have been given to companies instead of being auctioned. Only a per-capita distribution can meet equity standards. Even though the United States has yet to ratify Kyoto, many companies recognize these new profit opportunities in reducing their polluting emissions and investing in less-polluting technologies. Countries can take full advantage of these new revenue streams allowable as they shift toward natural gas (with 50% reductions in CO_2 emissions) and for all cleaner processes and investments in renewables. To take full advantage of these new revenues, countries will need to overhaul their national accounts (GNP/GDP) to fully account for their existing infrastructure as assets as the United States did in 1996 and Canada followed suit in 1999. Such asset accounts should fully calculate all un-priced ecological assets: water services of forests and watersheds, biodiversity resources for pharmaceuticals, tidal and wind energy assets and their huge daily insolation rates.[20] For example, sunlight reaching Amazonia each day contains the energy equivalent of some sixty hydrogen bombs, which is usefully captured by the forests. *The Ecologist*'s Peter Bunyard warns that current plans to exploit these forests will lead to massive fires and desertification. With all these ecological assets and energy sources fully accounted, countries will be in much stronger negotiating positions vis-à-vis industrial countries of the OECD.

There is much good news brought by the globalization of the new networked information economy, including distance-learning, pioneered in Mexico, and college courses for people confined to their homes. Other positive aspects of today's uneven globalization are the rapid proliferation and sharing of concepts of sustainable development. The United States, Europe and other industrial countries are well into a new phase of the New Economy of Information. We are transitioning to the Age of Light, not only of light wave technologies (photonics, solar energy, etc.) but also of deeper knowledge of our world and ourselves. Scarce human time and attention, as well as living ecosystems, are recognized as more valuable than money. At the same time, we live in "mediocracies" where a few media moguls now control the attention of billions of people—for better or worse. This has changed politics forever. We are already living in the new Attention Economy,[21] and shifting away from material goods, still measured by the traditional Gross National Product (GNP). Burgeoning services are slowly added to GNP and such re-calculations account for much of the recent "rise" in productivity. More intangible factors in living standards are measured by new scorecards such as the *Calvert-Henderson Quality of Life Indicators*, mentioned earlier—a co-venture of mine with the Calvert Group, Inc. A pioneering Latin American initiative to correct the GDP was the 1989 Caracas Report, "New Ways to Measure Economic, Social and Environmental Change" for the South Commission.[22] Costa Rica has also provided leadership in re-vamping its national accounts to include ecological assets.

As our economies dematerialize toward more services, it will be harder for business and governments to hype wasteful goods-based GNP-growth in the global economy. They will be accountable for and need to assess progress in human health, education, human rights and environmental quality. This requires measuring toxic wastes, resource-depletion, health, water and air quality, public safety, poverty gaps and overall quality of life. Newly-aware citizens, consumers, employees, investors and advanced management training such as that of Amana-key in São Paulo are driving the growth of socially-responsible corporations, codes of conduct, the Global Reporting Initiative (GRI) in accounting, and the $2.2 trillion invested in "clean, green, ethical" companies in the United States alone.

If GDP was re-categorized and re-calculated for the United States and similar Attention Economy sectors in other countries, we would find that these information/services sectors already are even more dominant than they appear in the revisions. Mass media and entertainment are a growing percentage of global trade, much of it promoting the worst in human behavior and values. Global e-commerce is predicted by Forrester Research to reach $3 trillion by 2003. Yet, 28% of US citizens are "down-shifting"— in typical Attention Economy style, tuning out this culture of information overload and costly mass consumption-oriented value system.[23] They are choosing more free time and less money income and moving to quieter, less expensive, rural towns where life is slower, commuting easier, and communities are still intact. Consumers are seeking their own (not advertisers') definitions of "quality-of-life." In addition, Attention Economy consumers increasingly demand global corporations to reduce emissions and employ fair labor standards and promulgate codes of conduct.

Today's haphazard globalization can be shaped, democratized and shared. Education and health care are now recognized in many political campaigns as urgent public issues, because they are key sectors of information economies. Knowledge, intellectual, social and ecological capitals are the key factors of production. Fossil fuels have served as platforms for the Industrial Age. The Information and Solar Age sectors will continue to grow worldwide—particularly in Brazil, Malaysia, China and India.

Both "public" and "private" sectors in our economic and political textbooks must now move over, as the third, civic sector where most of the world's poor exist, takes its rightful place in human affairs. University courses now study these civic sectors; economists and politicians misunderstand them. After the battles of Seattle, Washington, London, Prague and Davos, both governments and corporations have learned to respect them. Even the World Bank, in an unpublished study, "Beyond the Washington Consensus: Institutions Matter" (1998), at last allowed that "human capital," civil organizations, social structures, families culture and values must be studied and accounted in economic development. The Prague Declaration of 2001, the 1993 Statement of the Parliament of the World's Religions and the Earth Charter, together with the many UN conventions on human rights, all point toward the evolution of ethics and global standards necessary to address our Age of Global Interdependence.

The world is slowly and unevenly moving toward balancing win-win strategies and domains of international agreements and laws to tame cutthroat competition and exploitation, both of people and ecosystems. Democracy is slowly spreading and primitive industrial technologies are slowly giving way to decentralizing ecologically benign information and energy technologies. These transformations do not rely on new religions. Human populations have increased, so that today our species consumes 40% of the planet's biomass photosynthesis. We will become ever more interdependent. We must learn the lessons of this interdependence and build a win-win world if we are to survive. Today, the planet is our programmed learning environment. All our self-interests—seen from this larger perspective—coincide. Morality, as Charles Darwin speculated over a century ago,[24] is becoming ever more pragmatic.

NOTES

1. See for example, D. Landes, *The Wealth and Poverty of Nations* (W.W. Norton & Co., 1998), an important interpretation of economic development that embraces culture, climate and geography.
2. R. Morgenthau, "On the Trail of Global Capital," *New York Times*, November 8, 1998, 125.
3. *Business Week*, "The Globo-Cop at Treasury," April 14, 2000.
4. My late friend Nicholas Georgescu-Roegen, *The Entropy Law and the Economic Process* (Harvard University Press, 1971) grounded erroneous economic theories of "productivity" and "efficiency" in thermodynamics following British chemist, Frederick Soddy, who shared a Nobel Prize with E. Rutherford for the discovery of isotopes.
5. *The Economist*, "World Investment Prospects," February 24, 2001, 80.
6. See for example, Arthur Levitt, *Take on the Street* (Pantheon, 2002).
7. H. Henderson, *Building a Win-Win World*, Ch. 9 "Information, the World's New Currency, Isn't Scarce" (San Francisco: Berrett-Koehler, 1996).
8. H. Henderson and Alan F. Kay. *Futures*, Vol. 31, October 1999 (UK: Elsevier Scientific), 759-777.
9. *The Economist* "Making the Web Worldwide," October 2002, 76.
10. H. Henderson, *Building a Win-Win World*, ibid.
11. *Rocky Mountain Institute Newsletter*, Vol. XVI, #1, Spring 2000, 8.
12. *Calvert-Henderson Quality of Life Indicators*SM, eds. H. Henderson, J. Lickerman, P. Flynn, The Calvert Group, Bethesda, MD, pg. 93.
13. John A. "Skip" Laitner, US Environmental Protection Agency, Washington, D.C.; e-mail for a copy: laitner.skip@epa.gov.
14. *The Economist*, "Oil and The New Economy," April 1, 2000, 72.
15. See my review in *Harvard Business Review* (1971).
16. See for example, D. Lamberton, ed. *The Economies of Information and Knowledge* (Penguin Book, 1971).
17. Rómolo Betancourt, *Venezuela: Oil and Politics* (Boston: Houghton Mifflin, 1979).
18. A.F. Kay, *Locating Consensus for Democracy*, Americans Talk Issues Foundation, US, 1998.
19. See for example, the US-based Solaria, Inc.'s, joint project in Nigeria with Worldspace Satellite, Inc., to provide village access to the Internet.

20. Graciela Chichilnisky, *Development and Global Finance: The Case for an International Bank for Environmental Settlements* (New York: UNDP, 1997).

21. H. Henderson, *Building a Win-Win World*, Ch. 5, "Government by Mediocracy and the New Attention Economy" (UK: McGraw-Hill, 1996; 1997).

22. "Redefining Wealth and Progress," *The Caracas Report on Alternative Development Indicators* (New York: TOES Books, 1990).

23. Merck Foundation, Harwood Group, Silver Spring, MD (1995).

24. David Loye, *Darwin's Lost Theory of Love* (Writers Club Press, 2000).

FUTURE OF INFORMATION ERA COMMUNICATION TECHNOLOGIES

by

Graham T.T. Molitor

SCIENTIFIC BREAKTHROUGHS AND TECHNOLOGICAL SUBSTITUTIONS

Better means of communication have been consistently introduced throughout history. Improved methods of communication displace the less effective and become the dominant mode. Spoken words preceded the handwritten word, which gave way to the mechanically printed word that was eclipsed by the telegraph and telephone. Four major communication modes, each one more efficient than the preceding one, dominated eras of US economic growth over the past century:

- Low cost *"penny press"* which made inexpensive mass-circulation newspapers and periodicals available to an increasingly literate populace.
- Regular *radio* broadcasting that began in the mid-1920s.
- *Television*, starting in the 1950s.
- *Computers* that flooded consumer markets by the late-1970s.

Computers of the 1960s and 1970s were big, costly, few in number, and limited to top management use. During the 1980s, desktop PCs lopped off middle-management paper pushers, and decentralized decision-making. Take-off during the 1990s greatly enlarged computer networking and the Internet provided access to the fund of human knowledge.

Science constantly seeks faster, better, more efficient, less costly, and more streamlined technologies. Communication advances can be categorized into at least seven successive stages of development that follow this pattern:

1. *Physical/mechanical stage.* Edison's primitive phonograph, utilizing a mechanically vibrating pickup and diaphragm to reproduce sound, commercially introduced in 1877, exemplifies this introductory stage. Forerunners of modern computers can be traced back thousands of years to the hand-manipulated abacus. Later on, came Charles Babbage's calculating engine that was partially constructed between 1822-1871.

2. *Electro-mechanical stage.* Alexander Graham Bell's telephone,

Graham T.T. Molitor *is a well-known speaker and widely published author on trends and developments. He is president of Public Policy Forecasting and vice president and legal counsel of the World Future Society. He may be contacted at gttmolitor@aol.com.*

introduced in 1876, demonstrates this type of innovation using electric pulses to vibrate a diaphragm or open and close an audible circuit. Computer antecedents are characterized by Herman Hollerith's electrically operated tabulator using printed punched cards that was used to process 1890 census data.

3. *Fully electronic stage.* Marconi's first wireless telegraph signals (precursor to the radio), demonstrated in 1895, represents this principle. Continuing to track computer development, the earliest numeric analog computer, the Electronic Numerical Integrator and Computer (ENIAC), was developed by Eckert and Mauchly in 1946.

4. *Electro-optical stage.* Telephone analog switching systems converting signals to photonics characterize this development.

5. *Optical/photonic stage.* Light transmission is the latest communications frontier. Light changes polarity more than one quadrillion times per second. Scientists already succeeded in switching light 100 trillion times per second (100 terabits). Emerging evidence that the speed of light may be exceeded by a factor of 10-1,000-fold, perhaps even ten-million-fold, suggests future threshold potentials.

6. *Bio-electronic stage.* Some foresee organic semiconductor devices and bio-computers as the next (science-fiction-like) stage of potential development. Crude experiments already have demonstrated these possibilities.

7. *Extra-sensory stage.* Much more speculative are the possibilities inherent in development of extra-sensory perception (ESP)—clairvoyance, precognition, prodigals, "tongues," telepathy, telekinesis, faith healing, hypnotic states, out of body experiences, and so on—suggest the possible potentials. Dismissed as "quackery," ESP might become the preferred communication mode at some future date.

COAXING THE MOST OUT OF AVAILABLE RESOURCES: DOING MORE WITH LESS

Smaller, faster and cheaper are hallmarks of communication technologies. Technological advances wrest more and more from basic raw materials. Falling prices bring such conveniences to mass markets.

Clocks, the forerunner of mechanical invention, initially occupied entire temples. Pocket watches, ponderous and thick at the outset, steadily diminished in size. By 1700 the average thickness slimmed down to 1.5 inches, trimmed to one-half that thickness (0.75 inch) by 1800, and shrank to 0.25 inches by 1850. Today, LED display timepieces measuring the thickness of a sheet of paper and molecule-thick versions have been developed. Once again, this underscores how science provides ever newer ways of doing the same thing better, utilizing even fewer resources.

The first programmable computer (ENIAC) filled an entire room. This huge computer included 17,468 vacuum tubes and semiconductor diodes, 70,000 resistors, 10,000 capacitors, 6,000 switches, and 1,500 relays. It weighed 30 tons. Standing 10 feet tall it occupied space measuring 80 X 30 feet. The dimensions were equivalent to an oversized 18-wheel tractor trailer. This is not exactly the sort of device you could carry around in a briefcase, a shirt pocket, or on a wrist. Electrical consumption was enormous—140,000-174,000 watts per second—enough to provide power to an average home for over a week. This enormous machine performed a mere 5,999 basic mathematic operations per second. It cost a whopping $450,000.

By the 1950s, computers shrank to refrigerator-size. Recently, massive mainframe computers filling an entire room have been reduced to PCs with "footprints" the size of a telephone book or even smaller ones that slip into a shirt pocket. Now, computer devices occupy postage-stamp dimensions. Meanwhile, R&D focuses on quantum computers the size of a pinhead!

Virtually every facet of communications benefits from ephermalization—doing much more, with much less.

• Birthday cards that tinkle the "happy birthday" tune when the card is opened incorporate more computing power than the first room-size computers.

• Wristwatches may contain more computing power than existed in the entire world before 1961!

• Palm-size computers and video games today possess more computational capability than the best supercomputers of the mid-1970s.

• Motor vehicles—some with 30-100 onboard dedicated computers that constantly check and adjust oil pressure, fuel mixture, tire air pressure, seat adjustments, headlights, and navigation—surpass the computational ability of Apollo 11!

• Gigantic satellite-receiving antennae 10-100 feet in diameter have been replaced by receptors as small as 12-16 inches in diameter.

• CD-ROM disks plummeted from 12-16 inch diameters to 5 inches, shrinking to 2-3 inch diameters, then to units the size of a quarter. Diminutive disks storing one trillion bits have been developed.

• Tape cassettes shrank from 12 inches, to 4 inches, to as little as 2-3 inches, and smaller.

• A few thousand-pound communications satellite outperforms copper lines more than a trillion-fold.

Fiber optical cable, fashioned from silicon, replace (and/or complement) vast tonnages of copper wires. The first copper transmission lines, measuring about one-fourth inch in diameter, carried but a single message. Coaxial cable voice channel capacity rose from 48 in 1955 to 4,200 by 1976. Fiber optics boosted the number of voice channels which rose from 8,000 in 1988, to 16,000 during 1991, and greater than 500,000 around 1998. Fiber optic cables with ten terabit capacity emerged by 1998, and others carrying 10 trillion bits per second have been demonstrated. Photonic transmission rates will reach 100 terabits per second by 2004, and transmissions at 200 trillions bits per second are projected.

Science typically starts out using cruder and larger dimensions. Inevitably, and step-by-step, as mastery is accomplished, artifacts become better, less resource-intensive, and more efficient. Moore's law, which anticipates computer capabilities double every 18 months, is easily understood in terms of the basic parameters of packing density and speed. Smaller scales increase packing density, involve shorter travel distances, and enhance speed. Electrons have a certain speed and photonics possess still more diminutive dimensions. Knowing the range of those parameters reveals basic limitations that indicate the highest level potentials attainable.

Integrated circuits etched using extreme ultraviolet (EUV) lithography can create features smaller than 0.1 micron (about one five-hundredth a hair's width). This development can increase microchip capacity by 1,000-fold, and boost speed of the fastest chips currently available by at least 100-fold. Lithographic chip etching will reach a limiting threshold—70 nanometers—around 2100. "Short-channel effects" involving uncontrollable leakage across channels compromise functionality at this scale by disrupting and compromising semiconductor effectiveness. Quantum effect phenomena in the 50-nanometer range and below pose other limits to miniaturization. Double-gate technology may help reduce channel width to as little as 20-25 nanometers. But, other obstacles emerge at this scale. Nanotechnologies—artifacts constructed at scales measuring one-billionth of a meter (about the length of ten atoms), or lower—open up a new frontiers for development.

Experimental silicon germanium chips—50 times faster than standard chips—outperform currently top-performing gallium arsenide. All told, nanotech products hold promise for using fewer materials, consuming less energy, minimizing wastage, and stretching out finite resources.

Technological resources that once dominated economies often

find new uses and much higher value-added uses over the millennia. Sand (silicon dioxide), for example, has been a linchpin resource in varying applications over thousands of years. Back in 3400 BC, beads became a significant factor in commercial exchange, and acquired greater importance when intricate beakers were fabricated around 1500 BC. Later on, use in cement, beginning around 300 BC in Pompeii, followed by concrete in Rome, 240-190 BC, gave rise to a new epoch of building construction. Sand in its purified forms (and doped with traces of rare earth elements) provides the basic building block of current Information Era technologies.

COMMUNICATION INVENTIONS—INCREASED RATES OF COMMERCIALIZATION

Time lapse between discovery and large-scale commercial penetration of new scientific technologies steadily decreases. Thousands of years lapsed between development of spoken words to written forms, and hundreds of years more between handwriting to printing. Radio took 30 years to amass 50 million users. Television required 13 years to match that feat. World Wide Web introduction attracted 100 million users within a mere six years. The Pony Express was displaced by airmail, which in turn has been supplanted by overnight mail, facsimile transmissions, and instant e-mail messaging.

Information/computer guru Ray Kurzweil delineates the following pattern for computer successive development: mechanical computing devices, 1900-1928; electromechanical (relay-based) computers, 1939-41; vacuum-tube computers, 1968-1998. Kurzweil points out that "The speed of computation has been doubling every three years (at the end of the twentieth century), regardless of the type of hardware used." He expects this pace to continue.

Less material intensive technologies cut communications equipment costs and lead to reduced pricing. Material cost of copper wire, for example, amounts to 80 percent. Material in fiber optic cable amounts to less than 10 percent. And during the early 1980s, material and energy cost in semiconductor chips amounted to as little as 2 percent of product total cost.

Kurzweil suggests that PCs costing around $1,000 will be able to process 20 quadrillion calculations/second by 2025. Nor does he stop there. He speculates that the brain's 100 trillion synapses represent one quadrillion bits. Specifying that one billion bits (128 megabytes) of computer RAM cost $200 in 1998, and that capacity doubles every 18 months, he estimates by 2023 quadrillion-bit memories will cost $1,000. Staggering the imagination, he contends that computer chips will operate one billion times faster than human brains!

All of this sounds a bit far-fetched. For perspective, bear in mind that even the best of the best don't get it right all the time. IBM founder Tom Watson erred, for example, when he contended "...there is a world market for about five computers" (1943). Ken Olson, president of Digital Equipment Corporation, asserted, "There is no reason for any individual to have a computer in his home" (1977). Bill Gates contended that "640K ought to be sufficient enough for anybody" (1981). Settings within which projections are made change. Great thinkers continually adjust their ideas as new potentials emerge. Ideas discussed in this article provide a framework for sizing up the future of communications.

"BIG SEVEN" TRANSFORMING COMMUNICATIONS TECHNOLOGIES

Telecommunications technology will experience more change in the next five years than occurred over the past 95 years. Seven vital technologies contribute to this outcome:

1. Transmission rates
2. Supercomputer speed
3. Artificial intelligence
4. Satellite communications
5. Wireless communications devices
6. Broadcast digital technologies
7. Internet resources.

Transmission Rates

This is an age of near-instantaneous communications. During the Stone Age early ancestors communicated at the rate of about one visual or audible message per second, the time required for simple gestures, grunts, body language, fire or smoke signals or reflected light to be conveyed. Today, mind-boggling terabit per second communications usher in rates of speed that divorce time from human capabilities.

Advanced rates of communications took off during the mid-1800s. Invention of the telegraph in 1884 enabled transmitting 5 bits per second. The telephone, developed in 1876, boosted the rate to the equivalent of 2,000 bits per second. Rates escalated rapidly from that point, rising from the equivalent of 30,000 bits with transcontinental transmission of three voice channels per wire pair. By 1940, the rate over coaxial cable rose to 480 voice calls over a single cable, the equivalent of 7,680,000 bits per second. The first programmable computer, ENIAC, operational in 1946, was capable of 5,999 instructions per second. In 1994 a DEC computer was capable of processing 1 billion instructions per second.

To help maintain perspective, bear in mind that one billionth of a second (one gigabit) is to a second what a second is to 31.7 years! By one estimate, the amount of information an individual uses in a lifetime is equivalent to a mere 20 billion bits of data. That amount of data, taking full advantage of current communication technologies, can be transmitted in the fleeting fraction of a second. In other words, the entire knowledge base individuals amass over an entire lifetime can be shunted from place to place, literally in the blink of an eye.

Wavelength division multi-plexing (WDM) of photonic signals tilted the entire field. Transmission rates skyrocketed from 20 billion bits per second using eight channels in 1995; 40 billion using eight channels in 1996; 400 billion utilizing 40 channels in 1997; to 800 billion using 80 channels in 1998; to a capacity of 1 trillion using the highest rated commercial cable available mid-2000. Bell Labs achieved speeds of 3.28 trillion bits per second utilizing 82 different wavelengths in early 2000.

Transmission rates at trillion bits per second also require some perspective. Laboratory demonstrations achieved transmission rates of 10 trillion bits per second in 1998. At 10 trillion bits per second, the 24 million books in the Library of Congress could be transmitted in about 18-24 seconds time! Transmission speeds will not end at this point. Alastair Glass (Bell Labs) speculated in 1998 that rates of 200 trillion bits per second would soon become possible. More astounding yet are the breakthrough potentials of ongoing research into quantum computers theoretically capable of transmitting at quadrillions of bits per second.

Supercomputer Speed

America's speediest computer, dubbed ACSI White, will cost $110 million to build. Like ENIAC, it will fill a large room, about twice the size of a basketball court! This supercomputer, situated at the Lawrence Livermore Laboratory, engages 8,192 IBM PowerPC microprocessors. It consumes enough energy to power 10,000 homes, considerably more than the huge power requirements of ENIAC. All of this sounds familiar. Scientific change, as noted, typically occurs at an increasing tempo and, over time, it scales inputs down to Lilliputian levels. When this ACSI White becomes operational in 2004, it will be capable of churning out 100 trillion bits per second (100 teraflops), or performing 16 trillion calculations per second!

Accolades to IBM's impressive achievement have been outdone elsewhere. No nation, after all, has a monopoly on invention. As of 2002, the world's fastest supercomputer kudos go to Japan. The NEC-built Earth Simulator, situated at the Institute for Earth Sciences in Yokohama, operates at a blistering 35.86 trillion (floating point) operations per second.

IBM's biggest and fastest computer now under development—Blue Gene—will operate at one quadrillion operations per second—when it becomes operational in 2005. IBM's Web site shows two versions under development: Blue gene/C/CU-11 and BG/P/CU08. IBM's Web site also lists two other supercomputers: QCDOC—CMOS7SF operating at 20 teraflops, and ASCI-Q operating at 30 teraflops.

The truly extraordinary thing about Blue Gene is the fact that the machine will be dedicated to biomolecular simulation, protein folding and protein reactions. One report asserts that this single-purpose machine will be devoted, over the course of an entire year, to explicating exactly how a single protein (composed of 150 amino acids) folds into its peculiar shape in a millisecond.

Rudimentary quantum-based computers have already been developed. Eventually, these devices are expected to operate at blistering quadrillion per second speeds. Grasping some concept of what quadrillion rates means helps to comprehend what's involved. The Library of Congress' 24 million volumes, assuming a megabyte per book (and 8 bits per byte), equals 193 terabits. This means that the total contents of the world's largest book accumulation could be transmitted in the merest parsing of a second!

Artificial Intelligence

Computers and artificial intelligence (AI) will be taking over more and more split-second human response. IBM's supercomputer that beat grand master chess player Garry Kasparov in 1995 led to speculation concerning reasoning powers and self-learning potentials. Problems that once required armies of people working their entire lifetimes to solve now can be solved in seconds. Ray Kurzweil, author of *The Age of Spiritual Machines*, foresees increased computer speed and transmission rates leading to voice entry and automatic language translation. These developments, he contends, pave the way for machines overtaking and surpassing capabilities of the human brain.

Computer Speech Recognition. Computers capable of speech recognition and direct data input were in use by 1998, and more primitive models considerably earlier. Voice recognition achieved a 10,000 word capacity with 95-98 percent accuracy by 2000. The English language utilizes 450,000 words, more than almost any other language. Those big numbers don't pose that big a barrier. The Merriam-Webster Third International Dictionary listed 70,000 words in the late 1990s. Usage is quite another matter. A learned person uses an average of 20,000 different words. Regularly used words total only 10,000. Average persons use about 5,000, and casual conversation involves a modest 2,000 words. Dealing with so few words, relatively speaking, amounts to kid's stuff.

Multiple language capabilities. The huge number of languages worldwide poses additional challenges. In 1995 there were 9,500 different languages and 96 official state languages worldwide. Although the number of languages is expected to decrease to 8,000 by 2025, the number of official state languages may increase to 150, thereby posing (at bare minimum) a 50 percent increase in translation needs. Word recognition software covering so many translations is not insurmountable.

Automatic language translation. While rudimentary voice translation software systems have been available for years, Kurzweil foresees sophisticated ones taking over chores like telephonic automatic language translation by 2007. Language translators capable of converting foreign languages into real-time audible signals or hard copy, once perfected, necessitates massive computer capabilities. Automated translation of telephone conversations—US/Japanese— was developed in 1998. Simultaneous language translation tears down one more barrier between peoples. International travel, tourism and diplomatic interchanges will benefit enormously.

By 2010, computers are expected to match computational capabilities of the human brain, an estimated 3.2 million instructions per second. A decade later, Kurzweil foresees personal computers capable of 20 billion instructions per second, equivalent (he claims) to the human brain. By 2029, Kurzweil predicts computers will be executing 200 trillion instructions per second. At this point, he speculates supercomputers could become so advanced that conferring "human rights," of a sort, will be widely discussed.

Kurzweil begins his straight-away path to AI by specifying the baseline of 100 billion neurons in the human brain. Assuming 1,000 interconnections between neurons, he arrives at a grand total of 100 trillion connections. Sounds impressive. It is. Unraveling and deciphering how and why the human brain works is not likely (in my opinion) to be understood for well over another 100 years. Back to Kurzweil's projections. Next, he assumes that neural circuits operate at a mere 200 calculations per second. Mathematic calculations, based on these numbers (100 trillion X 200), yields 20 quadrillion operations/second.

Dispensing with calculating potentials of human brains, Kurzweil proceeds to spell out where computers have been and where they are headed. Supercomputer speed increases as development time shrinks, suggesting ongoing trend potentials (within the physical limits of physical constants, as we know them). Kurzweil starts with a baseline of 2 billion computer calculations per second in 1997, assumes that speed doubles every year, and calculates that 23 interim doublings, indicating speeds of 20 quadrillion by 2020. That's how Kurzweil arrives at supercomputer capabilities similar (if not equivalent) to human brains within 20 years. Considerable controversy rages around Kurzweil's technological optimism.

Satellite Communications

The 1990s have been characterized as the era of optical fiber. The next several decades may be touted as the era of wireless communications. By 2005-2007, satellite service improvements, coverage and cost will encourage widespread use of this mode. Early use is largely taken up by commercial users. Consumer use will follow as costs drop. Some indicators of this trend:

• Commercial satellite operations in 1998 included 1,700 payload launches. Commercial satellite launches over the next 10 years were valued at $140 billion worth (May 1999). Additional cost for launch systems and ground services were tagged at $70 billion.

• Mobile and cellular phone subscribers, growing by leaps and bounds, could reach 32 million by 2007, generating $31.6 billion annually in revenues.

• Annual revenues from telephone services, high-speed Internet access, and imaging expected to be generated by satellites during 2008 were expected to reach $150 billion (International Space Business Council estimate).

• US commercial satellites, 200 of the 500 in orbit during 1997, were estimated to be worth at least $100 billion.

Satellite receivers initially were prohibitively costly and beyond consumer reach. Receiving antennas were so large and unsightly that zoning laws and nuisance restrictions barred them from use in residential neighborhoods. Smaller and less unsightly parabolic dish receivers, measuring a foot or so in diameter, pose little objection.

The first Earth stations established in the 1960s cost upwards of $10 million. By 1963, versions measuring 100 feet in diameter cost between $3-5 million. Second generation stations available in 1975 brought dish costs down to $100,000. Upscale retailer Neiman-Marcus' famed Christmas catalogue several years ago offered to install home satellite receiver dishes for $36,500. A short while later prices dropped to $10,000-$12,000. Currently, dishes measuring less than three feet in diameter can be purchased for about $100.

Wireless and Mobile Telecommunications

Cell telephone technology was developed by Bell Laboratories during the 1960s. Commercial US cell phone operations commenced in 1983. Units were cumbersome, costly and subject to restrictive regulations. Cell phones costing as much as $5,000 in 1986—a rich person's toy, or conspicuous consumption novelty—plunged to less than $100 today.

Economics play a key role in burgeoning wireless telecommunications growth. Installation costs are considerably lower than land-based lines. Telecommunication costs have dropped from stratospheric levels. A three-minute phone call between New York City and London costing $245 in 1920, and $19 in 1950, was only 78 cents in 1999. Soon, a telephone call to anyone from anywhere will cost the same as local calls. Distance will not matter. Wireless communication cost per minute dropped from 35 cents in 1998, to 27 cents in 1999, and 23 cents in 2000. The cost is projected to continue dropping from 21 cents in 2001, to 19 cents in 2002, and 18 cents in 2003 (The Strategis Group estimates).

Wireless and mobile communications devices of all kinds have come into their own. Unwieldy telephones of yesteryear have been replaced by featherweight versions with billions of times the capability of their predecessors. Cell phones weighing 4-5 ounces, pack the punch of a 1960s mainframe computer. Broadband system costs will come down, use will soar, and revenues will grow. Consumers will enjoy the added convenience of Internet and multimedia communications on the go.

Telecommunication handsets initially were designed and constructed to last 50 years. Today, handsets have relatively short life spans that no longer require "battleship specifications." User friendly operation, diminutive size, blinding and capacious sending and receiving rates, Web browsing capability, rapidly changing designs, and new styles encourage rapid turnover of mobile handsets. Obsolescence is measured in months, not years. The turnover and replacement rate for 1999 stood at 40 percent. Industry analysts expect nearly 50 percent of handset sales to be replacement purchases.

Overall, the trend is toward a universal communicator, a single unit used for digital transmission capabilities ranging from voice to video. Coalesced units will operate as a video-telephone, fax machine, computer, and smart card module database with all the data handling capability needed. Melding of multiple communications capabilities into mobile communications attracts mass consumer interest. As practical capabilities to access multimedia and Web retrieval develop, growth will explode. Older single-purpose devices and systems will become obsolete.

Added convenience of being able to pull up bits and pieces "on the fly" makes a valuable addition to overall computer/digital capabilities. That capability should not be confused with an "open ticket" to becoming the platform of choice. Acceptance of Web-surfing platforms depend, in large part, upon ease of use. Screen size and display capabilities pose a major roadblock to runaway use of hand-held diminutive screen devices for heavy-duty full-size screen tasks. Users may not like using one inch or other diminutive screen sizes to access Internet capabilities.

Powerful wireless phones and handheld or portable communication devices have been made possible by advances in materials sciences, especially solid state physics. Vacuum tubes the size of a potato shrank to peanut-size, only to be replaced by transistors. Next, transistors were miniaturized to the size of a fly-speck and densely packed into integrated circuits smaller than the size of a fly's wing.

Miniaturization, lighter materials, and long-life batteries make the devices enticingly convenient and attractive. This trend of doing more with less is characteristic of most technological advances.

Digital optical broadband telecommunications offer advantages that totally overshadow copper lines. Signals don't fade (as they do with analog); are immune to static and noise interference; operate with lower energy demand; and transmit at rates far surpassing the capabilities of wire. Perhaps most important, broadband allows multiple users to utilize channels simultaneously.

Mobile full-time communication access is being nurtured from birth these days. Parents rely on continuous monitoring of babies left in their cribs by two-way radio transmitters. Teens and fast-trackers everywhere wouldn't leave home these days without packing their mobile telecommunications device, whether it be telephone handset, personal communicator device, or other gadget. The modern world increasingly is bent on staying in touch.

Standard setting—surmounting incompatibilities. Obstacles involve surmounting system incompatibilities, and moving beyond slow and prohibitively costly transmission rates. Competing operating standards are diverse and incompatible, in many instances. All of that is about to change.

Europe utilizes the most widespread digital protocol, the Global System for Mobile Communications (GSM). Harmonization of operating protocols enabled the leading mobile systems companies in Europe to plow straight ahead forthright. The result was that Vodaphone, Ericsson and Nokia acquired market domination. Mobile phones achieved highest penetration levels early on in Europe (63 percent). Scandinavian nations achieved the highest market penetration anywhere, reaching 100 percent among teenagers. Some major metropolitan areas in the US have reached penetration levels approaching those in Scandinavian nations.

American cellular and personal communications services (PCS) squabble among themselves and jockey for position. Basically, three different digital wireless telephone technologies vie for market share: CDMA (Code Division Multiple Access), TDMA (Time Division Multiple Access), and GSM. CDMA involves three additional protocols. CDMA One (widely used for cellular phones), CDMA 2000 (eight channel capacity), and WCDMA (Wideband CDMA for speediest data handling). CDMA uses two air interface standards: cellular (824-894 MHz) and PCS (1850-1990 MHz). Further complicating matters, other standards apply to network interfacing, service options and performance standards. Special interfacing adaptations enabling telecommunications to operate on all three technologies have been developed—at a cost.

Underscoring the importance of operating standards, other protocols dealing with optical transmission systems also jockey for position and dominance. Competing standards—not interoperable— for the new G3 broadband systems pose problems, including wavelength division multi-plexing (WDM), dense WDM (DWDM), and synchronous optical network/synchronous digital hierarchy (SONET/SDH). Setting compatible operating systems is crucial to growth of these new modes.

Bringing the Internet to wireless communications devices represents another problem involving competing standards. Wireless Application Protocol (WAP) and Bluetooth have been put forward. WAP is an open system but it requires that Web pages be written in wireless markup language (WML), not hypertext markup language (HTML) typically used on the Internet

A single uniform standard would greatly advance commercial development. As major players vie for position, such squabbles are not uncommon—in any industry. Incompatible systems and interfaces have plagued many emerging technologies, ranging from railroad track sizes to fire hydrant couplings, nut and bolt thread-sizing, or VHS versus Beta videotape. The begrudging path to settling uniform standards hallmarks most competitive new technologies.

Broadband Digital Technologies

Melding of information and communication technologies creates a new force—tele-power—that is the driving force of global change. All-purpose personal communicator systems geared to societies "on the go" involve multi-functions: cell phone, e-mail capability, PC, Web surfer, fax, video-television, picturephone, AM-FM radio, global positioning system, and so on. "Teleinformatics," "telematics," and other new words have been coined to convey the coalescing of television, telephone and telecommunications of all kinds, with computers, data processing terminals, facsimiles and other elements of the microelectronics explosion.

Bottleneck to the newest generation of digital communications needs is the lack of bandwidth in existing systems. Broadband involves communications channels that handle frequencies above the narrow band range of voice frequencies, thereby enabling many simultaneous voice or data transmissions at high speeds. In an age of multimedia signal handling, such a communication "pipeline" becomes imperative.

Although prodigious teraflop transmission rates are coming, how soon will those capabilities be available to consumers? The answer depends, to a large extent, upon bigger "pipes." Telephone services, designed to carry short voice transmissions, fall woefully short of being able to handle prodigious amounts of multimedia digital data. Fortunes beyond belief are being invested by telecoms, wired and wireless providers, cable servers, television broadcasters, satellite systems, even radio, microwave and a host of other carrier/transmission technologies. Titanic-dimensioned struggles are under way. Vast fortunes have been waged on these technologies. Many fortunes have been lost. Timing is everything, as the saying goes.

A new generation of wireless service (third generation—3G) is being modified to handle transmission rates of up to 384 kilobits per second in wide area coverage, and 2 million bits per second in local areas. European and Asian nations enjoy a leg up with their greater use of wireless technologies. Experts place the US as much as 10 years behind other postindustrial nations in adopting these technologies. US conversion to 3G broadband technologies is not expected until 2005.

Coalescing of information technologies. Universal "digital language(s)" encourage melding of communications functions and purposes. Communications of all kinds—computers, consumer electronics, information, education and entertainment sectors—are all evolving, albeit slowly, into one seamless communications web. Boundaries disappear between voice and data, wireline and wireless, voice to text, and text back to voice. A single interactive information industry, based on standardized interfaces, was expected to generate more than $3.5 trillion in revenues by 2001.

Television's commanding 99 percent US household penetration makes it a strong candidate for morphing into the unified household information appliance of the future. Federal Communication Commission rules requiring the change-over from analog to digital signals by 2006 lend encouragement to that end. It isn't the only mode in the running. Indicative of these rivalries, television set sales were surpassed by computer sales during 1993.

Internet and World Wide Web

Interconnecting computers began in 1969 with a hookup of four computers. Developed by the Defense Department's Advanced Research Project Agency (ARPA), the system existed until 1990. By 1971 things hadn't changed much; a mere 15 sites with 24 connected computers were operational. The milestone event in 1972 was the first electronic mail exchange between two computers by Ray Tomlinson, who also established the @ signage icon. By 1974, 62 computers were hooked up. Seven years later (1981), there were 200, and 500 computers in 1983, then 28,000 in 1987.

During 1989, the World Wide Web (WWW) was created at the European Center for Nuclear Research (CERN), a Geneva-based particle physics lab, by Tim Berners-Lee. This breakthrough made multimedia available on the Internet in August 1991. During the early 1990s, WWW opened to commercial uses. Less than 1 million users were online in 1991. The turning point for opening up the Web was laid in 1991 when the first Web browser or software was released. During 1993, the National Center for Supercomputing Applications released versions of Mosaic, the first graphical Web browser for Microsoft Windows (developed by Marc Andreesson at the University of Illinois). Now marketed as the Netscape browser, this system facilitated navigating among the multimedia offerings. The Netscape Navigator browser was released by Netscape Communications in 1984, and host computers or servers swelled to 3 million. Users jumped to 28 million in 1996, 57 million in 1997, and 97.2 million in 1998. High tech enthusiasts insist that one billion users is big enough to dub the virtual world of the Internet as the eighth continent!

Not only has the volume of Internet users grown by leaps and bounds, but the kinds of digitally-dense transmissions (graphic material, streaming video, and so on) impose huge demands in carrying capacity. Telephone lines, which still carry most of the Internet traffic, are reaching limits of their carrying capacity. The infrastructure is rapidly being converted to broadband information-carrying pipelines of vastly increased capacity. As the quality, speed, clarity and low cost of the new mode take hold, consumers will switch over in droves.

CONCLUSION

Propagation and dissemination of digital communication of all types is becoming accessible to anyone and everyone, anywhere and anytime—for a price. Faster transmission rates and increasingly powerful computers propel development. Rapidly improving satellite communications, wireless and mobile communication devices, broadband, digital technologies, and Internet resources constitute the communication backbone. Territorial constraints and time of day no longer limit communications. *The Death of Distance: How the Communications Revolution Will Change our Lives,* written by Frances Cairncross, captures the nature of wrenching changes under way. Mind-bending potentials of artificial intelligence loom as communication changes reach toward surpassing human brain power. Perhaps one day far off, ESP will virtually moot the entire panoply of "traditional communications technologies." Time will tell.

FOUR MISCELLANEOUS TOPICS

MANAGING IN THE FUTURE:
WHAT MANAGEMENT SKILLS WILL BE NEEDED?

by

Raymond S. Kulzick

As we enter the new millennium, management is faced with many new challenges—not the least of which is a significant shift in the types of management skills that are essential for business and career success. Although the old skill set emphasizing hard work and task success will remain important, it is likely to be overshadowed by new competencies. The manager who wants to succeed in the new business environment will need to shift his or her emphasis towards the new critical management skills, developing these new abilities rapidly, or be left behind.

Ultimately, the internal dynamics of organizations are driven by external demands from the marketplace. In order to understand why these new managerial abilities will become of paramount importance, we need to look at the major environmental trends that businesses will face.

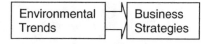

To succeed in this changed environment, businesses will need to adopt a new set of business strategies.

To successfully implement these business strategies, managerial strategies of the organization will need to change in some fundamental ways.

Environmental Trends → Business Strategies → Managerial Strategies

These changes, in turn, will require a new management skill set.

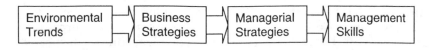

Environmental Trends → Business Strategies → Managerial Strategies → Management Skills

Raymond S. Kulzick *is an associate professor of management at St. Thomas University, Miami, Florida. He may be contacted at rkulzick@stu.edu.*

THE MAJOR LONG-TERM TRENDS IMPACTING BUSINESS

Although there are many trends that can be forecast to occur over the next 20 years, I believe that these can be narrowed down to eight primary environmental trends that will have a major influence on the American business environment. Similar impacts can be expected for businesses in other developed countries and some of the more advanced developing countries. Although listed separately, many of the trends interrelate and reinforce one another.

Level of Complexity

The world we live in has become increasingly complex. This trend will continue, with most human endeavors becoming even more complicated, confused, and convoluted. This will include markets, products and services, organizations, vendors, laws, regulatory agencies, technology, competitive relationships, and business problems.

Rate of Change

The rate of change has been steadily accelerating and will speed up even more in the future. Faster change will affect many areas, including the life cycles of markets and products, technologies, organizations, alliances and joint ventures, competitor relationships, industries, and consumer tastes.

Population Demographics

The population is aging rapidly. This means a major increase in the retired population (particularly those over 75) as well as a shorter-term increase in the 45 to 65 age group. This shift will impact areas including capital accumulation and consumption patterns, political and governmental policies, characteristics of both the workforce and consumers, and economic growth patterns.

Information

There will be a major shift away from products and services as the overwhelmingly dominant economic goods in society. These traditional goods will increasingly be replaced by information as the "product" that consumers, businesses, and individual managers most seek and need. Additionally, business processes (both internal and external) will become increasingly dependent on sophisticated information systems.

Ethics and Accountability

Recent corporate scandals and reactive legislation have only served to emphasize a growing demand from Americans that corporations become more ethical and responsible citizens—both domestically and internationally. This is not limited to the financial and investment community, but cuts across all aspects of the organization. This includes both internal aspects, such as employees rights, to external aspects, such as whether customers are treated fairly and ethically.

Economic Growth

Real economic growth has been nonexistent (or close to it) in the developed countries for the last 25 years. The only growth that has occurred can be accounted for by increased external borrowing, longer work hours (including growth in second jobs) and the rapid growth in the number of women in the workforce. These moderating factors have now been mostly exhausted, so there is likely to be very little real economic growth in the future for developed countries. Longer term, actual declines in the labor force are projected for most of the developed countries. Although the United States is forecast to have an increase, it is very small. It will be difficult to create much real economic growth when the labor force is declining rather than growing as it has in the past.

Internationalization

Although there may be short-term problems caused by regional trade blocs or sporadically rising nationalism, the trend toward increasing international interdependence and rising levels of trade will continue. Providers of goods, services, and information will increasingly compete in international marketplaces for customers, technologies, operations, and resources.

US Competitive Advantage

In international competition, the United States will continue to pursue a competitive advantage in leading-edge technologies, knowledge-based industries, and the "higher-level" knowledge portion of other industries. This would mean that, for example, manufacturing will decline, but not necessarily the design and marketing of manufactured products by US companies on a world-wide basis. The United States is not alone in this competitive strategy. The other developed countries are also pursuing the same strategy, although perhaps not on as broad a front.

STRATEGIC IMPERATIVE FOR BUSINESS

In order to compete successfully within an environment characterized by the above long-term trends, US business must be able to
respond simultaneously to three primary strategic imperatives that
traditional management approaches have found incompatible.

In the future, a successful business must (1) focus on delivering
real value to customers, but (2) be able to anticipate and take
advantage of rapid change (3) in an increasingly complex, ethical and
technical environment.

BUSINESS STRATEGIES

Leading American business firms are already experimenting with
and, in some cases, implementing a broad range of business
strategies in response to these environmental changes. Taken
together, the major, specific long-term business strategies listed below
are essential for businesses to successfully respond to the three-part
strategic imperative.

Core Competencies

Businesses will increasingly shrink the scope of their operations
to their core competencies. Vertical integration, in the traditional
sense, will continue to decline. However, businesses will carry this
much farther through a redefinition of which parts of their business
are critical to success and then retain only those core portions. This
de-integration of the basic business unit will be accomplished
through increased use of other firms to provide these "nonessential"
elements to the organization. This will include not only increased use
of subcontracting and functional outsourcing, but also a variety of
partnering arrangements.

Flexibility

The ability to respond flexibly to rapid environmental changes
will result in even more flexible organizations. Increasingly, even
large organizations will be restructured into smaller, self-supporting
units that can more quickly adapt to new conditions. The need for
increased flexibility will also lead to an increase in the use of more
temporary forms of organizational structures.

Value Sourcing

Just because an organization may view part of its operation as
"noncritical," and outsource it, does not mean that it does not play
an important economic role in the organization. Subcontracted goods
and services will be controlled increasingly tightly in order to assure

a high level of value to the acquiring firm. There will be an increasing shift toward assuring total value received rather than the narrower lowest-cost model.

Industry Interdependence

As organizations shrink to their core competencies, reducing the scope of their operations, organizations will become more dependent on others. Many more industries will follow the pattern of the personal computer industry, where, for example, even large companies like IBM are dependent on chip suppliers (like Intel) and software suppliers (like Microsoft). Even though IBM and Apple are trying to reduce this dependence, this will be unsuccessful in the long run as the industry interdependence model provides more flexibility and technological options to respond to rapid change. It is projected that this type of industry model will spread to more industries as change acceleration broadens and impacts additional industry groups. A current example is what is happening within the communications industry. Even though there is a major trend toward mergers and "bigness," simultaneously, the industry is splitting into specialized pieces within each delivery mode.

The Ethical Organization

Organizations will dedicate increasing amounts of effort and resources to guaranteeing not only compliance with a growing body of laws and regulations, but on assuring all their various internal and external stakeholders that they are conducting business in an ethical manner. This will become increasingly difficult to do as more demands are placed on organizations to act ethically and certify that their growing number of suppliers, subcontractors, distributors, and outsourced service providers are also behaving to the same high standards as the organization itself.

Small Business

In a time of huge merger announcements, it is hard to believe that the small business share of the economy is actually growing. But, because of massive layoffs that continue within these behemoths, it is. As large organizations shrink, the importance of smaller enterprises will continue to grow. Attempts by larger organizations to form smaller, more responsive internal units will be generally unsuccessful, which also will increase the importance of small businesses. However, the role of small business as a low-cost self-sufficient unit will increasingly change as small businesses adopt the same strategies as larger firms and become more tightly linked to both other small businesses and larger firms in the roles of vendors, customers, and partners. These ties will tend to become of shorter duration as changing needs drive frequent reshuffling of business relationships.

Joint Ventures

Just as small business and industry partnerships become of shorter duration, so will joint ventures. The "permanent" joint venture of the past will become a marriage of convenience for the short term, with each partner seeking to add to their own long-term goal accomplishment, rather than establishing a new permanent organization. Joint ventures and other forms of temporary partnering will increase in their potential rewards, but will also become far more strategically dangerous for the unwary.

Forced Turnover

Organizations will increasingly utilize strategies of forced turnover (such as layoffs and short-term employment contracts). External hiring at all levels will replace the historical reliance on internal promotions and retraining. These changes will allow the organization to quickly acquire new skills and knowledge, either for the long term or on a project basis. As a result, average tenure at a given organization and within a specific job will continue to decline.

Role of Consultants

As organizations seek to remain lean, yet responsive to rapid changes, consultants will find an increasing role as providers of specific technical, market, and management skills and knowledge. However, the long-term use of "feel good" consultants will decline sharply as both unnecessary and inappropriate to the smaller, more focused organizational environment. Consulting organizations will either become "total solution providers" or highly competent in narrow areas.

External Connections

As the environment changes faster and inter-business dependency rises, it will be increasingly important that organizations become more porous and externally connected, both formally and informally, at all levels. Although information systems may be able to provide some of this, interpersonal networking will be the predominant method. In a related area, the importance of a rapid and reliable method to assure the widespread internal dissemination of this external intelligence will become highly critical. The tools and approaches to succeed at this will, of course, vary widely between large and small organizations.

Internationalization

Increasing internationalization of business will occur at all levels. This will include ideas, technologies, information, markets, suppliers, production and operations, and capital sources. Although large transnational organizations will continue to expand, increasing internationalization will impact mainly on smaller firms as they are forced to expand their horizons beyond national borders on all fronts.

Flattening of Organizations

Organizations not only will shrink in scope, but also will continue to become flatter in their structures. This will lead to smaller, more self-sufficient decentralized organizations and a reduction in the size of central staffs. Staff units at the decentralized locations will need to be more generalist (less technical), and will be judged increasingly on their ability to contribute to the success of the business unit, and less on technical expertise. The model of a methodical and highly technical staff unit is becoming increasingly obsolete.

Information Systems

Major changes will occur in the area of information systems, as organizations try to accomplish two formerly disparate objectives. First, efficient centralized database control is essential if the organization is to maintain quality in its core information resources. Without such centralization, duplication and grossly excessive costs are inevitable and the firm will be unable to deliver value to its customers. Additionally, the smaller business units that are forecast for organizations will require a broader range of information to accomplish their objectives. The only way to provide this with efficiency is through centralized database control. At the same time, however, it is essential that individuals and smaller units have a high level of personalization and powerful tools that allow easy access and manipulation of a vast array of sources and types of information. People will become highly dependent on sophisticated and flexible information systems, yet the organization will need to provide these capabilities in a very efficient manner to small units without large support staffs.

Communications Systems

Organizations and individuals will become more dependent on computerized communications systems. The significant reduction in face-to-face communication and a corresponding increase in the use of electronic media for effective communication (both formal and informal) will become more critical to business success. The organization will need to maintain large, high-capacity, but flexible communications networks and improved communications tools to meet these needs. Because of the increasing geographical and time dispersion of workers and work times, traditional voice communications will decline over the longer term.

Core Stability

Many of the business strategies discussed involve the intentional creation of various forms of temporary and permanent instability in many parts of the organization. Such instability will dissolve rapidly into uncontrolled chaos, anarchy, and the ultimate demise of the organization, unless there is a strong, stable core within the organization that provides continuity, coordination, ethics, and a long-term view. The traditional means of providing this stability through long tenures in technical and staff departments will be counterproductive and unsuccessful in the future. Such stability and continuity must exist within the destabilized and changing operational units themselves. In other words, within the critical line functions, not in increasingly tangential staff areas. It appears that the only way to provide this continuity within line units without stifling change is through long-term employment of a carefully selected core of line managers. These people will need to be generalists, who are comfortable with technology and can manage technical people, but are not committed to specific technologies themselves.

MANAGERS IN THE NEW BUSINESS ENVIRONMENT

Changes in the business environment and new business strategies adopted in response will require a different blend of management skills, knowledge, and capabilities than in the past. This will be reflected in several significant ways.

Performance

Managers no longer will be able to hide within large bureaucracies, behind techno-babble, or play the role of follower-of-the-procedures. In the new flat organization with small units (or small businesses), everyone not only will have to perform reliably and productively, but be able to demonstrate their level of contribution to organizational goals.

External Yardsticks

In line with the shrinking of organizational scope, not only individuals, but also organizational units will need to prove their value versus external organizations who will be seeking to take over their functions. Just appearing to do a good job won't be enough. The question will become, Are you doing as good a job, and as efficiently, as an external contractor could do?

Strong Ethics

The ethical organization requires that a strong sense of ethics is infused throughout the organization and is respected and demanded as an essential part of the corporate culture. This means that our future managers must truly believe in and model ethical behavior if they are to instill it within their own units. This requires a strong sense of self and a willingness to speak up for what is right, not just what is easiest. The best organizations will increasingly seek out and value managers with strong ethical perspectives.

Job Mobility

Careers will span many organizations and a variety of job types. Although more managers may seek security within this fluid environment, they are unlikely to find it. The successful manager will welcome change and seek out advantageous transitions. Even those within large organizations will need to accept primary responsibility for finding their own way to their next position as their old one is phased out.

Adaptation

The increasingly fluid work environment will place a premium on the ability of managers to quickly and appropriately adapt themselves in many ways. This will include adaptation to new knowledge, new organizations, new people, new cultures, new products, new customers, new viewpoints, and new technologies. This adaptation will be required both within current jobs and in preparation for new positions.

Change

Managers will need to understand and be able to manage the process of change. This includes how and why change occurs, when change is positive, and how to channel and direct change. Since change can occur at different levels—organizational, cultural, and individual—the manager will need to understand multiple facets of the change process. Managers who cannot proactively manage change are likely to either try to prevent it or allow it to degenerate into counterproductive chaos—both equally deadly to a career short term and the organization long term.

Change Context

Being able to manage change will not be enough. The new

environment is more likely to produce an excess of pressures for change rather than too little. Managers will need to understand the overall context within which change is occurring if they are to determine which changes are beneficial and thus should be encouraged, and which change is not going to lead the organization in the right direction. Expertly guiding which changes will occur, and when, will be more important than being able to implement specific desired changes.

Flexibility

The organizational environment can range from rigidity to flexibility to anarchy. The manager will need to be able to balance the need for responsiveness and flexibility against an equally powerful organizational need to be productive and efficient. This balancing act will need to be orchestrated carefully to prevent chaotic and destructive swings in direction.

Shorter Work Relationships

Because of the shorter work relationships caused by frequent job shifts, temporary teams, project orientations, and the like, managers will need to be able to assess quickly and accurately the competencies and abilities of others in their new work environment. Equally important, they will need to be able to prove their own competence and value to other team members.

Managing Others

Managers will be overseeing the work of a wide variety and shifting range of technical specialists. Although not technical themselves, managers must be capable of effectively leading such work groups. In order to do so, they will need to be able to quickly judge the goals the group must achieve and determine the critical success factors that will be necessary to reach these goals. This will allow them to focus on managing these critical factors and not get overly involved or sidetracked by technical issues.

Distance

Face-to-face contact among managers and professionals will decline as team members retain their old physical locations within the company, work from their homes, or are based at customer or other external sites. Managers must face the reality that they will have to lead, motivate, communicate, monitor, and coordinate more and more of their staff in an environment of infrequent physical contact. This will require the proficient use of a broad range of electronic media.

Information

One of the major roles of the new managers will be to provide access to information needed by their unit, and coordinate information flows between their unit and the balance of the organization and the external environment. In order to accomplish this, managers will have to thoroughly understand the organizational information systems and be aware of the many changes that will be occurring continually within the structure, content, and capabilities of that system. Additionally, they will need to be adept at utilizing information systems as management and communication tools.

THE FUTURE

Will tomorrow's organizations be able to adopt the new strategies the changing environment requires? Will managers be able to successfully adapt to these new strategies? It won't be an easy task for either, but the time to start planning for these changes is now. Those organizations that can successfully implement the new strategic imperatives through appropriate business strategies are likely to succeed in the marketplace. Concurrently, those managers who can adapt to the new management skill and capability requirements will be rewarded with long, interesting, and challenging careers in the new business world.

DIVERSITY WITHIN UNITY

by

Amitai Etzioni

While traveling during the summer of 2001, I became deeply troubled by the rising level of animosity directed at immigrants and minorities in various countries. After doing some initial exploration, I found that my anecdotal observations were backed up by social science data. Polls done over the past two years show that 66 percent of Britons said there are already too many immigrants in the United Kingdom[1] and two-thirds of Germans opposed relaxing of Germany's immigration laws.[2] One out of every five French confessed to harboring racist and xenophobic views of some kind.[3] According to a Eurobarometer survey taken in 2000, about a quarter of all Europeans are dissatisfied with the idea of a society made up of different races, religions and cultures, and half reject the notion that multicultural diversity is a source of social strength.[4]

It also became clear that the existing political framework was, and in large part still is, unprepared to meet this challenge. Right-wing political parties and fringe groups have nurtured a heightened sense of nationalism and fostered a spirit of xenophobia. At the same time, many on the left have simply embraced an approach that condemns the anti-immigrant sentiments of the majority, typically characterizing them as shameful. Neither response, it seems to me, can adequately address the underlying problem. The right's xenophobia will lead only to more strife; the left's refusal to address the underlying tension will merely prolong the tension.

After consulting with fellow Communitarians, I drafted a new framework for addressing the relationships that majority populations have with immigrant and minority communities. As one reporter recently wrote, it was my intention to "stake out an alternative to unbounded multiculturalism and forced assimilation."

In time, my colleagues and I at the Communitarian Network generated a new project entitled "Diversity Within Unity" (DWU). The DWU approach presumes that all members of a given society will fully respect and adhere to those basic values and institutions that are considered part of the basic shared framework of the society. At the same time, each group in society should be free to maintain its distinct subculture—those policies, habits, and institutions that do not conflict with the shared core—and a strong measure of loyalty to its country of origin, as long as doing so does not trump loyalty to the society in which it lives. Examples of the element of unity—which all must share—are a respect for basic human rights, for democratic government, and for existing laws (until they are changed). At the same time, diversity in cultural tastes and religious

Amitai Etzioni *is the founder and director of the Communitarian Network and the first university professor of The George Washington University. He may be contacted at etzioni@gwu.edu.*

traditions would be welcome—and not just tolerated—as would immigrants' special interest in their country of origin.

After consulting with dozens of scholars and experts around the world, I drafted the DWU Position Paper. That document, portions of which follow this introduction, was then submitted for a two-day dialogue at a Communitarian Network meeting of 40 scholars and leaders from eight different countries during November 2001 in Brussels. Following the conference, the Position Paper was redrafted and sent out for endorsement. To date, more than 170 leaders and scholars from 21 different nations have signed on. Among them are a number of elected officials:

- Australian Minister for Citizenship and Multicultural Affairs and MP: Gary Hardgrave
- Belgian MP: Fauzaya Talhaoui
- Canadian MP: John Godfrey
- Costa Rican former President: Miguel Rodriguez
- German former Minister of Health and MP: Andrea Fischer
- German former MP: Cem Ozdemir
- German former President of the Bundestag: Rita Sussmuth
- Dutch MP: Oussama Cherribi
- Member of the Dutch Council of State: Ernst Hirsch Ballin
- Member of the British House of Lords: Lord Bhikhu Parekh.

Today, the Communitarian Network has moved the project to its next stage: introducing DWU to the world of policy makers. With the Communitarian Network staff, I am presently organizing a second transnational Diversity Within Unity Conference. Four or five dozen leaders from center-left and center-right parties in developed democracies will meet to discuss the DWU Position Paper, its implications, and its future. In furthering its mission to provide policy makers with the tools and background required to address the crisis currently crippling much of Europe and the rest of the world, the DWU Project promises to have a dramatic impact on the framework in which immigration law is created for years to come.

Below is an *abbreviated* version of the DWU Position Paper. (See www.communitariannetwork.org for the full text of the statement. Please address any feedback and questions to the director of the Diversity Within Project, Marc Dunkelman. His e-mail address is mdunkelman@communitariannetwork.org.)

We note with growing concern that very large segments of the people of free societies[5] sense that they are threatened by massive immigration and by the growing minorities within their borders that hail from different cultures, follow different practices, and have separate institutions and loyalties. We are troubled by street violence, verbal outbursts of hate, and growing support for various extremist parties. These are unwholesome reactions to threats people feel to their sense of identity, self-determination, and culture, which come on top of concerns evoked by globalization, new communications technologies, and a gradual loss of national sovereignty. To throw the feelings of many millions of people in their faces, calling them "discriminatory," "exclusionary," "hypocritical," and worse, is an easy politics, but not one truly committed to resolution. People's anxieties and concerns should not be dismissed out of hand, nor can they be effectively treated by labeling them racist or xenophobic. Furthermore, telling people that they "need" immigrants because of economic reasons or demographic shortfalls makes a valid and useful argument, but does not address their profoundest misgivings. The challenge before us is to find legitimate and empirically sound ways to constructively address these concerns. At the same time, we should ensure that these sentiments do not find antisocial, hateful, let alone violent expressions.

Two approaches are to be avoided: promoting assimilation and unbounded multiculturalism. Assimilation—which entails requiring minorities to abandon all of their distinct institutions, cultures, values, habits, and connections to other societies in order to fully mesh into the prevailing culture—is sociologically difficult to achieve and unnecessary for dealing with the issues at hand, as we shall see. It is morally unjustified because of our respect for some normative differences, such as to which gods we pray.

Unbounded multiculturalism—which entails giving up the concept of shared values, loyalties, and identity in order to privilege ethnic and religious differences, presuming that nations can be replaced by a large number of diverse minorities—is also unnecessary. It is likely to evoke undemocratic backlashes, ranging from support for extremist, right-wing parties and populist leaders to anti-minority policies. It is normatively unjustified because it fails to recognize the values and institutions undergirded by the society at large, such as those that protect women's and gay rights.

The basic approach we favor is Diversity Within Unity. It presumes that all members of a given society will fully respect and adhere to those basic values and institutions that are considered part of the basic shared framework of the society. At the same time, every group in society is free to maintain its distinct subculture—those policies, habits, and institutions that do not conflict with the shared core—and a strong measure of loyalty to its country of origin, as long as this does not trump loyalty to the society in which it lives if these loyalties come into conflict. Respect for the whole and respect for all is at the essence of our position.

THE LAW: VARIANCES, BASIC RIGHTS, AND COMPELLING PUBLIC INTEREST

Assimilationist models favor maintaining universal laws—those that apply to all citizens and other people within a given jurisdiction. They tolerate some variations and exemptions, but those are to be based on individual needs (e.g., mental illness) or demographic categories (e.g., minors), not on ethnic or racial groupings. Group rights are not recognized.

Unbounded diversity favors allowing each community to follow its traditions, even if they conflict with prevailing laws (for instance, allowing for forced marriages and female circumcision), although most pro-diversity approaches recognize that some universal laws must be observed.

The DWU model favors a bifocal approach: It sharply distinguishes between those laws that all must abide by and those for which various group-based variances and exemptions are to be provided.

STATE AND RELIGION

Most of the states here under discussion have historically had (or still have) one religion they formally recognize as their only one—Christianity in many of them (including a specific version of it, such as Lutheranism in Sweden). Almost all of these nations now face massive immigration and growing numbers of minorities that believe in different religions, especially Islam.

Where might one go from here? One option is to maintain the official church. A second option is to lift all religions to the same status as the official one. A third option is for the official standing of the prevailing religion to gradually lapse (as it did in Sweden). Under this model, no new religion would be recognized as the official religion of the state, but financial support for the clergy and places of worship of all religions would be provided. The amount would be determined by the number of people who indicate, annually, that a given religion is theirs. This third model is most compatible with the DWU approach because removing formal recognition of any state religion puts all religions on more equal footing (at least in legal terms and financially) without directly challenging history and identity.

DWU SCHOOLING

Schooling should neither be used to suppress all cultural differences and distinctions, nor to reinforce the segregation and ghettoization of minorities. A DWU approach, based on the concept of neighborhood schools, suggests that (A) a major proportion of the curriculum—say, 85 percent or more—should remain universal (i.e., part of the processes that foster unity). The commonalities of sharing 85 percent or so of the curriculum are intended not merely to ensure that all members of the next generation are exposed to a considerable measure of the same teaching materials, narratives, and normative content, but also that they will mix socially. Hence, teaching the same material but in ethnically segregated schools is incompatible with our approach. (Granted that the segregating effects of such schooling can largely be mitigated if they teach a considerable amount of the "universal" material and endeavor to provide for social mixing, if not in their own confines, elsewhere.) Although teachers of all backgrounds should be welcomed, insisting that children must be taught by teachers who are members of their ethnic group is not compatible with the DWU model. (B) Minorities should have major input concerning 15 percent or so of the curriculum; this could be in the form of electives or alternative classes in which students particularly interested in one subject or history or tradition could gain enriched education in that area. The universal, unity-related content of the curriculum should be recast to some extent to include, for instance, more learning about minority cultures and histories.

CITIZENSHIP FOR QUALIFYING, LEGAL IMMIGRANTS

A Diversity Within Unity approach emphasizes that societies are best served if those who are legal immigrants, and have met educational requirements, are allowed to become full citizens rather than treated as guest workers, which is often a term that conceals their true status as permanent, but second class, residents. The key to a democratically defensible and economically viable approach to immigration is to make decisions up front about the scope and nature of immigration that the nation favors. Then the government can provide permanent status for those admitted and facilitate their access to citizenship. This approach offers a more sensible way to staff the labor market, unite families, and allow citizens to assess the way immigration is shaping the national economy and culture.

All in all: Citizenship constitutes a critical way a person becomes a responsible and accepted member of a community. Hence it should not be awarded without proper preparation nor denied to those who have completed the required measure of acculturation.

LANGUAGE: AN INESCAPABLE ELEMENT OF UNITY?

A DWU approach recognizes the strong advantages of having one shared language (two if necessary) and teaching it to all immigrants, minority members, and people whose education is lagging for other reasons. However, the state should provide ample translators and translated documents for those who have not yet acquired the shared language, even if this results in some lowering of the motivation for immigrants to learn the prevailing language.

CORE SUBSTANCE, SYMBOLS, NATIONAL HISTORY, HOLIDAYS, AND RITUALS

In numerous situations, differences arise concerning matters that are relatively limited in importance in their own right, but acquire great symbolic meaning regarding the rejection, or partial or full acceptance, of people of diverse cultures. These include dress codes (e.g., regarding girls wearing headscarves), boys and girls swimming together, the display of ethnic vs. national flags, areas in which ethnic celebrations can take place, noise levels tolerated, and so on. In effect, practically any issue can be turned into a highly charged symbolic one, although some issues (such as flags) tend more readily to become such. These symbols serve as expressions of people's sense that their culture, identity, national unity, and self-determination are all being challenged. Only as these deeper issues are addressed might societies be able to work out satisfactory resolutions of the symbolic issues.

A DWU position indicates that we understand why people feel the way they do, but also assures them that the cultural changes that they must learn to cope with will not violate their basic values, will not destroy their identity, nor end their ability to control their lives. Indeed, it is the prime merit of the DWU approach that it allows such a framing of the issue, not as a public relations posture or a political formula, but as a worked-out model of laws, policies, and normative concepts that gives substance to such assurances.

The most challenging issue of them all is to consider, beyond changes in symbolic expressions and even in laws and policies, what would be encompassed in a modified but unified core of shared substantive values? Commitment to a bill of rights, the democratic way of life, respect for basic laws (or, more broadly, a constitutional faith or civic religion), and mutual tolerance come (at least relatively) easily. So do the communitarian concepts that rights entail responsibilities, that working differences out is to be preferred to conflict, and that society is to be considered a community of communities (rather than merely a state that contains millions of individuals). However, as important as these are and as much as they move us forward, these relatively thin conceptions of unity (and those limited to points of commonality—overlapping areas of consensus—among diverse cultures) constitute an insufficient core of shared values to sustain unity among diversity.

The challenge for the DWU model is to ask how the realm of unity, however restated, can be thick enough without violating the legitimate place of diversity. The answer may be found in part in secular humanist values and ethics (including respect for individual dignity and autonomy) and thicker communitarian values that spell out our obligations to one another. It may encompass a commitment to building still more encompassing communities (such as the European Union), to assisting those in need in the "have-not" countries, and to upholding the United Nations Universal Declaration of Human Rights. Still, the question stands as to what will provide a source of shared commitments to define and promote what is right versus wrong, and what will provide an answer to transcendental questions of life, as far as they concern public life, if it will not be based on religious doctrines, nor be sheerly relativistic or based on the beliefs of particularistic groups.

The DWU approach is a work in progress. It does not claim to have all or even most of the answers needed to bridge the schisms that have opened up between many immigrants and the majorities in the free societies in which they live. It does offer, we state, a basic orientation that respects both the history, culture, and identity of a society and the rights of members of the society to differ on those issues that do not involve the core of basic values and universally established rights and obligations.

NOTES

1. Anne Karpf, Recent Press Reaction to "Asylum Seekers Arriving in Britain Seems Uniquely Virulent," *The Guardian*, June 8, 2002.
2. Derek Scally, "Germany Requires a Change of Image to Attract Workers," *The Irish Times*, July 20, 2001.
3. Jon Henley, *The Guardian*, August 14, 2001.
4. Stryker McGuire, "The Fear Factor," *Newsweek*, May 6, 2002.
5. To allow for productive deliberations, we limit this initial examination to well-established nations and those with democratic governments, including those in Western Europe, North America, Japan,

and Australia. We do not deal with immigration and identity issues in countries that are in the nation-building stage (and hence might need to first build a shared identity and shared institutions before they face the question of how these might be protected or changed) or in those that rely on a non-democratic government to deal with the issues at hand. The discussion covers both immigrant and minority groups of citizens within a country.

THE MODERN SIGNIFICANCE OF WOMEN'S LIBERATION AND MARRIAGE FOR LOVE

by

Charlotte Waterlow

The United Nations' Universal Declaration of Human Rights of 1948 may be regarded as the moral code of the modern age. Most societies are now struggling to implement these rights, and violators of human rights are condemned around the world. This 200-year-old development—its token birth date may be taken as 1789, the year of the French Revolutionaries' Declaration of the Rights of Man and of the signing of the American Constitution—represents, I suggest, a mutation in human consciousness, a leap forward into psychological maturity.

The specific rights proclaimed in the Universal Declaration are well known: the civil rights, freedom of speech, assembly, travel, worship, to form associations, to have a fair trial, and so on; the political right to take part in the government of one's country; and the social rights to a decent standard of living and to education. And included is the right of men and women freely to choose their marriage partners, and to enjoy equal rights during marriage and at its dissolution (Article 16). In the Western world we tend to take these rights for granted. We do not realize that their philosophical basis is revolutionary: the simple concept that they belong to *persons*, as such, because the purpose of human life is "the full development of the human personality" (Article 26 [2]) the development of the *creative potential of each person, male and female....*

With the partial exception of those of ancient Greece and Rome, traditional societies were organized on the basis of the idea that the purpose of an individual's life was to perform his or her *duties* as a cell in the social organism, for example as a peasant, a slave, a scholar, a warrior, a landowner, a priest, a housewife or a courtesan. In traditional Japan, a person who behaved in an "other-than-to-be-expected-way" could be executed.[1] In traditional East Africa an expression of personal originality led to ostracism from the tribe, a fate worse than death.[2] In traditional India a similar fate befell anyone who broke the innumerable rules of the 3,000 sub-castes; at the end of her life, Gandhi's sister cursed her great brother for condemning her "to a lifetime of humiliation and ostracism by the people about whom she minded, the orthodox of her own sub-caste and neighborhood," because he broke all the caste rules and attacked the whole system.[3] The concept of human rights is therefore as explosive, in terms of the release of psychic and spiritual energy, as the splitting of the atom has been in terms of the release of physical energy.

Perhaps, therefore, the key question for the modern world is: *Who*

Charlotte Waterlow *is an author and retired school teacher from Cirencester, Gloscestershire, United Kingdom. She may be contacted at (+44) 01258 640075.*

is a person? The freedom of self-expression, which the implementation of human rights promotes, means that a person is free to be creative or destructive. The abuse of this freedom has produced immense tensions, massive violence and profound psychological alienation. But a reaction into authoritarianism is not the answer. We must struggle forward towards maturity, transmuting destructive urges and developing personal creativity—in freedom. And freedom implies love.

How shall a person realize what his or her inherent *potential* is? As Pascal said: "Thou wouldst not have sought Me if thou hadst not already found Me." This brings us face to face with the key concept of *archetypes*. The contemporary relevance of the key concepts of Plato and Aristotle falls outside the scope of this article. Suffice it to say that Plato's concept of archetypes as "perfect forms," ideas in the Mind of God, emanating from a transcendent Source beyond Time and Space, represents the loftiest vision of the human potential expressed in metaphysical terms. Add to this Aristotle's "teleology," the idea that each organism is *evolving* towards its inherent end (telos); add also the Christian teaching that the soul has available for its "redemption" the divine power of Grace focussed through a supreme Person, Christ, and you have a logically coherent and comprehensive metaphysical basis for answering the key question. (In this context Jung's archetypes, although useful at the psychological level—see below—are inadequate metaphysically because they are "subjectivized"—if I may coin such a clumsy word—rather than related to the objective, transcendent spiritual reality of God.)

In its present stage of development the modern world is inevitably secular. The Founding Fathers of the United States were clear that the rights set out in the Constitution's Bill of Rights stem from God. The United Nations' Universal Declaration of Human Rights makes no such claim. Science, which complements human rights as the second foundation stone of modernity, is by its nature concerned with the physical, not the metaphysical, world, and the prevailing scientific climate of thought has therefore promoted secularity. The traditional religions are discredited, at least in their traditional form, because they supported social, economic and political structures in which the development of personhood had no scope. The fact that humans are now able, for the first time, to steer the evolutionary process itself and the fact that they have it in their power to destroy or transform the planet, poses the vital challenge: to grow up or blow up. The world today is like a supersonic plane whose pilot, humankind, does not know where he is supposed to go. Only by growing up, that is, by growing into the archetypes, which are inherent in our souls, can we discover the goals for the evolution of humankind. And "marriage for love" is, I suggest, central to this great process of growing up.

TRADITIONAL ATTITUDES TOWARD WOMEN AND MARRIAGE

In traditional societies the general nature of the man/woman relationship and the social structures based on it were decided by *men*. We may distinguish three basic attitudes: first, the woman is man's property, and marriage is a contract concerning this piece of property; second, that woman represents man's lower nature, the "get-thee-behind-me-Satan" projection; and third, that woman represents man's higher self, the "pedestal" projection.

Woman as Property and Marriage as Contract

Traditional marriages were normally arranged by the parents on the basis of such factors as ethnicity, caste, wealth, religion, and ability to bear sons. Often the partners were still children—Gandhi and his wife were both 13 when they were married in 1882—and met for the first time on their wedding day. In Africa the husband's family often bought the bride by offering a "bride price" in the form of cattle. In India, China and medieval Europe the bride's father bought her a husband by offering a dowry, often ruining himself in the process. Although dowries have been illegal in India since the early fifties, young brides without adequate dowries are still being murdered by their rapacious in-laws. Marriages arranged on the basis of such factors are not out of date in modernized countries; *The New York Times*, on December 31, 1977, quoted an advertisement from Japan: "Oteocho, Japan: 'Wanted: 8,000 brides for 8,000 grooms. Young women must be willing work hard in house and fields. Daily cooking. Also husband's bath preparation. Desire for many children imperative. Must be respectful of and obedient to in-laws. Taste for long winters away from town preferable. One-way fare provided. Apply Hokkaido Farmland Bride Liaison Bureau.'" If the wife did not fulfill her part of the contract, in particular, if she did not produce a son to carry on the family line in this world and the next, he could get rid of her. If she broke her contract by committing adultery he could, in many societies, kill her, while in most societies, with the exception of Christendom and European Jewish communities, polygamy or concubinage was institutionalized. Men had control of their feminine property; and they often ensured that their women had no contact, throughout their lives, with any men other than those in their immediate family, or with any women other than those with whom they worked in the fields. "Women led a strangely huddled life," wrote a British official of colonial India. "You hardly ever saw them. If you went through a village they quickly veiled their faces and shrank indoors. If you entered a house there would be a great rush of scampering feet as they made for some inner room.... Men sat and ate with men—not with women.... Of women as an active part of life, as a valued source of love and sex, there was not a trace."

In many societies, notably those of the Far East, India and Islam, the position of women deteriorated as the centuries rolled on. What were the men doing, not only to their women but to themselves? The answer is hinted at in a striking African custom: "In the Ivory Coast ... initiation (of boys into manhood) has two denouements: one when the masked dancers who have represented the gods and the social forces suddenly take off the masks and put them on the boys; the other when the innermost secrets of the men's religious societies is exposed to them—and turns out to be a woman." Men were suppressing their own feminine nature.

The "Get-Thee-Behind-Me-Satan" Projection

Through the centuries men who were seeking God projected certain emotional attitudes on to women. The negative projection is that of the theologian who, over-emphasizing the rational intellect as he pours over the scriptures, becomes unable to love and therefore obsessed with fear of lust. This fear inspires him to treat women as temptresses luring him to Hell. "I feel that nothing more turns the masculine mind from the heights than female blandishments and that contact of bodies without which a wife may not be had," wrote Saint Augustine, who abandoned the woman who had been his devoted mistress for 20 years to follow Christ. Saint Jerome, the famous translator of the Bible into Latin, wrote to a Spanish Christian who had vowed to live physically apart from his wife: "You have with you one who was once your partner in the flesh but is now your partner in the spirit; once your wife but now your sister; *once a woman but now a man; once an inferior but now an equal.*" A modern Indian scholar writes that "Buddhist thought gives honor to women to this extent, that it never doubts the possibility of her putting off woman's nature, and even in this life becoming, as it were, a man." Those religions, which developed an excessive dogmatism and legalism, viz. Orthodox Judaism, Orthodox Islam and Protestant Christianity, tended to conceive God in exclusively masculine terms. This masculine denigration of the feminine aspect of the cosmos has tended to foster built-in attitudes of arrogance and domination in men and of submission, inferiority and childishness in women.

The "Pedestal" Projection

The mystical tradition enshrined in the ancient Mysteries, which flows like a deep undercurrent through all the great religions, makes two affirmations regarding "the feminine." First, the cosmos is bi-polar in nature. The creative tension and unity between masculine and feminine, Father and Mother, Sun and Moon, Heaven and Earth, Yin and Yang, god and goddess, pervades all things. To the ancients, therefore, the mind was illuminated and the heart purified when the light of Heaven brought masculine and feminine into perfect harmony in the soul. The Greeks embodied Wisdom in a goddess, Pallas Athenae, not a god; and the last line which Goethe wrote was: "Das ewigliche Weibliche sieht uns hinan"—"the eternal feminine leads us upwards."

Secondly, this balance can be described as the archetypal marriage. If archetypes in the Platonic sense exist, then each of us fulfills our inherent potential, and becomes the celestial being which we truly are, when united with our celestial "counterpart." This idea is to be found in many of the mystical traditions, leading to the concept of human marriage as a sacrament, "made in heaven"—as in Hinduism and Christianity—rather than as purely a contract; and it is found in some of the greatest poetry, for example, in Shakespeare's strange poem "The Phoenix and the Turtle":

> So they loved, as love in twain
> Had the essence but in one:
> Two distincts, division none:
> Number there in love was slain....
>
> Reason, in itself confounded,
> Saw division grow together:
> To themselves yet either-neither,
> Simple was so well compounded.
>
> That it cried how true a twain
> Seemeth this concordant one!
> Love hath reason, reason none
> If what parts can so remain.

Shakespeare's poem gives the impression that the phoenix and the turtle stand on the same ground, whether it be on earth or in heaven, and love as equals. The same may be said of the prince and the princess in Mozart's opera *The Magic Flute*, another great artistic portrayal of the archetypal marriage based on Freemasonic teachings. But often this lofty concept of the celestial marriage, formulated by *men*, suggested that the man was drawn upwards to heaven by his "better half" who was already there, either objectively, a risen soul, or subjectively, through her purity of heart. He projected his spiritual aspirations on to the archetypal woman. This "pedestal projection," was of course, the major inspiration of European chivalry, and found one of its highest expressions in Dante's poetry. Dante hardly knew his paramour, Beatrice. She died at an early age, and he subsequently married and led a life of normal sexuality. But it was the image of Beatrice, not that of his wife, that inspired his great poetry, which "makes the love of woman a pathway from heaven to earth," and "sets forth a creed of love, as ideal as human nature can well sustain."[4] A secret teaching of Judaic mysticism puts the situation bluntly. When a *man* is away from his wife on a journey, or studying the scriptures with other men, he is accompanied by a heavenly mate, an angelic female presence, in order that his spirit may remain stable in the "male/female" consciousness. When he returns home it is his religious duty to have conjugal intercourse with his wife, and if she should conceive, "the heavenly partner bestows upon the child a holy soul."[5] But there is no word in these teachings of the *wife's* heavenly mate, an angelic masculine presence; thus when *men* have thought about the mystical concept of the twin soul they have tended to concentrate on their own feminine counterpart, and to ignore the concept of the masculine counterpart of the human woman who ministers to them. What would happen to the man's ego if he had to contemplate the existence of a glorious male presence brooding over, loving and inspiring his wife?

The pedestal projection is marvelously developed in two of the most famous works of modern literature, Goethe's *Faust* and Ibsen's *Peer Gynt*. What happens, at the hands of these great writers, to the loving and saintly woman while she waits to redeem and uplift her man? Peer Gynt spends a lifetime of ego-centered experience and experiment before he returns in old age to Solveig, the sweet love of his youth, now old, blind and apparently celibate. Because she has spent her whole life waiting for him, he now discovers, through her love, the meaning of *his* life.

Peer Gynt: Tell me, then—where was my real self,
                Complete and true, the Peer who bore
                The stamp of God upon his brow?
Solveig: In my faith, in my hope and in my love....
Peer Gynt: Mother and wife! You stainless woman!
                Oh, hide me, hide me in your love!
(Clings to her and buries his face in her lap. There is a long silence. The sun rises.)[6]

The fate of Goethe's Gretchen is much worse. Seduced, ruined and abandoned to her execution for murdering her baby by Faust at the age of about 15, she is not in a position to save his soul until both have been in the next world for some time. At the level of ordinary life, therefore, the pedestal projection seems to the realistic advocate of women's liberation to be but another example of the way in which the male ego "uses" women. Yet, as we shall see, there may be more to it than this.

THE MODERN ATTITUDE TOWARD WOMEN AND MARRIAGE

The modern attitude is that men and women should relate to each other essentially as *persons*; and it is therefore necessarily a *shared* attitude. For the first time in history a *woman's* attitude to the man/woman relationship is being expressed. It has two aspects. First, the central relationship of a man or a woman's life, his/her marriage, is now regarded as not essentially contractual—though a legal contract may be necessary for practical purposes, as clothes are to the body—but a union of minds and souls as well as of bodies. The partners are expected to relate happily and equally in terms of character, intellect, interests, habits and styles, so that they can share every aspect of their lives. The force which unites persons, as such, is love: and love, unlike the factors on which the contractual relationship is based—duty, obedience, hard work, possessiveness, dependence, desire and so on—is spontaneous and can only flourish in freedom. And so, in the modern world, an entirely new situation has arisen at the heart of society: Men and women are expected to "marry for love," to choose their partners themselves and to give each other freedom of self-expression and self-development.

The institution of the contractual marriage is therefore breaking down. The Cuban Family Code of 1973 exemplifies the universal development. The old Code defined marriage as a "contract," and implicitly recognized the husband as lord and master of the family. The new Code defines marriage as "the voluntarily concerted union of man and wife legally joined, to live their lives in common." When the core of the relationship was a contract there were dire penalties for breaking it. But now that the core of the relationship is expected to be "love," people feel that they have a "right" to break the contract, that is, to divorce, if love has died out or proved to be a mirage. "Is it a sacrament to tie people up to bite each other and hate each other?" asked Jawaharlal Nehru, India's first prime minister, when he introduced India's first secular divorce law in the early 1950s.

This raises the question: What is "love" between a man and a woman as *persons*? No amount of "Women's Lib" can alter the physiological fact that nature has assigned to women alone the role of producing children. And there is a spiritual factor. Modern psychology has helped to make modern man aware that lust, like gluttony, diminishes his personhood. The "get-thee-behind-me-Satan" fear of sex has been rightly debunked; but those who, like the novelist D.H. Lawrence, have sought to substitute for this fear the idea that sex *is* spiritual love, have identified the actual phenomenon with the archetypal ideal. Common sense and life's experience tell us that the union of souls (if the soul exists) is one thing, which we share with the angels (if they exist); and that the union of bodies is another thing, which we share with the animals. If, however, the two experiences can be blended, then the reproductive process might be spiritualized, and a higher race be born. The idea that a new and higher race is emerging as a result of the evolution of consciousness is in the air today. A hundred years ago an English poet wrote:

These things shall be! A loftier race
Than e'er the world has known, shall rise
With flame of freedom in their souls
And light of science in their eyes....

New arts shall bloom of loftier mould,
And mightier music thrill the skies,
And every life shall be a song,
When all the earth is paradise.[7]

(To take this idea and then give it a perverted twist—the "new man" is "Aryan man," or "proletarian man"—has been a secret source of the psychological power of the modern totalitarian ideologies.)

These concepts—that people should marry for love, and that out of their love a higher race may be born—have two major implications for the modern world. First, biological relationships are no longer the dominant relationships in the lives of many modern people. They have their obligations, naturally, to their biological relations. But *friends*, people they love as *persons*, increasingly constitute their most important relationships. And these friends may be found in different countries and social classes, and among the other sex. Modern communications are providing the physical basis for a global network of personal relationships. As education, sophistication and higher standards of living spread, as human rights are implemented, what the French Jesuit theologian Teilhard de Chardin has called the *noosphere* is developing. The blending of consciousness on a planetary scale would seem to be in the trend of things. The vision of a global family is emerging.

This means that, secondly, the biological situation is beginning to reflect the archetypal pattern. Matter *is* being spiritualized. The introduction of "family planning," a concept hitherto unthought of, is an important adjunct to marrying for love. In the biologically-oriented society children are desired in order to provide labor, to satisfy *machismo*, to carry on the ancestral rites, to care for their parents in old age, and so on. In the spiritually-oriented society they are desired in order to enrich the world with new personalities. In the first case poverty and ignorance produce large families—leaving the girl who has been producing a child a year from the age of 15 to 25 or 30 a haggard old woman at 35. In the second case, parents plan to ensure that they will give the two or three children whom they decide to bring into the world conditions for the development of their personalities. Men and women are taking the creative process into their own hands; and this opens up the possibility of bringing the human family into the line with the archetypal family.

At present the situation is, inevitably, very confused. In the modernized countries, the scientific and agnostic climate of thought tempts many people to identify spiritual unity with sexual unity.

And when the biologically-based family breaks down before its members are sufficiently mature to establish the spiritually-based family, the result is a dangerous state of psychological alienation. It is no wonder that marriage for love is profoundly difficult to fulfill. The implications of an urge which links the depths of the biological with the heights of the spiritual are beyond the comprehension of the vast majority of people who are responding intuitively to it. But if this thesis be sound, more and more people will gradually find themselves feeling and expressing a deeper and more marvelous quality of love; the human race, as it matures, will *learn to love*.

This means that in the modern world the treatment of women *as persons* is transforming society. For the first time in history, men are having to relate to women outside the home, the bedroom and the field. Everywhere a man goes in a modern society he finds women around, and he is forced to cope with them as intellectual and social equals. He cannot behave like the don at Cambridge University, England, who, entering a lecture hall which contained only some women students said: "I see that there is no one here," and walked out. If the creative tension between male and female is part of the universe, then the establishment of a balance in all spheres of life could have as profound an effect on the psyche of the planet as marrying for love. The opening of professional careers to women and other aspects of "equal rights" have not yet done much to achieve this, because so far the emancipation of women has meant that women have had to scramble into the men's world, and there to ape the men. In this context Jung's psychological archetypes are relevant. According to Jung, every person, male and female, is a complex of qualities which can be regarded as masculine (*animus*) and feminine (*anima*). Rationality, organization, initiative, courage and "toughness," for instance, are *animus* qualities; while intuition and compassion are *anima* qualities. Psychological maturity is achieved when *animus* and *anima* are harmoniously developed in a man or a woman. The traditional societies have tended to cultivate the masculine qualities in men and the feminine qualities in women, producing immature and unbalanced personalities. The emergence of women into the men's world is impelling them to develop their *animus*, their masculine qualities. The fact that women are being equipped to look after themselves and to contribute the product of their minds and hearts to the general pool of human creativity is surely a supreme human benefit. Meanwhile, the effect of their presence as partners is to stimulate, in men, the development of the *anima* qualities. Thus the emancipation of women is a vital factor in the maturation of the human race. When women are rational and men are intuitive, wisdom will illuminate their joint counsels.

There is however, more to it than this. Jung himself, although no metaphysician, called his *animus* and *anima* concepts "archetypes"; each man and each woman is seeking his or her ideal in someone of the opposite sex. Normally, of course, this search involves a large element of projection: The person who inspires the *animus* or *anima* ideal in the heart of the lover is normally a fallible and ordinary human being. But Jung's concept persuades us to look again at the phenomenon of "pedestal projection." Anyone who has experienced romantic love knows the wonderful sensation of fundamental happiness and enhanced consciousness which love quickens. What is this elixir which touches the core of my being, which in a strange way hurts, yet with the hurt brings an indescribable blessing? Perhaps my beloved has awakened in me my own archetypal qualities because he or she has seen his *anima* archetype in me. Perhaps Dante, Goethe and Ibsen had a valid vision, although they expressed it only in masculine terms. If so, the modern mixing of men and women as equal *persons* is providing the conditions for a far deeper love to flourish between them than ever before on a general scale. Men will discover their true selves through women, and women through men, as love illumines the mirror which each holds up to the other. Those who have looked in this mirror will have gained wisdom; they will know what it is right to do; love will give them the strength to do it; and irrationality and anger will fade away like mists before the rising sun. A new era of human fraternity, peace and creativity will dawn.

As the 19th century English scholar Matthew Arnold[8] wrote:

> If ever the world sees a time when women shall come together purely and simply for the benefit and good of mankind, it will be a power such as the world has never known.

NOTES

1. Lafcadio Hearn, *Japan: An Interpretation* (London: Macmillan, 1904), 193.
2. Sir H.H. Johnson, *The Opening Up of Africa* (London: Home University Library, 1937).
3. Taya Zinkin, *Caste Today* (London: Oxford University Press, 1962), 49.
4. Edmund G. Garner, Introduction to *The Divine Comedy of Dante*, translation by Rev. H.F. Cary (London: J.M. Dent, 1948) p. viii.
5. *Zohar: The Book of Splendor: Basic Readings from the Kabbalah*, ed. Gershom Scholem (New York: Schocken Books, 1975), 34-35.
6. Henrik Ibsen, *Peer Gynt*, translated by F. Farquasson Sharp, (London: J.M. Dent, 1930).
7. John Addington Symonds, 1840-1893.
8. Matthew Arnold, 1822-1888.

LABOR UNIONS, COMPUTER POWER, AND THE NEAR FUTURE

by

Arthur B. Shostak

When in 2025 savvy scholars discuss over the Internet the unvarnished history of organized labor in the early 21st century, much is likely to be made of the fact that the use of the Internet in 2003 by labor's anti-war plurality demonstrated once and for all the extraordinary power of information technology (IT) in shaping labor's fate (Lee, 1997).

Until that time it was easy for decision makers in the AFL-CIO and its 64 International Union to direct, constrain, and control the uses and impact of IT. Most of labor's Web sites were uni-directional, weighed down by top-down sanitized material, or, "business as usual." Only a few activist zines and listserves ventured into the high quality zesty material that always beckoned (e.g., Eric Lee's Labour start.org; tkatona@portup.com, OPEIU Local 512's On Line 'Zine!; MODEM, brimitch@springnet1.com; Solidarity4Ever-subscribe@igc.topica.com) (Shostak, 2002).

A veritable "explosion" occurred in the late winter of 2003 when anti-war union rank-and-filers reached out via the Internet to hobble together overnight the most powerful juggernaut of membership opinion the Labor Movement had seen since the rush in the 1930s to create the CIO. (According to a spring issue of *Labor Notes*, "By March 2003 roughly 130 local unions, 45 central labor councils, 26 regional bodies, 11 national/international unions, and the AFL-CIO Executive Council had passed resolutions condemning the Bush administration's actions around Iraq in varying degrees of criticism.")

Labor leaders scrambled to get back in front of the parade, and the general public and the media were treated to the unprecedented sight of a cadre of dedicated members actually taking the lead. Organized labor, in the United States and worldwide as well, was never the same—as this demonstration of what CyberUnionism could, should, and would mean in labor's reinvention of itself was clear, emphatic, and empowering (Shostak, 1999).

To think usefully about organized labor today is to think immediately about tomorrow, so fast and thoroughgoing are the changes with which labor must deal. In particular, expectations concerning labor's current and prospective use of computers are very exciting: little wonder certain academics now contend "employee organizations will prosper in cyberspace because the Internet is the bridging technology between an increasingly heterogeneous workforce and individualistic workers and the collective activity and solidarity that lie at the heart of trade unionism." (Freeman and

---

Arthur B. Shostak *is professor of sociology at Drexel University, Philadelphia, Pennsylvania. He may be contacted at shostaka@drexel.edu.*

Diamond).

As for computer use tomorrow, organized labor should be busy preparing for mind-boggling changes: Internet cognoscenti, for example, "are betting they will soon rekindle the mega-innovation of the Web's early days (a mere ten years ago)—a world of pervasive computing that lets people communicate more efficiently than ever" (Ante).

For example, by the end of 2003 there may be more mobile devices than PCs accessing the Internet, so powerful appears the next "killer ap," the "teleputer" (otherwise known as an advanced wireless mobile phone). Keen competition in 2003, however, is expected from Microsoft's Tablet PC, a portable book-sized, three-pound wireless "wonder." Proponents hail it as "a revolutionary device that actually replaces the laptop in your briefcase and the PC on your desk" (Levy, April 30, 2001). By 2007, as many as 59% of all Americans are expected to own a device that can access mobile data (Gunther).

Where stationary PCs are concerned, knowledgeable forecasters expect household penetration to plateau at about 73% by 2005, up from 57% in 2000, an expansion that underlines the increasing number of unionists able to use labor Web sites and access labor e-mail from their living room (Baker).

Union households already outdistance all households in possession of at least one PC (some 60% in January 2000), and this gap is likely to persist, if not widen (Lazarovici). By 2007, then, a significant number of union influentials (officers *and* members) may carry a compact picture-phone and computer and dictate to it by voice and listen to it in turn. They may use it to access any type of information, anywhere, at anytime. To stay in touch with significant others all the time. To send and receive messages in all languages, as if their own. To surf the Internet and Web with the stress-less help of "smart" software that provides useful information even before they ask for it.

As if these hardware advances are not exciting enough, organized labor should be studying group collaborative software now touted as "the next great turn of the wheel" (Ellis). Known as peer-to-peer (p-to-p) programming, it circumvents centralized computer infra-structure and allows PCs to talk directly with one another. Its creator, Ray Ozzie, believes it offers the "directness and spontaneity of a phone call, the visual immediacy of a fax, the asynchrony of e-mail, and the privacy of a closed-door meeting" (Ozzie). Proponents expect p-to-p to enable users (such as far-flung union activists) to work easier and more creatively with one another than ever before possible. Skeptics agree it will be used very broadly, but dismiss it as "only" another technology (Gomes).

If only half of these glittering possibilities are soon realized, the rest are likely to be very close behind. The impact is likely to continue to change reality dramatically, as it has since we entered the Information Age—especially for social movements like organized labor, and for everyone and everything else.

LABOR'S CHALLENGE

The central question for labor in the early years of the 21st century asks—What is labor to do about its computer use challenge? Plainly, ongoing efforts by the AFL-CIO and its 64 affiliates to use computer power may help slow, stem, and possibly even reverse labor's long-term, ongoing decline. The harder question asks if labor has the will and "smarts" to go *beyond* conventional uses and dare to employ a fresh model, one with computer use at its core, rather than its periphery, one I call the F-I-S-T model (more on this later).

While emphatically not a "magic bullet," computerization makes possible wide-scale communications of dazzling speed and enormous outreach (national and international). It enables unprecedented access by members to office-holders, and timely exchanges of views among them, as well as among the members themselves (via electronic bulletin boards and chat rooms, including some valuable ones run unofficially by the "Loyal Opposition"). It bolsters mobilization for political action and strike support. And it facilitates corporate campaigns that would otherwise overwhelm with complexity and data.

Where locals are concerned, computerization enables international representatives and business agents to download reams of relevant material (grievance and arbitration records, previous contracts, etc.). This enables them to use their laptop on the spot to do a high quality job directly on the shop or office floor. As well, locals can create electronic listserves to link together an entire membership, appeal to prospective members, address sub-cultures differently, and in other overdue ways, build a new form of "electronic community," a 21st century adaptation of solidarity.

Where labor militancy is concerned, intriguing new tools are under consideration. Unions might encourage members to shut down or in other ways impede the use of their computers at work. Or they could create "picket lines" in cyberspace. Or urge boycotts of the products or services of targeted employers, and do this faster and with far wider coverage via the Internet than was ever possible relying on old-fashioned mailings.

Contrariwise, concerning a rare, if desirable possibility, a local's effort to co-create a high-performance workplace in partnership with a cooperative employer, a labor computer system (like Groove, discussed above) could facilitate employee dialogue about overdue workplace boosts to productivity—complete with a union imprimatur.

Accordingly, although unable alone to "rescue" labor, gains from computer use in efficiency and effectiveness might help attract many new members. Computer use could also help bolster support of existing members (always labor's best organizers). And, in 101 other significant ways, it could rapidly aid labor's urgent efforts at recovery. (See, in this connection, workingfamilies.ibelong.com/ and afscme.org/publications/puttc.htm).

Of late, computerization has begun to challenge the status quo in many critical aspects of modern unionism (and modern life alike). Components of trade unionism all the way from A (accountability) to Z (Zeitgeist) are being substantially altered, especially where decisive matters of internal administration are concerned (Lee, 1997).

Today, reliance on computers means electronic files that can save space, are timely, and can with reasonable effort be kept current—thanks to e-mail exchanges designed to update information. Phone calls give way to real-time e-mail exchanges (complete with a "paper trail"). As well, a union or a local can discretely assess the Web site of a prospective allied organization. It can determine privately whether to seek a new alliance in a coordinated boycott, educational venture, lobbying effort, picket line, or the like. And it can determine—in discrete dialogue with other labor bodies—whether to offer assistance.

Today, millions of members of AFL-CIO's affiliates with a Web site can, at a click of a mouse, have access to facts, figures, documents, archives, rules, regulations, photos, videos, etc. They can resort this material to suit their own purposes, and they can request additional material—including streaming video subject matter and other fascinating forms of communications they are coming to expect from their locals and international unions.

Shop stewards, for example, can access revealing profiles of active mediators and arbitrators (their biases, idiosyncrasies, standards, etc.). They can access data on labor law cases and precedents. And they can secure field-proven clues as to how best handle a grievance, arbitration, etc., in light of yesterday's major decisions, clues the computer can format as an electronic tutorial or rulebook.

Members can be briefed immediately about fast-breaking developments and kept abreast almost in a real-time mode. E-mails can now go out in a 24/7 (day-long; everyday) format as part of a remarkable new "web" of timely communications never possible before with mail, phone, or fax.

Especially novel is the opportunity computer-based communication has made possible for a vast upgrade in a very old effort to forge strong bonds among unions around the world (an effort Marx and Gompers alike aided). With over 2,700 labor union Web sites online now, and more being added weekly, the opportunities for networking are enormous (Freeman and Diamond).

Although not well known by most unionists here, various federations overseas have tried to promote international solidarity for decades (such as the ICEM, with its 403 union affiliates in 113 countries). But making phone connections and/or airmail use has always been a hindrance. Today, e-mails flash back and forth almost in real time, aiding the conduct of far-flung port boycotts, intricate corporate campaigns, and other coordinated international activities.

Perhaps *the* most far-reaching change in labor's communications involves the newfound ability of members to reach one another, independent of officialdom. Until recently, a member could to do so only through the union's newspaper or magazine, and then only if the editors agreed. Today, grass-roots activists are busy on a 24/7 basis exchanging uncensored advice, views, and visions. Caucuses of like-minded members can link together in an e-mail list serve or through a shared Web site. Solidarity is built, and the cause of union democracy can receive a very strong boost. (More on this, known as transactional computing, later).

Organizing has previously been a neglected stepchild, receiving only about 5% of the annual budget and little respect from many stand-patters (often waiting out their retirement, or disinclined to assume the heartaches that came with having to service a lot of new members with unreasonable and untutored expectations).

Today, however, in response to the crisis posed by labor's steady numerical decline, and the unrelenting pressure from the Sweeney administration, many unions and locals are spending more money and effort than ever before—with computers strategic in the process. Many leads are coming in cyberspace to union Web sites specifically designed to attract non-members reaching out for help. Organizers are immediately advised by Web masters via e-mail whom they are to rush to contact. The computer also draws a roadmap to the home of a prospective member, and provides an analysis of the company, industry, and labor market history involved in this specific case.

Especially intriguing is the possibility that unions might soon use the Internet to organize "minority" locals inside a workplace as yet unorganized. Incubators for unionism, these computer-based "locals" could collaborate via listserves with one another around the country, trading field-proven advice and lending precious morale support. These unofficial "locals" could make a case for formal unionization by proving useful to their surreptitious members and promoting solidarity—even as participants wait until the times are propitious for seeking an open card count or NLRB election (Freeman and Diamond).

Another less-heralded aspect of this matter, organizing the *organized*, can also receive a major boost from labor's use of computer power. Local unions in particular can use their Web site as a 24/7 "newspaper," rich in very current coverage of the activities of members. Photos of participants in a rally, a picket line, a union picnic, or a meeting can appear within a few hours of the event (or sooner!). Immediate news of births, deaths, retirements, etc., can be proudly carried, the sort of homey material that used to grow stale in a once-a-month prosaic union paper, but now can excite and please members who appreciate a bit of positive recognition.

Especially creative Web masters can use their site to offer members a swap service. Or for a garage sale outlet. Or for a recipe-exchange page. Or for other "down home" services valued by a membership that comes thereby to think first of the local's Web site when seeking valuable information. In this way, new bonds can be forged between local officialdom and dues-payers, bonds that may yet help secure the highly rewarding volunteer services of rank-and-file organizers.

Staff development efforts, while not as poorly treated as was organizing, have also suffered from neglect and low priority. Staff obsolescence threatens unacceptable chaos, especially where getting the staff up to speed in computer use capabilities is concerned. Accordingly, tutorials online or through computer workshops are increasingly common, and are budgeted for as a necessity.

As if this wasn't enough, a new type of staffer has been added to the lineup: a labor union computer specialist. These talented (and often expensive) individuals help assure the adequacy of the union's computer system, offer staff training, prop up the computer work of key officers, prepare power point presentations, and in general, keep the organization "online" (Katz).

In all, then, four key aspects of internal administration—building alliances, getting the word out (and back), recruiting new members (and re-organizing old ones), and upgrading the human capital of the union's or local's staff—would seem to benefit considerably from computer use.

Many in labor, however, worry about a potential erosion in face-to-face contact, arguably labor's greatest asset in earning and holding onto members. Dues-payers like to feel recognized (and valued) by union officialdom, a feeling that impersonal e-mails may not convey. "Pressing the flesh" and "showing your face" are practices many in labor think indispensable, regardless of the time-and-energy-saving (cyberspace) alternatives championed by labor's digerati.

Many in labor also worry about loudmouths and troublemakers monopolizing dialogue in non-moderated chat rooms and bulletin boards. They fear that "crazy talk" will drive others away, and undermine the entire medium. They also worry that thin-skinned officers will be hurt by outrageous posted criticism, and insist on either strong censorship or a shutdown.

Many in labor worry about a generation gap that separates older leaders from young "hot shop" types. The younger leaders are often impatient to get on with it, to rush the computerization process faster than the older (pre-computer) leaders are comfortable with—a rift that exacerbates the natural divide between the generations—and undermines solidarity.

Many in labor worry about loss of confidentiality. They fear that hackers and others possibly in the pay of government RICO "snoops," union busters, union-hating employers, or the dangerous like, will break into union databanks and files, much to the union's dismay.

Finally, many in labor worry about the overload that e-mails entail in work lives already stretched to the limit. Union staffers complain of their inability to keep up with electronic messages rushing in, and earmarked for rapid response, almost regardless of the situation of the receiver. Many staffers resent heightened expectations on them to respond almost immediately via e-mail to scores of daily e-mail queries, even while their previous workload weighs heavy. As well, top officers often shift their e-mail response load to staffers with blithe indifference.

Some staffers grumble about an unreasonable speedup, made all the less bearable by the absence of any commensurate increase in salary. Paltry utterly fail to assuage the pain. And rumors of high salaries required to hire and retain computer specialists only rub salt in the wound.

All five current anxieties—possible erosion in face-to-face relations, loss of control over the medium, generation rift, loss of confidentiality, and (unappreciated) work overload—*can* serve as a valuable call for overdue reforms: None need prove a paralyzing self-fulfilling prophecy.

Remedies *are* available, such as special schooling (private, discrete, and exceedingly sensitive) for older union leaders in how to use computers. Password protection schemes (as used now by the AFL-CIO and various unions) would help (Levy). And, redistributed workloads, the hiring of additional aides, and overdue salary increases for those genuinely overloaded by computer inputs would go a long way in remedying problems.

THREE PATTERNS OF COMPUTER USE: A DIVISION OF THE HOUSE

Given the pattern above of gains and pains associated with current computer use by labor, three models seem to dominate the scene. Arranged below in an original typology boldly designed to cover 64 international unions and 35,000 or so local unions, the typology obviously cannot exhaust all the variations extant. However, it does highlight major variations, and, in the absence of any alternative scheme, should help advance study of the subject. Better yet, it invites attention to a fourth model (the F-I-S-T variation), one without an earthly counterpart to date, an ideal type of union and local that beckons from the horizon.

The first contemporary model, which I call *Cyber Naught*, involves minimum employ of computer potentialities. Cyber Naught unions and locals generally hesitate to go beyond staid reliance on computer-based bookkeeping. They pretend little has changed around them, deny being under pressure to modernize their use of computers, and essentially sleepwalk through time. Their members, although grievously under-served by the absence of progressive computer uses, seem only to shrug and focus their attention elsewhere, a dereliction of responsibility that serves no one well.

The second model, *Cyber Drift*, has labor organizations move spastically first in this direction where computer uses are concerned, and then in other directions, unable to maturely guide their own efforts. Crippled by unthinking adaptation of incompatible, if glitzy and trendy, equipment and software, Cyber Drift unions and locals disappoint unionists eager to believe labor has much to gain from computer use. They remind one of the drunk found searching under a lamppost for his keys because of its light overhead, and not because that is where he thinks he may have dropped them.

The third model, *Cyber Gain*, wins accolades for its state-of-the-art accomplishments where computers are concerned. Ironically, however, its lasting significance may be to set the stage for the emergence soon of its necessary successor, the *CyberUnion*, today only an alluring distant possibility. Unless and until Cyber Gain organizations are succeeded by the CyberUnion variety, organized labor will continue to sub-optimize its possibilities here, and remain far more vulnerable than is necessary or tenable.

GETTING TO A THIRD WAVE CYBERUNION F-I-S-T MODEL

If labor is to reinvent itself as rapidly, as thoroughly, and as meaningfully as appears necessary, a new model appears necessary. Specifically, early 21st century unions might well experiment with an ambitious and creative alternative that incorporates four matters newly enhanced by computer uses—namely, futuristics, innovations, services, and labor traditions (F-I-S-T).

Futuristics would have CyberUnions employ all of the tools of forecasting to help get clues to where relevant industries are heading, why, and what labor might do about it. Forecasts would scrutinize demographic changes in the labor force the union and/or local draws on, and help develop plans that get out ahead of shifts. Forecasts would enable labor to test the warring claims of antagonists in public debates that beckon for labor's taking of sides, as in the global warming or energy embroilment. Above all, forecasts would enable unions and locals to better anticipate training upgrades for members, and continue thereby to distinguish dues-payers from less well-prepared competitors.

Innovations would have CyberUnions trying this, that, and the other thing in a responsible and earnestly assessed pursuit of ever-better processes, things, services, and so on. The union or local would gain a proud reputation for early adoption of cutting-edge items, and members would look to the organization for assessments and advice when considering testing a novel option themselves. Above all, innovations would mark the CyberUnion as forward-looking, self-confident, and thereby worth the membership of all intent on making, rather than inheriting, a future.

Services refers to the ability of CyberUnions to use computer power to vastly enhance 101 old and another 101 new services of keen value to the membership. Typical would be arranging for the sale of computers and software at great discount, thanks to the volume buying labor can arrange (as demonstrated already in Sweden, Norway, and elsewhere). Another service might have a local facilitate car-pooling, using a listserve of members sorted by zip code. Or arrange for swap meets in cyberspace, as managed (and policed) by a local.

Traditions refers to the dedication of CyberUnions to honoring the culture and lore of a union and/or local. Every effort might be made to create an oral and video record of the reminiscences of older members, complete with archival storage. The history of the organization might be recreated by actors and actresses, videotaped, and placed permanently on the Web site. Many relevant labor songs, anecdotes, and historic speeches might be added to the site, along with streaming video celebrations of special days and events in the organization's past.

Labor urgently needs the computer-aided rewards possible from reliable forecasting. From innovations, such as computer data mining. From computer-based services, such as p-to-p software dedicated to meeting labor's groupware needs. And from the computer-aided celebration of traditions, as in the production of interactive software or CDs rich with labor history material. Together, these four items (F-I-S-T) just might help labor go beyond its necessary, but insufficient, Cyber Gain strengths (Shostak, 1999).

BRIEF CAUTIONARY NOTE

None of the advances possible in hardware and software will suffice unless there are commensurate advances in "thoughtware." That is, unless the quality of thinking and imagining in labor circles soars alongside market-driven advances in machines and computer code, organized labor will not profit as it should—and must. Computers only deliver messages, and at present do not create them or vouch for their merit. The quality of labor's messages remains far more important than the message infrastructure ... although proponents like this writer believe that when the F-I-S-T model is employed, the quality of thought and vision necessarily soars.

SUMMARY: LABOR UNION PROSPECTS?

American labor unions five years from now are likely to be very different from their 2003 counterparts. Their hallmark will either be irrelevance, or they will draw handsomely on CyberUnion attributes (F-I-S-T). While computerization cannot "rescue" labor, unless organized labor soon makes the most creative possible use of it, labor probably cannot be rescued.

At least where four areas of advancement are concerned—

alliance-building, communications, organizing (external/internal), and staff development—labor would seem well on its way. Provided, that is, that labor remembers "high tech" computerization works best when aiding such "high touch" efforts as "one-on-one" organizing, "shoe leather" vote-getting, "button hole" lobbying for labor law reform, and so on—the *humanizing* dimensions of unionism that constitute its unique "value added" dimension.

Where five major anxieties are concerned—losing its personal touch, being battered by internal criticism, hurting its older leaders, suffering breaches of confidentiality, and work overload and speedup —labor has several available remedies to employ, and other reforms it can readily create and apply. Alert to advances that other similarly challenged organizations—businesses, NGOs, schools, etc.—are busy making in their use of computer power, labor can adapt reforms pioneered elsewhere (as explained, for example, in issues of *Business 2.0, Fast Company*, etc.).

Building on this foundation, early in the 21st century a new model of computer-based unionism—one celebrating the F-I-S-T model—may help labor finally make of computer use all that has always been possible in this revolutionary communications mode. At that time, and not until then, organized labor will once again be a player of significance, and its power and vision will have all respectfully acknowledge that—in the richest possible sense of the term—labor "computes."

REFERENCES

Ante, Spencer E. "In Search of the Net's Next Big Thing," *Business Week*, March 26, 2001, 140-141.

Baker, Stephen. "A Net Not Made in America," *Business Week*, March 26, 2001, 124.

Dowd, Maureen. "Drill, Grill, and Chill," *The New York Times*, May 20, 2001, WK-17.

Ellis, John. "Grove Makes It Possible to Light Up the Edge," *Fast Company*, May, 2001, 101.

Fiorito, Jack, Paul Jarley, John Thomas Delaney, and Robert W. Kolodinsky. "Unions and Information Technology: From Luddites to CyberUnions?" *Labor Studies Journal*, 24 (Winter 2000), 3-34.

Freeman, Richard, and Wayne Diamond, as quoted in Robert Taylor, "Trade Unions: Workers Unite on the Internet," *Financial Times*, May 11, 2001.

Gomes, Lee. "P-to-P, B-to-B—R.I.P?" *Wall Street Journal*, April 4, 2001, B-1, B-4.

Gunther, Marc. "Wireless E-mail," *Fortune*, March 19, 2001, 76.

Katz, Jon. *Geeks* (New York: Villard, 2000).

Lazarovici, Laureen. "Cyber Drives: Organizing, Bargaining, and Mobilizing," *America@Work*, March, 2001, 9.

Lee, Eric. *The Labour Movement and the Internet: The New Interna-*

tionalism (Chicago: Pluto Press, 1997).

Levy, Steven. "Bill Gates Says, Take This Tablet," *Newsweek*, April 30, 2001, 67.

Levy, Steven. *How the Code Rebels Beat the Government—Saving Privacy in the Digital Age* (New York: Viking, 2000).

Ozzie, Ray, as quoted in Bill Green, "Jazzed about Work," *Fast Company*, May 2001, 194.

Shostak, Arthur B. *Robust Unionism: Innovations in the Labor Movement* (Ithaca, NY: ILR Press, 1991).

Shostak, Arthur B. *CyberUnion: Empowering Labor Through Computer Technology* (Armonk, NY: M.E. Sharpe, 1999).

Shostak, Arthur B., ed. *The CyberUnion Handbook: Transforming Labor through Computer Technology* (Armonk, NY: M.E. Sharpe, 2002).

Toffler, Alvin. *Future Shock* (New York: Bantam, 1970) 452, 480-483.

Townsend, Anthony, Samuel M. Demarie, and Anthony R. Hendrickson. "Information Technology, Unions, and New Organization: Challenges and Opportunities for Union Survival," *Journal of Labor Research* XXII (Spring 2001): 275-286.

Wieffering, Eric and Tony Kennedy. "Search Raises Privacy Issues," *Star Tribune* (Minneapolis, MN), February 8, 2000, 1, 3.

THE
PROFESSIONAL MEMBERSHIP PROGRAM

The World Future Society offers a special program for members who are involved professionally in futures research, forecasting, corporate or institutional planning, issues management, technology assessment, policy analysis, urban and regional planning, and related areas.

Professional Membership includes:

♦All benefits of regular membership in the World Future Society, including a subscription to *The Futurist*.

♦A subscription to *Futures Research Quarterly*, the Society's professional journal.

♦Society supplement newspaper *FutureTimes*.

♦Invitations to meetings arranged specifically for professional members. The registration fee for these occasions is very modest. Recent forums were held in Washington, D.C., Houston, Texas, Minneapolis, Minnesota, and Philadelphia, Pennsylvania.

♦A copy of *The Futurist Directory: A Guide to Individuals Who Write, Speak, or Consult About the Future*. Published in January 2000, this comprehensively-indexed, 436-page volume lists nearly 1,400 futurists.

♦The monthly e-mail newsletter, *Futurist Update*.

Dues: The dues for Professional Membership are $118 per year.

Comprehensive Professional Membership includes:

♦All benefits of Professional membership plus a subscription to *Future Survey* and complimentary copies of all other books published by the Society during the term of membership.

Dues: The dues for Comprehensive Professional Membership are $225 per year.

These programs are available to individuals only. To join, or for information about Institutional Membership, contact Society headquarters.

World Future Society • 7910 Woodmont Avenue, Suite 450 • Bethesda, Maryland 20814 USA
tel.: 301-656-8274 • fax: 301-951-0394 • e-mail: sechard@wfs.org

Schedule of Upcoming World Future Society Meetings

July 29-31, 2005
Chicago Hilton and Towers
Chicago, Illinois
August 1, 2005
Professional Members' Forum

2006 Annual Meeting
Dates and Venue to be Announced

July 29-31, 2007
Hilton Minneapolis and Towers
Minneapolis, Minnesota
August 1, 2007
Professional Members' Forum

July 26-28, 2008
Washington Hilton and Towers
Washington, D.C.
July 29, 2008
Professional Members' Forum

July 17-19, 2009
Chicago Hilton and Towers
Chicago, Illinois
July 20, 2009
Professional Members' Forum

World Future Society
7910 Woodmont Avenue
Suite 450
Bethesda, Maryland 20814
Call 301-656-8274 or
toll-free at 800-989-8274;
sechard@wfs.org

For further information visit our Web site at www.wfs.org

FUTURING:
The Exploration of the Future

By Edward Cornish

This comprehensive new guide to the study of the future will give you a detailed look at the techniques futurists use, what we can know about the future and what we can't, and the role that forward-looking people can play in creating a better tomorrow.

Topics Include:

History: From ancient times to the Futurist revolution, including religious views, the doctrine of progress, the rise and decline of optimism, science fiction, great blunders of forecasting, futurist pioneers.

Methods: Trend analysis, trend scanning, scenarios, stages of development, Delphi polls, historic parallels, creativity techniques, matrices, visioning.

Basic issues: Change vs. continuity, time, chance, chaos, systems, cycles, explaining cultural evolution, hyperchange, what we can know about the future.

Outlook: The global transformation, three techno-economic revolutions with a fourth in prospect, supertrends, the world of 2040.

BIBLIOGRAPHY, INDEX, AND MORE

Publication date: October 15, 2003
6x9 hardcover with jacket
Approx. 350 pages
ISBN 0-930242-57-2

World Future Society
Bethesda, Maryland, U.S.A.
www.wfs.org